Psychology Revivals

Lifes Preservative Against Self-Killing

This book, first published in 1637, was the first full-length treatise on suicide published in English. Originally published in 1988 as part of the *Tavistock Classics in the History of Psychiatry* series, the introduction by Michael MacDonald places the book in the context of attitudes to suicide in its day, as well as showing some of the ways that this theological book is also a study of the psychology and sociology of suicide. He discusses the evolution of the law of suicide and analyses the religious beliefs held about it at the time, before going on to look at John Sym himself and the structure of his book.

I0891178

Lifes Preservative Against Self-Killing

John Sym

Edited with an introduction by
Michael MacDonald

Routledge
Taylor & Francis Group
LONDON AND NEW YORK

First published in 1988
by Routledge

This edition first published in 2014 by Routledge
27 Church Road, Hove, BN3 2FA

Simultaneously published in the USA and Canada
by Routledge
711 Third Avenue, New York, NY 10017

Routledge is an imprint of the Taylor & Francis Group, an informa business

Publisher's Note
The publisher has gone to great lengths to ensure the quality of this reprint but points out that some imperfections in the original copies may be apparent.

Disclaimer
The publisher has made every effort to trace copyright holders and welcomes correspondence from those they have been unable to contact.

A Library of Congress record exists under ISBN: 0415006392

ISBN: 978-0-415-73080-8 (hbk)
ISBN: 978-1-315-84990-4 (ebk)
ISBN: 978-0-415-73083-9 (pbk)

LIFES PRESERVATIVE
AGAINST
SELF-KILLING

BY

JOHN SYM

Edited with an Introduction by

Michael MacDonald

ROUTLEDGE
London and New York

First published 1988
by Routledge
11 New Fetter Lane, London EC4P 4EE
29 West 35th Street, New York, NY 10001

Printed in Great Britain at the University Press, Cambridge

British Library Cataloguing in Publication Data

Sym, John
Lifes preservative against self-killing
——(Tavistock classics in the history
of psychiatry).
1. Great Britain. Suicide, history
I. Title II. MacDonald, Michael,
1945– II. Service
362.2

Library of Congress Cataloging in Publication Data

Sym, John
Lifes preservative against self-killing/John Sym: edited with an introduction by Michael MacDonald.
p. cm.——(Tavistock classics in the history of psychiatry)
Includes index.
ISBN 0–415–00639–2
1. Suicide—England—Prevention—History—Sources. 2. Suicide—Social aspects—England—History—Sources. I. MacDonald, Michael, 1945– . II. Title. III. Series.
RC569.S945 1988
616.85′8445——dc 19

ISBN 0–415–00639–2

CONTENTS

PREFACE

The Tavistock Classics in the History of Psychiatry series meets a considerable need amongst academics, practitioners, and all those who are more broadly interested in the development of psychiatry. Psychiatry as a discipline has always paid considerable heed to its own founders, its history, and emergent traditions. It is one field in which the relevance of the past to the present does not diminish. There is a high professional awareness of the history of the subject, and many aspects of this are now benefiting from fruitful dialogue with the now rapidly expanding investigations of historians and historical sociologists.

Yet two factors greatly hamper our grasp of psychiatry's past. On the one hand, a considerable number of the formative texts in the rise of psychiatry are exceedingly difficult to obtain, even from libraries. As a small discipline in earlier centuries, many of the major works were published only in short runs, and many, even of the classics, have never been reprinted at all. This present series aims to overcome this problem by making available a selection of such key works. Mostly they are books originally published in the English language; in other cases where the original language was, say, French or German, we are reprinting contemporary English translations; in a few cases, we hope to present entirely new translations of classic Continental works.

On the other hand, in many instances little is commonly known of the life and ideas of the authors of these texts, and their works have never been subjected to thorough analyses. Our intention in this series is to follow the model of the now defunct Dawson series of psychiatric reprints, edited and introduced by Richard Hunter and Ida Macalpine, now, alas, both dead, and to provide substantial scholarly introductions to each volume, based upon original research. Thus the book and its author will illuminate each other, and one will avoid the dilemma of a text isolated in an intellectual vacuum, or simply the accumulation of miscellaneous biographical data. It is our hope that this series will break new ground in the history of psychiatry, and secure a new readership for a number of illustrative works in psychiatry's rich and fascinating past.

INTRODUCTION

Michael MacDonald

John Sym's *Lifes Preservative Against Self-Killing* was the first full-length treatise on suicide published in English. Sym himself stresses the novelty of his work. He has, he tells us, 'met with no single, nor compleat *Treatise* of it', and so he has launched his book onto uncharted waters (sig. a1^{v}).* Like the identical claims that adorn the beginnings of books and theses today, Sym's assertion that he is the Columbus of self-killing was, though true in the strictest sense, distinctly exaggerated. There was already a considerable body of literature that treated suicide from sharply differing points of view. Clerical writers had frequently condemned it as a sin and a crime; humanist intellectuals and imaginative writers had popularized ancient philosophies and examples that condoned it.[1] A small but growing number of medical writers – many of them, as was the custom of the day, divines first and doctors second – had also briefly discussed the subject. John Donne had already written a large and highly iconoclastic theological tract to prove that it was 'not so naturally Sin that it may never be otherwise'.[2] And yet Sym was right. For despite the very large number of sermons, chapters in devotional works, essays, passages in plays, prose dialogues and poems discussing self-killing, he was the first to publish a comprehensive study of suicide. Donne's book, too controversial to print and distribute openly, remained in manuscript until after his death.

That a large amount of literature, discussing the legitimacy of suicide in religious and secular terms, already existed in 1637 is crucial to understanding Sym's arguments. *Lifes Preservative* is a thoroughgoing condemnation of self-murder, an expression of protestant zeal, and a reaction against humanist secularism.

From the first page until the last, Sym's main aim is to show that deliberate self-destruction is a heinous sin. And although he moderates his harsh attitude slightly, his position is absolutely clear. Hostility to suicide was neither new nor unusual, but it had been aroused to a new pitch by the early seventeenth century, as we shall see. Self-murder 'hath in sundry Sermons preached, and published, and in other printed Treatises, beene spoken against', the famous puritan divine William Gouge points out, a little uncharitably, in his address 'To the Christian Reader' that opens this book (unpaginated). The orthodoxy of *Lifes Preservative*, rather than its originality, is the chief reason why it is an important work in the history of attitudes to suicide. It is absolutely representative of the prevailing opinion of its day. Furthermore, it fused theological discourse, moral condemnation and psychological insight in a way that none of the shorter works by divines and medical writers had. To understand *Lifes Preservative* is to grasp precisely what suicide meant to pious Englishmen in the early seventeenth century, to see something of the now forgotten attitude of mind that interpreted behaviour and emotion in terms both of natural and supernatural forces, psychological motivations and religious meanings.[3]

It is fashionable nowadays in the 'human sciences' to interpret texts in ways that defamiliarize them. It is a vogue to which the most celebrated and most controversial historian of psychiatry, Michel Foucault, contributed early and powerfully. But time has defamiliarized *Lifes Preservative* more effectively than the most dazzling French Prospero could have. The main business of this Introduction will therefore be to 'familiarize' the text, as it were, to situate it in the context of attitudes to suicide in its day and to point out some of the ways in which this book of theology is also a subtle study of the psychology and sociology of suicide. I shall proceed in stages from context to text. Because, by Sym's era, suicide had come to be considered a crime and a sin, the first part of the Introduction will discuss the evolution of the law of suicide and the second will analyse religious beliefs about it. Some attitudes and practices, that ran contrary to the prevailing trend toward legal and religious severity to suicide, will then be considered. The changing legal and religious context shaped the content of Sym's book, and so did the undertow of toleration that accompanied growing severity.[4] I shall therefore next turn to describing Sym himself and analysing the formal structure of his book, suggesting what his intentions were in writing it, explaining how and why it is organized as it is, and stating what its principal themes are. Finally, I shall analyse some of the important features of his discussion of 'direct bodily self-murder', suicide as we usually understand the term.

The law of suicide

Suicide was a terrible crime in Tudor and early Stuart England. And during Sym's lifetime it was harshly punished. Self-slaughter was a species of murder, condemned by the law, by religion and by folklore. 'For the heinousnesse thereof', observed Michael Dalton in a standard legal handbook, 'it is an offence against God, against the king, and against Nature'.[5] People who killed themselves were tried posthumously by a coroner's jury, and if they were found to have committed suicide when they were sane, the jury returned a verdict of *felo de se* (felon of himself). The suicide's goods, leases and loans were forfeited to the crown or the holder of a royal patent. His body was turned over to parish churchwardens and interred profanely, denied the usual rites of Christian burial. Old popular customs that expressed a profound horror of the act of self-murder governed the disposal of the body, which was buried at night in a public highway, tossed face down in the grave and pinioned there with a wooden stake. These savage punishments expressed profound abhorrence at self-destruction. They had originated long before Henry Tudor took the throne in 1485, and they were not formally abolished until the nineteenth century. But this perdurable continuity in the laws and customs penalizing suicide disguises striking changes in attitudes and responses to it. The punishments for self-murder were seldom enforced before 1500, and they gradually fell into disuse after 1660. The era of greatest severity toward self-murder, during which Sym lived and wrote, was the product of concatenated political and religious changes. His book both epitomized the results of those changes and helped to advance them.

Punishment for suicide was not new in the sixteenth century, nor was it unique to England. Similar laws and customs existed in many parts of Europe. Both the forfeiture provisions of the law and the rites of desecration had their origins in the ancient world. By the early Middle Ages most western governments seem to have adopted forfeiture as a means of punishing suicide.[6] In England the common law condemned suicide as self-murder by the time of Bracton, in the thirteenth century. Bracton himself articulates the distinction between *felo de se* and *non compos mentis.*[7] *Felo de se* verdicts were occasionally returned in the thirteenth century, and by the end of the fourteenth the crown had realized that they could yield windfalls that were an attractive kind of patronage. Richard II gave part of the property of a number of suicides to courtiers, and like other medieval monarchs he also granted away the rights to the goods of felons of themselves to noblemen and lesser landlords.[8]

The rituals that were used to desecrate the bodies of suicides were based on early, pre-Christian religions. Their symbolism varied greatly from region to region in Europe, and they were only belatedly sanctioned by the Church. The canon law merely forbade suicides the normal rites of Christian burial; the civil law embraced the forms of punishments, used in parts of France and Germany, at a later date, sometime in the late Middle Ages.[9] In England the Council of Hertford adopted a canon denying suicides normal funerals and burials in 672, and a canon of King Edgar reiterated the prohibition and exempted madmen in 967. After that, the English Church was silent on the subject of suicide until 1662, when a rubric forbidding ministers to read the burial service over 'such as have laid violent hands upon themselves' was at last included in the Book of Common Prayer.[10] No ecclesiastical legislation – in England or elsewhere – stipulated the forms of burial to be used to punish self-murderers. The rites of desecration were genuine popular customs, accepted by the Church and the State as an essential part of punishing suicide but not enjoined by either institution. They expressed a deep fear of and hostility to suicide.

The monarchy thus realized it had a financial interest in the enforcement of the law of suicide in the Middle Ages, and the Church sanctioned popular rituals that expressed a deep abhorrence for self-destruction. And yet *felo de se* verdicts were very rare in the thirteenth and fourteenth centuries. The crown challenged the verdicts of coroners from time to time, but supervision of their activities in this sphere of their duties seems to have been rather lax. Furthermore, coroners were unpaid and easily corruptible.[11]

Enforcement of the law of suicide was thus largely left up to local officials and local communities. Barbara Hanawalt has argued convincingly that many suicides were concealed as accidents. 'Community feeling', she concludes, 'would [have been] with the surviving family'.[12] Take but one example. Although the crown later proved that a Bedfordshire man who drowned in a well in April 1278 had been a suicide, a jury from the four townships around where he died returned a verdict of misadventure and concealed his goods.[13] Medieval juries were also more willing to return verdicts of *non compos mentis* than their Tudor and Stuart successors. Even when they did not return verdicts that were bogus or favourable to the deceased and his survivors, medieval juries seem often to have undervalued the goods of suicides, like those of other felons. It would not be going too far, I think, to say that the law of suicide was enforced only when it was unavoidable.

All that changed in the half-century after 1500. The law was enforced with increasing rigour, and the result was a massive increase in the numbers of suicides reported to the central government. The shift from locally-based leniency to centrally-directed severity was one small facet of the Tudor 'revolution in government', the administrative reforms undertaken to strengthen the crown in the reigns of Henry VII and Henry VIII. Reform of the law of suicide began soon after the battle of Bosworth Field. In 1487 Henry VII passed a statute ordering coroners to hold inquests on every violent and suspicious death in the realm and establishing a regular procedure for supervising their work. Coroners were supposed to hand in all of their inquisitions at semi-annual meetings of the assizes, and they were forwarded to King's Bench, the premier criminal court, where they were reviewed by officials, who made sure that property forfeited to the crown was turned over to the king's almoner or his deputies. This ordinance was finely tuned with a writ and a second statute in 1509 and 1510 that clarified the duties and pay of coroners. Soon after these reforms the number of suicides reported to the court of King's Bench began to climb.[14]

The keystone of the Tudor system of enforcing the law of suicide was put in place in the late 1530s or early 1540s. At that time a protégé of Thomas Cromwell, Henry VIII's great reforming minister, established the king's almoner's right to sue for concealed goods in the court of Star Chamber. The Privy Council sitting in judicial session, Star Chamber was probably the most prestigious tribunal in the land. It dealt out justice swiftly, and although the penalties it could exact for evading the law of suicide were usually not in themselves crushing, the court was an intimidating weapon. Unlike most other Tudor law reforms, which typically substituted prerogative courts for common law courts, this reform resulted in a complementary, and far more efficient jurisdiction. Routine supervision of coroners was handled by King's Bench, and so were the routine sorts of evasion. More complicated cases – or ones that escaped the vigilance of King's Bench – were tried in Star Chamber, where the almoner could expect a much faster and less complex prosecution of his cause. By about 1540, therefore, the two most prestigious courts in the land were working in tandem to enforce the law of suicide.[15] The man apparently responsible for establishing the almoner as a privileged prosecutor in Star Chamber, Nicholas Heath, was a moderate reformer in religion during Cromwell's lifetime, who reverted to conservatism and later catholicism. Almoner from 1539–47, he was on the Privy Council in the reign of Mary I and had a hand in reorganizing the business of Star Chamber. This probably explains why there was no slackening in the activities of Star Chamber in this area throughout the 1540s and 1550s.[16]

The results of these reforms were spectacular. Between 1500 and 1560, the number of *felo de se* verdicts returned to King's Bench rose rapidly, far outpacing the growth of the population. After 1560 a kind of jagged plateau was reached, in which yearly and decennial totals of suicides jumped up and down, until 1630 or so, when reported suicides began to fall.[17] Because the statistics are so difficult to interpret, incomplete in ways that cannot be accounted for, it is impossible to confirm or refute the truth of Sym's assertion that he was living through an epidemic of suicides. What is irrefutable is that *reported* suicides had risen sharply in the century or so before *Lifes Preservative* was written[18] (see Figure 1).

The law was enforced with a rigour that went far beyond mere compliance. Juries returned verdicts of *felo de se* when it was impossible to prove with certainty that a suicide had occurred. A great many suicides, for instance, chose to drown themselves. And frequently no one saw them go to their watery graves. Sixteenth and seventeenth century suicides seldom left notes – the odds are that the vast majority of them were illiterate – and physical evidence of

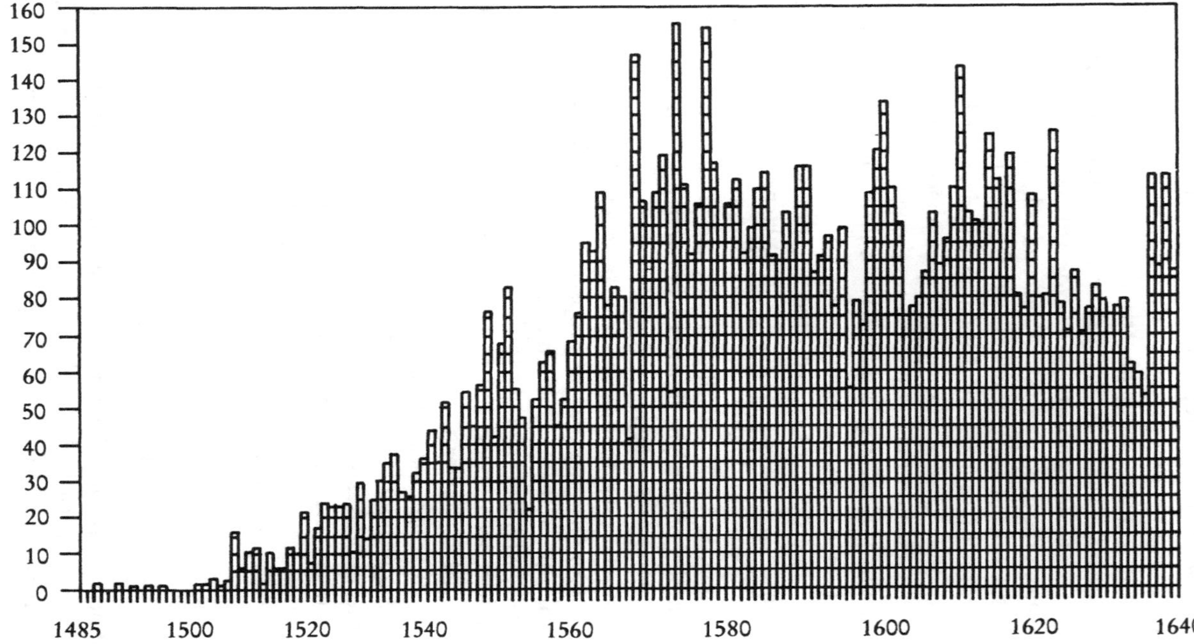

Figure 1 Reported suicides, 1485–1640
(Suicides enrolled by King's Bench)

Source and note: PRO, KB 29/116–289. As it took up to eighteen months for some inquisitions to be returned to the court, actual yearly totals of suicides were often somewhat higher or lower than the numbers enrolled. This is a graph, therefore, of the pattern of suicide as it looked to the clerks supervising compliance with the law.

deliberate immersion was rarer still. It is evident from the time and place of death and the description of the body's discovery in many inquests that it was impossible directly to prove that the deceased had jumped into the water. As we shall see, juries relied on circumstantial evidence to determine that a suicide had taken place: mostly testimony about the dead person's moods and behaviour just before his death. But even if such evidence was frequently persuasive, a high proportion of suicides by drowning could easily have been judged accidental. One authority says that almost half of them could be reclassified on the basis of the surviving evidence.[19]

A similar pitch of severity can be seen in juries' handling of the problem of insanity. *Non compos mentis* verdicts were rare – too rare. Less than 2 per cent of reported suicides were excused on account of insanity between the accession of Henry Tudor and the Restoration.[20] Now it is highly improbable that so few of the people who killed themselves were legally insane, and in fact it is not hard to find examples of outright lunatics who were declared felons of themselves. After the suicide, in 1560, of Thomas Spryngold of King's Lynn, the jury found him *felo de se* and his goods were confiscated. Complaining that his property should have been used to relieve his 'poor infant children', Spryngold's family sued the town officials, who had the right to the goods, on the grounds that the suicide had been 'madd and frantyke' when he killed himself. They produced no fewer than ten witnesses, including the local minister, all of whom swore that Spryngold had been long insane. When asked questions, said one neighbour, 'he answered Lyke A mad old fole, as he was wont to doe'. And when the parson tried to persuade him to forsake his mad fancies, he 'toke up a pype and pyped, nothing regarding his instrucion and good Counsell'.[21] None of this testimony had inclined the jury to mercy.

The Reformation

The harshness with which Tudor and Stuart juries enforced the law of suicide was only partly due to the government's coercive vigilance. The Tudor revolution in religion – the protestant Reformation – also promoted greater severity. Medieval theologians had long condemned suicide: the most august authorities were united in their opinion that no circumstances justified taking one's own life. Augustine faulted even the most heroic pagan suicides and excused only grudgingly the biblical and early Christian martyrs who killed themselves. Aquinas echoed his views and added the new idea that suicide was unnatural, a violation of the natural law of self-preservation. Many lesser figures, to be sure, had granted that there were exceptional cases in which suicide might be permissible.[22] But by the fourteenth and fifteenth centuries the emphasis in both theology and popular religious teaching – sermons and iconography – was on the sinfulness of self-killing. Suicide was the product of despair, an act instigated by the devil or by some evil spirit.[23] This theme was amplified and extended by protestant clergymen after the Reformation. Tudor and early Stuart divines insisted that suicide was invariably wrong. In 1600 the future archbishop of Canterbury, George Abbot, summed up clerical opinion when he declared that suicide was 'a sin so grievous that scant any is more hainous unto the Lord'. Abbot was a Calvinist. At the other end of the theological spectrum, Abbot's friend, Lancelot Andrewes, argued that 'it is worse than beastly to kill or drown or make away with ourselves; for ... the very swine would not have run into the sea but that they were carried by the devil'.[24] Sym is echoing the views of a very long line of clerical writers when he declares in *Lifes Preservative* that killing oneself is the sin 'most hainous and most to be abhorred in humane *society*' (p. 47).

To clerical writers suicide was not merely wrong, it was diabolical. At the very beginning of the Reformation Hugh Latimer warned that some men are so vexed by the assaults and temptations of the devil that 'they rid themselves out of this life'.[25] The great Elizabethan puritan divine, Richard Greenham, worried that 'Satan doth make many now adaies' end their lives.[26] According the devil a role in God's providence as a scourge of sin, William Willymat declared emphatically that the Fiend's way with 'lewde and willful sinners' was to draw them into despair, so that they would 'shorten their lives by killing and murthering them-selves'.[27] Among the principal causes of self-murder, Sym asserts, are 'the *strong impulse, powerfull motions, and command of the Devill*' (p. 246). Thomas Beard went so far in his best-selling *Theatre of Gods Judgements* as to claim that the circumstances of some suicides offered material proof of Satan's immaterial presence:

> For otherwise it were not possible that they should perish so strangely as they doe: as when some have beene hanged with their knees almost touching the ground; others upon a weake twigge, not strong enough to beare the weight of one tenth part of their bodie; others [have] beene drowned in a puddle of water; which plainely sheweth, that the Divell, either as the principall actor, or at least as a helper, was the procurer of their murders.[28]

Although the clergy were united in their hatred for suicide no matter how radical or conservative their theological opinions, the leading puritans were particularly interested in the psychology of self-murder. As William Haller pointed out many years ago, puritan divines conceived of themselves as physicians of the soul. They believed that by ministering to troubled minds they could convert unregenerate men and women to the godly life, perhaps even save them from damnation:

> Sinners had to be helped out of the slough of despond and up the hill of difficulty before they could proceed upon the later stages of their pilgrimage toward the heavenly city and the Puritan commonwealth. Hence the reiterated praise bestowed upon the spiritual brethren for comforting perplexed consciences.[29]

Many of the leading puritan divines – men like Richard Greenham, William Perkins, Richard Sibbes, Robert Bolton and William Baxter – published treatises explaining the religious significance of emotional distress and describing how to overcome it. Richard Sibbes, for example, observed that carnal men sank deeper and deeper into despair until at last they killed themselves. But godly men could recover themselves, for 'there is an art or skill of bearing troubles, if we could learn it . . . as in bearing of a burden there is a way so to poise it that it weighth not over heavy'.[30] Meant to serve both as handbooks for ministers and self-help books for godly laymen, these tracts depicted despair and suicidal urges as the antithesis of faith and assurance of eternal life – the state of mind to which every religious soul ought to aspire.

The struggle to overcome self-destructive feelings was often described in terms of the venerable metaphor of spiritual combat.

Haller, once more, describes most effectively the puritans' aims and methods.

> They set out to describe the warfare of the spirit, to portray the drama of the inner life, to expound the psychology of sin and redemption. This, they found, was what the people would come to hear. ... For them the ancient Christian images of spiritual struggle were the thing wherewith to catch the conscience of the common man. ... It is to be the drama of sin and grace, of the war between Christ and Satan, experienced immediately in the soul.[31]

They stressed above all that the vast struggle between God and Satan, the angels and the demons, the saints and the unregenerate, took place on every plane of existence. Human emotions had their counterparts in the unseen world of the supernatural: the spiritual warfare was fought in the mind and the heart as well as in the heavens and on earth in the affairs of nations. Like medieval preachers and writers before them, protestant divines used the symbolism of the psychomachy to categorize behaviour and to dramatize the spiritual significance of emotions. And in fact temptations to despair and suicide were a key moment in the drama of spiritual redemption in protestant sermons and tracts, just as they had been in medieval moralities.[32]

The preachers' views amplified old demotic beliefs. The rites of desecration symbolized the widespread conviction that suicide had spiritual causes and consequences. The ghosts of suicides were believed to be restless and malevolent; the stake driven through the suicide's body was supposed to fix his spirit in its grave. In William Sampson's play, *The Vow Breaker*, a faithless woman whose lover kills himself after she has married another man remarks spitefully:

> My best counsell is that you bury him as the custome of the Country is, and drive a stake through him; so perhaps I that had not quietnes with him, whilst he liv'd, may sleep in peace now he's dead.[33]

Whether this aspect of the punishment of suicide was invariably observed, we do not know. Because ritual burials were performed by laymen and were not prescribed by law, records of them were not kept. But coroners were customarily supposed to order that bodies were to be buried profanely, and handbooks for legal officials noted that they were not to receive the rites of the church.[34] A few descriptions of the whole rites do survive. The Aldgate parish register, for example, contains a brief account of the interment of Amy Stokes in 1590:

> Judgment was given ... by the sayd crowner that she should be carried from her sayd howse to some cross way neare the towns end and theare ... should ha[ve a] stake dreven through her brest and so be buried with the stake to be seene for a memoryall that others goinge by seeinge the same myght take heede [be]fore comittinge the lyke faite. And the sayd Amy Stokes was so buried in the crossway Beyond sparrowes corner neare to the place wheare the owld cross ded stand.[35]

By Sym's day it had become an article of popular faith that self-murder had demonic causes as well as spiritual consequences. The belief that the devil enticed people to kill themselves long antedated the Reformation– it may be found in medieval moralities and iconography. But it was almost certainly strengthened by the preachers' repetition and reinterpretation of it. Queen Elizabeth's godson, John Harington – a libertine famous to posterity for his epic celebrating the water-closet – repeated the conventional belief in his otherwise decidedly unconventional dialogue on the legitimacy of self-killing: 'SATAN is not only dampned, but a Suggester, a mover, and perswader, readie to entice, willing to betraye, earnest to bewitche, strong to envince [sic] ... to bring to desperacion'.[36] At least 138 of the patients of Richard Napier, an early seventeenth-century astrological physician, were 'tempted' to kill themselves, and some of them had actually seen the Tempter himself. Elizabeth Hayford, for instance, saw the devil, who told her that she could never be saved, and Robert Toe believed that the 'black boy' from whom he had bought a knife was Satan himself. The anguished Richard Lea told Napier that a malevolent spirit 'will speak often to him and appear in the likeness of a man, and to kill him, and would draw him away'.[37] A victim of one of Matthew Hopkins's witch hunts confessed that thirty years before he had given his soul to the devil, who had appeared in the likeness of a dog and tempted him to hang himself.[38] Stories like these could be multiplied many fold.

Some counter trends

Suicide was thus condemned by law, by religion and by folk belief. The Tudor reforms in the enforcement of the law of self-murder and the clerical emphasis on the sinfulness of despair and suicide surely intensified popular hostility to self-killing. And yet at the very time that attitudes and responses to suicide were growing harsher, some contrary opinions began also to be heard. The revival of classical texts popularized Roman ideas that were at odds with traditional condemnations of suicide.[39] What educated Elizabethan did not know that Seneca, long in love with death, had opened his veins at Nero's command, that Lucretius had slain himself, that the aged Zeno had divined God's permission to commit suicide when he stubbed his toe? Stoic and epicurean arguments excusing suicide were openly published. Montaigne's famous essay on 'A Custom of the Isle of Cea', which offered a limited defence of suicide, was translated by Florio in 1603, and Pierre Charron's popular *Of Wisdome*, which also contained a Stoic justification for rational suicide, appeared in English in 1608.[40] Playwrights, notably George Chapman, dramatized stoic ideas about the nobility of suicide in their Roman plays. Chapman's play *Caesar and Pompey* ends with the suicide of the republican hero, Cato, a terrible death that the playwright presents as a wholly noble deed. Just about to fall on his sword, the great Roman addresses the gods and leaves no doubt that he expects to meet them in heaven:

> Now wing thee, dear soul, and receive her, heaven.
> The earth, the air, and seas I know, and all
> The joys and horrors of their peace and wars,
> And now will see the gods' state, and the stars.[41]

So far as I know, no Englishman followed the French sceptics' example and ventured to publish a fully-developed stoic or epicurean defence of suicide, but these radical ideas had greater currency than one might suppose. In 1578, when he was still an undergraduate at Cambridge, John Harington wrote a dialogue on the legitimacy of self-killing that displays close familiarity with the arguments of the sceptics. The piece is an inept performance, an anachronistic debate among Samuel, Saul and Solomon, who keep referring to post-Christian and even contemporary events. But its most daring assertion, that whenever a man has a 'necessary cause' to die, his suicide is vindicated, for 'yt is no matter what death a man dyeth', is pure epicureanism.[42] More importantly, at least one full-length defence of suicide was composed in England. John Donne's *Biathanatos* expounded the 'Paradox or Thesis, that Self-Homicide is not so naturally Sin that it may never be otherwise'.[43] Donne eschewed classical arguments and examples and relied instead on theological analysis and authorities to prove that suicide was not always contrary to divine, natural and civil law. He stressed in particular that self-killing is nowhere explicitly forbidden in scripture, and that many suicides in the history of the Church had been excused and even venerated as martyrs of the faith. His arguments were complex, deliberately conforming to the model of 'scholastic and artificial men', and they were exceedingly radical. At one vertigious moment, he actually asserts that Christ's passion was the model suicide.[44] Not surprisingly, Donne concluded that his book was too controversial to be published in his lifetime. It circulated in manuscript – how widely we do not know – until his son finally had it printed in 1647.

Medical writers, who revived classical psychology, popularized another set of views about suicide that conflicted with the prevailing notion that suicides were wilful rebels against the laws of God and nature. Philip Barrough, whose medical textbook was reissued for three generations after its first publication in 1583, observed that people suffering from the disease of melancholy 'desire death, and do verie often behight and determine to kill them selves'.[45] His words were echoed in La Primauday's popular *The French Academie*, which warned that the black humour caused 'some to grow so far as to hate themselues, and so fall to despaire, yea many kil and destroy themselues'.[46] Robert Burton, in his famous *Anatomy of Melancholy*, went so far as to argue that religious and legal condemnation for suicide ought to be suspended for people who had been sorely afflicted with the disease for a long time:

> In some cases those hard censures of such as offer violence to their own persons . . . are to be mitigated, as in such as are mad, beside themselves for the time, or found to have been long melancholy, and that in extremity.[47]

Melancholy was the most fashionable malady of the age, and gloomy lovers, sad philosophers, and unhappy religious fanatics, abounded in its literature. A character in one of Chapman's plays who has lost his wife falls into a long, suicidal torpor, which he explains in humoural terms:

> A kind of false, sluggish, and rotting sweetness
> Mix'd with a humour where all things in life
> Lie drown'd in sour, wretched, and horrid thoughts.[48]

'I am mop't', exclaims a lovesick maid in Beaumont and Fletcher's *The Two Noble Kinsmen*, using a popular synonym for melancholy, 'Let not my sence unsettle/ Least I should drown, or stab or hang myself'.[49] And of course the most famous meditation on suicide in English literature is voiced by Hamlet, who declares himself melancholy before he speaks it and is diagnosed as a melancholic after he has finished his soliloquy and abused Ophelia: 'There's something in his soul/ O'er which his melancholy sits on brood'.[50] That melancholy was frequently the prelude to suicidal thoughts was a literary commonplace.

It is easy to see why clerical writers like Sym felt constrained to reiterate that suicide was sinful and to rehearse the arguments against allowing it. Sir Thomas Browne even worried that some preachers had grown so fond of stoicism that they 'allow a man to be his owne *Assassine*, and highly extoll the end and suicide of *Cato*'.[51] And yet, despite Browne's alarm, arguments condoning suicide failed to weaken the prevailing trend toward harshness. Robert Burton, after a thorough review of the arguments, railed against classical defences of the crime: 'But these are false and pagan propositions, profane Stoical paradoxes, wicked examples; it boots not what heathen philosophers determine in this kind, they are impious, abominable, and upon a wrong ground'.[52] His own views may well have been more ambivalent than this, but his diatribe certainly stated the orthodox opinion. Moreover, medical explanations for suicide neither resulted in greater numbers of *felo de se* nor posed any significant intellectual problems for clerical conservatives. They simply integrated medical science into religious interpretations of self-murder. Melancholy, wrote Richard Sibbes, 'is, without great watchfulness, Satan's bath; which he abuseth as his own weapon to hurt the soul, which, by reason of its sympathy with the body, is subject to be misled'.[53] Almost everyone agreed that diabolical effects and natural disorders were fully compatible explanations for despair and suicide and other sorts of remarkable states of mind and actions. But there was a good deal of learned dispute over whether the devil worked entirely through natural means or could actually perform supernatural deeds.[54] Sym is inclined to finesse the problem. His language strongly implies that the devil has powers that are at the very least preternatural: 'In a mans sufferings and distractions the *devill* is most busie to work his owne ends thereby, who subtilly intermingles himselve in all *stormes* of troubles, against man' (p. 247). Melancholy and diabolical temptation were not, therefore, alternative explanations for suicide. Prior to the middle of the seventeenth century, the widespread acceptance of the notion that melancholy was a cause of suicide did not excuse those who succumbed and killed themselves. Indeed, one of the most uncompromising advocates of the notion that suicide was the product of divine vengeance and diabolical temptation was the author of the earliest English treatise on melancholy, Timothy Bright.[55]

John Sym and his book

Attitudes and responses to suicide, even during the period in which they were more severe than ever before or afterwards, were thus complex and contradictory. The rigour displayed by government officials and coroners' juries concealed continued ambivalence about the justice of confiscating suicides' property; the severity of clerical opinion was redoubled by the emergence of more tolerant views and models. *Lifes Preservative* was very much a product of these currents and eddies of change. It was, Sym tells us, on one level a direct response to his conviction that suicide had become epidemical: 'In these dayes, wherein so many doe wretchedly, and unnaturally *kill* themselves, it is a *Tractate* too nessessarie and usefull' (a1^{v}). In his preface to *Lifes Preservative*, William Gouge is even more emphatic, and more eloquent:

> I suppose, that scarce an age since the beginning of the World hath afforded more examples of this desperate inhumanity, than this our present age, and that in all sorts of people, Clergie, Laity, Learned, unlearned, Noble, meane, Rich, poore, Free, bond, Male, Female, young and old. (unpaginated)

It was a conviction others shared. John Bradford had complained as early as 1553 that 'the hanging and killing of men themselves . . . are, alas! too rife in all places', and George Abbot asserted in 1600 that the times had grown so iniquitious that people killed themselves almost daily.[56] Leaving aside the issue of how much suicide may have gone unreported and thinking only of the trend in cases that were identified, punished and reported, these alarums may well have been right. An unusually large number of suicides – over twice the average for the preceding decade – were reported to the government in 1637–8.[57] The long-term trend, is, of course, plainer – at least in retrospect. Thanks mainly to the Tudor reforms, the numbers of suicides reported to royal authorities rose dramatically during the course of the sixteenth century. And if they were not at their height in the 1630s, as Gouge claimed, they were still much higher than they had been when Henry Tudor took the throne. One historian has reckoned that the suicide rate in Kent at about this time was around 10 per 100,000, roughly the same as it is in England today.[58] Men living through these times would certainly have been justified in believing that suicide was much more common than it had been before the 1560s.

Sym's book was thus occasioned by the upward trend in reported suicide, which was in turn rooted in legal and religious change. The form that his response took was determined by his position, his background and his religious outlook. Sym was a militant puritan, born and bred in Scotland, where Calvinist theology and presbyterian church government had been perfected to a pitch that English puritans could only envy. The Scots taught the most advanced version of predestinarian theology, devised in Geneva by Calvin's disciple, Theodore Beza, and endorsed by the Dutch Calvinists at the Synod of Dort in 1618. They had swept away the traditional church hierarchy with the reformation, establishing in its place a kirk run by the clergy in a General Assembly and synods. James VI and I had restored a bench of bishops, but they were men of no great standing or authority, and until the 1630s the crown made little progress in moderating Scottish Calvinism or remodelling the church. In England, on the other hand, puritan attempts to reform the doctrines and practices of their church had met with only very limited success. James's refusal to implement moderate puritan reforms debated at the Hampton Court Conference in 1604 had precluded change on the national level.

Moderate Calvinism flourished in the English church, but activists found that they could implement their programme of preaching and liturgical reform only on the local level, with the help of lay patrons who possessed the right to appoint rectors and lecturers to parish churches.[59]

Sym somehow caught the eye of one of the most important of these lay patrons, Robert Lord Rich, who installed him in August 1609 as rector of Leigh-on-Sea in Essex, where he remained until his death in 1638. The Rich family was determined to transform their county into a puritan stronghold, and Leigh was near the family seat, at the heart of the little Zion the Riches were creating. They sponsored prophesyings – a sort of religious 'teach-in' hated by the bishops – and when these were suppressed, they continued to supply parishes under their control with godly preachers. Sym was picked to succeed William Negus, a puritan firebrand whose nonconformity had resulted in his suspension by the authorities.[60] When Robert Rich, now the Earl of Warwick, died in 1619, his son assumed along with his title his mantle as a champion of the puritan clergy. Perhaps the most influential puritan layman in the nation – the Earl of Bedford was his only real rival – Warwick numbered among his friends and clients a distinguished group of divines, including John Preston, Richard Sibbes and William Gouge. These men acted as talent-spotters for Warwick, identifying the best and most energetic young Calvinists, and following their advice, he used his powers of appointment gradually to transform much of his home county of Essex into a hotbed of zealous Calvinism. Sym's praise for Warwick's '*noble* and *pious* care of providing *able, paineful*, and *godly Ministers* to the Churches under your speciall *Patronage*' (sig. A3) was not merely an example of the sycophantic rhetoric characteristic of seventeenth-century book dedications: it was a statement of fact.[61]

Sym was evidently the model of a godly divine, much respected by his parishioners. Gouge claims that the people sought his advice about spiritual matters (sig. B), and Sym proclaims himself devoted to his parishioners and their welfare (sig. a3). In 1636 his congregation joined him in a day-long session of fasting and prayer in defiance of the ecclesiastical authorities' ban on such activities. It was an audacious act. The anti-Calvinist offensive launched by Charles I and Archbishop William Laud was by then in full swing, and a crack-down in Essex had just begun. The archbishop's commissary, Robert Aylett, was active in the county, ordering parishes to conform to more conservative rules regarding church furnishings and worship and suppressing fasts. 'On Wednesday in Ascension week', he wrote angrily to the dean of the Arches, the archbishop's court, 'the people ... remained all day in the church, fasting, praying, and Mr. Sym preaching'.[62] He enclosed a letter of explanation he had demanded from Sym. In it, Sym admits that he had preached two sermons that day in addition to the appointed service, 'with prayer before and after the sermons for the cessation of the pestilence and for seasonable rain'. He excuses himself with a medley of disingenuousness and legalism, claiming that he had not really observed an unauthorized fast day, since everyone who attended was free to leave and break his fast if he chose to do so, pointing out ironically that it was Rogation (a festival hated by puritans as a relic of the pagan past that the authorities had ordered ministers to observe) and including extracts from the canon law (another distasteful relic from the past), purporting to show that his actions had been perfectly legal.[63] This was a kind of response with which Laud and his agents were all too familiar, and it enraged Aylett, who referred to it scornfully as 'a kind of excuse'.[64] At the time he was writing *Lifes Preservative* Sym was thus in deep trouble with the government. What the consequences for him were, I do not know. The destruction during the puritan revolution of the papers of High Commission, the ecclesiastical arm of the Privy Council, makes it unlikely that a record of any severe punishment meted out for his bold resistance to the Laudian regime survives. And in any case, he died two years after he and his flock aroused Aylett's wrath.

Lifes Preservative was Sym's only book.[65] He explains in his preface that he had long before promised to produce a tract 'about the *body* of *Practicall* and *Case-divinity*' (sig. a2^{v}), but that he had changed his mind. Casuistry was a speciality of many of the leading puritan divines, who were especially concerned with 'practical divinity', personal and written advice to laymen struggling to reconcile their religious faith with the realities of life in the world.[66] Sym was, Gouge notes a little regretfully, particularly well-suited to add to the corpus of puritan casuistical literature:

> For he is an expert *Casuist*, by learning and experience so fully accomplished, as he hath for many yeares beene accounted an

> Oracle where he lives: and by all sorts, resort is made to him to be resolved in intricate doubts. (sig. B)

Why did he abandon his earlier plan for a more comprehensive work, which would have been in the mainstream of puritan divinity, for a more narrowly focused study of a comparatively neglected problem? Partly, as we have seen, the answer lies simply in his conviction that suicide was an especially urgent social problem. He no doubt also felt that he could still fulfil the aim of providing help to those who were struggling to live a godly life, even in this narrower compass. Gouge points out that *Lifes Preservative* retains traces of Sym's earlier plan: 'Many pertinent cases are here and there, yea every where in this *Treatise* judiciously discussed and resolved' (sig. B). But there were, I think, at least two other motives for his change of heart, both of them personal. First, despite his disclaimer about 'the precipitating *zeale* and bold undertakings of less considerate *youth*', Sym seems to have wished to make a name for himself by producing a book that was novel and timely. There were, he remarks, plenty of excellent works of casuistry in print already, while there was no full treatment of suicide (sig. a2^{v}). Second, as I shall argue below, Sym may have seen a treatise on suicide as a better vehicle for propagating puritan and anti-arminian views at a time when he was under close scrutiny, and the government was vigilantly censoring books critical of its religious programme.[67] A treatise arguing the conventional view that suicide was unlawful, would attract less suspicion than one that by its very nature would have had to raise controversial doctrines. As we shall see, Sym constructed his book according to a plan, derived from conventional rhetoric, that allowed him to discuss a much wider range of subject-matter than suicide. And in the course of those discussions, he propounded Calvinist theology and views about ministerial obedience that were every bit as defiant as his Rogation Week fast, although they were far less conspicuous.

Organization and principal themes

'So good is the wine here to be had, as there needs no bush to draw thee to it', Gouge writes in the preface of *Lifes Preservative*, 'Let mee but perswade thee to taste it, I shall need to set no greater commendation upon it' (sig. B). Tastes change, and a brief description of the structure and arguments of Sym's treatise may help the modern reader better to appreciate its virtues. The book is organized around a series of antitheses or binary contrasts that are in turn subdivided into further antitheses. This sort of plan was commonplace during this period. It reflected both the vogue for Ramist logic and for the rhetoric of contraries.[68] The book opens with a statement of its fundamental antithesis: '*Life* and *Death* are *two* things of the greatest importance in this *world*' (p. 1). The discussion of life dominates the first part of the book; the consideration of death occupies the rest. There are, Sym argues, two sorts of life and death, natural and spiritual, corresponding to the body and soul of man. Natural and spiritual death are further subdivided into direct and indirect, active and passive forms of dying. Reduced to the format favoured by Renaissance logicians, the plan of the book would look something like that depicted in Figure 2.[69]

A nearly contemporary handbook of rhetoric advises writers to begin an essay with a brief definition of its subject: 'Having chosen a Subject, express the nature of it in two or three short Definitions, or Descriptions'. Its author goes on to say that the essayist should then 'shew the severall sorts or kinds of it with their distinctions', and 'shew the severall causes, ajuncts, and effects of each sort or kinde'.[70] Although he was not writing an essay, this is just the procedure Sym followed. He opens with a familiar-sounding definition of just what self-murder is: 'Self-murder is the voluntary destroying of a mans owne life, by himselfe, or by his owne meanes or procurement' (p. 2). Then the logic-chopping begins. Observing that this definition was comprised of three distinct ideas – that suicide deprives a man of his life, is premeditated and therefore murder, and is by his own procurement – Sym immediately broadens the scope of his topic beyond suicide proper to include a very wide range of material about conduct, religion and morality. Although the central argument of *Lifes Preservative*, stated again and again throughout the work, is that self-murder is a heinous sin instigated by Satan, Sym assumes that a full demonstration of this truth requires an equally elaborate consideration of the antithesis of suicidal despair.

Indeed, the long opening chapters on natural and spiritual life (chs 3–5), justified by the assertion that self-murder is a base

- Life
  - Natural Life
  - Spiritual Life
- Death (May be passive or active)
  - Spiritual Self-Murder
    - Indirect
    - Direct
  - Bodily Self-Murder
    - Indirect
    - Direct
      - Means
      - Motives
      - Predisposition
      - Lawfulness
      - Consequences
      - Prevention

Figure 2 A Synopsis of *Lifes Preservative*

privation of life, are for Sym the crux of his work. They establish that while existence in this world is precious, the object of every Christian's life must properly be salvation. Much of this part of the work is of mainly theological interest, epitomizing nicely the Calvinist view of salvation and godliness. Sym is rather cagey about precisely how many might reasonably hope to attain eternal life, a politic strategy in the circumstances, although he makes his commitment to the doctrine of predestination clear enough later on (p. 157). He reiterates his call for godliness in his treatment of spiritual self-murder in the next part of the book, describing conversion metaphorically as a kind of legitimate self-murder, the destruction of carnal man (pp. 54–7), and stressing the wide range of sinful actions that lead to spiritual self-murder (ch. 8). Sym's conviction that spiritual life is far more important than natural life does not preclude him from making observations about secular matters that are highly practical. Consider, for instance, his discussion of the proper uses of physic (pp. 15–16). Medicomania was rampant in Sym's day, and so was medicophobia – some people killed themselves with physic, others refused to be saved. Sym's advice on the use and abuse of physic is a commonsensical treatment of a genuine peril.

From the perspective of the modern historian of medicine and psychiatry, the religious framework and language of Sym's work tends to obscure the fact that it is a discussion of actual psychological afflictions and offers a realistic set of observations about their causes, prevention and cure. The religious psychology of the seventeenth century, which constantly elided the spiritual and the mental, is as unfamiliar now as the cosmologies of non-western peoples. From our perspective, the importance of Sym's discussion of natural and spiritual life lies in its depiction of states of body and mind prophylactic to suicide. The transcendent purpose of maintaining physical health and cultivating godliness is salvation; but these practices also afford protection against the assaults of diabolical despair. Contrary to our usual picture of the psychology of puritanism, Sym promises that those who persevere in godliness and live the spiritual life will achieve the highest degree of mental health and happiness. Regeneration places a man 'in a glorious estate; farre above all other earthly creatures, in this world and in the world to come: whereby he becomes so happy, that nothing can make him miserable, but even in tribulation he hath cause of rejoicing' (pp. 27–8). This promise of perfect happiness is tempered elsewhere by the recognition that since godliness is not easy to sustain, even the saints are subject to doubts, and even spells of desperation. But it was not therefore an empty promise, for Sym and other puritans believed entirely that the new birth led to joy and increased emotional strength.[71] There are in puritan autobiographies many examples of pious men and women who were saved from profound and even suicidal gloom by embracing the godly life that he describes.[72] Sym, in other words, was, through the logic of opposites, led to write a description of the positive and joyful state as well as the negative and desperate condition, a normal psychology as well as an abnormal psychology.

His rhetorical method also led Sym, unusually, to discuss forms of self-destruction that other authors did not treat as suicide. These he comprehended under the names spiritual self-murder and indirect bodily self-murder. Sym uses these categories both subtly to advance his political agenda and also to broaden the concept of suicide to include kinds of self-destructive behaviour that have only recently been again treated as 'suicidal'. Spiritual self-murder, Sym implies, includes not only the usual sorts of irreligion and vice, but also hindering the puritan programme of godly reformation. Consider, for example, this passage:

> All sins are not alike, (as the *Stoicks* affirm:) but, some are more mischievous, and repugnant to *God* himselfe, and to our *salvation*, and to the *good* of *others*; and are more incompatible with justice, and charity, than others are: as Idolatry, perjury, &c. (p. 76)

Idolatry was precisely what ministers like Sym felt required to commit if they followed the government's injunctions and railed in their altars and began using vestments and ceremonies they had abandoned on principle; perjury was what they would have to risk committing if they tried to avoid punishment for refusing to obey its commands, as Sym himself just had in the 'kind of excuse' he gave Aylett. In this context the government was guilty of driving people to commit a kind of self-soul-murder. The subject of obedience and its implications arises again, and in a more explosive form, in his consideration of indirect self-murder. Here the position

Sym adopts is partially concealed by some uncharacteristically convoluted prose. Making a distinction between the obedience subjects owe to the magistrate in secular and religious callings, Sym argues that it is the duty of ministers to accept suspension from their cures, rather than to conform to practices that are contrary to the truth of the gospel, except when there are not enough clergy to carry on the proper functions of the true church. In that case, he goes on to say, defiance is justified. Who is to judge when such a situation has arisen is left unstated. The *true* church, he remarks with pointed irony, could not suspend or deprive men to its own detriment, and if it did, then 'transgressing of such restraints is no disobedience to the *Church*' (pp. 148–9). This is an artfully ambiguous passage, but its main emphasis is on the situations in which ministers may defy suspension, the limitations of the powers of the church and the *manner* of resistance that is legitimate. Now Sym is describing the situation in which many puritan divines, some of them Warwick's clients, found themselves. He is, I think, justifying a policy of covert disobedience, in which ministers might choose to obey official orders rather than to suffer deprivation and yet go on disregarding injunctions that were not 'edifying', just as Sym did by holding an unauthorized fast day. That the whole discussion is intended to encourage resistance of some sort is made pretty plain by a marginal note that identifies the suspending authority as the 'Church of Rome'. The charge puritans levelled at the Laudians, after all, was that they were papists and hence not legitimate authorities over a true protestant church.[73]

Just in case sympathetic contemporary readers did not understand that he was referring to the trials of the puritan clergy under the idolatrous arminians, Sym turns immediately to the subject of persecution and the duty to resist false religious commands. He opens this discussion with the declaration that a man is justified, and indeed required, to risk his life rather than to sin against God's word. Among the biblical examples he adduces to prove this point, one stands out – 'the three *children*, that would not, upon the *Kings* command, worship the golden *Image* to save their lives' (p. 149). It is tempting to construe this as an explicit allusion to the three famous puritan martyrs, Henry Burton, John Bastwick and William Prynne, who were in June 1637 condemned to mutilation and perpetual imprisonment for defying the Laudian reforms. Their trial and sufferings were the most dramatic events in the puritan struggle against arminianism, and they became instant heroes among the godly. Alas, I cannot prove that Sym had these contemporary reincarnations of Shadrach, Meshach and Abednego in mind. *Lifes Preservative* was printed after 18 April 1637, when Gouge dated his preface, and Sym may still have been working on revisions when the trials occurred.[74] It is impossible to believe that his audience would have overlooked the parallel. If he did not intend the reference, Sym would have called the coincidence of its appearance in this context providential.[75]

Sym's other uses of the concept of indirect bodily self-murder require less decoding and conjecture. They also show once more how his religious concerns could be a vehicle for concepts that look strikingly modern when their language is translated into secular terms. Sym comprehends and condemns as forms of indirect self-murder a familiar list of sins that puritans railed against: drunkenness, gluttony, excessive passions and so on (pp. 109–10). He also argues that excessively dangerous ways of making money, such as thievery, are indirect bodily self-murder, as is the practice of duelling, even though it may be justified by a code of honour. He also includes irrational risk-taking by soldiers and sailors (pp. 112–18). Sym's preoccupation with sinfulness and eternal life thus leads him to conceive of suicide, not merely as a simple and straightforward act of deliberate self-killing, but also as a complex of behaviours that embody a self-destructive impulse. The language may be alien, but the concept is one that has only recently become a scientific orthodoxy among suicidologists, who have invented the word 'parasuicide' to describe a person who deliberately performs an act of non-fatal self-injury and reinvented the concept of indirect suicide.[76] The classic modern work in English on the elision between self-destructive behaviour and suicide is, of course, Karl Menninger's *Man Against Himself*.[77] Menninger follows Freud in postulating two antithetical and instinctual drives, Eros and Thanatos, and he presents a very wide range of actions as examples of the ascendancy, in varying degrees, of the death wish over the desire to live. There are some striking similarities with Sym's book, not only in the recognition that certain specific behaviours are suicidal – religious asceticism, alcoholism, self-mutilation and unnecessary surgery, for instance – but also in the overriding desire to see the human condition in terms of a conflict between positive and negative forces.

Sym conceives of those forces in theological terms, Menninger in psychoanalytic ones, but both of them are grappling with the same problem, the manifold varieties of self-destructive behaviour. Both see suicide as a spectrum of actions, rather than as an easily identifiable form of death. And Sym, no less than Menninger and others who adopted a broad conception of suicide, should be recognized as a perceptive and thoughtful analyst of the elusive meanings of self-killing.

Direct bodily self-murder

It is not until the twelfth chapter of his book that Sym turns his attention fully to ordinary suicide, or 'direct bodily self-murder' as he calls it. Throughout his treatment of self-murder, Sym is concerned above all with its moral and religious implications, and he structures this part of the book so that it leads up to his proof of its unlawfulness. His observations nevertheless show a strong awareness of the secular dimensions of the problem. Once more he defines suicide as self-murder, 'an advised, witting and willing intention, and effectuall endeavour of a man, by his owne hands, or meanes, to take away or destroy his owne life, whereby he doth indeed kill himselfe' (p. 159). This definition, which seems at first quaintly meticulous, actually embodies a prescient appreciation of the complexities raised by any attempt to define suicide. Nothing seems more self-evident than suicide, and yet it is actually quite difficult to distinguish conceptually from other kinds of self-destruction and still harder to separate in practice from other kinds of death. One central problem is that western conceptions of suicide have always turned on the intentions of the dead. Like the lawyers, Sym insists that self-murder is a premeditated action that proceeds from a man's own will, and he describes the self-murderer's resolution to commit suicide in some detail: After

> premeditation in his minde of killing *himselfe*, *and* after approbation of the *fact* in his judgement, he resolves upon his unwarrantable *motives* to doe it: *and* devises and plots the means and manner how to doe it, and conflict with himself between opposite *reasons*. (p. 160)

Sym is mainly concerned to establish that suicide is capable of being judged morally wrong, and so he seeks to eliminate any hint of ambiguity that might excuse, even partially, its perpetrator. But he also inadvertently calls attention to one of the many paradoxes in contemporary attitudes and responses to suicide. Everyone insisted that self-murder was a premeditated crime, and yet many realized that reconstructing the thoughts of a dead person with certainty was often impossible. Thomas Hobbes made the point bluntly and precisely:

> How can that be proved of a man dead; especially if it cannot be proved by any witness, that a little before his death he spake as other men used to do? This is a hard place; and before you take it for common-law, it had need to be cleared.[78]

We know that the difficulties of establishing intent and sanity notwithstanding, suicide was prosecuted as self-murder thousands of times.

Sym's definition hints at his awareness of some of the other complexities implicit in contemporary conceptions of self-murder. He insists, for instance, that to be a self-murderer, a suicide must die by his own 'effectual endeavour'. This was often not easy to establish. For example, when people died some time after they attempted to kill themselves, considerable problems could arise in connecting the self-destructive act with the medical cause of death. The legal authorities tried to solve the difficulty with a crude, temporal rule: a person who wounded himself intending to commit suicide was *felo de se* if he died within one year after he struck the blow.[79] In practice this test was not very helpful. Illnesses that arose after a suicide attempt were especially problematical. When Anthony Joyce died of pneumonia after throwing himself into a pond in 1668, his kinsman Samuel Pepys ran to the Town Clerk of the City of London to find out what the customs of the city and the nation were in such cases. The official assured him that Joyce was unlikely to be convicted of self-murder, whatever the legal rules, and after a period of intense manoeuvreing he was proved right when the jury returned a verdict of natural death.[80]

Sym's definition specifically excludes certain kinds of self-killing (pp. 172–4). He mentions five kinds of exceptions: suicides by persons who are not mentally competent; by people who kill themselves by mistake; by persons whose deaths are unintentional; by men who kill themselves intentionally for some justified end; and by people who are delirious because of physical illnesses. All of these categories of non-suicidal self-killing presented difficulties for actual juries. Because of the rigour of Tudor and Stuart responses to suicide, comparatively few people were excused because they were *non compos mentis*, as we have seen. Attitudes were so harsh, in fact, that juries occasionally returned boys and girls not yet in their teens as self-murderers. Over 10 per cent of the *felones de se* whose ages were recorded were under fourteen years old; ten were eight and nine.[81] Physical maladies presented similar difficulties. Men and women were sometimes spared the penalties for self-murder when they killed themselves in feverish fits, but this exception seems to have been made more readily after 1660, when the rigour of the prohibitions against self-murder began to be relaxed. Accidents are, of course, still hard to distinguish from suicides, and given the primitive state of forensic medicine in the early modern period, the problem was even greater. Poisonings could and did happen accidentally, as Sym himself notes, and even hanging could be accidental. To give a very late example, the Norwich jury judging the death of Peter Browne, a youth of sixteen who hanged himself in 1729, for instance, decided that he had done so 'with a designe to Scare and fright his friends but not with a designe to make away with himself' – and maybe they were right.[82] Perhaps the rarest problem for juries was one of the commonest forms of legitimate self-killing – death in battle. One of the few cases in which the heroic death of a soldier was even rumoured to have been a suicide happened in 1643, when Lucius Cary, Lord Falkland, threw away his life by charging between the lines of infantry at Newbury. The gossip John Aubrey was convinced that he had killed himself out of shame or grief.[83]

Turning to the methods that people used to kill themselves, Sym points out certain features of suicidal behaviour that also tended to complicate the identification of suicides. The self-murderer, he rightly asserts, 'affects *secrecie*', and often showed considerable cunning in achieving his desperate end (pp. 187–8). Any perusal of a large sample of inquests on suicides from this era will show that Sym was absolutely right. He was also correct in his assertion that there were variations in the means of suicide among people of different temperaments, genders and callings. Suicides who were stark mad or tormented with guilt occasionally inflicted terrible, and sometimes symbolic, wounds on their bodies. Oliver Heywood related the horrible story of a man who had castrated himself and thrown his genitals into the fire in 1682. The victim claimed he had had a vision commanding him to do so and to go on a pilgrimage for Jesus. Heywood remarked that 'there is more than ordinary grounds of suspicion there hath been some antecedent filthiness, both from his own expressions and other circumstances'.[84] A majority (53 per cent) of Tudor and Stuart suicides hanged themselves – it was easy to do and the necessary implements were handy. Farmers frequently strung themselves up in their barns with halters; weavers hanged themselves from their looms with skeins of wool. Men and women also preferred different methods. Drowning was popular with both sexes, but it was the most common way for women to kill themselves, while it took second place among men. Military weapons, notably guns, were almost exclusively male means of suicide; poisons, domestic potions that usually required a little mixing, were almost as exclusively female. In a large sample of King's Bench inquisitions, the ratio of male shooters to female was about 40 to 1; of female poisoners to male, about 3 to 1.[85]

As an observer of suicide in his culture, however, Sym is probably at his best in his discussion of the psychology of suicide and people's motives for committing it. His list of the 'signs of self-murder' is a masterly analysis of the behaviour betokening suicidal moods. It includes solitariness, 'a strange change in outward behaviour', 'a mindlessnesse and close dumpishness' and speeches and actions implying that something important was about to happen (pp. 259–61). These are precisely the actions that witnesses, juries and other officials regarded as evidence that a person had killed himself and not died accidentally. Disputing a verdict of accidental death returned on John Stoner in 1621, the king's almoner asserted that he had been 'desperately minded and having, as it seemed by the sequel, a purpose and full resolution . . . to destroy and make himself away'. The day before his death, the crown claimed, Stoner said that he could not sleep and 'doubted he should go beside himself'. He had also become reclusive, avoiding a visitor who came to the house and dressing to leave home only to change his mind and lie down on his bed. He had told someone that 'he was growing into such a humour as that he doubted he should make them all afraid shortly'.[86] Like most other contemporaries, Sym thought that many of these sorts of actions were at least in part symptoms of melancholy. Among those most prone to suicide he numbered in first place, '*melancholic* people; *because* they are most *cogitabundi & tristes, given to musing and sadnesse*, on whom Satan works most; *and* they are most subject to discontentment, and apt thereupon to entertaine impressions and resolutions of *self-murder*' (p. 254). Describing melancholy in his *Art of Memory*, John Willis personified it succinctly: 'a man very sad, who having his arms wreathed up, and his hat pulled downe in his eyes, goeth up and down in a discontented manner'.[87] The medical writers agreed that those who showed the tokens of melancholy were apt to become suicidal, as we have seen.

Sym's concern with the religious and moral causes of suicide did not blind him to the calamities and disappointments that drove people to take their own lives. He devotes over fifty pages to a discursive review of at least eight kinds of motives for self-murder. They are, to modern eyes, a strange medley of the religious and the psychological, the metaphysical and the social. Aside from Satan's meddling, those that now seem most far-fetched are mistakes in religious doctrine. And indeed suicide for such reasons was unquestionably rare. But as their critics constantly charged, puritans like Sym preached doctrines that occasionally resulted in despair and even suicide. Religious melancholy was a genuine problem among the godly. Among those in peril of committing self-murder, Sym noted, were 'Christians under great *spirituall temptations*, upon their want of apprehension of the presence of *grace*, and favour of *God*' (p. 254). The puritan Nehemiah Wallington kept a catalogue of pious men and women who were driven by anxiety over their salvation to kill themselves.[88] And even among non-puritans the language of religious psychology was so pervasive that people who fell into suicidal moods sometimes declared that they despaired of their salvation.[89] It was essential from Sym's perspective to show that such deaths were not prompted by adherence to true doctrines.

In his discussion of the strictly secular motives for suicide, Sym identifies afflictions that arose from contemporary material conditions, social organization and cultural values, including poor health, bereavement, the loss of love or money, dishonour and shame. These were the motives mentioned most often in accounts of actual suicides as well. Illness was the malevolent shadow that followed everyone as he lived every day. Contemporary medicine was psychologically rich but scientifically impoverished, and pain and death were much more in evidence than they are today. Sym illustrates the frightening litany of maladies he gives as reasons for self-murder with examples of ancient sufferers. But such afflictions caused people to slay themselves in Sym's time too. The most frequently mentioned illnesses that caused suicide were fevers, for not only were these the most common and dangerous of diseases, they also presented at least the possibility of a *non compos mentis* verdict. One that did not was the suicide in 1590 of Enoch Greve, who drowned himself because his gonorrhoea 'so burned that he could not abide the pains'.[90] Surprisingly, perhaps, love and money were mentioned more often than illness as the motive for self-killing. Tudor and Stuart society was composed of small families that lived cut off from daily contact with their wider networks of kin. Romantic love was the common prelude to marriage among the middling sort and the poor. As Sym recognizes, the importance of love and people's dependence on their husbands and wives, parents and children, for emotional support made them vulnerable to mortal disappointment when strife or death severed a crucial relationship[91] (pp. 213–14). Despite the constant warnings of preachers not to love earthly creatures too dearly, ordinary people persisted in forming intimate attachments. Lovers really did die from time to time when they could not obtain their beloved. 'Grief taken for a wench he loves', Richard Napier wrote of one lovesick youth who consulted him, 'he sayeth if he may not have her he will hang himself.'[92] Widows and widowers killed themselves rather than survive their spouses. Mothers like Winifred Goose took their lives when their children died, as children often did. 'Sonday, about none', the Elizabethan magus John Dee wrote sadly in his diary, 'Wenefryde Goose, her sone born and died, and she did [there] uppon for old melancholick pangs destroy herself'.[93] Financial disaster was just as common as the loss of love as a cause for suicide. Farmers were vulnerable to bad weather and the death of their animals; businessmen were wiped out with astonishing frequency. A battery of examples could be given of suicides precipitated by each of the economic calamities Sym lists (pp. 214–15). Indeed ruin was so comprehensible an explanation for suicide that observers were amazed when a rich man killed himself. Unaware of the fact that his acquaintance, Thomas Creech, had strung himself up in his rooms at Oxford because he had lost the hand of Miss Philadelphia Playdell, John Evelyn was astonished at his suicide. He seemed 'to be of a grave and sollid temper', Evelyn remarked, and yet he was 'found hanged, none knowing upon what occasion or apparent discontent or Cause, his Circumstances being so very easy.'[94]

The motives for suicide, as Sym realized, were therefore to be found in perils inherent in the environment and in the basic social and economic structures of society, unendurable distress that arose from disease, the family system and from pre-modern capitalism. He hoped, unrealistically, that the remedies for these dangers might be found in changing people's attitudes to other people and to things, refocusing their love and desires on God. He also recognized that traditional codes of behaviour precipitated and sometimes were supposed to justify suicide. Honour and shame were less important values in Sym's England than they were or are in Mediterranean cultures, but they were still crucial to people's self-esteem. Sym was right to assert that '*disappointment* of their expected dignities', loss of respect from luminaries and dismissal from preferments caused some people – particularly gentlemen and aristocrats – to kill themselves (pp. 215–16). When the newly-created Earl of Berkshire shot his face off with a crossbow in 1622, he was responding in the only way he knew how to complete disgrace. A few months earlier he had got into a shoving match with Lord Scrope in a narrow passage at the House of Lords. The commotion attracted the House's attention, and Berkshire, who seems to have been a volatile and dislikeable man, was committed to the Fleet until he calmed down. Humiliated by his peers, he fled to his county seat as soon as he was released and killed himself.[95] Honour was not solely the possession of men of rank, whose code of conduct was highly publicized. It was the most precious asset of ordinary men and women, whose reputation for honesty and sexual probity was crucial to their economic survival and social standing. Sym needed no example from ancient Greece to show that suspicion of theft might be enough to cause a man to go out and hang himself. It happened often. Convicted criminals were also prone to commit suicide. Just before he poisoned himself in the Tower of London in 1657, Miles Sindercome was overheard to say: 'I take this course, because I would not have all the open shame of the World executed upon my Body'.[96] Nor did he need to invoke the legendary figure of Lucretia to illustrate the devastating consequences that sexual disgrace could have on women. Pregnant and unmarried girls were a distinct and recognized class of suicides. An unusually compassionate coroner's jury ruled that a young woman who drowned herself in 1672 had died by accident. But Oliver Heywood noted that the neighbourhood thought they knew better: ''Tis vehemently suspected that the young woman was with child'.[97]

It is, in fact, the very plausibility of such motives for suicide that both leads to and requires Sym to consider at last the lawfulness of self-killing, the climax of his treatise. For he knows that although suicide was in the abstract hated and feared as a diabolically evil act, in reality there was a good deal of potential sympathy for its perpetrators. Their motives were commonly calamities that could befall almost anyone. And so Sym seeks to underline the absolute interdict against self-killing by showing that it is utterly forbidden by divine, natural and human law. The arguments were familiar and becoming more so. Little very novel had been added to them since St Thomas Aquinas had elaborated St Augustine's condemnation of suicide. And Sym himself does little more than rehearse assertions that a good many other seventeenth-century divines had reiterated recently. The chief difficulty that all Renaissance writers on the subject faced, and which Donne exploited to the hilt in *Biathanatos*, was that suicide is not explicitly condemned in the Bible. Moreover, certain early heroes of the Church, for example, the Christian Lucretia, St Pelagia, had taken their own lives and been hailed as heroes by the Fathers. Following Augustine, Sym declares that the law against self-murder is comprehended in the Sixth Commandment, which forbids all murder, including the murder of oneself. Following Aquinas, he adds that suicide effaces God's image and usurps his authority. He also follows Aquinas's lead in arguing that suicide is unnatural, adopting his argument, hugely popular with many later opponents of suicide, that God had implanted in each person a self-protective instinct that was one of the axioms of natural law (p. 283). Finally, again following Aquinas, who in turn was developing an argument advanced by Aristotle, Sym declares that suicide harms the commonwealth, which may therefore outlaw it. Like Augustine, Sym dismisses the examples set by Samson and St Pelagia, claiming that they were not really suicides at all. Their deaths were acts carried out at the command of God (pp. 303–6). (And how do we know that, Donne asked quite reasonably, since nowhere in scripture or history are such commands recorded?[98])

All of the arguments in condemnation of suicide that Sym advances were repeated by other divines.[99] There was only one point on which clerical opinion showed some sign of ambivalence toward suicide. Some churchmen felt, as Luther had, that it was uncharitable to presume that self-murderers were damned. William Vaughan, for example, declared that 'Nothing is more damnable, nothing more ungodly, then for a man to slay himselfe'. But he also maintained that 'Albeit Augustine thinketh hardly of them that kill themselves, saying, that there is no place of repentance left to them, wee must not presume so cruelly to judge of their despaire.'[100] George Abbot also admitted grudgingly that God might pardon a self-murderer *inter pontem et fontem*, but he added that it was monstrous to presume that he would do so, for he was just as well as merciful.[101] In general, however, the clergy felt that instances in which self-murderers might have escaped eternal damnation must be rare. John King made the key point: suicide was worse than other sins because it left no time for repentance, and so it was difficult to believe that many, if any, self-slayers were spared.[102] On this question Sym tended to adopt a rather severe interpretation. He acknowledges that it would be uncharitable to suppose that every suicide is damned, but he devotes himself afterwards entirely to explaining why it is unlikely that any self-murderer would not be. Self-murder, he declares at a high point in his denunciations, is a transcendent sin beyond mercy. Exclusion from the churchyard is an expression of the Church's judgement on self-murderers. Suicide is, he concludes in words terrible to any Christian, the sin against the Holy Ghost, the unforgivable offence to which the Bible darkly alludes (pp. 288–311).

It would not be fair to Sym, however, to leave the impression that he was simply a narrow-minded zealot. He detested self-murder, but he genuinely believed that by persuading people to embrace a godly way of life, he could help them to overcome the desperation that drove them to suicidal despair. He also took an unusually limited view of the kinds of suicide that were utterly to be condemned. His elaborate definition of self-murder, while it was designed to clarify the sinfulness of the act, paradoxically led him to a broader conception of the states of mind that excused self-killing than contemporary juries held. His list of accidental kinds of self-destruction, for instance, includes rash and unconsidered actions. He thinks that people who killed themselves without premeditating their crime were probably not guilty in 'the *Court* of *heaven*' (p. 173). This was an opinion few juries shared, although it probably expresses an ambivalence that many people felt. Moreover, had his requirement, that a suicide had to make a fully considered moral choice to kill himself in order to be a self-murderer, been strictly observed, many fewer men and women would have been disgraced and desecrated for their desperate deed. Sym's treatise is marbled with paradoxes. An unyielding opponent of self-murder, Sym was actually prepared to be more tolerant in practice than many of his contemporaries. A work that is animated by a profound concern with the religious implications of suicide, *Lifes Preservative* is nevertheless full of prescient observations about its secular causes.

Notes

* References in brackets refer to pages in this edition. The prefatory matter in books published prior to 1700 was often paginated using a system that assigned letters to each gathering of pages and numbers to each leaf in the gathering. Gatherings are called 'signatures' (abbreviated sig.), individual pages are indicated by numbers (where they have been added) and the front and back of the page by recto (r) and verso (v). Thus sig. a1^{v} may be found at the back of the first page in the gathering lettered a. Sym's printer complicated the usual system by using both upper and lower case letters.

1. Richard L. Greaves (1981) *Society and Religion in Elizabethan England*, Minneapolis, pp. 531–7, is the best survey of clerical opinion; Rowland Wymer (1986) *Suicide and Despair in Jacobean Drama*, New York, is the best discussion of suicide in secular literature.
2. John Donne, *Biathanatos*, Michael Rudick and M. Pabst Battin (eds) (1982), New York, p. 1.
3. The best discussion of contemporary beliefs about the natural and

supernatural worlds is still Keith Thomas (1971) *Religion and the Decline of Magic*, London. See also Michael MacDonald (1981) *Mystical Bedlam: Madness, Anxiety and Healing in Seventeenth-Century England*, Cambridge.

4. A fuller discussion of these themes will appear in my forthcoming book, *Suicide in Early Modern England*, chs 1–3.
5. Michael Dalton (1626) *The Countrey Justice*, 3rd edn, London, p. 234.
6. Research on suicide in the Middle Ages is still rudimentary, but at least two important studies are underway, a book by Alexander Murray and a doctoral dissertation by Abigail Freedman. In the meantime, see Charles Moore (1790) *A Full Inquiry into the Subject of Suicide*, 2 vols, London, 1: 286–305; F. Bourquelot (1841–3) 'Recherches sur les opinions et la législation en matière de mort volontaire pendant le moyen âge', *Bibliothèque de l'Ecole des chartes*, 3: 539–60 and 4 (1842–3): 242–66; Jean-Claude Schmitt (1976) 'Le suicide au moyen âge', *Annales, E.S.C.*, 31: 3–28; Albert Bayet (1922) *Le suicide et la morale*, Paris; Henry Romilly Fedden (1938) *Suicide: A Social and Historical Study*, repr. New York, 1972.
7. Henry de Bracton, *Bracton on the Laws and Customs of England*, Samuel E. Thorne (ed. and trans.) (1968) 5 vols, Cambridge, Mass., 2: 423–4. Bracton, of course, was but the compiler and not the author of this work; its sources are somewhat earlier.
8. For enforcement of the law, see C.F.A. Meekings and David Crook (eds) (1979–83) *The 1235 Surrey Eyre*, 2 vols, Surrey Record Society, 32–3. Guildford, 1: 109–10, 2: 387; Helena M. Chew and Martin Weinbaum (eds) (1970) *The London Eyre of 1244*, London Record Society, London, 6: 16, 49, 55; M.T. Clanchy (ed.) (1971) *Civil Pleas of the Wiltshire Eyre, 1249*, Wiltshire Records Society, 26 (1970), Devizes, no. 183; R.F. Hunnisett (1961) *The Medieval Coroner*, Cambridge, p. 30, note 4. For confiscated goods as patronage, see *Calendar of the Patent Rolls, 1381–1385*, p. 339; *CPR, 1391–1396*, pp. 239, 266; *CPR, 1396–1399*, pp. 184, 291, 326, 459. I have been unable to tell from the calendared rolls precisely when this practice began. I would hesitate to attribute it to Richard.
9. Fedden (1938) *Suicide*, op. cit. (note 6), pp. 139–40; Bayet (1922) *Le suicide et la morale*, op. cit. (note 6), pp. 439–42.
10. Moore (1790) *Full Inquiry into Suicide*, op. cit. (note 6), 1: 307–9, provides what is still the best history of early ecclesiastical legislation in England, although it is now outdated in some of its details. The Council of Hertford's adoption of earlier prohibitions against normal funerals was implicit in its agreement to a compendium of earlier

canons. Suicide was, however, discussed explicitly in Theodore's penitential, which was contemporaneous: Arthur West Haddan and William Stubbs (eds) (1871) *Councils and Ecclesiastical Documents Relating to Great Britain and Ireland*, Oxford, 3: 197–8. For the original text of Edgar's canon and a Latin translation, see Benjamin Thorpe (ed.) (1840) *Ancient Laws and Institutes of England* [London], p. 406. For the Book of Common Prayer, see Francis Procter and Walter Howard Frere (1902) *A New History of the Book of Common Prayer*, London, p. 636.

11. Hunnisett (1961) *Medieval Coroner*, op. cit. (note 8), ch. 7.
12. Barbara A. Hanawalt (1979) *Crime and Conflict in English Communities, 1300–1348*, Cambridge, Mass., pp. 101–4. See also Hunnisett (1961) *Medieval Coroner*, op. cit. (note 8), p. 21.
13. R.F. Hunnisett (ed.) (1961) *Bedfordshire Coroners' Rolls*, Publications of the Bedfordshire Historical Record Society, Streatley, 41, no. 197.
14. 3 Henry VII, cap. 1; 1 Henry VIII, cap. 7; R.F. Hunnisett (1969) *Calendar of Nottinghamshire Coroners' Inquests, 1485–1558*, Thoroton Society, Nottingham, 25: xviii–xix; R.F. Hunnisett (1985) *Sussex Coroners' Inquests, 1485–1558*, Sussex Record Society, Lewes, 74: xiii–xiv. The latter provides a very clear picture of the procedures of supervision used by King's Bench.
15. The language of the bills from the 1540s and the answers given to the charges in them show that the jurisdiction of Star Chamber was still novel. For early cases, see Public Record Office, London, STAC 2/1/101–8, 110–12. See also J.A. Guy (1985) *The Court of Star Chamber and its Records to the Reign of Elizabeth I*, Public Record Office Handbooks, London, 21: 37.
16. The practice of sueing in Star Chamber may have originated with Heath's predecessor Edward Foxe (almoner 1532–8), who was even more closely allied with Cromwell. Just one of Foxe's cases regarding suicide, initiated by his executors after his death, survives: Public Record Office, London, STAC 2/6/75–77. For the relationship of Heath and Foxe to Cromwell, see, e.g., G.R. Elton (1977) *Reform and Reformation: England 1509–1558*, London, pp. 184–5.
17. These figures are based on the heroic research of Professor Terence R. Murphy, who examined all of the surviving inquisitions on suicides in the records of the courts of King's Bench, the Palatinate of Lancaster, and High Court of Admiralty for the period 1485–1714, almost 13,000 in all: Public Record Office, KB 9, 10, 11; PL 26; HCA 1/83. Murphy's notes have been tabulated and analysed statistically by the present author.
18. Michael Zell (1986) 'Suicide in Pre-Industrial England', *Social History*,

11: 303–17; S.J. Stevenson (1987) 'The Rise of Suicide Verdicts in South-East England, 1530–1590: The Legal Process', *Continuity and Change*, 2: 37–75.

19. For examples of ambiguous cases, see Hunnisett (1969), op. cit. (note 14), *Nottinghamshire Coroners' Inquests*, nos 292, 294, 304; PRO, STAC 5/A43/1; STAC 8/2/42. Stevenson (1987) 'Rise of Suicide Verdicts', op. cit. (note 18), pp. 63–5 is the source of the high estimate of the prevalence of such cases.
20. PRO, KB 9, 10, 11; PL 26; HCA 1/83.
21. PRO, REQ 2/84/12.
22. Augustine, *Concerning the City of God against the Pagans*, trans. Henry Battenson, David Knowles (ed.) (1972), Harmondsworth, pp. 26–39; St Thomas Aquinas, *Summa Theologiae*, 38, London, 1975: 30–7 (Pt 2 of Pt 2, Q. 64, art. 5). And also the sources cited above in note 6.
23. Susan Snyder (1965) 'The Left Hand of God: Despair in Medieval and Renaissance Tradition', *Studies in the Renaissance*, 7: 18–59. Various aspects of the theology of suicide and its complex relationship with despair and *acedia* in medieval thought and art are illuminated by Siegfried Wenzel (1966) '"Acedia" 700–1200', *Traditio*, 22: 73–102; Siegfried Wenzel (1967) *The Sin of Sloth: Acedia in Medieval Thought and Literature*, Chapel Hill, N. Carolina; Arieh Sachs (1964) 'Religious Despair in Medieval Literature and Art', *Mediaeval Studies*, 26: 231–56.
24. Lancelot Andrewes (1854) *The Works*, Oxford, 6: 219. See also Jeremy Taylor (1852) 'Doctor Dubitantum', in his *Whole Works*, A. Taylor and Page Eden (eds), London, p. 93.
25. Hugh Latimer, *The Works of Hugh Latimer*, George Elwes Corrie (ed.) (1844–5), 2 vols, Cambridge: Parker Soc., 1: 435.
26. Richard Greenham (1599) *The Works of the Reverend and Faithfvll Servant of Iesus Christ M. Richard Greenham*, London, p. 239.
27. William Willymat (1607) *Physicke, To Cvre the Most Dangerous Disease of Desperation*, London, pp. 7, 12–16, 24–34, 70–1.
28. Thomas Beard (1618) *The Theatre of Gods Judgements*, London, p. 307.
29. William Haller (1957) *The Rise of Puritanism*, New York, p. 155.
30. Richard Sibbes, *The Complete Works*, Alexander Bolloch Grosart (ed.) (1862–4), 7 vols, Edinburgh, 1: 148, 319. For other works with the same aim, see, for example, Richard Greenham (1599) 'A Sweet Comfort for an Afflicted Conscience', in his *The Works of the Reverend and Faithfvll Servant of Iesus Christ M. Richard Greenham*, London, pp. 233–86; Robert Bolton (1635) *Instructions for a Right*

Comforting of Afflicted Consciences, 2nd edn, London; Richard Baxter, 'The Cure of Melancholy and Overmuch Sorrow, By Faith and Physic', in his *The Practical Works*, William Orme (ed.) (1830), 23 vols, London, 17: 236–85.

31. Haller (1957) *Rise of Puritanism*, op. cit. (note 29), pp. 33–4.
32. Ibid., esp. chs 1, 4. See also J. Sears McGee (1976) *The Godly Man in Stuart England*, New Haven Conn., ch. 2; Owen C. Watkins (1972) *The Puritan Experience*, Oxford.
33. Quoted in Wymer (1986) *Suicide and Despair*, op. cit. (note 2), pp. 118–9. This play was based on an actual incident, which was the subject of a pamphlet and several ballads. In all of them the ghost of James Bateman returns to haunt his former fiancée: Joseph H. Marshburn (1971) *Murder and Witchcraft in England, 1550–1640*, Norman, Okla., pp. 88–90.
34. See, for example, Dalton (1626) *Countrey Justice*, op. cit. (note 4), p. 234.
35. Thomas Rogers Forbes (1971) *Chronicle from Aldgate*, New Haven, Conn., pp. 164–5, 169. See also J. Charles Cox (1910) *The Parish Registers of England*, London, pp. 114–6.
36. British Library, London, Additional MS 27, 632, fo. 122^{v}.
37. Bodleian Library, Oxford, Ashmole MSS 217, fo. 67^{r} (Hayford); 414, fo. 194^{v} (Toe); 199, fos 11^{r}, 28^{r} (Toe); 215, fo. 298^{v} (Lea). See also, Ashm. 404, fo. 289^{v} (Morton); 227, fos 57^{r} (Neale), 94^{v} (Chalice); 409, fo. 83^{v} (Payne); 218, fo. 42^{v} (Southan). For other examples of satanic temptation to self-murder, see Keith Thomas (1971) *Religion and the Decline of Magic*, New York, pp. 474–5, 521.
38. C. L'Estrange Ewen (1933) *Witchcraft and Demonianism*, London, p. 294; see p. 298 for a similar confession.
39. Theodore Spencer (1960) *Death and Elizabethan Tragedy*, New York, pp. 141, 158–79, 218, 233, 251, 252; Clifford Leech (1962) 'Le dénouement par le suicide dans la tragedie elisabéthaine et jacobéenne', in Jean Jaquot (ed.) *Le theâtre tragique*, Paris, pp. 179–97; Paul D. Green (1979) 'Doors to the House of Death: The Treatment of Suicide in Sidney's *Arcadia*', *Sixteenth Century Journal*, 10: 17–27.
40. Michel de Montaigne *The Essayes of Michael Lord of Montaigne*, John Florio (trans.) (1603), London; Pierre Charron *Of Wisdome, Three Bookes*, S. Lennard (trans.) [1608], London. Note also Montaigne's essay in praise of Cato the Younger, which is interestingly expounded by Jean Starobinski (1985) *Montaigne in Motion*, Arthur Goldhammer (trans.), Chicago, pp. 70–5.
41. George Chapman, *The Plays of George Chapman*, Thomas Marc Parrott (ed.) (1961), 2 vols, New York, 2: 398; George Chapman, *The Tragedy of Caesar and Pompey*, V, ii, 157–61.

42 British Library, London, Additional MS 27, 632, fo. 125[r].
43. Donne, *Biathanatos*, op. cit. (note 3), p. 1.
44. Ibid., pp. 169–70. I follow here the reading of the editors, Rudick and Battin, whose argument is far more persuasive, if less ingenious, than those of other critics, who have (I think) overemphasized Donne's irony. Contemporary readers thought he meant just what he said.
45. Philip Barrough (1596) *The Method of Physick*, London, p. 46.
46. Quoted in Lawrence Babb (1951) *The Elizabethan Malady*, East Lansing, Mich., p. 105.
47. Robert Burton, *The Anatomy of Melancholy*, Holbrook Jackson (ed.) (1972), 3 vols, London, 3: 439.
48. Quoted in Babb, *Elizabethan Malady*, op. cit. (note 46), p. 106.
49. Ibid., p. 166. A melancholy lover in John Davies's *The Scourge of Folly* likewise 'seeks a rope, and then ... a knife': ibid., p. 168. See also Wymer (1986) *Suicide and Despair*, op. cit. (note 2), pp. 118–19.
50 Shakespeare, *Hamlet*, III, ii, 171–3.
51. Browne, *Selected Writings*, p. 50.
52. Burton, *Anatomy of Melancholy*, op. cit. (note 47), 1: 438. For rejections of classical arguments and examples, see John King (1618) *Lectures Upon Jonas, Delivered at York in ... 1594*, 6th edn, London, pp. 184–90; William Vaughan (1608) *The Golden Grove*, 2nd edn, London, chs 23–4.
53. Sibbes, *Complete Works*, op. cit. (note 30), 1: 136, 160. See also Burton, *Anatomy of Melancholy*, op. cit. (note 47), 1: 429, 3: 395; William Perkins (1626–31) *The Workes of that Famous and Worthy Minister of Christ in the University of Cambridge, Mr William Perkins*, 3 vols, London, 2: 46–7, 3: 381.
54. For a brilliant discussion of the debate over the devil's powers and their relation to natural forces, see Stuart Clark (1984) 'The Scientific Status of Demonology', in Brian Vickers (ed.) *Occult and Scientific Mentalities in the Renaissance*, Cambridge, ch. 12.
55. Timothy Bright (1586) *A Treatise of Melancholy*, London, pp. 193, 208–9, 225–30, esp. 228.
56. John Bradford, *The Writings of John Bradford*, Audrey Townsend (ed.) (1848), 2 vols, Cambridge, 1: 60; George Abbot (1600) *An Exposicion upon the Prophet Jonah*, London, p. 125.
57. Public Record Office, London, KB 29/286 notes 113 returns for suicide in 1637–8. Most of these deaths had occurred up to a year earlier. The totals for the next two regnal years were 89 and 113. Some jejune technical problems prevent one from connecting in a statistically precise manner this surge in inquisitions into the central

court with price fluctuations. But worsening economic conditions, which culminated in the catastrophic harvest of 1637, might plausibly explain why the incidence of reported suicide was undergoing a short-term rise when Sym undertook to write his book.

58. Zell (1986) 'Suicide in Pre-Industrial England', op. cit. (note 18), p. 309. For many reasons, this figure should be regarded as a good illustrative guess and not a talisman. Zell notes one problem with the figures on p. 308, note 6; Stevenson (1987) demonstrates many others he has not explored, 'Rise of Suicide Verdicts', op. cit. (note 19), *passim*; still others are evident in Murphy's nationwide data. The rate of reporting to King's Bench varied greatly from county to county, for reasons having little to do with social conditions.
59. The literature on these subjects is huge and highly controversial. For a sampling of current work, see Patrick Collinson (1982) *The Religion of Protestants*, Oxford, and (1983) *Godly People*, London; William Hunt (1983) *The Puritan Moment: The Coming of Revolution in an English County*, Cambridge, Mass., which describes puritanism in Essex.
60. *Dictionary of National Biography*, art. 'William Negus'. This article contains much useful information about puritanism at Leigh.
61. Barbara Donagan (1976) 'The Clerical Patronage of Robert Rich, Second Earl of Warwick, 1619–1642', *Proceedings of the American Philosophical Society*, 120: 388–419; Hunt (1983) *Puritan Moment*, op. cit. (note 59), pp. 104, 163–4, 176, 178, 179, 193–4, 197, 199, 201, 203, 220, 223, 252–4, 258, 259, 274, 278, 280–1. Donagan insists that the conventional picture of Warwick's patronage is too one-dimensional, but her own views seem to me to swing too far in the other direction, turning as they do on examples of men who wavered in their choice whether to defy the government openly. Hunt's treatment is closer to Sym's own perspective.
62. *Calendar of State Papers, Domestic, Charles I, 1636–1637*, London, 1868, p. 29. For the background to this incident, see Hunt (1983) *Puritan Moment*, op. cit. (note 59), ch. 10, esp. p. 274; Nicholas Tyacke (1987) *The Anti-Calvinists*, Oxford.
63. *Calendar of State Papers, Domestic, Charles I, 1637*, p. 260. This undated letter must be the excuse to which Aylett refers, and so it has been misfiled among the state papers of June 1637 instead of June 1636.
64. *Calendar of State Papers, Domestic, 1636–1637*, p. 29.
65. He also co-authored the preface to William Negus (1619) *Man's Active Obedience*, London.
66. Haller (1957) *Rise of Puritanism*, op. cit. (note 29); George L. Mosse

(1957) *The Holy Pretense*, Oxford, chs 4–5; Norman Pettit (1966) *The Heart Prepared: Grace and Conversion in Puritan Spiritual Life*, New Haven, Conn., ch. 3; Camille Wells Slights (1981) *The Casuistical Tradition*, Princeton, ch. 1.

67. Christopher Hill (1985) 'Censorship and English Literature', in his *Collected Essays, Volume One: Writing and Revolution in 17th Century England*, Brighton, Sussex, ch. 2; Stephen Foster (1978) *Notes From the Caroline Underground*, Hamden, Conn.
68. William G. Crane (1937) *Wit and Rhetoric in the Renaissance*, repr. Gloucester, Mass., 1964, p. 224; Stuart Clark (1980) 'Inversion, Misrule and the Meaning of Witchcraft', *Past and Present*, 87: 105–9, which is a concise, brilliant treatment of this theme.
69. Cf., e.g., Burton, *Anatomy of Melancholy*, op. cit. (note 47), 1: 126–9.
70. Ralph Johnson (1665) *The Scholar's Guide from the Accidence to the University*, quoted in Crane (1964) *Wit and Rhetoric*, op. cit. (note 68), p. 224.
71. This theme is very effectively developed by Charles L. Cohen (1986) *God's Caress: The Psychology of Puritan Religious Experience*, New York.
72. The title of one such work gives the full flavour of the conviction these healed souls felt: Hannah Allan (1683) *Satan His Methods and Malice Baffled: ... Reciting the Great Advantage the Devil Made of Her Deep Melancholy; and the Triumphant Victories, Rich and Sovereign Graces God Gave Her Over All His Strategems and Devices*, London.
73. Donagan interprets this passage as evidence of Sym's willingness to conform with arminianism, and thus his 'falling away' from puritanism. She notes that Sym's actual practices do not support her reading: Donagan (1976) 'Clerical Patronage of Robert Rich', op. cit. (note 61), p. 413. For a riveting account of how a puritan could chart a middle way between open defiance and abject compliance, see Hunt's (1983) analysis of the actions of Samuel Collins: *Puritan Moment*, op. cit. (note 59), pp. 253–8.
74. The book was entered on the Stationers' Company register on 18 November 1636; there is no way to tell when it was actually published – long delays between registration and publication were not unusual: Edward Arber (1877) *A Transcript of the Register of the Company of Stationers of London, 1554–1640*, London, 4: 343.
75. For Burton, Bastwick and Prynne, see Foster, *Notes From the Underground*, op. cit. (note 67), ch. 5; Samuel R. Gardiner (1884) *History of England, From the Accession of James I to the Outbreak of the Civil War, 1603–1640*, 10 vols, London, 8: 224–35.

76. See, for instance, N. Kreitman (1977) *Parasuicide*, New York; Richard Farmer and Steven Hirsch (1980) *The Suicide Syndrome*, London, chs 1, 3; N. L. Faberow (ed.) (1980) *The Many Faces of Suicide*, New York. A comprehensive list of works on these topics is in John L. McIntosh (1985) *Research on Suicide: A Bibliography*, Westport, Conn., pp. 23–32.
77. Karl Menninger (1938) *Man Against Himself*, repr. New York, 1966.
78. Thomas Hobbes (1840) *The English Works*, William Molesworth (ed.), London, 6: 89.
79. For a brief review of this and other difficulties, see Matthew Hale, *Historia Placitorum Coronae: The History of the Pleas of the Crown*, new edn, ed. Sollom Emlyn and George Wilson (1800), 2 vols, London, 1: 12–13.
80. Samuel Pepys, *The Diary of Samuel Pepys*, Robert Latham and William Matthews (eds) (1970–83), 11 vols, London, 9: 32–4, 78. For a similar case, see Cumbria Record Office, Carlisle, D/Lec/CR I, 5/3.
81. PRO, KB 9, 10, 11; PL 26; HCA 1/83.
82. Norfolk and Norwich Record Office, Norfolk, Coroners' Inquests, Peter Brown, 11 May 1729. For a similar incident in 1510, see PRO, KB 9/458, m. 7.
83. John Aubrey, *Aubrey's Brief Lives*, Oliver Lawson Dick (ed.) (1972), Harmondsworth, p. 153.
84. Oliver Heywood, *The Rev. Oliver Heywood, B.A., 1630–1702: His Autobiography, Diaries, Anecdote and Event Books*, J. Horsfall Turner (ed.) (1882–5), 4 vols, Bingley, 4: 38.
85. These statements are based on figures from PRO, KB 9, 10, 11; PL 26; HCA 1/83. For a break-down of data on suicides in Kent, see Zell (1986) 'Suicide in Pre-Industrial England', op. cit. (note 18), p. 311.
86. PRO, STAC 8/3/10.
87. Quoted in Bridget Gellert Lyons (1971) *Voices of Melancholy*, London, p. 22.
88. Paul S. Seaver (1985) *Wallington's World: A Puritan Artisan in Seventeenth-Century London*, Stanford, pp. 60–1.
89. For examples, see Michael MacDonald (1981) *Mystical Bedlam: Madness, Anxiety and Healing in Seventeenth Century England*, Cambridge, pp. 134, 220–1.
90. F. G. Emmison (1973) *Elizabethan Life: Morals and the Church Courts*, Chelmsford, p. 35.
91. For a discussion of the part the problems of courtship and family life played in causing mental disorders generally, with additional

examples of the situations mentioned below, see MacDonald (1981) *Mystical Bedlam*, op. cit. (note 89), ch. 3.

92. Bodleian Library Oxford, Ashmole MS 406, fo. 21^{v}. See also, Ashmole 182, fo. 77^{r}.
93. John Dee (1842) *The Private Diary of John Dee*, James Orchard Halliwell (ed.), Camden Society, O.S., London, 19: 40.
94. John Evelyn, *The Diary of John Evelyn*, E. S. de Beer (ed.) (1955), 6 vols, Oxford, 5: 417.
95. *Dictionary of National Biography*, art. 'Francis Norris'.
96. Anon., *The Whole Business of Sindercome*, London, 1657, pp. 14, 19.
97. Heywood, *Oliver Heywood*, op. cit. (note 84), 3: 197.
98. Donne, *Biathanatos*, op. cit. (note 3), p. 181.
99. See, for example, William Ames (1639) *Conscience with the Power and Cases Thereof*, n.pl., pp. 186–7 [mispaginated]; King (1618) *Lectures upon Jonas*, op. cit. (note 52), pp. 184–90; Abbot (1600) *Exposition upon Jonah*, op. cit. (note 56), pp. 125–35; Vaughan (1608) *Golden Grove*, op. cit. (note 52) chs 14–25; Jeremy Taylor (1852) *The Whole Works*, A. Taylor and Page Eden (eds), 10 vols, Edinburgh, 10: 96–7.
100. See Vaughan (1608) *Golden Grove*, op. cit. (note 52), chs 19, 29; Taylor (1852) *The Whole Works*, op. cit. (note 99), 10: 96–7.
101. Abbot (1600) *Exposition upon Jonah*, op. cit. (note 56), p. 132.
102. King (1618) *Lectures upon Jonas*, op. cit. (note 52), pp. 185–6.

VERA EFFIGIES R: VIRI D: IOHANNIS SYM·RECTOR: ECCLESIÆ LEENSIS. INTER ESSEXIANOS. ÆTATIS SVÆ: 70.
Pro Vita Vota atq; conatus.
Will: Marshall
Anno 1637

LIFES PRESERVATIVE AGAINST SELF-KILLING.

OR,

AN VSEFVL TREATISE

Concerning *Life* and *Self-murder*;

SHEWING

The *Kindes*, and *Meanes* of them both:
The *Excellency* and *preservation* of the *former*:
The *Evill*, and *prevention* of the *latter*.

CONTAINING

The *Resolution* of manifold *Cases*, and *Questions* concerning that *Subject*; with plentifull variety of necessary and usefull *Observations*, and *practicall Directions*, needfull for all *Christians*.

Is it lawfull—to save life, or to kill? Mark. 3. 4.

Non est nostrûm mortem arripere; sed oblatam patienter ferre. Hieron. *in* Jonam.

By JOHN SYM Minister of *Leigh* in *Essex*.

LONDON,
Printed by *M. Flesher*, for *R. Dawlman*, and *L. Fawne*, at the Brazen Serpent in Pauls-Churchyard. 1637.

TO THE RIGHT HONORABLE AND MOST NOBLE *LORD*,

ROBERT

EARLE OF *WARWICK*,

Lord RICH, Baron of LEEZE, *&c.*
My very good LORD, and most noble PATRON:

Increase of *Grace*, *Honor* and *Happinesse*.

Right Honourable,

THat *Eminencie* that is in a most *excellent Mæcenas*, to supply the *defects* and *meannesse* of an obscure *Author*; and that *Relation* and *obligation* that a poore *Clerk* may have to a most

 noble,

noble, worthie, and *respective Patron,* hath made me presume to make choise of your *noble Lordship* for a *Guardian* of this my poore *tractate* : which is of a compounded *Denomination*, consisting of contrary *ingredients*, of *life*, and *death*; of *saving* and *killing*; by such reflecting acts of the *doers* upon themselves, as make the *Agents* and *patients* thereof to be the same *individualls.*

The *discourse* is of a mixt and various nature; and the theame of *self-killing* is the *subject* both of *Divinity*, and of *humanity*; of *Religion*, and of *Law* : the full handling whereof may be serviceable to the *Kings Majestie*, for preservation of the *lives* of his *people*, against the blowes and mortall wounds of a *self-killing* hand: and may be usefull for the publick good of the *Church* and of the *Common wealth*; both for the safety of the *soules* and *bodies* of their members; and also, in point of *Honour*; that the *government* of so gracious a *King*, and the glory of so famous a *Nation* may not be ignominiously stayned, by *self-murdring practises.*

In

In which *respects*, it was most requisite that I should *dedicate* the *treatise* of that nature to such a *noble Guardian*, as hath a most speciall care to uphold and advance both *Religion* and *Iustice*; the *honour* of the *King* and *kingdome*, and the *welfare* both of *Church* and *CommonWealth*, in all the *members* of the same, as your *Honourable Lordship* alwaies hath, in the places of your imployment and residence: which, in cognizance of us in the *Ministery*, is specially apparent, by your *noble* and *pious* care of providing *able*, *painefull*, and *godly Ministers* to the Churches under your speciall *Patronage*, bestowing your Church-livings, both freely, and to the *fittest* and *best* deserving that you can finde for those places; and countenancing and furthering the *Clergie*, what you can, in all godly and legall courses; whereby multitudes of *soules* being saved, and the *Church* of *England* (under our *Soveraigne* the *King*) advanced and supported in the *Honour* of her *Ministery*, all have cause to praise *God*, and to pray to *God* for your *Lordship*, and for your *noble Family*, the ho-

 nourable

nourable instruments of so much divine and publick good; whereof many blessed *soules* in *heaven* (saved by that meanes) are witnesses before God, to your eternall praise, honour and comfort, with your renowned *progenitors*, of that practise.

And I confesse, it is the dutie specially of us of the *Ministery* to write your most *Illustrious name*, and highest *Commendations* with the poynt of a *Dyamond*, in letters of *Gold*, upon the most durable *pillars* of *perpetuity*; and ever to celebrate your due *praise*, both, for honour of your *noble* deservings, and also for vertuous and pious *example* and incouragement to all *posterity*, and *noble Peeres*, in that poynt specially of upholding and advancing true *Religion* and *piety*, both in and by that carefull and conscionable course of bestowing your *Church-livings*, and regarding of your *Ministers*; and also, by your constant *profession* of the *truth*; and, according to the same, professedly worshipping the true *God*; thereby publickly obliging your selfe to such *holines* of heart and conversation in *walking with* *God*,

God, according to the rules of true *Religion*; as may give your *Lordship* sound and grounded *hope* of eternall life, and may verifie in you the realitie of that most Christian and *heroick motto*,

Garde ta foy.

In a word, *Divine Providence*, and *Heavens favour* hath made your *Lordship Rich*; not onely by *nature* and *name*, but also in *honor* and manifold *blessings* upon you, and in much good done by your meanes, whereby you stand bound to be accordingly thankfull to *God*; and to be ever mindfull that your *Eminency* objects your *Lordship* to the worlds prying *observation*, and to mens rigid *censure*, which requires your more carefull circumspection in your whole conversation, that you may be as farre distant from all *ignoble vices*, and sinfull courses, (which staines and abases *Honour* and *greatnesse*) and as *Illustrious* in all *vertues*, and commendable *actions*, as your *noble condition* is elevated above the common ranck of men; which conciliates and

procures

procures *Honour* and *comfort* of a higher *nature*; and of more lasting *continuance*, than that which can be had from, or by *Titles*, and *humane dignities*, or from sycophantizing humoring and flattering, that so you may attaine to eternall glory and happines after this short life ended.

Most noble Lord, I commed this *treatise* to you, not onely that you may put credit and respect upon it, for publick favour and entertainment, and to give encouragement to the *Author*: but also, with all *observancie*, to subject it to your *judicious censure*; and my selfe to the *service* of your *Honour* and noble *Family*, for the furtherance of the *good* and *salvation* of you and yours, by the dayly *prayers*, and faithfull labours of him that ever remaines

From your Lo^{ps}. Leigh in Essex.

Your Lordships

devoted, faithfull and

obsequious servant in Christ,

Iohn Sym.

THE PREFACE TO THE READERS OF THIS TREATISE:

AND

To my Auditors in my Ministery; specially my ever much respected loving Friends, and respective Parishioners, the Inhabitants of *Leigh* in *Essex*:

Grace and Peace be multiplyed.

THis Treatise *I can neither commend to you, from the pleasantnesse of the* nature *of the* subject *of it, which is about* Self-murder; *that is a wickednesse not to be named among* Christians, *in regard of* likeing, *or* practice *thereof*: *nor yet can I magnifie it to you for any thing that is simply mine in it; although there is much more mine in it, than might have beene, if there had been full and compleat* Tractates *made by other men of that* subject; *whence I might have borrowed more, and have had more*

help,

help, than now I could, to have made this a more perfect and better polished peece.

I doubt not but it shall be found, in the advised and candide perusall thereof, to carry in all the passages thereof the impresse and stamp of truth *; for which it may be worthy of your acceptation, both for* information *of* judgment*; and also for* direction *of* practice, *in many important* points *and* cases.

Although I did not obtrude it to the presse *for publique use, upon mine owne meere* motion, *or presumptuous* self-conceit *; yet I need not make* Apologie *for my publication thereof, from the incouragements and furtherance of such persons, whose worth of* Judgement *and power of* godlinesse *is such, as might be sufficient to put mee forward to it ; seeing that, in these dayes, wherein so many doe most wretchedly, and unnaturally* kill *themselves, it is a* Tractate *too necessarie and usefull; which sufficiently warrants mee, upon and with the approbation of the* Church, *to* divulge *the same to the worlds view and service.*

Although many men of learning and worth, Casuists, Schoolemen, *and other* Divines : Protestants, and Papists, Ancient *and* moderne, transmarine, *and* Domestick *have occasionally, or but brifely touched and condemned* Self-murder ; *yet I have met with no single, nor compleat* Treatise *of it. And therefore, seeing how requisite and needfull it is that there were in these dayes, such an entire* Tractate *of that* subject, *when as of most other* subjects, *and of many lesse necessary there is a surcharge of* bookes *and pamphlets ; and finding my selfe, in this particular*

unprevented

unprevented by others of a Birth *and opportunity free for me to adventure to the* Sea *of publicknesse, I have imbarqued my selfe in this bottome of dismall* denomination *from* Self-killing; *which notwithstanding spreads and carryes in the* fore-top, *and in the* Ensigne *upon the* Poup, *the white and comfortable* Colours *of* Lifes preservation, *having all her force and ordnance bent against* Self-murder; *to overcome and sink the same; for which purpose it displaies the* Flagge *of bloody* colours against *it in the* maine Top *of every page. And thus I have, for the good both of* Church *and* Common-weale, *and of the* soules *and* bodies *of men, (all which this* subject *doth neerly concerne,) adventured to commit my self to the stormie and unconstant Ship-wrecking* Ocean *of this tumultuous and tempestuous world, under the* sailes *of the* presse, *with flowen sheets,* quò fata ferunt, *whither divine* providence *will carry me. I pray for* heavens favour; *for the* worlds faire weather; *and for a prosperous* voyage: *desiring that my* auspicable *attempt may occasion and provoke* others *of better abilities to perfect my good meaning and weake* Assay, *by their more exquisite performances; and that my* selfe *may not be discouraged, by counterblasts, or ill successe, in my first setting saile out into the* worlds *view.*

The Contents *and* worth *of the* Treatise *will bee apparent to the judicious* Readers, *upon the advised perusall thereof: and the* fruit *of the same will shew it selfe, in the* Effects *of it: and according to your esteeme in* both, *I doubt not but you will entertaine and regard it. I pray you read considerately every* passage *thereof, and the* whole *to the end, before you rashly censure, condemne. or reject any thing therein, upon the first mistake; either of the* matter, *or of the* Authors *meaning. What shall be, upon good* reasons, *manifested to me to be therein amisse, I will willingly endeavour to amend and correct; with respective thankfulnesse to the* Informer.

I affect not to stand upon the pinacle *of publicknesse; objected to the contrary blasts of every bodies impetuous* censure, *neither agreeing within themselves, nor many times with the truth; where* passion, prejudices, *or their owne private unsound* principles, *and* by-respects *yeeld them the* premises *of their* conclusions.

Although I am, in some sort, under an obligation *of ancient* intention *to have made some thing publick, about the* body *of* Practicall *and* Case-divinity; *yet I may be excused for not performing; because the precipitating* zeale *and bold undertakings of lesse considerate* youth *are often commendably moderated, or recalled, by more mature and beter advised* age.

I find so much, and so wel, scatteredly done by others *(of great worth for judgment, piety, and experience,) touching that subject; which collected into one body, out of their writings publick and private, may suffice. And also I doe perceive that it may be hurtfull, besides the difficultie of it, to descend particularly and punctually to the speciall definite and publick determination in* Print, *of all incident* cases, *as the same may be diversified, by their severall* circumstances *and* accidents: *whereupon I have beene hitherto deterred*

terred from that taske; which requires the united wisdome and experience of all the most practically-judicious, pious, *and* profound Divines.

For the present, this Tractate *I commend to your use. And above all, as I stand most bound, I commend it to you my much respected* Auditors *and* friends *of my peculiar* charge; *whereupon I have faithfully, although in weake manner, attended and bestowed my labours in my ministery these seaven and twenty yeares, and upward; (in succession to a most* Reverend, Iudicious *and* godly Divine, *a* Father *both to you and me,) endeavoring to doe you* all *the best service and good that I could: and (I thank God) not without comfort of some fruit of my paines among you; although it be not so much as I would, for the salvation and welfare of you all; from whom neither any intestine* discontents, *nor externall* invitations *could ever hitherto prevaile to draw mee, to whom I found my selfe so strongly obliged and tied, both by my comfortable calling, and the* Churches order, *to bee yours; and also by our mutuall entire affection and respects each of us to other; begun with your* Ancestors, *and continued with your selves as the same ought to be betweene a* Minister *and his parishioners or people.*

In which regard I leave and commend unto you this Treatise, *for a monument and witnesse, in times to come, of remembrance of your* true *and* deare Friend; *whose last farewell, he would be loath should be concluded with this lesse-pleasant* subject. *Wherein (I confesse) my care is most for you, that you may have benefit, by that now subjected to your* eyes; *which for the most part of it, you have heard sounding in your* eares.

 For

For which purpose, I beseech God through Iesus Christ, *to give a blessing; and to watch over, and keep, build up and strengthen you all in his grace, love and feare unto the end; and in the* End *give both you and me the* Crowne *of eternall* glory *with all the blessed* Saints *in heaven. Amen.*

And so he leaves you

that remaines ever

Your owne

Leigh in Essex.

JOHN SYM.

To the Christian Reader.

SOLON, *the wise Law-maker among the* Athenians, *being asked the reason why hee made no penall law against such as should kill their parent, returned this answer, that he supposed no man would doe it. He was thought to doe wisely, in enacting no penalty against that which had not then beene done; lest he might seeme rather to put men in minde to do such a villany, than to restrain the doing of it. But after that wofull experience had given too great evidence of mens impudency in committing this inhumane and unnaturall sinne, most severe lawes were made against the same. In like case hath more woefull experience given more abundant evidence of the more then most inhumane*

Cic. in orat. pro Rosc. Amerin.

Sapienter fecisse dicitur, cum de eo nihil sanxerit, quod antea commissum nō erat, ne non tam prohibere, quam admonere videretur, &c.

humane and unnaturall sinne of Self murder. *And I suppose, that scarce an age since the beginning of the World hath afforded more examples of this desperate inhumanity, than this our present age, and that in all sorts of people, Clergie, Laity, Learned, unlearned, Noble, meane, Rich, poore, Free, bond, Male, Female, young and old. It is therefore high time that the danger of this desperate, devilish and damnable practice be plainly and fully set out: which to my best remembrance hath not before this beene performed by a full and just Treatise.*

Chrysost. Hom.84. in Ioh.19. Augustin. epist. 61. alijsque in locis. Hier. comment. in Ion. cap.1. Cic. de Fin. bon. & mal. l.5. & Somn. Scipion. Proxima deinde tenent mœsti loca qui sibi lethum Insontes peperere manu &c. *Virg. Æn. 6.*

It hath in sundry Sermons *preached, and published, and in other printed Treatises, beene spoken against, and the hainousnesse and danger thereof, somewhat to the quick, yea and life too, beene declared: and that both by the Ancient* Fathers, *and also by late Divines. Yea Heathen men by the light of nature have damned it to the pit of hell: where they have placed* Self-murderers, *making them againe and againe to wish themselves alive on earth, though there, poverty, griefe, shame and all other evills should befall them.*

Surely

To the Christian Reader.

Surely most seasonably is this Treatise here published by an Author well fitted and enabled thereto. For he is an expert Casuist, *by learning and experience so fully accomplished, as he hath for many yeares beene accounted an Oracle where he lives: and by all sorts, resort is made to him to be resolved in intricate doubts. In handling this Treatise, like a skilfull Artist and wise builder, he hath digged deep to lay his foundation sure: he hath begun with life, and artificially distinguished the severall sorts thereof, and shewed the excellency of every sort, that the hainousnesse of taking away so precious a thing, might thereby be the more aggravated. Many pertinent cases are here and there, yea every where in this Treatise judiciously discussed and resolved. So good is the wine here to be had, as there needs no bush to draw thee to it. Let mee but perswade thee to taste it, I shall need to set no greater commendation upon it. I make no question but that wheresoever it findeth entertainment, it will prove a most soveraigne preservative against this horrible temptation to* Self-murder. *The Lord give such a blessing to it, as it may be a meanes of keeping men from laying* Luke 6.48. Vino vendibili non opus est hederâ.

B violent

violent hands upon any, especially upon themselves, and of directing and inciting them so to preserve their temporall and spirituall life, as they may bee reserved unto eternall life.

18. Apr.
1637.

WILLIAM GOUGE.

IN DOCTISSIMVM, ET ELABORATVM HVNC *TRACTATVM*,

Technas Diaboli homines ad horrendum scelus τῆς αὐτοφονίας provocantis, mirâ arte & pietate denudantem.

Mortalibus vitæ semèl scintillulam
Natura cunctis indidit,
Tuendam ab omnibus virili pro sua: ad
Imaginem quæ condita est
DEI, *cruore et sacro* CHRISTI *parta: huic*
Larvatus invidet Serpens.
Hanc suffocare cordis pendulus (*cujus*
Curæ anxiæ cor vellicant)
Contendit: alter *nescius probi, qui se*
Nequitiâ totum fædat,
Illam æstimat parvi; scelestâ dexterâ
Extinguit illam tertius.
Sic à DEO *creata vitæ scintilla, et*
CHRISTI *redempta sanguine*
(*Quæ charior lapillis est, & purior,*)
Morte interit repentinâ.

Quis non beatum prædicabit Symeum
*(*CHRISTI *facit ſolertem quem*
Gregis *tuendi cura :) qui pandit viam,*
Quâ poßit hæc ſcintillula
Vitæ foveri : pendulum cordis (cui
Iter dolores obſtruunt
Vocis) per anfractus doloris dirigit
Ad ſempiterna gaudia.
Acumine inſigni qui pandit ſubdolas
Technas diaboli, quibus
Vitæ ſtruit dolum : qui cunctos inſtruit
Vitam caducam degere,
Vt illius peracto curſu gaudijs
Vitæ fruantur æternæ.
Gregem ô beatum, qui Tuo doctiſſimo
Labore *ductus, abſtruſa*
Cœleſtium ſcitorum ediſcit dogmata!
CHRISTUS *diu* Te *ſoſpitet,*
Gregem *ut Tibi commiſſum poſſis (quod facis)*
Fovere, ſcriptis, & vitâ.

T.Y.

Hæc amoris ergò appoſuit, qui graviſſimum hujus Tractatus Authorem verè ſuſcipit, & ſincerè colit.

A deare Friend to the Author.

FRom *Albion* (whence now we *all* be *one*)
with healthfull *salves*, thou doest assay to cure
Self-murders griefe; that many long agone
doth kill; and fill dark *Hell*, with soules impure:
Which sage *Hippocrates*, and *Galen*, (sure,)
could not *prevent*, nor *heale*, with all their skill.
But thou, by thy receipts, that will indure,
most skilfully canst soundly cure this *ill*.
Goe to, therefore *deare Sym*; God give successe,
Like to thy skill, thy will, this to redresse.

S. H.

A TABLE OF THE *Chapters* and ſeverall *Sections*, with their *Contents*.

Chap. 4.

Chap. 4. *Of mans naturall life more specially.*

Chap. 5. *Of mans spirituall life.*

§ 9. How

Chap. 6. *Of lifes destruction, and of murder in generall.*

Chap. 7. *Of murder as it is of ones selfe.*

Chap. 8. *Of spirituall self-murder in speciall.*

§ 16. Of

Chap. 9. *Of bodily self-murder in speciall.*

Chap. 10. *Of the kindes of bodily self-murder, direct and indirect.*

Chap. 11. *Of indirect self-murder of the body.*

§ 11. Of

Chap. 12. *Of direct bodily self-murder.*

Chap. 13. *Of direct self-murderers.*

§ 3. How

Chap. 18. *Of the finall estate of direct selfmurderers; whether they be all everlastingly damned with the devils in hell, or not.*

LIFES

LIFES PRESERVATIVE AGAINST *SELF-KILLING.*

CHAP. I.
The generall deſcription of Self-murder.

§. 1. *Concerning life and death.*

LIfe and *Death* are *two* things of the greateſt importance in this *world*; both in reſpect of what they *are*; and whereto they *tend*: that is, their *Eſſence*; and the great *conſequences* that depend upon them: and yet there is nothing whereof many *men* are more regardleſſe, than of their *lives*; how *wretchedly* they *ſpend*, and *end* them; and of their *Deaths*, how deſperately they incurre and contract *them*; caſting themſelves into the danger of *it*, by the hands of *others*, or of

Life and death things of great importance, and much to be regarded, are not rightly cared for.

themselves; although the *sinnes* in which they *die*, can never afterwards be recovered, or eternall *destruction* be avoided.

And therefore, considering the dangerous and damnable *practise* of divers *persons* desperately destroying their owne *lives*, and *murdering themselves*; with so great *prejudice* to the *Honour* of *God* and his *truth* imbraced amongst us; and with so much *hurt* to *themselves* and *others*: I have adventured to treat more largely of the *point* of *self-murder*, than yet I have seene the same done by others.

Touching which I will *first describe* in *generall* what it is.

§. 2. *Self-murder described.*

What it is. *Self-murder is the voluntary destroying of a mans owne life, by himselfe, or his owne meanes and procurement.*

1. *In* which *description* we are for the better understanding of it, to consider, *First*, the *object* of *self-murder*, and that is the *life* of man.

2. *Secondly*, the *act* it selfe; which is the voluntary taking away of *life*, or unjustly destroying of it; which makes it to be *murder*.

3. *Thirdly*, the *efficient cause*, or meanes of the destruction of mans *life*, and that (in this case) is a mans *owne selfe* by his owne procurement; which *specifies* the *act*, and makes it to be properly *self-murder*.

§. 3. *Self-murder is knowne by life.*

Life. In explicating these in order, I will begin at *life*; as *first* in *nature*, and more *auspicable*; which is the *object* of *self-murder*. For, *self-murder* being *death*, and *death* being onely a *privation*, it cannot be knowne what it is but by the knowledge of *life*, which is its contrarie: for, no

privation

privation can be defined (in regard of its want of *entitie* in it selfe) but by its opposite *habit*: as no man, that knows not in some measure what light is, can know what darknesse is.

And self-murder being in it selfe *evill*, it cannot be but in and about that thing which of it selfe is *good*. *For evill* cleaves and adheres to *good* for *two reasons*; *first*, that it may subsist, which *extra subjectum bonum*, without the *subject* of *good* cannot be: for, *evill* is like to the disease called the *woolfe, which* maintains it self by eating & feeding upon the body wherein it is. For, as *non datur summum malum, nec datur merum malum per se existens*: There is nothing absolutely *evill*, neither is there a meere *evill* subsisting by it selfe, but in that which is *good*.

Evill cleaves to good.

Reason 1.

2.

Secondly, *evill* adheres to that which is *good*, that it may convert and turne the *good subject* wherein it is, into the quality of it selfe, so making it nought, and destroying it; as *leaven* that sowreth the whole *lump* wherein it is: the nature of all *evill* is ever *active* and destructive of that *good* that entertaines it, or that it is exercised about, it being as the worm that destroyes the tree wherein it breeds and harbours.

Observe. All things are subject in this world to contrarie passions.

From whence we may *observe* that, *as all created substances are mutable, so are they capable of, and subject unto contrary passions and qualities in this world*; and by how much the more excellent any *good* thing in this world is, so much the worse is the contrary *evill* that attends upon and corrupts it; and therefore the better that any *created thing* is on earth, the more danger it is in, and needs the greater care and indeavour to be had about it, to preserve it against its opposite *evill*: so, *life* being of the nature and number of the best things, it is in danger of the worst *evils*, and therefore is with the greater care and circumspection to be watched over, for its preservation.

Chap. 2.

Of the kindes of the life of man.

Kinds of life, naturall and ſpirituall.

THat we may know what *life* is,& (becauſe there be divers *kinds* of it) wch it is that in *ſelf-murder* is deſtroyed by death;we are to conſider there are *two kinds of the life of man*; the *firſt* is *naturall*, the *ſecond* is *ſpirituall*; according as he conſiſts of two *natures*, and is an inhabitant of two *worlds* ; being made of heaven and earth, to inhabit both : *there* is no creature in the world that conſiſts of ſuch various & different compoſition as *man*; nor is indowed with ſuch multiplicity of vitall operations,or ſuch variety of *properties* and qualities,fitted for diverſity of *actions* of ſo many kindes ; and thereupon is ſubject to ſo many and oppoſite *motions* and *temptations*.

Obſerv. Mans care muſt be of two lives.

From the divers *kindes* of mans *life*, we may obſerve, that *mans* care muſt not bee (as the brute beaſts) to live according to the *inſtinct* of *nature*, but that he may live by a *ſupernaturall principle*, and divine direction, a *ſpirituall life*, even here in this naturall life, as he expects to arrive, and attaine to a more excellent and heavenly end of advancement,than other earthly creatures do,or ſhall: *and* there is a *taske* of more and greater *performances* required to be done by him, than from any other creature on earth.

Chap. 3.

Of naturall life in generall.

§. 1. *Of divers ſorts of life.*

Kindes of naturall life.

FOr our better underſtanding of naturall *life*, wee are generally to conſider that, according to the diſtinction

ction of earthly living creatures, there be *three kindes* of *naturall lives*.

First, that which is called the *life of vegetation*; which is the life of trees, plants, corne, and the like; whereby they grow and encreaſe, both in their ſeverall *kindes*, and in their *individuals*. 1. Of vegetation.

Secondly, the *life* of *ſenſe*, whereby *irrationall* and *ſenſitive* creatures do, beſides their life of vegetation common with plants, live inlived with ſenſe and motion. 2. Life of ſenſe.

Now theſe two *kindes* of *lives*, conſidered *ſpecifically* in the aforeſaid ſeverall kindes of creatures, fall not under the conſideration of, nor are ſubject to *ſelf-murder*; becauſe the law againſt *murder* is not given to them, who are not properly capable of the ſame, by meanes of their want of *reaſon*: neither are they ſubject to this fact and ſin of *ſelf-murder*, which by *inſtinct* of *nature* they abhorre, and doe alwaies naturally indeavour their owne preſervation.

The third kinde of *naturall life* is that which is called *rationall*, or of *reaſonable creatures*; which is proper to *men*; whereby they live, (beſides the life of vegetation and ſenſe, common with other earthly living creatures,) according to *reaſon*, or in a *rationall* manner; both for the *eſſentiall forme* of their *natures*, whereby they are called *rationall* creatures; and alſo for their *thoughts* and *actions*; which for their *originall principle*, whence they flow, and for the *rule* whereby they are ordered, are reaſonable, morall, and more divine in all their motions, than are other earthly creatures; if the ſame be not perverted by ſome other exorbitant *principles*, or *accidents*. 3. Rationall life.

In and under this *rationall life* of man, both the other lives are comprehended; as things inferior and ſubordinate are contained in their *ſuperiour* and *ſummary* head. The *perfections* of all other earthly creatures are in *man*, together with, or comprehended in that which is proper to himſelfe, whereby he tranſcends them all. *Note.* Mans perfection.

§. 2. *Man only is subject to self-murder.*

Notwithstanding that *man* indowed with *understanding* hath the greatest helps against *self-murder*, and hath the greatest reason of all worldly creatures to preserve his life, it being so excellent above theirs, yet he onely of them all is subject to this fault and mischiefe of *self-murder*.

The greatnesse of the sin of self-murder.

Note.

And as all the aforesaid *three kinds* of *lives* are comprehended, for *faculty* and *vertue*, in mans *reasonable life*, flowing from his *reasonable soule*, as we see in the ceasing of them all in man at once, upon the departure of his *soule* from the *body*; so the *killing* & destroying of *mans life*, is absolutely farre greater than the destroying of the lives of all other earthly creatures; *because*, both the *lives* of them all for *kinds*, and also *mans* own proper *life*, that farre excells them all, in the destruction of *mans life* are destroyed: and also, all other creatures were made for man, for the comfort of whose *life* all their *lives* do serve.

§. 3. *How naturall life is knowne by man in whom it is.*

This life is knowne 1. by sense.

Touching the knowledge of the *naturall life* of *man*, a reasonable living creature apprehends the same, both by *sense* and *understanding*: by *sense*, a reasonable creature not onely *descernes* that it lives; but also feeles this *life* by the *effects* of it, to be a quickning power of inlivening the body *inwardly*, and disposing and inabling it to action *outwardly*.

2. By understanding.

By understanding, a man knowes that this *life is an act of the spirit, or soule in the body of man*; or a quickning vertue of it, in a continued *fluxe*, by the personall union of the soule and body together.

§. 4. *The*

§. 4. *The soules double act of life in man.*

This act of the *soule* in its *union* with the *body*, is *two-fold. First*, that which respects the *bodie* it self; or rather mans *person*, in that worke, or lively *energie*, which we may, in some respect, call *opus ad intra*, or a reflexe worke of man upon himselfe; upon the *personall union* of the *soule* and *bodie*, whereby he becomes a *living soule*, *Gen. 2. 7.* for *extension*, in all his parts; and for *intension*, in fulnesse of lively power; for his *subsisting* and *growth* to his appointed period; and for use of all his *organs* and *faculties*, for their proper function; being thereby also able to discerne, take notice and judge of himselfe, his state and actions: For, not the *soule* only, nor the *body* onely is to be properly said to *live*, after their *union* together; but the *person*, consisting both of *soule* and *body*, doth live this *life*; which is not the *life* of either of the *natures*, or parts of man by themselves considered; but the *life* of the *person* of man consisting of both *natures* personally united. And *therefore*, when one *kills* a man, we say not properly that he hath onely killed an earthly body; but we say properly that he hath *killed* such a person, as consists of a *soule* and a *body*: and therefore, it is said in Scripture, that there were so many *soules slaine* [a]; not that the immortall *spirit* is in it selfe subject to such a death, or can be slaine; but in regard of its *acting* and *working* in its personall union with the *bodie*; whereby both of them live *personally* together, that *life* which is the *life* of the *person*; which is destroyed, and ceases upon death, *which* is further apparent by this, *because* the *murder* of a *man* is so hainous a crime, in regard of the destruction of the *Image* of *God* in man; which is not onely in the *body*, or onely in the *soule*, but is in the whole *person* of man, so long as the same lives.

The *second* lively *act* of the *soule* in this union with the

The soules act of life in man.

1. Making the subject to live.

Man lives or dies personally considered.

[a] *Joshua* 10. 28.

Reason.

2 Making the subject to worke.

the body personally considered; is that whereby it makes the body *organically-fitly disposed* and *active* to those duties, which we call *opera ad extra*, works about *objects*, not it selfe : which works are the common outward workes of the *person* consisting of those two *natures*, and not of either of them apart.

Observe. Upon life depends the subsisting and working of the person.

Whereupon wee may *observe*, that upon this *life* depends, both the subsisting of the *person* of man in its *being* ; and also all its *actions* naturall, civill and morall: so that, he that *kills* a *man* destroyes his *person*, and abolishes all his *personall actions* and activity, whereby he might be serviceable and usefull to God, to *himselfe*, to the *Church*, or *Commonwealth*. And yet we see no thing more *passionately* and rashly enterprised than *killing* of *men*, than the which nothing should be more *deliberately* and upon weightier causes done, it being no lesser matter than to dissolve heaven and earth, by destruction of a *person* consisting of an heavenly *spirit*, and of an earthly *body*, to destroy the noblest naturall *life* ; and to deprive *God*, and the *world* of the most glorious and profitable workes. Such a thing is this *naturall life* of man generally considered.

Chap. 4.

Of mans naturall life more specially.

§.1. Wherein the naturall life of man consists.

Mans naturall life is fraile. *Phil.1.22.* expounded.

Mans *naturall life* consists (as in part wee have heard) in the *Act* of the *soule* united *personally* with the *body*, by meanes of the *animall*, *naturall*, and *vitall spirits* : which the *Apostle* calls *living in the flesh*, *Philip.1.22.* which is to live neither to the *flesh* to *fulfill* the *lusts* thereof, nor yet is it to live according to the *flesh*,

flesh,directing our waies by our owne carnall *wisdome* and *will*: but,thereby is intimated living in a fraile and sinfull *body*, subject to manifold *troubles* and *infirmities*: in which regard, it is a *fading* and temporary *life*, as *Saint Iames* tels us, *Iam*.4.14. comparing it to a *vapour that vanisheth away*.

With the which *life* all men that come into this *world* are indowed, as *Saint Iohn* affirmes, *Ioh*. 1. 9. and this *naturall life* is onely for this *sublunary* world, and not for the world to come; for,our *lives* do differ according to our estates, and places wherein we are to live.

§.2. *The sweetnesse of naturall life.*

Even this *naturall life* is *sweet*, in regard of the *union* of the *soule* and body together; and in respect of the *preservation* of our persons by it; and for the workes that we may doe in it, for *Gods glory* and our owne *salvation*. (In what respect naturall life is sweet.)

So that the lesse *certainty* that a man hath of a *better life*,the more deare this should be unto him, that therein he may enjoy the present, and may provide for a better; and also the more *zeale* and desire that a man hath to doe good, in glorifying of *God*, and in benefiting of others; (and the more care he hath of advancement of his owne eternall happinesse,) the more is hee to respect his *life* wherein the same is to be done. (*Observe.* 1. 2.)

§. 3. *The losse of naturall life is horrible and painefull.*

God hath so ordained that,the departure of the *soule* from the *body* should ordinarily be horrible to mans apprehension, and with paine and griefe; not onely in respect of parting two such sweet Companions, which separated are *imperfect* the one without the other; but also in respect of the utter *destruction* of their common, (How death is naturally horrible.)

naturall, *personall life*; and the cutting off of all these comfortable *actions* and *affections*, that depend upon, and do tend to the perfection of the same: Which is to the end, that man may naturally endeavour the *preservation* of his *life*, against all *dangers*; and may abhorre *self-murder*, that deprives him of so much good.

§.4. *How life is deare and precious.*

Life deare.

There is nothing in the world more *deare* to a man than his *life*; in which regard it was that *Satan* said to the *Lord* touching *Iob*, *all that a man hath will he give for his life*, *Iob*.2.4. and, for the *excellency* and use of it, *Salomon* calls it the *precious life*, *Prov*.6.26. and *therefore*, he should not part from it, or cast it away for a trifle, or in a humour; specially seeing he can never redeeme, or recover it againe from *death* [a].

[a] *Psal*.49.7.

Reasons.

1. It preserves the person in being.

For three reasons especially is the *life* of man *precious*: *First*, because by it the *person* of man is *preserved* in its *esse* or *being*, by personall union of soule and body; which otherwise would be dissolved and undone. Now, betweene *being* and *not being* there is so vast a distance and opposition, that a creature doth naturally desire rather to *live miserably*, than not to *live*; as is apparent by that naturall *instinct*, whereby the *creature*, to save its *life* or vitall parts, objects and offers its lesse principall *members* to undergoe the danger: choosing rather to *live* mutilate and wretched, than, for prevention thereof, to *die*. For, the losse of *life* is not onely irrevocable, and unmatchable in worth, compared with that worldly thing for which it is exchanged; but also, it includes all other worldly losses in it; and *therefore*, it is farre the greatest losse that man can suffer.

2. It makes capable of comfort.

Secondly, it is by *life* that the creature is capable of any *comfort*, or of the use and benefit of the blessings of good things,

things, that *God* gives us to rejoyce in, in this world: for, to a *dead man* all this world and pleasure of it is gone; and to him that wants *sense*, the use and delight of all sensible things is lost: in which respect *Solomon saith, to him that is joyned to all the living there is hope: for, a living Dog is better than a dead Lyon*, *Eccles.* 9.4. so it is, under *God*, by the blessing of *life*, that other good things are blessings to us; and that the miseries and calamities, that betide us here, are lesse *evills* than *death*: for that, partiall and initiall *evills* are ever lesse than those that are *compleate* and full; those that *afflict*, than those that *extinguish*.

Thirdly, *life is precious* for the *use* and *improvement* of it: First, to *Gods glory*, in spending of it in manner according to his holy word; with respect to God, for the *end* that we aime at: in which regard, godly *Hezekiah* said, that *not the dead, but the living praise God*[a].

3. For the use of it.
1 To Gods glory.

[a] *Esay* 38. 18, 19.

Secondly, the *preciousnesse* of *mans life* is seene in the use of it, for the good that thereby is done to *others*; both in *civill* and *divine* good offices, in *Church* and *Commonwealth*: as the *Apostle Paul* confesseth of himselfe, that he did live for the spirituall benefit of the *Philippians*, *Phil.* 1.24,25.

2 To others.

As for the *dead*, they are unprofitable to the living, as appeares by *Esay* 63.16. saying, *that Abraham is ignorant of us*: and the *Psalmist* tels us, *that we should not put our trust in Princes, nor in the sonne of man, in whom there is no help*: and then gives the reason of it; *His breath goeth forth, he returneth to his earth, in that very day his thoughts perish*[b].

[b] *Psal.* 146. 3, 4.

Thirdly, the excellencie and necessity of *life* is seene, in the *use* and *benefit* of it to a *mans selfe*; in fitting him for *heaven*, by working up of his *salvation* here in this life, and in advancing himselfe in *glory*, both by adorning his person with divine and saving *graces* of Gods spirit; and also, by holy actuall *obedience*, and dutifull perfor-

3 To a mans selfe.

mances to *God*, in tract of living. For, if a man doe not at all live this naturall *life*, he cannot be capable of eternall *life*: and although he do live this naturall *life*, yet if he do not endeavour to extend and employ it to the attainment of salvation, but that it be cut off, before salvation be wrought, he cannot but of necessity perish for ever. For, as *the tree falls, so it shall lye*, there is no amendment of our estate and errors after *death*: as appeares by the *parable* of the *rich man, Luke* 16.25,26. if *God* doe give a man *life* and *time*, he puts a *price* into his hand, and gives him a great blessing, for his advancement to a better life.

And therefore, in all the aforesaid respects, it is apparent that life is the most *precious* thing, that *God* bestowes upon man, whereby all other blessings to us are expressed: as appeares by *Abrahams* speech to the *Lord*, saying, *Oh that Ismael might live before thee*[a].

[a] *Gen.*17.18.

Use. To preserve life.

The chiefe use of the former doctrine is, to provoke and move us to use all lawfull meanes to *preserve*, and prolong our *lives*: for hee that wills the end, should also will the meanes, whereby he may attaine to that end.

§.5. *Of the meanes of lifes preservation.*

The meanes. 1. Prayer.

Those meanes are, *first, prayer to God* for to sustaine and preserve our *lives*, especially in apparent dangers: as *David* did, *Psal.* 102.24. saying, *Oh my God take me not away in the midst of my dayes.* For, as our lives depend upon him, that is the fountaine of life,[b] so our eyes must be to him for a continuall *influxe* of continuing the same: in regard of outward dangers, and inward mortality dayly putting our lives in jeopardy, which of our selves we are not able to resist.

[b] *Ioh.*1.4.

2. Foode, cheerefulnesse, &c.

The second meanes of the *preservation* of mans *life*, is the moderate and cheerefull use of necessary *foode* and *raiment*, with other convenient comforts and delights, needfull

needfull to cherish and preserve our lives: according to *Solomons* direction, that *there is nothing better for a man, than that he should eate and drinke, and that he should make his soule enjoy good in his labour*, *Eccles.* 2.24. according to *Iacobs* desire, *Gen.* 28.20. intreating *God*, that he might have *bread to eate, and cloathes to put on:* not to hoard and lay up, but for his use.

For a man to have plenty, and yet to be in want, is a miserable condition; for, so he defrauds and wrongs himselfe; he is injurious to the creatures, in not imploying them to the use for which God made and gave them; and is ingratefull to *God*, in not rightly using his blessings, so as he may thereby doe *God* the greatest honor and service.

Cheerefulnesse is an excellent meanes of *life*; for, as *Solomon* saies, *by sorrow of heart the spirit is broken*; *and all the dayes of the afflicted are evill*; *but a merry heart maketh a cheerefull countenance*; *and he that is of a merry heart hath a continuall feast*[a]: and therefore, *Eccles.* 8.15. he commendeth mirth; *because a man hath no better thing under the sun, than to eate, and to drinke, and to be merry; for, that shall abide with him of his labour, the daies of his life, which God giveth him under the sunne*: and for this purpose, *God* gives us some things that are onely for *delight*, and of other things he often bestowes such plenty, upon us, as shewes it to be his pleasure that we should use them, not onely for necessity, but also for *cheering* of us; that we may both taste thereby how good he is to us; and also, that we may the more joyfully serve him, with gladnesse of heart, in health and in plenty of all things.

Of cheerefulnesse.

[a] *Prov.* 15.13, 15.

The grounds of this *Cheerefulnesse* are *two*; *First*, inward *peace* of *conscience*, in the apprehension of *Gods* favour and love to us in *Christ Iesus*; in the comfortable evidence of the pardon of our sins; in the undeceivable enjoying of the saving graces of Gods spirit; in the truth of

Grounds of cheerefulnesse.

1 A good conscience, grace and hope.

of our conformity and obedience to *God*; and in assured *hope* of everlasting life and happinesse, all which will make us to rejoyce, yea *even in tribulation, Rom.* 5. 3. with joy unspeakeable and glorious.

2. Outward blessings.

The second ground of our *cheerefulnesse* is, the *outward favours* and *benefits* that God in mercy bestowes upon us; whereof wee are to take the present use and sweetnesse; not depriving our selves thereof, nor deading our spirits with feares of uncertaine, or remote future evils: according to the direction of our *Saviour*, *Mat.* 6. 34. *Take no thought for the morrow*: forbidding anxious tormenting care for feare of ensuing crosses, and according to the practise of *Hezekiah*, to whom the *Lord* had denounced fearefull judgements upon his posterity, who said, *Good is the word of the Lord: for there shall be peace and truth in my dayes*, *Isai.* 39. 8.

3. Physick.

Thirdly, to *preserve* our *lives* it is requisite that we use the seasonable, fit and moderate help of *Physick*, to prevent or remove diseases; which are not onely the enemies of *life*, but are also an *inchoate*, or begun *death*; as *Hezekiah* did take a *lump of figgs*, and laid it on his *boile*, for his recovery, 2 *King.* 20. 7. according to Gods direction by *Esay* the *Prophet*: in this respect did *Saint Paul* direct *Timothie to drinke no longer water, but to use a little wine, for his stomacks sake, and his often infirmities*, 1 *Tim.* 5. 23. that so a man may not be a *deficient cause* of the preservation of his owne life, when God gives meanes to save, or prolong it.

§. 6. *How to use Physick.*

Cautions about Physick.

1. That wee trust not to it.

In taking of *Physick* wee are alwaies to *observe* these subsequent *cautions*: *First*, that wee *dote not* upon, nor *trust*, or *ascribe too much* to physicall meanes; but that we carefully looke and pray to *God* for a blessing by the warrantable *use* of them. For, it is *God* that both directs the

the *Physitians* judgement, and conscionable practise about a *patient*; and also puts vertue into, and gives healthfull operation to the medicines.

Secondly, that we use *Physick moderately*; not out of wantonnesse, but for necessity: nor as our daily diet, bringing our selves under a necessity of ever using it; and so by repairing of the house of our *body*, wee may waste and overthrow it: neither are we then to use *Physick*, when there is no needfull cause, nor yet in such desperate cases, where there is no hope of life, but apparent signes of approching death; lest under an intent of prolonging life wee doe shorten it, or of curing wee doe kill; where there is not strength of nature to help *physick* to work its due effect.

2. Use it moderately.

Thirdly, our care about *Physick* must be, that wee doe not *unadvisedly* and *rashly* use it; *either* by practising upon our selves, or others beyond our skill, or calling: or else by taking *Physick* from others, that be either presumptuous-ignorant *Empericks*, or prophane and desperate *dispensers* and undertakers, neither conscionable in their owne lives, nor tender of the *lives* of others: but, are more desirous of their patients monies, than of their healths: and *therefore*, our endeavour should be to take *physick* both seasonably for time, and also by the counsell and direction of such, as be *both skilfull* persons in that facultie, and also *conscionable*, for religion and piety; that *God* may blesse their labours the better; who will be tender and carefull of mens lives, working by safe courses, and in manner fit for their *patients* good: and *herein*, what ever the effect be, men may have comfort, when *they* shall have insisted in a warrantable way.

3. Use it not rashly.

Fourthly, wee are to take heed that we be not anxiously perplexed and troubled, when upon the using or forbearing of *Physick*, upon warrantable grounds, the *effect* answers not our desire or expectation: But, suppose the *patient* dies, or labours under any griefe unrecovered,

4. Not to be perplexed about the event.

vered, without hope of *cure* : it is folly to vexe our selves, because we have not used this body, or that body, this medicine or that medicine, thinking, or saying, if we had done this, or that, *our selves*, or some other *patient* belonging to us, had beene recovered : just as *Mary* said to *Christ, Lord, if thou hadst beene here my Brother had not died*[a].

[a] *Ioh.* 11.32.

When a thing contrarie to our desire is done, wherein we are not faultie, when wee worke according to our present knowledge and meanes, we should rest content with the *will* of *God*, how adverse, or crosse soever it seemes to us : considering that, as *God* appoints the *end* and thing that doe come to passe, so doth he likewise direct and order the meanes to accomplish the same. *For, God* oftentimes over-rules our purpose, mens skill, and the nature and effects of *Physick*, to the bringing to passe of his owne purposes, contrary to our expectation: which must bee attributed *to God* the soveraigne *Lord*, and is not to bee imputed to unblameable men and meanes, that are but the instruments under *God*, and subject to his controle and disposition : and therefore, touching the events thereupon following, wee must bee content to be crossed of our wils sometime, that God at all times may have his.

§. 7. *Of deadly things to be resisted.*

4. Opposition of deadly things.

Fourthly and lastly, to preserve his life, every man is bound to *decline*, and *oppose* all things that tend to the unlawfull taking of it away : for, that which other creatures do, by *Antipathie*, and *instinct* of nature, for shunning that which is contrary or pernicious to them ; man is, by the meanes of his *reason* and *will*, to do the like for his preservation : who, by his intellectuall parts, can better foresee and discerne what is hurtfull and dangerous to him or his life.

The

The things that especially he is to *decline* and beware of are: First, *Forcible invasion*, whereby his *life* is assaulted or indangered, and his death attempted by others: For, besides the perill that a mans life is in, by that inbred poyson of diseases and mortality in himselfe, it is lyable to death, by meanes from without himselfe, whereof a man is to be carefull, both to foresee the same, and to prevent it, or to extricate and free himselfe out of it: as we see how *Paul*, (understanding of a conspiracy of above 40. men lying in waite to take away his life,) used his best indeavours to decline and prevent the same, by discovery thereof to the chiefe *Captaine*, *Act*. 23. 17. and so our *Saviour* himselfe gave commandement to his *Disciples*, that when their enemies did *persecute them in one citie they should flee to another*, *Mat* 10. 23. according to his own practise, who to avoid and escape the bloody hands of *Herod*, was carried into *Egypt* [a]: which course is abundantly warranted by manifold arguments and examples in *Scripture*, and upon just reason, is so good, that necessity of saving a mans life, against unjust and violent invasion, warrants him, both in the Courts of Heaven and Earth, in his owne lawfull defence, to kill, rather than to suffer himselfe to be unjustly killed: because, that *love*, which is the fulfilling of the *Law* [b], begins at a mans selfe, it being the *rule*, that *we should love our neighbours as our selves*. How can it bee expected that he will preserve other mens lives, that is carelesse of his owne?

1 Invasion.

[a] *Mat*. 2.

[b] *Rom*. 13. 10.

Qui sibi nequam cui bonus?

Secondly, for preservation of mans life, he must not onely not submit himselfe *passively* to private deadly cruelties of others: but also he must not *actively* expose himselfe to hazard the losse of his life, upon self-will'd dangerous undertakings, without a lawfull calling, and sufficiency of strength to undertake, or go safely through the enterprise: as our *Saviour* intimates, *Luk*. 14. 31. in the parable of the *King* going to warre, that would

2. Dangerous undertakings.

not undertake above his power.

3. Motions of self-murder.

Thirdly, the thing that a man is to decline, for preservation of his life is, that he do abhorre and reject all unnaturall *motions*, or resolutions of *self-murder*. That the *heart* of man may neither be suffered to breed, nor to entertaine the thoughts of his owne destruction; like *a viper* conceiving and fomenting such an issue, as in the birth thereof destroyes the parent that gave it being. The *thoughts* of *evill*, that a man doth at first but dally withall, and fearelesly beholds in his mind, (presuming of his power over them;) at length possesse him, and master him: and *therefore*, above all things, wee are to keep our *heart*, for, *out of it proceeds all evill. Prov.*4.23. *Mat.*15.19. if the seed and spawne of sin in the motions of it in the heart be extinguished and destroyed, then there is no feare of the breaking of it out in act: for, as *Saint Iames* saith, *Lust* first *conceives* before it *brings forth sin* [a].

[a] *Jam.*1.15.

§. 8. *Of spending our lives well.*

To spend our lives well.

Another generall use of the former doctrine of the *pretiousnesse* of *mans life* is, *that wee be the more carefull to husband and spend it well; to the glory of God; our owne good and comfort; and for the good of others, among whom we live:* considering that our life is too good to be spent away in idlenesse, to bee wasted prodigally; or to bee mis-imployed in the service of *sinne* and *Sathan*; and is irrevocable, when it is past, that it cannot be had backe againe; that it might be better spent, and former errors be undone: and therefore, we doe ever need, with the *Psalmist*, to intreat that *God would so teach us to number our dayes, that wee may apply our hearts unto wisdome* [b]: being ever mindfull of the *Apostles* admonition; *redeeme the time, because the dayes are evill, Eph.*5.16.

[b] *Psal.*90.12.

Motives.

The motives that may move us to spend our time, and

and *life* well, are specially these *three* following. *First*, the wickednesse of the world, which should make us more watchfull, to catch at all opportunities to do good; that our *life*, that will waste away with the rust of doing nothing, may bee comfortably spent, in well doing: *Happy shall that servant be, whom his Lord, when he comes, shall find doing so. Mat.* 24.46. 1. Badnesse of the times.

Secondly, *the shortnesse and uncertainty of our lives*, (which passes as a shadow, or a vapour, that appeares no more,) puts us in mind, not to deferre; but, while it is called to day, requires us, with sobriety and watchfulnesse, to be couragious and incessant in well doing. *Post est occasio calva, the morrow is not ours*; and if we be cut off before it comes, our worke being undone; how then will it grieve us that we were so slothfull? 2. Shortnesse of our lives.

Thirdly, *the weightinesse of that which depends upon well-spending of our lives here*; as, the comfort of our soules, and everlasting salvation hereafter, calls upon us to consider, that no estate or stock need be so frugally spent, as the short life and few dayes of man; than which, nothing is more wastefully, worthlesly, vainely, nor worse mis-spent; specially *three* wayes: to which we may adde a *fourth*. 3. The benefit of well-spending them.

First, *in doing of naughtinesse and evill*; which wee ought not to doe, it being forbidden by God: whereby many men take great paines in vile courses of prophanenesse, filthinesse, drunkennesse, fighting against the truth, and the like, mis-spending their meanes, and lives, to oppose God, and to get, and goe to hell; by rightly imploying whereof, they might, with farre lesse trouble and adoe, happily do much good, and attaine to *heaven* and everlasting glory. How men mis-spend their lives. 1. By doing evill.

Secondly, *by doing that, which is little, or nothing to the purpose*; *for a mans true happinesse and comfort*; as impertinent studies, pursuite of curiosity and vanity, hunting immoderately, and prosecuting eagerly after the profits 2 By doing things impertinent.

 and

and pleasures of this world; that before *God* will availe a man nothing for his salvation, and eternall, or spirituall comfort; when the things whereupon the same depends have beene neglected: for as the *Apostle* sayes, *bodily exercise profiteth little; but godlinesse is profitable to all things* [a].

[a] 1 Tim.4.8.

3. By idlenesse.

Thirdly, men do often mis-spend their *lives*, by *wasting* it in *sluggish idlenesse*; when they minde and indeavour nothing so much as *how they may* sleepe at ease, or passe away their time in sloath, or sottishnesse; so driving their dayes and lives to an end in doing nothing, although none have more to do than they: while others complaine of want of time in their imployments, about their commendable affaires; these object, that *they* have more time than they know what to doe with. *Such* are, *iners & inutile pondus, an unprofitable burthen, and the excrements of the Church and Commonwealth*; dead while they live, and, as hoggs, more profitable by their deaths than by their lives: like *ciphers*, they keepe a place, but are of no value or worth: they go out of the world, before they regard why they came into the world; when they are present, they are unprofitable, and when they are gone, they are not missed, for any good they ever did.

Causes of idlenesse.

The causes of which idle course of life, are, affectation of their owne bodily and worldly ease, contenting the flesh with doing of nothing; and care onely to avoid trouble, which attends upon active and industrious godly imployment: but wee finde the sentence of condemnation passed no lesse against those that omitted to doe their duties [b]; than against them who committed that evill which was forbidden. *Wilfull defects* and omissions of doing good bring damnation. He that wanted his *wedding garment* was thrust out of doores, and cast into *utter darkenesse Mat.22.13.*

[b] Mat.25.43.

Why was *Meroz* cursed? *because they came not out to the helpe of the Lord against the mighty, Judg.5.23.* An idle

idle and slothfull spending of a man life, is every where in Scripture condemned; and by nature the Bees expell the Droanes.

4. By over-charging ones selfe in doing good.

There is another way of *mis-spending* a mans *life*, proceeding from good *affection*, in a pious manner; *by his over-tasking, or overcharging himselfe, in religious performances, or good duties, above his strength:* as in *fasting* and *prayer*, in *studies* and *labours* in the *Word*, and the like: whereby a mans life is soone spent; like a sudden blaze consumed in a present flame; which, by more frugall ordering of it, according to his ability, might last much longer, to the greater benefit both of *Church* and *Commonwealth*: and thus I have done with the discourse of *mans naturall life*.

Neque immoderata imperamus jejunia. Hieron. *ad Demetriadem.*

CHAP. 5.
Of mans spirituall life.

§. 1. *What spirituall life is.*

Spirituall life what.

WEe are now to consider of mans *spirituall life*; which is not properly the life of his *spirit*, whereby the spirits of all men doe live: but, it is the *life of a man, whereby he, personally considered, lives a spirituall, and supernaturall life.*

Which consists in the gratious union of man with *God* in *Christ*; who is our *life* [a]: whom *God* sent into the world, that we might live through him, 1 *Ioh*.4.9. by whom we are delivered from death by his *spirit*; because of the spiritualnesse of this our *life*, it is said to be *hid with God in Christ*, *Col*.3.3.

[a] *Ioh*.14.6.

§. 2. *The acts of spirituall life.*

Acts of it.

1. *Of* this *spirituall life* there are *two acts*: *First*, that

 whereby

whereby we, that were dead in trespasses and sinnes, are quickned. *Ephes* 2.1. being translated into a state of spirituall and eternall *life*; and indowed with a new lively *principle* of *grace*; inabling us to spirituall motion.

2. *The second act* of this *life* is, that, whereby we *walke*, and *worke*, according to the direction of Gods word; and the good motions of the good spirit: so being made conformable to *God*, and walking with *God*, as new creatures, in the estate of *regeneration*.

§. 3. *The degrees of spirituall life.*

Degrees of it. 1. *Of* this *life* there are *two degrees*: *First*, that which is by *faith*, in the state of *grace* in this world, as our *Saviour* tells us, *that hee that beleeveth on him hath eternall life*, *Ioh*.6.47. by this life we are to live *according to God in the spirit*, 1 *Pet*.4.6. and also, *if wee live in the spirit, wee are also to walke in the spirit* [a]. *Faith* and good *workes*, as the cause and effects, are alwaies together, *Iam*. 2.2[illegible].

[a] *Gal* 5.25.

The second degree of our *spirituall life*, is that which is by *vision* or sight, in *glorie*: whereof *Saint Iohn* tells us, *that we shall be like to Christ, for we shall see him as he is*, 1 *Ioh*.3.2. and touching those things wherein it consists, *Saint Paul* saies, *that eye hath not seene, nor eare heard, neither have entred into the heart of man, the things which God hath prepared for them that love him* [b]. And he himselfe, having beene rapt up into the third *heaven*, confesseth that there he heard *unspeakable words* [c]; which was not lawfull for him to utter [d], in regard of impossibility; there being want of words to expresse such *supernaturall* matter, and his *conceiving* being lesse than could comprehend what was represented to him. This *spirituall life*, in the estate of grace in this world, is apprehended, first, in the *understanding*, *Heb*.11.1. but in the state of *glory* in heaven, it is visibly injoyed, by way of a spirituall *sensiblenesse*. In the former state, *life* is put into us;

[b] 1 *Cor*.2.9.

[c] ἄῤῥητα ῥήματα.

[d] 2 *Cor*.12.4.

Note.

us;but in this latter state,wee shall be put into *life*; filled with it, within us; and fully compassed about with it, without us ; as vessels cast into the *sea* are filled with water within and without: so being comprehended by it, as well as it is comprehended by us according to our modell and capacity.

Although these *degrees* of *spirituall life* bee severall; yet the life it selfe is but *one*, whereupon these subsist. This life is one.

This life is *begunne* here in the state of *grace* by faith in *Christ*, and is *consummate*, and fully accomplished by vision, or sensible fruition, in the state of *glory* in heaven, according to our hope, & Gods promises to us: although at death faith doth cease, yet the *spirituall life*, thereby wrought in us, is not extinguished; for, or by the introduction of the *life* of *glory*; but the manner onely is altered, and degree of spirituall living *intended* to perfection.

A mans severall and *graduall kinds* of lives do stand in *subordination* one to another thus, to the life of *glory* in heaven with the *Lord*, none can attaine, but those that first live by *faith in Christ*, in the state of grace; in manner conformable to Gods word and will: neither can any attaine to the *life* of *grace*, but those that first live the *naturall life*; which is the materiall, or passive foundation of the other twaine: for this naturall life gives *beeing* to a man; the other two doe adde *perfection* and happinesse to him: so that if the first be a blessing, much more are the other lives blessings, and highly to be esteemed. The degrees subordinate.

These three *degrees*, or kinds of *life are like* to the three roomes of the *Temple*, where all entrance into the most *Holy place* was made by the *Holy place*; and into *this* by the *outward Court*; so, none could come into the *third*, but by the *second*, and none could come into the *second*, but by the *first*: whereby it appeares, that *naturall life* brings man under a possibility and capacitie of the *life* of *grace* and *glory*; and the life of *grace* brings us, that

certainely

certainely have it, into faire assurance of attaining the life of *glory*; for that they are *specifically* the same, but *gradually* different: as the *twilight*, and *perfect light* at noone.

§. 4. *Who may have spirituall life, and by whose fault doe any misse of it.*

Denyed to none.

Although all men, that doe live the *naturall life*, attaine not to the *spirituall*; yet spirituall life is denyed expresly to no man, *if they will* carefully use the meanes, and truly indeavour to have it: for, whosoever miscarries and misseth of this spiritual life, he himselfe is guilty, and cause thereof: for, *God* hath given sufficient meanes of salvation, and made a generall offer thereof to all men: as *Ioshua* did *call Heaven and earth to record that day, that he had set before the people life and death*, and so did put them to their choise, *Ioshua* 24. 14. if with *Mary* wee choose the *better part*, wee are happy: it were better for us that wee had never lived at all, than that wee should not live this *spirituall life*; without which we are *dead* while we live[a].

Lost by our owne fault.

[a] 1 *Tim.* 5. 6.

None can be excused, by pretense of want of particular *insinuation* of the *Gospell*; (that is) the *power of God to salvation*, to every *individuall* man; or, because it is not naturally ingrafted in every mans heart, as is the *morall Law*, in the generall *principles*, and *matter unformed* thereof; though not as it is perfectly *formed*, in every particular precept. For the *Gospell* is not contrary to the *Law*; but the *Law*, both *morall* and *ceremoniall*, is our *Schoolemaster* to drive and direct us to *Christ* for salvation[b]; and that for the same we should neither rest upon our selves, nor upon the Law.

[b] *Gal.* 3. 21. 24.

The Gospell to al published.

1. To *Adam*.

[c] *Gen.* 3. 15.

Againe, when *God* himselfe, at the *beginning*, first after the fall, preached and delivered the *gospell* to *Adam* and *Eve*[c], he did publish and give the same to every particular

ticular man and woman, then in them, that ever should be borne into the world; to whom their *parents* were bound successively to preach and deliver the *Gospell*, by a continued *tradition*. If any of their *children* should have died before they were capable of salvation by that mean; then (as it is most probable) they were to be saved, as dying *infants* of *beleeving parents* now are. *Note.*

2. To his posterity.

Furthermore, ever since the first promulgation of the *gospell* to *Adam*, it hath pleased *God* to repeat, and more and more fully to explicate the same by his *servants*, with invitation of all men to entertaine the same, from age to age, in such places and companies, where all men might take notice thereof, if they were not wanting to themselves, in adjoyning themselves to, and keeping union with the *Church*; where they might be within the hearing of the *Gospell*; which is sufficient to leave men *inexcusable*, in their ignorance of it: Although *God* by his providence and prerogative *Royall*, directs, dispenses, and applyes the Gospell, in the ministrie of it, to some people, and not to others; according to the good pleasure of his will, after the first promulgation: as wee see how the publication of *Lawes* and *proclamations* of *Princes*, (which are as little written in their subjects hearts as the *gospell* is in mankind) being *published* in manner, and in places, as *Princes* please, whereby, and whence their subjects are to take notice of them; *ignorance* of the same excuses not, but that the disobedient and transgressors of them may justly be punished; notwithstanding that they never knew them: seeing every man is at his owne perill to looke after, and take notice of those *Lawes*, or ordinances, whereby he is to *live*; whether they proceed from inbred *naturall* notions, or outwardly from the *will* of his *Superiours*. Comparison.

§. 5. *Of the excellency of spirituall life.*

Spirituall lifes excellencie

Mans spirituall life far excells his *naturall life*; in *three* respects especially.

1. For nature.

First, in regard of the things wherein it consists: the *naturall life* consists but in the *union* of *soule* and *body* which are but *naturall* things; and holds by a tie of naturall spirits in the blood; upheld by earthly naturall meanes, such as man is made and compounded of.

a Rom. 14.8. 2 Cor. 5.15. 1 Pet. 4. 2.

Spirituall life, which is now *supernaturall*, consists in a *spirituall* union with *God*, by his eternall *Sonne* and *Spirit*; and is upheld by supernaturall meanes, and divine influence, whereby we live the *life* of *God*; and also by *God*, and to *God* [a], and so, as the life of *naturall* or reasonable *men*, farre excells the lives of *brutes*; so doth this *spirituall life* of Gods regenerated people, farre surpasse the lives of meere *naturall* and unregenerated men: and therefore it is, that men are farre more beholding to the *meanes* and *instruments* of their *spirituall life*, than to the meanes of their *naturall*; for, naturall life without spirituall, makes a man but subject to misery; whereas the spirituall life, upon the naturall, makes a man everlastingly happy: which should quicken in us a desire, and endeavour to be *borne againe*, according to our *Saviours* speech, *Ioh.* 3. 3.

2 For continuance.

Secondly, the *spirituall life* farre transcends the *naturall*, in respect of its *continuance:* the *naturall life*, depending upon mutable and mortall ties and bonds, and subject to many externall harmfull accidents; is *fraile*, and, at last is swallowed up of *mortality*; it being *appointed for all men once to die*, *Heb.* 9. 27. and few and evill are our dayes in this world; wherein wee have no abiding city, the *spirituall life* is *eternall*, without subjection to death; because, it is in it selfe *supernaturall*, and advanced above the reach and power of all things that can destroy life and

and is preserved and upheld by such a fountaine of *indeficient* and omnipotent life, and undecaying lively vigour, and meanes of divine living, that never suffers the man, that hath and keeps communion with the same, to be subject to death: but makes him *passe from death to life*, *Iohn* 5.24. the faith whereof doth free a man from the feare of losing that happy estate, (while he continues to love it,) whereas others, in a loseable and mutable estate of life, are, (by feare of being deprived thereof, and being without hope of a better,) hindered in injoying the full comfort of the present good, that here is afforded.

Thirdly, *spirituall life* surpasses the naturall, in its *effects*: the *naturall life* enables a man to the doing onely of *naturall* actions, specially concerning mans naturall good; agreeable unto, and flowing from *naturall principles* in man; being, in the meane time, dead to any *divine*, or supernaturall good: neither *actively* doing that of goodnesse, which is truely *morall* or *divine*; nor passively receiving and enjoying that thereof which is *beatificall*, or which makes man blessed: and so he may, for all that life, the powers and actions thereof, be miserable and perish; *for, flesh and blood cannot inherit the Kingdome of God*, 1 *Cor.* 15.50. 3. For effects.

The spirituall life, by so neere conjunction of a man with the fountaine of *life Essentiall*, the well-spring of infinite goodnesse, not onely, by that touch and union, doth it make him so live, but also it causeth him to be most happy, both by making him able *Actively* to live the life of *God*[a], and *to live to the will of God*, 1 *Pet.*4.2. [a] *Gal.*2.19.
and also by endowing him with *passive* capacity, and with reall possession of all such *beatificall perfections* as are necessary for his advancement to, and in a glorious estate; farre above all other earthly creatures, in this world and in the world to come: whereby he becomes so happy, that nothing can make him miserable, but even

in tribulation he hath cause of rejoycing, *Rom.*5.3. and when he dyes, yet still he lives, in more excellent manner, as *Paul* said touching his afflictions, *as dying, and behold we live*, 2 *Cor.*6.9.

In regard of the aforesaid *excellency* of this *spirituall life* above the *naturall*, it was that our *Saviour* did command his *Disciples*, *not to feare them that kill the body*, but *are not able to kill the soule: but rather to feare him, which is able to destroy both soule and body in hell.* *Mat.*10.28.

§. 6. How to obtaine spirituall life.

Vse 1. To get spirituall life.

From the former doctrine, touching the *excellency* of this *spirituall life* of man, diverse very necessary *uses* are observable. *First*, it may provoke and stirre us up to *get* this *life*, above all things in this world: whereof we are borne destitute, yea dead in sin; to which life, by our manifold actuall transgressions wee doe indispose and unfit our selves: but yet the Lord of his mercy hath appointed us a way, whereby we may *get* this *spirituall life*: so that, by our conscionable use of the *meanes* appointed by *God*, wee may attaine thereunto, in regard of his promise, and faithfulnesse, that *those that seeke shall finde*. *Amos* 5.6.

By meanes.

And why to be used.

These meanes are wee to use, in regard both of Gods *commandement*, who thereby tries our obedience and faith: and also in respect of the *dispensation* of *God*, who gives his graces onely by, and in his owne way, which otherwise cannot be had. Also the worth and necessity of this *spirituall life* is such, as deserves our best endeavours to get it: our esteeme whereof is seene by our labours for it, in Gods appointed way, without which, God will not give it; because, hee will have us *active*, about our owne *salvation*; that the same may cost us the price of our labours, to come by it; that thereby we may the more comfortably know that we have it; when we know how we came by it: that wee may be the more carefull to keepe, what wee have so laboriously purchased; and may assuredly looke for the reward of our labours; which *God*, that cannot lie, hath promised to those that seeke life by his appointed meanes.

To use no *meanes* to get this *spirituall life*, is to contemne both it, and *God*: and to indeavour to get it, by using other meanes than *God* hath appointed for that *end*, is to *tempt God*, or to prescribe him his waies of dispensing his grace, and to preferre our owne *wits* and *wills* above Gods; whereby such men lose both their labour and expectation.

The meanes in particular, to get this *spirituall life*, are; *First*, the *word* of *God*, specially the *Gospell*; which is as the *materiall* and *seminall* cause of it, 1 *Pet.* 1.23. — Which they be. 1. The word of God.

Secondly, the meanes *vegetating* and *applying* the *Gospell* to quicken us: which is *fourefold*. — 2. Application.

First, the *ministrie* of the word; by reading, and preaching of it, to the enlightning of the understanding, and to the moving of the affections and hearts of the hearers, to embrace it; for, *Faith comes by hearing*, *Rom* 10.17. — 1. By the ministry.

Secondly, the *Company* and *conferences* of those Christians, that in this kind of life, are (by their motion, and example) *lively*, and vigorous; able, by their warmth and livelinesse, to heat and quicken those whom they touch: as *Elisha*, by his application of himselfe to the dead *child*, made it warme and alive, 2 *King*.4.34. and as *leaven* leavens the lump; and every thing affects to procreate its like. — 2. Christian conference.

The third meanes of the *Gospells* application to quicken us, is fervent and effectuall *prayer* to *God*; from whom is all the vertue and efficacy of it, that he would make it effectuall to us: for although *Paul do plant, and Apollo water, it is God that gives the increase*, 1 *Cor*. 3.6. — 3. Prayer.

Fourthly, the *Sacraments*, and in them the powerfull *operation* — 4. Sacraments, & the spirits operation in them.

operation of the *spirit* of *Christ*, is that which quickens us when wee are cast into the frame and mould of the *Gospell*; untill *Christ* be formed in us [a]: so that in this worke the *spirit* is the principall *efficient* cause: as our *Saviour* tells us, *Iohn* 6.63. *it is the spirit that quickneth.*

[a] *Gal.* 4.19.

§. 7. *How the Gospell workes life.*

1. How the Gospell workes not. 1. Not physically

So then, the *Gospell* works not this *life* in us, in a *Physicall* or naturall manner; as having *vertue* naturally inherent in the words, to produce such an *effect* in those that heare it. For then, men should be converted and regenerated in a naturall, and not in a divine manner: and also, then the *Gospell* would worke alike upon all men that heare it, that were alike disposed, and *did* not *ponere obicem*, or lay a barre of their owne to hinder it; except *God* should restraine the naturall power of it in working: but so, the conversion of man must be within the power of his owne *act*; and *God* could not be justified in his withholding grace.

The word is a supernaturall instrument of salvation.

But, the *conversion* of a sinner is wrought by a greater vertue, than can naturally and *subjectively* be in the words and sentences of the *Gospell*: for, the word of *God* is not *instrumentum physicum*, a naturall instrument, but a morall, or rather *metaphysicall* instrument of effecting such a supernaturall worke; according to the will of the first *agent*.

2. Not Ethically.

Neither in an *Ethicall* manner, doth the Gospell worke this *spirituall life* in us; onely by *morall* perswasion; as *morall Philosophers*, and *Rhetoricians* doe affect and draw their hearers; by reasons, and exhortations stirring up a *latent* power inherent in us, and inclining our wills, by rationall motives and objects, to be made alive: then must it depend upon us, that wee are saved; and be from a power of our owne, *exuscitated* by the *word*. *But God* works by his *word*, as a more puissant and

2. How God works by the Gospell according to his own will.

and independent *agent*; that *intends* and *remits* his power in working, according to his owne *will*, by the meanes; and uses meanes not as necessary for him; but that he can doe as much without them: in regard that the *effect* is his owne, and man the *passive* subject of it.

It is the *will* of a naturall man that is most dead to God-ward, and most averse from him; and *therefore*, it is the *will* that is chiefly to be wrought upon and made alive in conversion, whereupon all depends; but, wee know that nothing can make it selfe alive, when it is dead, but he that is the fountaine of life; the *Son* of *God*, *Rom.* 1.4. Mans will is the subject of conversion.

The illumination of the understanding, which is common to the *wicked* and the *godly*, is presupposed as requisite to fit a man for *conversion*: and therefore, in the worke of regeneration, the *scripture* takes notice specially of the *heart*, insomuch that the old *Testament* uses no other word to expresse the *understanding*; because, in *Divinity* no knowledge without intertainement in the heart, and without conformity of the *will* and practise to the truth, is saving; *action* being the end of *Theological* knowledge in this life; words of knowledge in *Scripture* commonly comprehend *affections* in them. *Note.* Of the heart.

§. 8. *Why God uses meanes.*

Although that *God* could, if he pleased, convey grace into a sinfull man, by immediate *influxe*, or inspiration; from which wee cannot utterly exclude all; seeing, the worke of grace depends absolutely neither upon the nature of the *meanes*, nor upon the abilities and *will* of the converted and elected, whereof many are not, by that method of meanes, capable; but upon God, who workes according to the good pleasure of his *will*: yet he uses *meanes*; not to help himselfe, as if otherwise he could not doe the worke; but in respect of *us*, that are naturall men,

indowed

Reasons of using of means.

indowed with senses as well as reason, hee appoints *meanes*, that by our using thereof, we may be *active* about the worke of our owne *salvation*; and may attaine the

1. same by a way and course within the compasse of our owne power and indeavours, as the reward and blessing of *God* upon our labours, to our *commendation before God and men*.

2. Againe, *meanes* are appointed by *God* for our obtaining of salvation, that by using of them, our *faith* in Gods promises and power may be tried, in expecting thereby so glorious effects, farre above their nature: and also, our *obedience* may be proved, by doing what God commands us to doe, within the reach of our power, to get *life*, albeit it doe transcend *reason*, how by this way it can be had: as appeares by *Naaman the Syrian*, 2 *King*.

3. 5.13,14. *And finally*, *God* appoints the use of meanes for our comfort, that by our constant conscionable using of the same, we may be assured of *grace* and *life*, as certainly as we are of the use of the meanes appointed to get, and by which *God* hath promised to give it, by the working of his holy Spirit.

§. 9. *How the Spirits power is manifested and seene.*

Use. To finde the Spirits power by the meanes in us.

Now further, from the consideration of the *excellency* of this *spirituall life* to be wrought in us by meanes, our *use* should be to endeavour to *find and feele*, both the Spirits quickning vertue of regeneration, by the *meanes*, powerfully working upon, and in us, and also, to discerne this spirituall life to be in our selves: seeing our comfort lyes herein, and that the one can never bee without the other.

Manifest in 4. degrees of operation.

The vertue of the *Spirit* in us by the *meanes* manifests it selfe in *foure degrees* of operation: not to speake of *illumination*. *First*, both in making us *see* and *feele*, with griefe of heart, our owne wretchednesse and sinfull deadnesse,

nesse, and also by turning us from our sins and ungodly courses, with detestation of them and with resolution and constant indeavours against them, it being the worke of the *spirit to lust against the flesh*; because they are contrary the one to the other [a], both in *nature* and *effects*.

1. Against sinne.

[a] *Gal* 5.17. *&c.*

In which respect, the *Prophet Hosea* tells us, that *if we will live we must turne*, *Hosea* 6.1. for, our sinfull courses are the waies of *death*: therefore, we should *labour* to be, and find our selves mortified to sinne, with some kinde not onely of voluntary indisposition, but also of strong *antipathie*, and detestation of committing the same; as formerly wee were prone, and *affected* with delight to doe; and that at the presence of sinne, in its *habit*, or *act*, we may with indignation be displeased and sad; having no joy nor contentment in that condition. For, *the motions of sin entertained, do worke in our members, to bring forth fruit unto death* [b].

[b] *Rom.* 7.5.

Which by a contrary life of grace, are mortified and subdued: but, I confesse that this degree followes after faith.

Secondly, the power of the *spirit* in us by the *meanes*, is seene, by the working of true *faith* in us; which the *Apostle* ascribes to the same, 1 *Cor.* 12.9. *Ephes.* 2.8.

2. Begetting faith

It is by this *faith* that wee do divinely and spiritually live [c], in the *act* of *beleeving*, uniting our selves to the saving and lively *object Christ Iesus*, with his gracious promises, by us adhered unto, and thereunto conforming our selves: without *Christ* we have no *life* in us: as himselfe tells us, *Ioh.* 6.57. and without *faith* wee can neither have him nor his blessed promises; but by *faith* we have them both; that so, by this *spirituall instrument*, spirituall blessings may be spiritually enjoyed, whereof the *soule* is the immediate *subject*; and secondarily the *body*, onely by the *soule*; to this *faith* our *Saviour* attributes this spirituall *life*, when he sayes *That whosoever beleeveth in him, though he were dead, yet shall he live* [d]: therefore,

[c] *Rom.* 1.17. *Habak.* 2.4.

[d] *John* 11.25.

therefore, it neerely concernes us all, to labour to get true saving *faith*; and that we doe make use of the same, in and about its proper *objects*: And for our *comfort*, it behooves us to know that we have this *faith*: but, because the signes how to discerne it, is the generall *subject* of most men in their bookes and sermons, I passe it over with reference to them.

3. Applying of Christ.

Thirdly, the *Spirit* of *God* manifests the *power* of it in us, by the *meanes*, in the *application* of *Christ* and his *merits* to us: whereby we become one with *Christ*, and being grafted into him, have the *adoption* of the sonnes of *God*[a]; and free *justification* from all our sins, sealed up and assured to us, by the same *Spirit*: whereupon, we may apprehend the sweet *favour* of *God* toward us; wherein consisteth *life*, *Psal.*30.5. and may be filled with a lively *vigour* of consolation, in the apprehension of the pardon of our sinnes, and upon the assurance of the graces and blessings of *God* to us, for our eternall happinesse, in which respect it is called the *Spirit* of *Consolation*[b]; which makes us cheerefully to endure afflictions, and to runne the way of Gods Commandements, when thus we are enlarged by the spirit, and by the same possessed of *Christ* and his *graces*; by and in whom we spiritually live: there is nothing in this world, that we should be so carefull of, as to bring forth the fruits of the *Spirit*, giving testimony of our adoption by our good works.

[a] *Ephes.*1.5. *Rom.*8.16.

[b] *Ioh.*14.26.

Evidences of the worke of the Spirit in us, applying Christ.

But, of the aforesaid *worke* of the *Spirit* in us, we may have some comfortable *evidences*, upon these ensuing *grounds*.

1. *First*, by the *sense* of the *vertue* from *Christ* quickning *us*, wee may assuredly discerne that we touch him, and have communion with him, being in him, as members under our head; and partaking in, and from him, of all his merits and graces.

2. *Secondly*, the same is evident by the *change* of our *estates*, morally considered, in regard of what our dispositions and lives formerly have beene, and now are, touching

touching vertue and vice, goodnesse and evill; concerning both which, a *supernaturall* change cannot be, but by a *supernaturall efficient* and divine principle: and so from the *effects*, we doe conclude the *cause* to precede or goe before.

3. *Thirdly*, the aforesaid worke of the *Spirit* is manifested and discerned, by our *subsisting* and keeping our standing in goodnesse, and in adhering to *God*, and to his *Word*, in states and times, of great and manifold *trialls*; wherein experiment is made of our strength, and sincerities, and cleaving to *God*: in which condition, when the unsound fall away, those that are built upon the *rocke Christ*[a], and from him are *supernaturally* furnished with all needfull *graces*; (by beholding and relying upon him that is invisible) they doe receive from above a continual *influxe* of assistance and abilities, whereby *they* stand fast and endure, as did *Moses*, *Heb.* 11.27.

[a] *Mat.* 7.24, 25.

4. The Spirits worke in sanctification.

Fourthly, the *Spirits* worke in us, by the *meanes*, is powerfully manifested, by these *lively seeds* and divine *principles* of *grace*; which it infuseth or worketh in us; called by the *Apostle Peter*, a divine nature. 2 *Pet.* 1.4.

Whereby the *regenerated* man is furnished, with all sufficiency of heavenly, and new inherent *principles*, for the right ordering of himselfe in *divine* manner: even as the *naturall* man is stored with his *principles* of *reason*, thereby to square his judgement and life, in *naturall* manner.

§. 10. *Of the degrees of the Spirits worke of holinesse in us.*

The degrees of grace.

The degrees of this worke of *grace* and *holinesse* of *Gods Spirit* in us, are *two*. *First*, that which consists in *habituall* divine qualities; diffused throughout all the powers and faculties of the *man*, in whom the same is; which are wrought, or infused *gradually*, from one degree to another.

1. Habituall. Which is the holinesse of mans new nature.

These

These are opposite to mans *naturall pollution* of sinne and malice inherent in him, upon the which they being *superinducted*, they doe by *degrees* weaken, dispossesse, and abolish the same: as the light doth the darknesse.

Use of it. So then, the office and use of this *habituall* holinesse, and qualification of man with *inherent graces* of Gods spirit, is *threefold*.

1. *First*, it *serves* to adorne, accomplish and beautifie, in spirituall manner, the *regenerate* man,

2. *Secondly*, it subdues, mortifies, and expells the contrary vice, in equall measure of extension and degree, as it selfe is.

3. *Thirdly*, it *qualifies* and inables a man that hath it, to the actuall doing of all holy duties; according to the quality and greatnesse of those divine principles of grace, that is the inherent originall of the same; so being both the *materiall* and also *exemplary* cause of actuall holinesse of life; *this* cannot be without *that*.

2. Degree is actuall obedience which is the holinesse of mans actions.

The second degree of this spirituall holinesse, is that which consists in *actuall obedience* to Gods will, in all holy performances, rightly ordering all our thoughts; all the inclinations of our wills; all the motions of our affections; all the *morall* postures of our behaviour; all the words of our mouthes; and all the actions of our lives; in abstaining; in sustaining; and in active performance, exactly according to Gods commandments; with perfection of integrity and sincerity.

The use of it. *The use* of this *degree* of holinesse, consisting in actuall

1. obedience, is *threefold*. *First*, to manifest the truth and power of mans inward and habituall grace.

2. *Secondly*, to oppose and keepe our corruption and sin out of that possession, which formerly they had of our *actions*, and *hearts*.

3. *Thirdly*, that the body, which is to be saved with the soule, may in all the organes and powers thereof bee honoured in holy imployment; for good example to others,

others, and for glory to God; before it be glorified with God.

The grounds and originall *motives* of this grace and holinesse, that consists in actuall obedience to *God*, are *three*. The grouuds of it.

1. *First, habituall grace* in man, not considered as in an *unformed* masse; but as *formed* in its severall *species* or kindes of definable vertues, is the ground and living spring, whence issues this actuall holinesse, according to the kinds and degrees of the seminall or radicall vertue whence it proceeds: without which all outward holiness is but vanishing hypocrisie.

2. Gods word. The *second motive* is the externall *impulsion* of Gods word, in the *ministery* and use thereof, directing and exhorting us, in way of *morall perswasion* to doe our duty: so stirring up the grace of God in us, to shew it selfe, in putting forth the vertue thereof in action.

3. The Spirit. *The third motive* is that *influence* and motion of the *Spirit of God*, which at times, both stirres up the graces of God in us, to make them lively, to put forth their strength, to make resistance against sinne; and to undertake and prosecute the doing of good; and also it *suppeditates* and conveyes increase of grace and spirituall abilities into a regenerated man; whereby he growes and goeth on, both in *habituall* and *actuall* holinesse: for being *dead* to sinne, it is requisite that we doe *live to righteousnesse*, 1 *Pet*. 2. 24. in regard that the *Prophet* tells us, *That he that doth that which is lawfull and right, shall live thereby*[a].

[a] *Ezek* 33.19.

§. 11. *Of the signes of spirituall life.*

Now it followes, that wee doe make inquiry and search, to find out the *signes* of this *spirituall life*, whereby we may know whether we have it, or want it, whereof I will give you some notes. Signes of spirituall life, are

1. Heavenly thoughts and affections. *First*, it is discernable by a mans *thoughts* and *affections*; for, if he have spirituall life, both his minde and thoughts will be taken up most with *God* and heavenly things; and also, his affections will be most set upon them, both with ardency of desires to have them, and also with abundant joy in the hope and fruition of them; according to the command of the *Apostle*, who bids us to *Set our affections on things above, not on things on the earth:* because, *our life is bid with Christ in God*, *Colos.* 3. 2, 3.

2. His life godly. *The second note* of this *spirituall life* is the powerfull *active effects* of it; whereby, the man that hath it, doth *live*: (for his divine and morall manner of living,) according to the direction of Gods holy *Word*, and the motion of the *spirit* of God; in manner and degree, farre surpassing the power of nature; and contrary to the disposition of flesh and blood; being hereunto moved and strengthened; not onely by outward *morall perswasions*; but, specially after a *divine*, or renewed manner, by a spirituall *principle* of supernaturall vitall motion within himselfe; whereby, after a sort, in some measure, he becomes a *rule* and *Law* to himselfe of good life: as those that have the law not onely written in their hearts, but have also a power, with activity of endeavour to do the same; with respect to a spirituall and supernaturall *end*: and in this respect also it is said, that the *Law is not made for a righteous man* [a].

[a] 1 *Tim.* 1. 9.

3. Patient suffering. *The third signe* of spirituall life in man, is his comfortable *suffering* for the things belonging to that *life*; when he subsists under afflictions for goodnesse, with unrelenting courage, adhering to the truth, and persisting in his integrity, against all opposition.

1. Which manifests it selfe, *first*, in the *measure* of these *afflictions*, when he beares the same with ability above naturall strength, as did *Moses*, *seeing him that is invisible* [b]: by whose vertue he was supported. *Secondly*,

[b] *Heb.* 11. 27.

2. by the *manner* of his undergoing of *afflictions*, in *voluntary*

tary and *active* submission, and not onely *passive*, or by way of coaction, and inforcement, wholly against his will subjected to them; but induring with joyfulnesse[a]; as those that the *Scripture* speakes of, who *tooke joyfully the spoyling of their goods*, *Heb.* 10. 34. which cannot bee done, but by such as are indowed with this spirituall life, whereby they live, even when they die.

[a] *Rom.* 5. 3.

The fourth note of this *spirituall living*, is the regularity of such a mans godly *behaviour* and conversation, in the worlds eye, in all his actions subject to the direction of God, and moving from, and according to *supernaturall principles* of habituall grace; not walking after the judgement and examples of the *world*, or of flesh and blood. *For*, he that is indowed with this spirituall life, is a compleat *new creature*, having *judgment*, *will*, *affections*, *qualities*, *senses*, and *deportment*, farre differing from the vulgar crew, and common course; in a life, as if not of the world, but as he were a *pilgrim* in the world, so his carriage in a manner is strange to the world.

4. Heavenly behaviour in the world.

And as the *life* of every *creature* is, so it affects the *element* fit for it; as, fishes affect the water; the *Salamander* to be in the fire; and other creatures, some to be on the earth, and others to flie in the aire; so that a man, that hath spirituall life, delights to live with God and good men, as did the *Prophet David*, *Psal.* 84. and doth desire to feed constantly upon such divine ordinances and graces as do cherish that life, delighting to be exercised therein, as in his proper element, as *David* confessed of himselfe to *God*, *O, how I love thy Law? it is my meditation all the day*[b].

[b] *Psal.* 119. 97.

§. 12. *How spirituall life may be preserved.*

I will now briefly shew you, how a man, that hath this *spirituall life*, may *preserve*, and strengthen it: which is done especially by *sixe* things.

Meanes of preservation of spirituall life.

First,

1. Use of the meanes whereby it is gotten.

First, by the constant and conscionable *use* of the same *meanes* still, whereby he got it: for, the *procreant* cause of any thing is also the *conservant* cause of the same; because of their *homogenean* nature, and *sympathie* between the *patient* and the *agent*, except in those things that are brought forth by *accident*, or by the power of an *efficient* overswaying the *instrument* and other *causes*, contrary to their naturall disposition. So that such a *Christian* must never be weary, nor give over the continued exercise of the same course of godly *meanes*, whereby at the first he found this life of grace wrought in him.

2. Exercise in spirituall workes.

The second meanes to preserve this spirituall life, in those that have it; is, to *exercise* it in all the *offices*, and *works* thereof; both in *beleeving* in *Christ* with application of the promises, and also in *doing* and *suffering* what *God* requires or imposes; for, as faith drawes this *life* from the fountaine of life, whereby we live, as men say, *actu primo*, so by the imployment and exercise of this *life*, in obedience to *God*, we live, *actu secundo*; preserving and nourishing this life. For, we see that by rest and idlenesse things are, not onely often frustrate of the end of their being, but doe also languish and die; which by action, according to their naturall faculties and proper use, are preserved. For, all things that are in the way to their *end*, (as spirituall life is here) are maintained and perfected by their *motion* to that end; where, at last, they are to rest, there not being an *ultra* or *more-over*, for them to aspire after.

3. Zeale.

Thirdly, this *spirituall life* is fomented and cherished by *stirring* up, and blowing the coale of godly *zeale* for goodnesse, and against evill; whereby a man may quicken the things that are ready to die: this *zeale* is, as the lively *spirits* that quicken this life, to make it active, whereby it growes and is vigorous.

The weakenes of zeale.

The things that weaken this *zeale*, are three. *First*, *wearisomenesse* and *satiety*, contracted by the length of time

time in assiduity, about good things and divine exercises. *Secondly*, by *discouragements*, from all *examples*, and from *opposition* of goodnesse. *Thirdly*, for the prevailing of *vice* in our selves, or generally in others, caried with a high hand; and from the languishing of *grace* in our selves; and from the generall discountenancing of it by others. 2. 3.

The *meanes* to *quicken* this *zeale* are; *First*, the serious consideration both of the *excellency*, and also of the *usefulnesse* of goodnesse, whereby wee may bee inflamed with the love and desire of it. *Secondly*, the *odiousnesse* and *dangerousnesse* of iniquity and sinfull prevailing courses in others; may, by *antipathie*, and *antiparistasis*, kindle our *zeale* the more against it: as *David* confesses of himselfe, *that rivers of waters did runne downe his eyes, because men kept not Gods Law, Psal.* 119. 136. Meanes to quicken zeale. 1. 2.

Fourthly, this *spirituall life* is *maintained* by observing and collecting the *promises* of the *word* of *God*; and marking how *God* fulfills the same to his people: and so by meditating and relying upon them, wee shall find incouragement, and a lively influence come from the same, to uphold this spirituall life in us, in all estates, when all other things do faile. As the *Prophet* saith, *unlesse thy Law had beene my delight, I should then have perished in mine affliction* [a]. 4. Gods promises

Fiftly, *spirituall life* is upheld in us, by having our *eyes fixt upon God*, in constant *perseverance* in all well doing, (as did *Iehosaphat* [b]) from whom there proceeds to us a gracious influence of divine life, as light from the sunne to the moone, when she is within the aspect of it. 5. Preseverance.

The sixt meanes of *preservation* of this *spirituall life*, is *hope*, set upon our future happinesse: as did our *Saviour Christ*; who, *for the hope that was set before him, indured the crosse*: by this *anchor* of *hope* a man rides safe in all stormes, as held up by the chinne, that hee can never bee drowned, when this *anchor* is cast upward *within the* 6. Hope of happinesse. Heb. 12. 2.

[a] *Psal.* 119. 42.

[b] 2 *Chro.* 20. 12.

[c] Heb 6.19. *vaile, whither Christ our forerunner is gone* [a] : drawing us after him.

§. 13. *Of mans care of spirituall life.*

Vse 2. Mans great charge.

The second use of the excellency of mans *spirituall life* is, to instruct us ; that man hath the greatest *adventure* and charge, to save, or lose, of any creature in the world: for, as he hath both a soule and a body, so hath he, both a naturall and a spirituall life to save, or lose : and upon the miscarying of the *spirituall*, depends the misery of the *naturall*.

Therefore it is, that *man* is subject to most dangers of all earthly creatures ; and needs to be most vigilant and carefull of himselfe : for, by how much the more excellent he may be, if he be saved, so much the more miserable shall he be, if he perish. And therefore, as of a ship lade with rich goods, more care is to be had, than of a ship lade with coales or chalke; so more care is to be had of a man than of any other worldly creature ; in regard of the greatnesse of the aforesaid adventure: which may be fitly represented by the answer of a certaine *Philosopher* to a wretched fellow, when they were both at *sea* in danger to be drowned together, whereof the *Philosopher* was much more fearefull than the other, who upbraided him for the same, and demanded the reason thereof ; to whom the *Philosopher* replyed, that the losse was farre the greater for him to miscarry, than for many such fellowes as the other was, who were nought worth.

Comparison.

Vse 3.

The third use observable from hence is; that if it come into competition whether wee should yeeld to lose our *naturall life*, or our *spirituall*; when both cannot be enjoyed together, then wee are to preferre the preservation of our *spirituall life* before our *naturall*, and, for saving of *this*, to do nothing to hurt or prejudice *that*: remembring that

that our *Saviour* saith, *he that loveth his life shall lose it;* *and he that hateth his life in this world, shall keepe it unto life eternall, Iohn* 12. 25. for obtaining whereof many of Gods people little respected their naturall life, as they who *Heb.* 11.35. *did not accept deliverance from death, that they might obtaine a better resurrection* ; *Paul* said that *his life was not deare to him* ; *but that he was ready to die for the name of Iesus Christ, Act.* 21. 13. which was the case of all the *Martyrs* ; such was their esteeme of, and affection to spirituall life. We that live (saith *Paul*) *are delivered to death for Iesus sake, that his life may bee manifest in us.* Which condemnes those, that *Esau-like* set light by this *spirituall life*; preferring the world, their lusts, their pleasures, or naturall life before it: because, they neither know the worth, nor comfort of it; nor have part or hope of it : which whosoever hath, will choose rather a thousand times to die this temporall death; than to lose his *spirituall life.*

Preferre Spirituall before naturall life.

CHAP. 6.

Of lifes destruction, and of murder in generall.

§. 1. *How mans life may be lost.*

HAving spoken of mans *life*, which is the *object* of *Self-murder* , now it followes in the next place, that we consider the *act* it selfe of taking away this *life*, specially in unjust manner.

Life may be lost.

Of both the aforesaid kinds of life, *naturall* and *spirituall*, a man may bee deprived, and that after *two* severall wayes : *First, passively*, as he therein is immediately but a sufferer, although mediatly, or by originall *merit*, he may be said to be *efficient* , in procurement of his owne

1. Passively.

 destruction;

destruction; but as he is meerely *passive* he cannot be deemed to be guilty thereof.

2. Actively.

Secondly actively, as he is an *agent*, in and about his owne death, working to effect the same, either meritoriously, or efficiently, and so he is a *self-murderer*, and guilty of his owne death.

§.2. *Of the meanes of losing life naturall.*

Meanes of losse of life are, 1. Internall.

Mans life is loseable by two sorts of *meanes* : *First*, *internall*, arising from, and within a mans selfe, that kills him, as the worme that breeds of, and in the tree, and destroyes it : so in mans bodie doe distempers and diseases breed of, and from it selfe; whereby hee is in deaths hands, and by degrees dies daily: also in the *soule* of man sinne doth breed, that kills his spirituall life : and so, he hath in himselfe the *principles* and *meanes* of the destruction, both of his *soule* and *body*; of his life, both *naturall* and *spirituall*.

2. Externall.

The second meanes is *externall*; inflicted from without a man; tending to that taking away of his life : and the same is either *casuall*, or *voluntary*.

1. Casuall.

Casuall, or *accidentall* is; when, besides the *intension* of the *agent*, and proper *nature* and *end* of the *action*, it falls out and comes to passe that thereby the *life* of man is hurt, or taken away : as when, in felling of wood, the axe flees off the *helve*, and unawares to him that uses it, kills a man[a], herein the life of man is taken away, not without concurrence of the providence of God, who is pleased, by suffering such an accident, to lay a crosse upon the agent, to whom it is a kinde of calamity or punishment to be a *meanes* (against his will) of the death of any man.

[a] *Deut.* 19.5.

Also, to this *casuall* destruction of mans *life*, belongs the perishing of the soules of those, that unjustly take offence

offence at other mens estates and lives [b]; for that which they lawfully and necessarily doe or suffer, in their callings and Christian condition; whereby such persons flee off from the truth; and fall into, or persist in evill and damnable course, to their eternall perdition; without any fault of theirs, by whose occasion they (of their own wretchednesse) stumble and miscarry; and so goe guilty of their owne *spirituall death*; by abusing of that, which is good, to their hurt and damnation; so falling and ruinating themselves, by other mens rising and standing. [b] 1 Cor. 1.23.

Or else, the *externall meanes* of taking away a mans *life*; doe of themselves, in their *proper nature*, and direct use, and in the intension of the *agent*, tend to the effecting thereof: which (about our *life* that is *naturall*,) is done either *justly*; upon lawfull causes; in just manner; by those those that are sufficiently authorized to doe the same: or else, it is done *unjustly*; when the same is without just cause; not by the hands of persons lawfully authorized to doe it; or is not performed in a just and warrantable manner. 2. Voluntary. Justly. Unjustly.

§. 3. *Of the meanes of the destruction of spirituall life.*

Also, touching our *spirituall life*, the same is *externally*, or by *meanes*, without a mans selfe, destroyed; *eyther* by the justice of God; when he most righteously, in his act of *vindicative* and *distributive justice* punishes man with eternall destruction, for his sinnes, *Mat.* 10.28. in which case man, in respect of his owne merits and deservings, is guilty of his owne perishing, and not God. 2. Of the soule. 1. By God.

Or else, our *spirituall life* may miscarry by meanes of *men*; who *First*, by their *corrupt doctrine*, and evill examples doe draw others with them to perdition: as did the *Scribes* and *Pharisees*; that did *compasse sea and land to make one Proselyte*, whom when they had wonne, they made 2. By men, two waies. 1.

made him *twofold more the child of hell than themselves*, *Mat.*23.15. or, by *depriving* them of the *meanes* of their salvation; they are subjected to destruction. *Secondly*, when men, by *compulsory meanes* of *unjust lawes*, and severe threatnings and punishments, are driven and forced from the waies of righteousnesse into sinnefull courses; as by *Ieroboam*, *Manasses*, *&c.* soules are destroied with a twofold guilt, both of them that force others; and also of them that yeeld themselves to evill, upon such constraint.

2.

Life is taken away: 1. By others. 2. By a mans selfe.

Againe, the *externall meanes* of depriving a man of his *life* is inflicted, either by others; sometime lawfully, sometimes unlawfully; *or* else, by a mans owne hands and procurement; which is ever, in all cases, unlawfull for him to doe, mediately, or immediately, directly, or indirectly. But, it is to be noted, that no man loseth his *spirituall life*, but by his owne meanes, and merits procuring the same: for the *spirituall life* of man is subject to no mans power; who *can kill onely the body and doe no more*, *Mat.*10.28.

And God, that is essentially and absolutely *just*, subjects not man to suffer that, which *actively* he hath not first some way procured, by his owne doings and deservings.

Observ. How subject man is to death.

From hence, it is *observable*, that the lives of no creatures are longer, and with more adoe hatched up, and maintained, than the lives of men; and yet, the lives of no creatures are subject to so many dangers, *inward*, and *outward* of destruction; and sooner overthrowne, than mans; we being like brittle *glasses*, that containe precious *balsame*; and as choise flowers, hardly cherished up, and soone blasted: which shewes, both our *weakenesse*, and want of self-sufficiency, to uphold our selves; and also, how we are possessed and compassed about, with things adverse and dangerous to our *lives*; both of soule and body: of all *creatures* man onely being a *stranger* and *pilgrim* on earth, hath, therefore, the least kinde entertainment in this *world*, and the most uncertaine possession of it; and is alwaies neerest to be thrust out of it; walking here but as a *shadow*.

Therefore, wee should be more carefull to *cleave* the more closely to our *God*, who is the *preserver* of men; that by him we may be upheld and protected against all dangers. *Vse* 1.

And againe, we should be the more *watchfull* against carnall security; that wee doe not presume upon our uncertaine lives; nor suffer our selves to be intangled with this world and the things of it; but that we be ever heavenly minded, and ready for our departure hence; labouring to get, and keepe that *spirituall* and *eternall life*. 2.

§. 4. *Of murder in self-killing.*

In a mans taking away of his *owne life*, *two* things are to be considered. *First*, that it is *murder*, in regard of the *nature* of the *act* of it. Killing of a mans selfe is murder. 1.

Secondly, that it is murder of ones *selfe*, in respect of the *object* thereof: and so *self-murder* is a compounded sinne of more degrees than one, and that in such a kind, as is the most hainous and most to be abhorred in humane *society*, in regard that this destroyes the *substantiall* being of that which ought to bee of all worldly things most deare to us; whereas other sinnes, spoile the *wel-being* of our selves, or others; which, so long as life lasteth, is recoverable. 2.

And therefore, whatsoever is to be thought of the vile quality, and of the damnable deserts of *murder* in generall, is to be conceived to be due, and much worse, to *self-murder* in speciall. For, *murder* is but the *genericall* or generall *matter*, and not the speciall and *formall* nature of *Self-murder*: and *therefore*, if it be horrible to murder another man, it is much more odious to kill ones *selfe*. Self-murder is horrible.

selfe. For, by naturall reason, the more that any *Genus*, or *generall matter*, is restrained, and *actuated*, by its superadded *formes* and *specificall* differences, the more it is intended, *active* and powerfull; according to the motion of *nature*, *ab imperfectioribus ad perfectiora*, proceeding toward that *perfection*, wherein it intends to *termine* and end. Now, the perfection of a *vice* (if I may so speake) consists in the highest exorbitancie of it, beyond which none can passe, and in murder, it is certaine that none can goe beyond self-murder, as afterward will fully appeare.

4. Things are observable in murder.

In taking away, specially, a mans *naturall life* unjustly and murderously, *foure* things are to be considered.

1. That death is undeserved.

First, that the *effect* done, or *death* of a man, in depriving him of his life, is without due desert on his part, at their hands that put him to death.

2. Done without lawfull authority.

Secondly, that the *act* it selfe, whereby that *effect* is accomplished, is *unlawfull*, on his part that doth it, in regard of his want of *authority*, and just calling to do that *act*: and if the *sufferer* have deserved *death*, and the *executioner* have a lawfull calling to kill him; yet, if his *manner* of doing of it bee contrary to the prescript and rules of his calling; and to the minde and disposition requisite for such an *agent* in that *act*; then the same is *murder*.

3. Done wittingly.

Thirdly, it is considerable in *murder*, that the *agent* therein both *knowes*, not onely that the *nature* of his action that he doth, tendeth to *death*; but also that *morally* it is an unlawfull *act*, or thing to be done: and also doth *voluntarily* and *wittingly* intend the doing of that action, without regard of the effect, or insuing of *death* thereupon.

4. Death intended.

Fourthly, touching *murder*, it is remarkeable that the *agent* doe not onely voluntarily and wittingly a lethiferous or mortall *act*; but that he doe also *intend*, and *desire* to effect the *death* of a man thereby; whom justly he cannot kill: otherwise, if a man should *ignorantly*, or *unwillingly*

lingly, in doing of his lawfull calling, be a meanes accidentally to take away the life of a man, he is not therefore guilty of *murder*. *For*, for such *God* provided *Cities of refuge*, for their preservation, against the *avenger* of *blood*. *Deut*.19.3,4,5. *Joshua* 20.3. by the *first* of these wee see, that an *innocent* suffers death; by the *second* wee see, that the *Agent* or *executioner* is such an one as ought not to kill him, although he were *nocent*: by the *third* and *fourth* it appeares that the *act* is *formaliter* murderous, in regard of the *knowledge*, and *intention* of the doer thereof.

So, in *Self-murder*, as it is murder, an *Innocent*, (never deserving of himselfe that himselfe should kill himselfe,) is slaine: the *Actor* whereof hath no authority, nor calling over himselfe so to doe: seeing, no man can be both *superiour* and also *inferiour* to himselfe: and for a man to doe an *act* upon himselfe, which he knowes to be both mortall, and unlawfull; and yet will doe it, with purpose and intent to bereave himselfe of his own life, it cannot be denyed to be *murder* in the highest degree, and he a *murderer* that doth it. Self-murder is most vile murder, in transcendent manner.

§. 5. *How murder is vile.*

The vilenesse of *murder* is not onely seene, by its contrariety to *Gods Law*, and the heavie censures and punishments thereof, and its incompatibility with humane *society*; but also, by the *effects* thereof upon the *sufferer*. The vilenesse of murder in its effects.

For, *first* the *act* of *murder* utterly so destroyes the *naturall life* of man, upon the departure of his soule from the body; that the same is never againe recovered. *For*, *naturall life* depends, not onely upon the presence of the *soule informing* the body; but even upon our *state* of *being* in this world; insomuch that after the *resurrection*, although soule and body shall be againe united; yet, as then our bodies shall be spirituall bodies [a]; so shall 1. It destroyes naturall life.

[a] 1 *Cor*.15 44.

our lives be. So then, a *murderer* takes that life away, which he can never give, nor restore; and destroyes that which he can never build up.

2. It destroyes mans person.

Secondly, the *act* of *murder* destroyes the person of man; which depends upon mans *life*. For, neither is the *soule* alone, nor the *body* alone the person of man; but the *whole man* consisting of *soule* and *body* with their properties *hypostatically* united. So that, when the soule is in heaven, he cannot say, but *Synechdochically*, that the *person* is in heaven. Nor, when the body is in the grave, can we properly say, that the *person* is in the grave. For, then, either a man must be two *persons*; one in heaven, and another in the grave, which is absurd: or else one created *person* should be in diverse places at once; which is impossible.

Observe where the person is after death.

If you say, where then is the *person* after death? I *answer*, it is not in *actuall being*, but *potentiall* in its constitutive *principles* of soule and body; that are to be joyned together, at the day of judgment. *And* therefore it is, that the soules separate from the bodies *thinke* nor, nor worke in that manner as they did *organically* in the body: whereupon the *Psalmist* saies of *Princes*, that when they die *their thoughts perish* [b]: and therefore, neither remember *they*, *in* that estate, things past; nor are capable of present, under those species and *notions*, as they did here in the body. So then, he that *murders* a man, destroies a *person*; although his distinct *natures* doe remaine.

[a] *Psal.* 146.4.

Thirdly, a *murderer* is injurious to *God*, not onely in breaking his *Law*, but also in destroying his *Image*; which is not properly in the body, or in the soule apart; but in the whole *person* of man, consisting of both soule and body, with their properties personally united: man was created in *Gods Image*: now, the soule alone, or body alone is not the *man*, but *both* united, as is said: so it is apparent, that wrong is done to heaven and earth, by a murderer.

§.6. Of

§. 6. *Of the originall of murder.*

We are to consider, whence it comes that man doth monstrously, *First*, fall upon his owne *kinde*, to destroy it; and *then* upon *himselfe*. Of *murder* in generall, mans wicked *heart* and the *devill* are the parents: for, the inward *principle* of *motion* to that vile sinne; and also, the *passive subject* entertaining the same, is mans owne wicked disposition inclining him, (by inbred hatred,) to that horrible mischiefe. For out *of the heart proceeds murder* [a], saies our *Saviour Christ*: which is a just recompence from *God*; that man, for his rebellion and disobedience against God, should be given over, in revenge of Gods quarrell, to destroy with his owne hands his owne *kinde*, and *selfe*. So that, he that will not agree with God and love him, cannot agree with, nor love himselfe, nor his neighbour.

Murder whence.

1. From our selves.

[a] *Mat.*15.19.

Satan is the *principall* and *active* parent of *murder*; *who was a murderer from the beginning*; and now is still, in spite against God and man, a provoker and stirrer up of man to *murder*; affording him occasions and opportunities to doe the deed; to the staining of the honor of *God*, and defacing of *mankinde*; and therefore, *murderers* are most especially the *children* of the *devill* [b]; and obedient to him, both in disposition and practise: they that wilfully doe the greater sin, do *habitually* and *dispositively* not stick at the lesser; seeing that the lesser are ever, in some sort, comprehended in the greater.

[b] *Ioh.*8.44.

This effect, in mans taking away the *life* of man, shewes that mans *ability* lyes specially in spoyling and destroying of Gods handiworks; and argues rather *impotency* than power in him; where there is no stronger power of preservation, opposing of him. For, the proper *effect* of power is *entity*, or *being*; and *non-entity* or not *being* is the effect of weakenesse. We see that, although

It was an act of impotency.

a man can kill, yet he cannot restore againe to life; because, it is *God* onely that hath power over the *spirit*, and that *kills* and *makes alive* againe.

Use To beware of murder.

And therefore, all men should be carefull how they take away the *life* of any man. For, although by repentance they may make their owne peace with *God*, for their *murder*; yet they can never restore the losse, or damage: none can call back the *spirit*, but the Father of *spirits*, to *animate* a dead body: *neither* hath any man absolute power over the creatures, to do with them as he list, but as he is limited by Gods commission and will.

Observ.

To terrifie a man from *killing himselfe*, he ought to consider how he is limited and restrained, by his *Soveraigne Lord God*, from rashly attempting, or medling to hurt the *lives* of any *men*, whom he may not *use*, or dispose of, according to his owne *self-will'd lust*; but, according to the good *will* of *God*, who is the supreme and absolute *Lord* and master of all mankinde, in speciall manner.

Man is restrained from murder.

Also, he is to consider the *odiousnesse* and *punishment* of simple *murder*, in any man; and how loath he himselfe would be to doe it, upon any other man: that so he may much more abhorre to doe it upon himselfe: sinnes are more discernable by us in others, than in our selves; as a visible *object*, close upon the *sense* of seeing, cannot bee seene so well, as at a greater fit distance: what wee doe see to be unlawfull and odious in others, others doe see to be no lesse, but rather more odious in us, if we excell them in place or personall parts; where there is no *accident*, or *circumstance* that may extenuate the same.

It is odious.

A man cannot possibly kill *himselfe*, but that thereby *he is*, in the lesser degree of this sinne, a *murderer*; in state common with *Barrabas* and others, that murderously kill other men than themselves: and thereby is lyable to the like detestation and punishment, but withall in a farre greater degree, for killing *himselfe*.

Note.

It is remarkeable, that no man can kill or murder *another*,

another, but withall he must kill *himselfe*, both *soule* and body. For, by his sinne of *murder* he stabs his owne *soule*, and subjects it to the vengeance of God: And also thereby hee makes his *person* obnoxious to the stroke of *justice*, by the hand either of *God* or *man*, to suffer death for that horrible sinne: according to the threatnings and judgements of *God*; and the apprehension of the *murderers* owne conscience; and the hatred wherewith all men doe prosecute such detestable persons, as enemies of mankind, and of humane society [a].

No man can murder another without murdring of himselfe.

[a] *Gen.* 9.5. *Deut.* 19. 12, 13. *Gen.* 4.14.

CHAP. 7.
Of murder, as it is of ones selfe.

§. 1. *Of the specificall difference of self-murder.*

BEsides the consideration of *murder*, in a mans killing of himselfe, the *third* point in the generall *description* of *self-murder* is the *efficient cause*, or meanes of it; and that is a mans owne selfe, by his owne procurement; who is also the immediate *object* of that vile fact; whereof now I am to speake.

Here is now the *specificall* difference of this sort of *murder*, wherby it transcends, and is distinguished from all other *murders*; and consists in restraint of the *act* of killing, in regard of its individual *object*, to a mans *own life* & self; which is the greatest and cruellest *act* of hostility in the world: when a man, who by nature is most bound to preserve *himself*, reflects upon *himselfe*, to destroy himselfe; the horriblenes whereof is so monstrous, that we read no Law made against it, as if it were a thing not to bee supposed possible. And this sinne of all others is most against the Law of nature, for that *self-preservation*, armes a man to turne upon others, unlawfully invading him to

Self-murders specificall difference.

kill him. And also, it is against that *self-love*, which is the *rule* of our *love* to others; and therefore what wee may not lawfully, in this *case*, doe to others, we can lesse lawfully doe it to *our selves*, against this generall *law* of *love*; in breaking whereof, specially towards our selves, we violate the whole *law*, the generall summe whereof is *love*.

§. 2. *Of the evill and greatnesse of self-murder.*

Whence it proceeds.

This is the malice of *Satan*, and our *own* wretchednesse, to set us at division and enmity against our selves; and in a monstrous manner to make a man both the *active* and *passive subject* of his owne *action*, and utter *destruction* of *himselfe*; (the greatest mischiefe that can betide him in this *world*) and so a mans *selfe* becomes his owne *executioner*, by his owne hands, or meanes; principall, or accessary; by command, or otherwise.

Comparison.

If parricide be a *grievous sinne*, as wilfully to kill our owne *parents*; *children*; *wives*; *husbands, &c.* who are distinct *persons* from our *selves*; much more is *self-murder* abhominable. For, by *unitie*, things are preserved; and individualls are principally *one*: and therefore, if *individualls* be divided against themselves, the world cannot stand; when things shall cease to be true, and amically disposed to themselves.

§. 3. *Of lawfull self-killing.*

Lawfull selfe-killing. Of our old man.

There is a *lawfull* and commanded *killing* of our *selves*. For understanding whereof, it is to be observed, that every one of us hath in him a *self-old-man* of *sinfulnesse*, lively and powerfull in manifold *lusts* and wicked *actions*: of which the *Apostle* tells us, *Rom. 7. 5. That when we were in the flesh, the motions of sinnes, which were by the Law, did worke in our members, to bring forth*

fruit

fruit unto death; when the Commandement came, sinne revived: the living whereof doth kill us.

In this *case*, even for our owne preservation, it is necessary, and lawfull for us to kill our *self-old-man*, with the lusts thereof: as the *Apostle* commands us *to mortifie our members, that the body of sinne might be destroyed: we should put off the old man. Ephes.* 4.22. *Col.* 3.9. so that we should become *dead to trespasses and sinnes, wherein* formerly *we were dead.*

This killing of *our selves*, is *metaphoricall* and *morall*; by which death we are made alive: For, if we doe not thus die, wee cannot live: as, the sowne corne must first die, before it can live and grow. The kinds of it. Comparison.

This our *self-old-man* is slaine by *three* severall *acts* or blowes. *First*, the same, after a sort, was crucified in *Christ*, *Rom.* 6.6. *That the body of sinne might be destroyed*; although, not the individuall persons; but the common nature of mankind assumed by *Christ* did suffer death in him. How done. 1. In Christ.

Secondly, our *self-old-man* is *killed*, by change of our *state*, upon our grafting into *Christ* by *faith*: so that we are, in that respect, said to be *dead to the Law, by the body of Christ, Rom.* 7.4.6. and *that we are dead to the Law, that we might live unto God, Gal.* 2.19. this is done at one entire *act* or blow; in the *act* of our *justification*; so, by this death, freeing us from him, that hath the power of death, even the *devill*. 2. By change of our estate in Justification.

Thirdly, our *self-old-man* and the lusts thereof are *killed*, as touching the dominion and corruption of them, by the *Spirit* of *God*, in the *act* of *sanctification*: touching which the *Apostle* tells us, *Rom.* 8.13. *That if we, through the Spirit, doe mortifie the deeds of the body*, (which is the worke of our whole life,) *we shall live.* 3. By the Spirit.

This killing of our *self-old-man* should be done by *our selves*, being the executioners of it; by assistance of divine power from *God*, in *three* severall *acts*. How we are actors in it.

First,

1. *First*, by our *act* of savingly *beleeving* in *Christ*, whereby our state is changed from death to life.

2. *Secondly*, by our constant indeavours to be conformed to *Gods Image* and will, by daily renovation.

3. *Thirdly*, by our continuall *warfare* against our corruptions and temptations, touching which, the *Apostle* saies, *that the flesh lusteth against the spirit, and the spirit against the flesh*, *Gal*.5.17. they are so contrary the one to the other, that there is no living for *either* of them, but by the death of its *opposite:* neither is there any peace, untill one of them be dead.

Observe. The use of our Christian armour.

Wee should therefore ever use our *Christian armour*, and imploy our utmost indeavours to destroy our *self-old-man*; against which, if we doe turne the edge of our spirituall sword to slaughter it, with the lusts thereof, we shall be diverted, not onely from unjustly killing of *others*, but much more from *killing* our selves, in any other respect, but when we, as *Saul*, doe spare the life of this *Agag*, or *self-old-man*, it causes us, by a just hand of *God*, to fall upon our selves; to take away that *life* of our owne which we should both spare and cherish.

§.4. *Diverse observations from the generall consideration of self-murder.*

Observ. 1. Man is in greatest danger.

From the consideration of *self-murder* we may *observe*: *First*, that man stands in more danger of *destruction*, than any other creature: for, no *creature* is subject to attempts against the *life* of it, by it *selfe*, but onely *man*; who is invironed also with mortall dangers from without, but specially of his owne procurement, by opening the way for others to invade and hurt him, by breaches and armes of his owne making.

2. God wants not executioners of his justice.

Secondly, wee here see that *God* wants not meanes of *execution* of his *judgements* upon man; seeing, he can leave a man to fall upon himselfe, and be his owne executioner.

The use hereof is, to make us *afraid* to *offend God*; or to provoke him to be our enemie; or to live unreconciled with him, destitute of the assurance of his peace and favour. *Vse.* Feare God.

Neither are we over-confidently to *trust* our *selves* with our *selves*; of whom wee have so little assurance for security and safety from self-mischiefe: and therefore, we are carefully to cleave to *God* for preservation, praying him not to give us up to our *selves*, who are mercilesly cruell to our *selves*, when wee fall into our owne hands: for the neerer that any are linked and knit together in condition, or affection, the more desperately *opposite* they are, when they fall into division; because of the want of a fit *medium* or *mediatour* of reconciliation, betweene a *mans selfe* and *himselfe*: what meane is there, either to keepe himselfe from himselfe, or to reconcile himselfe to himselfe, when himselfe is fallen out into murderous resolutions against himselfe? Distrust our selves.

CHAP. 8.

Of spirituall self-murder in speciall.

§. 1. *All perishing soules are self-murdered.*

OF *self-murder*, thus generally *defined*, there are *two kinds*, or *specialls*; to wit, *spirituall*, and *bodily*. Soule-murder.

Although some may be said to be *murderers* of other mens *soules*, by their scandalous *practises*; or by their corrupt *doctrine*, or by depriving them of the *meanes* of their salvation, and the like: yet no *soule* can perish without the intervening and concurring of the assistance and meanes of him that owes that *soule*: whereby it comes to passe, that all soules that miscarry are in some sort, *self-murdered*. Is also self-murder.

murdered. For, although it is against nature to desire to bee absolutely miserable, and that he should in his last *existing*, in his last *principles* bee undone, or wretched: albeit he may affect the dissolution of his personall *subsisting*, upon intention and hope, by his change, to bee bettered in his future estate: subsisting in his remaining *principles*: yet he may wittingly and willingly doe that, which may be the destruction of his soule: although he doth not intend that *effect*; and so commit not direct, but indirect *self-soule-murder*.

§. 2. *Spirituall self-murder defined.*

What spirituall self-murder is.

Now, that wee may know what it is: *Spirituall self-murder is the killing of a mans soule, or spirituall life by himselfe, or his owne meanes.*

That which *distinguishes* this from *bodily self-murder*, is the *subject* killed, which is the *soule*, or spiritual life: not that the *soule*, *essentially* considered, or its *naturall* life of *being*, and *acting* in it selfe, can bee destroyed by man, whereby it ever *lives*, to be capable of eternall *misery*, or *glory*. For, such a death it cannot die, without being reduced into *nothing*, and quite extinguished, in regard of the spirituall *simplicity* thereof, void of composition, and the *nature* of it is an *act*: but this *death* is onely of that *superadded* supernaturall *beatificall life* of grace and glory; whereof a man may misse and come short, and be guilty of the losse thereof, although he were never personally possessed of it: as those that are said 1 *Tim.* 1. 19. to *have put away faith and a good conscience.*

§. 3. *Of soul-murder, by deprivation of life.*

Two degrees of it.

Of *soul-murder* there are *two degrees*: the *first* is *deprivation of spirituall life*, which is *pœna damni*, *or punishment of losse*: the *second* is *subjection* to misery, in *positive*

1. 2.

manner,

manner, which is called the *second death*; and is *pœna sensus*, or *punishment of sensible feeling*; because, man was indowed at first, as it were *habitually*, with a *spirituall life*; in gracious indowments, and communion with *God*: and now, by mans owne fault, that *habit* of spirituall life being destroyed, it may be truly said, that hee himselfe hath killed it; in regard that he was *radically* and *implicitely* in *Adam*; when he first destroyed and lost the same.

§. 4. *Of mans deficiency to be saved.*

The principall *meanes* of mans *deprivation* of this spirituall life is, his neglect of *meanes*, when himselfe is the *immediate* cause and procurer thereof, by his owne *deficiency*: and that *two* waies. Meanes of mans deprivation of spirituall life, his deficiency.

1. In *Adam*.

First, as he is originally considered in *Adam*, who was the roote of mankind, and whose first sinne and effects thereof are equally reckoned to bee all *mens* in common, who then were in him: and so, thus *radically* in *Adam* all men have deprived themselves of *spirituall life*, by their owne act of neglect of eating of the *tree* of *life*, and of others permitted for their use, and by their eating of the forbidden *tree of knowledge of good and evill*.

2. By himselfe personally considered.

Secondly, as he is *personally* considered by himselfe, a man may deprive himselfe of *spirituall life*, and so in that respect be a *self-murderer* of his *soule*; which is done by his voluntary *omission* of duties, upon which life is promised: every man is dead in *trespasses* and *sins* [a], and thereby subject to death: but the *Lord* hath abundantly provided us of meanes to advance us to life; which if we do *wilfully* neglect, or contemne to use (there being no other safety,) of necessity wee must perish, and bee guilty of our owne destruction; as were the *Iewes*, by rejecting of the *Gospell*, *Act*.28.25.

[a] *Ephes*.2.

Foure-fold omission.

Of this *degree* of *self-soule-murder* or *deprivation* of life, a man may bee guilty, by a *foure-fold omission* of things, that ought to be done by him, for his salvation.

1. Neglect of the outward meanes.

First, when a man willfully *neglects* the conscionable and diligent *use* of the outward ordinances of *Gods word, worship* and *Sacraments*; the blessed *meanes* of life appointed by *God*; without which no man of discretion in the visible Church can be saved: the *Apostle, Rom.* 10. 13. limits salvation to *calling upon the name of the Lord*; which cannot be without hearing of the *word* of *God*.

This neglect of *spirituall meanes* is either, by not going where they may be had, and sincerely used: *or*, if hee may have them, his neglect may be in not frequenting, and carefully using them, in conscionable manner; nor submitting himselfe to bee wrought upon; that he may be *moulded* in the *forme* and frame of the *word*[a]. But, doth come to the *meanes*; either with a *prejudicate* opinion against the truth; or with a resolution to continue still in his unregenerated estate; and in his sinfull courses; as those that with *their mouth shewed much love*; *but their hearts went after their covetousnesse, Ezek.* 33. 31. and as those that *Ieremie* speakes of, *Ier.* 18. 12. who said, *Wee will walke after our owne devices*; and *wee will every one doe the imagination of his evill heart*: such persons are as guilty of their owne damnation, as a man is of *self-murder* of his body, that out of *stubbornnesse*, or *sullennesse*, will not eate, but in the midst of plenty *starve* himselfe to death.

[a] *Rom.* 6. 17.

§. 5. *Of mans neglect of the power of the meanes.*

2. The contempt of the power of the meanes.

The second omission, procuring *deprivation* of *spirituall life*, and so consequently effecting *self-soule-murder* in that degree, is a mans contempt and regardlesnesse of the spirituall *efficacy* and power of the *meanes*; for inward change of his *spirituall* and *morall state* and condition;

dition; and for power of enabling him to all holy practise of life and conversation; whereby he may be borne againe, and be made a *new creature*[a]: which is a thing most necessary and availeable for salvation, *Gal.6.15.* [a] *Io.3.3.*

Such men are either, utterly *carelesse* and regardlesse of grace and spirituall life; from their undervaluing of the worth of it, or from their esteeming of the same to be needlesse.

Or else, they harden their hearts, as did *Pharaoh*, and set themselves against the power of the *Word*; that it may neither enter into their hearts, nor make any divine change in their states or lives; as if they had made *a league with hell and death.*

Such, are ever learning, but never attaine to saving knowledge; they are ever sowing, but never reape; they are ever in the hand of the workeman, but are never framed anew: they are fairely featured by some outward profession, but are without life and sound grace: *the reason* hereof is, because such an one rests upon and pleases himselfe in his owne sufficiency, using the meanes, without consideration of the *end* why God gave the *meanes*, and why we are to use them; and without looking and seeking to *God*, for a blessing upon the meanes, that they may be effectuall to his salvation. What be those Contemners.

§. 6. *Of mans defect in obedience.*

The third omission, whereby a man *excludes* himselfe from this *spirituall life*, and so consequently subjects himselfe to *spirituall death*, is wilfull *want of obedience to Gods word*; and that in a double respect: 3. Want of obedience.

First, in regard of the *Gospell*; when he doth not savingly *beleeve* in *Christ*, as the *Gospell* requires: but remaines in *privative unbeliefe*, whereby a man is destitute, or deprived of *Christ* our life and *Saviour*; *For*, we are frequently said to *live by faith*[b]: and therefore, without it 1 Evangelicall.

[b] *Habak.2.4. Heb.10.38. Rom.1.17.*

it we are dead: and so, such as do not savingly beleeve and repent, (which are the *acts* of *Evangelicall obedience*,) doe deprive themselves of salvation, through their owne default: which is evident, because they are *willingly* impenitent *unbeleevers*, *resisting* the motions of the *word* and *Spirit*; not sorrowing for, nor striving against their unbeliefe and hard impenitency of heart; but are secure, and doe please themselves therein.

2. Legall. *Secondly*, want of *obedience* to Gods word, that deprives us of life, is in respect of the *law*; in omitting of performing and doing the *affirmative* Commandements thereof, upon observation whereof all the *promises* of life eternall are intayled, so that without the same wee cannot be saved: and *therefore* we should keep the *Commandements* as our life: the want of *obedience* to the *affirmative* Commandements excludes from life; as the breaking of the *negative* Commandements subjects the transgressors to destruction.

§. 7. *Of the reasons of defect of obedience.*

Causes of want of obedience. There are *foure* speciall *causes* of mens neglect of the *affirmative* Commandements, both of the *Law*, and *Gospell*.

1. Omissions. *First*, because the sinnes of that *kind* are but *omissions*, which are not so contrary to *God*, nor doe so much trouble the conscience, as sinnes of *commission*: neither do the *affirmative* Commandements binde *ad semper*, to the *ever* doing of them *all* at *all times*: and therefore, *intermission* being next to *omission*, men doe easily fall from the *former* into the *latter*.

2. Carnal reason. *Secondly*, because, *carnall* men would *subject Gods Lawes* and *ordinances* to their owne naturall *reason*, which neither allowes, nor likes the spiritualnesse, nor strictnesse of *Gods Commandements*: such men doe give *dispensations* to themselves for carnall *moderation*, or *omission*

omission of duties: as *Naaman* the *Syrian* did, 2 *King*.5. 18. pleasing themselves therein; so long as their owne wit can coyne them excuses, evasions, and pretenses, that they may preferre their owne will and waies, before Gods wisdome and Lawes.

Thirdly, because mens owne naturall dispositions and course of life, are contrary to the vertues commanded: therefore, in favour of their *old man* of sinne, that raignes in them; they forbeare to do what may *crosse* or hurt the same: as the naturall *mother* that would not have her owne *child* divided, 1 *King*. 3.26. the *law* of *sinne* within them, prevailing against the *Law* of *God* and his Spirit: neglect of duties and vertues ever attends upon their *opposite* contrary *master-raigning sins*.

3. Contrariety of nature.

Comparison.

Fourthly, because that the *observation* of the *affirmative Commandements* doth more crosse a mans *profit* and *pleasure*, and brings him under more opposition and hatred of the world, than the keeping of the *negative Commandements* doth; he, therefore, is the more apt, and inclined to omit the duties of the *affirmative*, as more *troublesome* to observe, *because*, they doe include the observation of the *negative*; and are more subject to the censure of men, being more sensibly discernable than the *negative*: and doth make a greater distance and difference from the world, than bare *omission* of evill: *because*, doing of *morall good* puts a man into a remoter *extreame* from worldlings and unconverted persons, than only not doing *evill*.

4. Profit and pleasure.

§.8. Of grace dying by mans neglect.

The fourth omission, whereby a man deprives himselfe of eternall life; is *neglect* to *cherish* and foment the graces of *Gods* Spirit, begun to bee wrought in him by the meanes; but lets them die, before *Christ* bee fully *formed* in him; *because*, he doth not constantly and con-

4. Neglect of cherishing grace.

The reason.

scionably

scionably use the *meanes*, to perfect them both in their *nature* and *degrees*; neither doth improve and exercise the *talent* and *gifts* that hee hath; but suffers them to perish, in languishing *idlenesse*: nor doth he indeavour to approve himselfe to *God* in all sincerity and holinesse, according to the utmost of his power; nor yet encourages himselfe to aspire after perfection; by the consideration and hope of everlasting glory: we should be carefull and industrious that we lose not the *things that wee have wrought*, 2 *Ioh*. 8. For, those *onely that hold out unto the end, shall bee saved*[a]: by neglect and sloth, that life of grace languishes and dies; which wee might seeme to have; and might be, in some *degrees* and *motions* of the *Spirit*, begun.

[a] Mat.24.13.

Vses. *The uses* of this point of doctrine touching this *degree* of *self-soule-murder* by omission of the meanes of life, are diverse.

§. 9. *The harme of omission of duty.*

1. Omission deprives men of life.

First, to *informe* our *judgement*, wee may see that by this neglect and *omission*, a man may cut off himselfe from spirituall life; and be, in this *degree*, a *self-murderer* of his owne soule. *Want* of *grace* deprives a man of happinesse: as the *Virgins* want of *oyle*[b]; and the *mans* want of his *wedding garment*, excluded them from the presence of the Bridegroome[c].

[b] Mat.22.12.

[c] and 25.12.

It is not enough that a man be not an *ill* man, by sins of *commission* against the *negative* Commandements of *God*; except he be also a good man, by his conformity to GODS *affirmative* Commands. For, it is requisite, that as a man would, not onely not be damned in *hell*, but would also bee glorified in *heaven*; that hee bee not onely carefull to avoid the sins, that may subject him to the former; but also, that he doe embrace the vertues, and doe the duties, whereby hee may be fitted for, and advanced

vanced to the latter: and as a man is made capable of vertue and glory, so should hee not onely labour to be cleare of *vice*; but also to be indowed with *vertue* and *holinesse*.

Negative righteousnesse, in abstinence from sinne, (whereof *bruits* and *inanimates* are free,) is an improper and lame *righteousnesse*; which is next to a *non ens*; so long as it is not accompanied with vertue. *Omission* of good duties is a more generall meanes of destruction, in exclusion from life eternall, than *commission* of evill. for, many doe die before they are able to doe actually any evill, and many others have beene *civill* harmelesse men; (as the Philosophers) and yet perished. For, *except our righteousnesse doe exceede the righteousnesse of the Scribes and Pharisees, wee shall in no case enter into the Kingdome of Heaven*[a].

Negative righteousnesse.

[a] *Mat.* 5. 20.

And againe, commission of evill is ever accompanied with omission of the contrary good; but *omission* of good is not alwaies so accompanied with commission of evill; as we see in *Infants*: the greatest losse and mischiefe, that can betide us, in our deprivation of life and happinesse; which consists in the fruition of God that is infinitely good; and is lost by want and omission of good; for, *without holinesse none shall see God.*

The losse of eternall life is *pœna damni*, the punishment of damage, which is farre greater than the punishment of feeling, and smart; (although it bee not so to mans seeming:) therefore, *Cain* complained that he was cast out from *Gods presence*[b]: because, the *objects* doe so farre differ, as *finite* and *infinite*: and the *glorified* in Heaven shall be more affected with that happinesse that they shall possesse; than the *damned* in *hell* can be, for that sensible misery, that they shall suffer: both, in respect of the differing degrees, and also of the *natures* of the things: *but*, punishment of damage, and privation of life and happinesse proceeds from want and omission of good, whereof wee are to beware.

Punishment of damage greater, than of feeling.

[b] *Gen.* 4. 4.

L §. 10. Of

§. 10. *Of indeavour after ſpirituall life, and of the lets thereof.*

2. *The ſecond uſe* is, to ſtirre us up to *indeavour* after life ſpirituall, both to get and keepe it; by the conſcionable uſe of the meanes thereof: For, as *God* gives not this life, without our *uſing* of appointed *meanes* : ſo, theſe *meanes* are within the reach of our power; and none do periſh, but ſuch as are wanting to themſelves therein. For, no man periſhes, or is ſaved by an abſolute *decree* of *God*, without reſpect to his owne *courſes*, in the accompliſhment thereof: as, *Act.* 13.48. it is ſaid, that *as many as were ordained to life, beleeved.*

By a mans conſtant carefulneſſe, in the *uſe* of the *meanes*, and *walking* in the *waies* of *ſalvation*, it is apparent, that he is *appointed* to *life*, as the *Apoſtle* tells us, 1 *Theſ.* 1.4. *Knowing your election*: for, *our Goſpell came unto you in power &c.* this *life* is worth the labouring for; if we doe our parts for a thing of that price, we may have aſſurance and comfort of it, againſt the ſervile *feare* of the contrary death.

Letts. *The lets* and hinderances of this *endeavour*, and the cauſes of this *omiſſion*, whereby men deprive themſelves of this *ſpirituall life*, are ſpecially *three*.

1. Perverted judgment. *Firſt*, a *perverted judgement*, and *ſtupid underſtanding*, undervaluing the worth of that *life*, as not ſo excellent, and neceſſary as it is; it being not ſubject to our preſent naturall *ſenſes*, nor regarded by the *world*.

2. Miſ-placed affections. *Secondly*, the *preferment* of the *world*, in the *profits* and *pleaſures* thereof, before it; in place or degree; after which, ungodly men doe more eagerly hunt, and therein have more content; *becauſe*, they have the ſame in preſent *poſſeſſion*, and it *agrees* best with their eſtate and diſpoſition: inſomuch that it may be ſaid of ſuch men,

that

that it is better to be their *bodies* than their *soules*; as the *Emperour* said of *Herod*, that it was better being his *hog*, than his *Son*, because he killed his *Son*, but spared, and fatted his *hogs*. Macrobius.

Thirdly, groundlesse *presumption*, that *either* he hath that life already; *or*, that he hath time enough to get it long afterwards; *or*, that it may be easily had without meanes, or at least without so much adoe; makes a man to omit endeavouring after it in due time, in use of the meanes: and so he misses that *life*. 3. Presumption.

§. 11. *Of spirituall self-murder by subjection to death, through commission of evill.*

The second, degree of *self-soul-murder* is *subjection* to spirituall *destruction*, in damnation and everlasting misery: whereof man himselfe is the *efficient* meritorious cause, by his owne activity in committing, and wilfully doing those sinnes, for which death and destruction is threatned [a], and is assuredly inflicted upon the impenitent perseverers therein. For, as by a mans omission of his duty he deprives himselfe of life; so by his *commission* of sinnes hee subjects himselfe to the contrary death: the *former* being as *terminus à quo*, the terme from which men move, the *latter* as, *terminus ad quem*, the terme to which they move: both which are inseparably united in the same *person*; in whom, thereby, this *spirituall self-murder* is consummate, to the highest perfection, or degree of it; whereby it properly may be called *self-soule-murder*.

The second degree of self-soul-murder.

[a] *Ezek*.18.4.

§.12. *Of the meanes of destruction, by breaking the Law.*

The deadly meanes, whereby men kill their owne soules, and subject the same to eternall *positive* destruction, By sins of commission.

struction, are the sins that they wilfully commit, and continue in; in such *kinds* and *degrees*, and manner, as cannot consist in them with grace and salvation: and are of *two* sorts.

1. Against the Law of negative commands.

First, such as be against the prime law of *Nature*, by transgressing the *negative* Commandements of God; *whereby* the transgressours doe subject themselves to that punishment, which is called *pœna sensus*, or *punishment of smart*, or damnation in hell. For, *by sinne entred death*, *Rom* 5.12. *Rev*.21.8. *Prov*. 19.16.

The properties of soul-murdring sinnes.

The properties of the course and *sinnes* of *Commission*, whereby a man becomes guilty of *self-murder* of his soule, are *foure*.

1. They are grosse.

Although the nature of all sinnes be *mortall*, deserves death, and disposes a man for it, yet those that be of the grossest *kinds*, and in the highest *degrees* of exorbitancy, such as *Hosea* speakes of, *cap* 4.2. are specially said to be *mortall*, for their extreame contrariety that they have to *God* and his *justice*; their *inconsistency* with grace; and for their apting and disposing of those to destruction, that live in them; so that, by committing such sinnes men doe cast their owne *soules* into the gulfe of *perdition*.

2. Wilfull.

Secondly, when they that commit those sinnes, or any of them, doe willingly doe the same; and live in them, against the light and checks of their owne consciences; as our *Saviour* charges the *Pharisees*, *Iohn* 9.41. then are they self-condemned; and do wittingly destroy their owne soules, without excuse of ignorance, or of want of power to have avoyded the same: *seeing*, as there is, in some, *naturall* notions of the Law in the minde, such as the *Gentiles* have, *Rom*.2.14. *So likewise*, all men have some remainder of *power* to forbeare sinnes, in their *grossest kinds* and *degrees*; if they were not wanting to themselves: and therefore, as all men, specially the *wicked* within the Church, shall be judged by the *Law*; so they shall have nothing to plead, to excuse why they should not

not be damned,for their grosse transgressing of it.

Thirdly, when men commit those sinnes, with *eager-nesse* and *delight*, from and upon advised judgment, and wilfull resolution; with contentment in the acting of them, and defending, or excusing them, when they are done; as did *Saul*, 1 *Sam*. 13.12. and do fall to opposing, censuring, and condemning the contrary course of vertue and godlinesse, in the persons that doe practise the same; whom, therefore, they hate and persecute[a]: such persons are in a course of destroying their owne soules, by setting themselves, with a high hand, against *God*; provoking him to his face, to fall upon them for revenge.

3. Obstinate.

[a] *1 Thes.2.15.*

Fourthly, by this course of sinning, a man *murders* his own soule,when he goeth on, and incorrigibly *perseveres* therein, passing from evill to worse; hardning his owne heart, against all reproofes, and amendment; storming against, and abusing all the meanes of his recovery,to his deeper plunging in wickednesse, and destruction; *for*, although hee would willingly misse *hell*, and bee rid of the *guilt* of his *sinne*, that troubles his conscience sometime; *yet*,the *corruption*,and *practise* thereof he loves and entertaines: which is *sweet in his mouth*, and which hee *hides under his tongue*, as *Zophar* saies[b]: *as* upon persevering in well doing attends eternall life; so unto them that are *contentious, and doe not obey the truth, but obey, and continue in unrighteousnesse, indignation and wrath is their portion;and tribulation and anguish shall be upon every soule of man, that doth evill, Rom*.2.6,7,8,9,10.

4. Presevered in.

[b] *Iob*.20.12.

§. 13. *Of the causes of mens adventure upon sinfull courses.*

The reasons, why men do so desperatly venture upon such deadly courses,and continue in them, to the destruction of their owne soules, are specially *two*.

Reasons of mens so living.

1. Seeming good. [a] 2 Pet. 1. 9.

First, because the same *seemes good* to them; in regard of the *blindenesse* of their minds [a], that cannot truly discerne things that differ; and in regard of their unregenerated *affections*, which do *sympathize* and comply best with such courses; and because they are self-deceived, by a seeming goodnesse of profit, or present pleasure in them; which they preferre before true *morall* goodnesse; and therewithall do rest and content themselves, in the ignorance and want of better comforts: but a wise man will beware of *self-deceit*; by trusting to his owne opinion, or sense; considering that there is a *way that seemeth right to a man; but the end thereof are the waies of death*, *Prov.* 14.12.

2. Want of faith.

The *second cause* of mans boldnesse, in adventuring to run an unlawfull course with the perill of the damnation of his soule; is *want* of true *faith* to beleeve the *threatnings* of *God* in his word against the same; *or*, at the least, they suppose that the judgments will not be so bad and intolerable, as is given out; *or*, they *hope* they shall escape them; *or*, they *comfort* themselves with conceit of their *fellowes* company; *and* doe imagine *God* to be all *mercy*, and no justice: the *reason* hereof is, both their not discerning, nor regarding of the *spirituall judgments* of *God* upon them; which are the greatest and worst, and such as they see not sensibly; *and also*, because *sentence against an evill worke is not executed speedily; therefore, the heart of the sonnes of men is fully set in them to doe evill*, *Eccles.* 8.11. the flourishing of men in their owne ill condition hardens them, and staggers the godly [b].

[b] Psal. 73. 12, 13.

§. 14. *Of spirituall self-murder, by sinning against the Gospell.*

The second kind of sinnes of commission are against the Gospell.

The second kind of *soul-killing* courses, are sinnes committed against the *Gospell*; which is the only remedy given

given for transgressors of the *Law*, that when they are condemned for their disobedience to the *Law*, they may be saved by their obedience to the *Gospell*; without which they cannot but perish.

This *Evangelicall* obedience differs from *legall* obedience, in *foure* points.

First, whereas *legall obedience* is originally required to be done by a mans *owne power* and strength; *Evangelicall obedience* is to be done by us, through the power of *Christ* and his *Spirit* working in us, and by us; inabling us above the power of nature. 1. Obedience of the Gospell differs from obedience of the Law. Done by Christs power.

Secondly, no obedience of the *Law* is acceptable to *God* from those doing it, as under the Law, for *justification* by their workes; except the doers thereof be pure from *inherent* corruption, and doe their actions in their highest degree of *morall* perfection, without any defect therein: but, for the obedience of the *Gospell*, it is accepted by *God*, from the hands of sinfull men, as perfect, if it be in truth and sincerity, although accompanied with many involuntary defects, in our beleeving and repenting. 2. Acceptable with infirmity.

Thirdly, *perfect legall obedience*, yea any obedience of the *Law*, as *legall*, whose performance respects *justification*; excludes *Evangelicall obedience*; with which, in that sense, it cannot consist: seeing, *justification* both by *workes* and *faith*, both by the *Law* and *Gospell*, are incompatible, as the *Apostle* proves, *Rom.* 3. 28. *Gal.* 2. 16. *But*, *Evangelicall obedience* includes *legall obedience*, as inferiour and subordinate to it: for, there is an *Evangelicall use* of the *Law* under the *Gospell*, *both*, for *preparation* to the beleeving of it; *and also*, for *sanctification* of life ordered thereby, by assistance of power from *Christ*; for manifestation of the truth of Gods grace in us; to the workes whereof, although imperfect, a reward is due. 3. It includes legall obedience.

Fourthly, the obedience of the *Law*, by it selfe considered, respects salvation by way of *morall works* in our 4.

selves,

ſelves, but the *Goſpell* reſpects the ſame, by way of appli-
It reſpects ſal-vation by another. cation of merit from another, to witt, from *Ieſus Chriſt*: the *Law* cannot cure nor excuſe the tranſgreſſions committed againſt the *Goſpell*; but the *Goſpell* can heale, and deliver us from the ſinnes and judgements of the *Law*, whatſoever they have beene: and therefore it is, that the tranſgreſſors againſt the *Goſpell*, are in farre more danger of deſtruction therby, than by their ſins againſt the *Law*.

§. 15. *Of Infidelity.*

Sins againſt the Goſpell. *Of* theſe *ſoul-killing* tranſgreſſions againſt the *Goſpell* there are *foure* branches.

1. Infidelity. *Firſt, poſitive unbeliefe,* or infidelity, when a man will not beeleve ſavingly in *Chriſt*, to have him to bee both his *Saviour* and *Lord*: neither beleeves truly the *Goſpell*, in its full latitude and contents, although litterally hee knowes the ſame, but holds and beleeves deceitfull errors, defending the ſame, and applauding himſelfe therein: and therefore, ſeeing that now there is no *ſalvation* but by true *faith* in *Chriſt*, thoſe that will not ſo beleeve,
[a] *Ioh.* 3.18. according to the Goſpell muſt needs periſh [a].

Cauſes of infidelity. The chiefe *cauſes* of this *infidelity*, are, *Firſt*, an innated
1. *habit* to beleeve error, before the truth.

2. *Secondly*, our *carnall reaſon*, deceitfull fancies, and humane preſumptions, upon falſe *principles*, overſwaying our *faith*, contrary to the word of *God*, whereby men turne aſide to their owne *crooked wayes*, and periſh (as it
[b] *Pſal.* 125.5. were) in the *gainſaying of Corah* [b]. For prevention of this
Cure. infidelity, I conclude with the *Apoſtle*, *take heed Brethren leſt there bee in any of you an evill heart of unbeliefe,*
[c] *Heb.* 3.12. *in departing from the living God* [c].

§. 16. *Of Impenitency.*

2. Impenitency. The *ſecond kind* of ſinnes againſt the *Goſpell*, whereby men

men kill their owne soules, is finall *impenitency*; when they neither care, nor indeavour to repent for their sins past; nor to reforme their lives, for time to come; but goe on in their sinnes, out of love, or carelesnesse of them: remorse for sinnes, in respect of the punishment of them, is not true *repentance*, if it bee not specially for the *offence* of *God* by them, and if a man bee sorrowfull for some *grosse* sinnes, committed by him, and doe restraine his practise therefrom, it is not sound *repentance*, so long as hee is not grieved for his sinnes of *omission*; nor makes conscience to doe his duty, in keeping the *affirmative* Commandements of *God*. *Of* the *danger* of this course of *impenitency* the *Apostle Paul* gives his censure, in these words: *But after thy hardnesse and impenitent heart, thou treasurest up unto thy selfe wrath, against the day of wrath, and revelation of the righteous judgements of God, Rom.*2.5. To prevent this *impenitency*, we must beware of *custome* in sinne, and of *slighting* our spirituall estates. Cure.

§. 17. *Of the sinne against the Holy Ghost.*

The *third branch* of the sinnes against the *Gospell*, whereby a man kills his owne soule, is the sinne against the *Holy Ghost*: which consists in hating, and opposing the knowne saving truth of the *Gospell*[a], and is called a *sinne unto death*, 1 *Ioh.* 5.16. from which there is no recovery; not onely because it is ever accompanied with *finall impenitency*; but, specially, for that the *nature* of that sinne is so directly *against* the *meanes* of salvation, that thereby a man cuts himselfe utterly off from it; and deprives himselfe of the *suffrages* and prayers of the *Church*[b]: every sinne disposes a man lesse or more to this sinne; which is the transcendency of all sinnes; and *therefore*, that all men may feare, and not presume upon any sinfull course, *God* hath set bounds to his *mercy*, how

3. The sinne against the Holy Ghost.

[a] *Mat.*12.31.

[b] 1 *Ioh.*5.16.

M farre,

farre, in what caſes, and to whom he will ſhew the ſame, and in what caſes, and to whom not. It behooves all men, as they would eſcape damnation, to beware of this ſinne; which at laſt often cauſes men to lay violent hands upon themſelves, and to end their lives in deſperation. The ſinnes neere approaching to it, are thoſe that men doe wilfully, with a high hand, commit, and ſtand in; with hatred and perſecuting of the contrary vertuous courſes in others. To avoid this ſinne againſt the *Holy Ghoſt*, wee muſt be carefull that wee ſinne not preſumptuouſly; nor hate goodneſſe, and good people.

Cure.

Things obſervable in it.

It is (by way of enlargement) further to be *obſerved*, that this ſinne againſt the *Holy Ghoſt* is both incident onely to perſons inlightned, with certaine knowledge of *Chriſt* and the *Goſpell*, by the Spirits *illumination*; and are indowed with ſome competent meaſure of *Evangelicall graces*, by the power and worke of the *Holy Ghoſt*: and alſo, that the *nature* of it conſiſts in an obſtinate malicious oppoſition of *Ieſus Chriſt* and his *merits*, and of the *Goſpell*, and of *Evangelicall* grace and goodneſſe; againſt divine light and convincing *illumination* of the *Holy Ghoſt*, in thoſe that doe it; who, in their very *act* of their oppoſition of Evangelicall truth, and the profeſſors and obeyers thereof, doe the ſame, with malicious reſiſting the very *motion*, working, and perſwaſion of the *Spirit* within them to the contrary, at that very inſtant.

[a] *Heb.* 6.4.

Obſerv. How many now do commit it.

Many more doe now, in the time of the *Goſpell*, commit this ſinne againſt the *Holy Ghoſt*, than could doe it in the time of the *Law*: and, many now doe come ſo neere unto it, that they fall into the deſperate eſtate of *impenitencie*, and of a *reprobate ſenſe*; in regard of the cleareneſſe, and abundance of the light of the *Goſpell*; *contrary* to which, and to their owne conſcience, they runne with greedineſſe to all exceſſe of wickedneſſe and prophaneneſſe; with hatred and oppoſition of goodneſſe;

an d

and of the power of the *Gospell*; and of those, in that respect, that are godly. None that are affraid they have committed the sinne against the *Holy Ghost*; or, are troubled about it; or, grieved for it, can (in that case,) commit it; neither have committed it: *because*, this sinne is done with the whole consent of will, and sway of affections in a totall *Apostacy*, with *impenitency*, and unreconcileable hatred, and persecution of the truth of the *Gospell*, and of the *professors* thereof. *Note.*

§. 18. *Of Apostacy.*

Fourthly, the *soule murdering* sinnes, committed against the *Gospell*, are, *apostacy*, from the profession, or power of it; occasioned by an evill heart of unbeliefe, by the profits, honors, pleasures, or examples and temptations of the world; in those that are *hypocrites* and unsound: as were *Demas* [a], and *Simon Magus* [b]: and by renouncing of *God* and the *Gospell*, by compact, explicit or implicit, with *Satan*; as *Witches* and *Magitians* doe; resigning their soules to him, and to eternall destruction. *Where* it is to be *observed*, that *Apostates* (in Gods just judgement) not onely runne into all excesse of impiety and prophanenesse; but, doe also become most bitter haters, and persecuters of the profession and professors; which formerly they seemed to embrace; being not content to perish themselves, but also are grieved that any should bee saved, and stand fast in the truth. *Apostates* are hardly ever recovered, and their damnation is greater; because, they fall from a *higher pitch* than other men; and against more *meanes* of knowledge, and reluctancy; whereby they are self-condemned; and often, at last, end their dayes in despaire: *graduall apostacy*, or *relenting* in the power and wayes of godlinesse, is incident to the godly, and recoverable, as wee see *Revel*.2.5. and therefore, is not comprehended in this

Finall Apostacy.

[a] 2 *Tim*.4 10.
[b] *Act*.8.21.

ranck of *soul-killing-apostacy*, which is not fallen into at once, but by degrees. To persevere in the truth, we must labour to be *sound* in the faith, and to love, and delight in the truth, above all things.

The difference of sinnes.

Although, it is certaine that all sinnes are damnable for *nature*, in regard of their contrariety to *God* and his *Law*; and are also of a condemning property, in respect of their *merit* of due punishment of damnation: *For, the soule that sins shall dye: Ezek.* 18.4. *yet*, all sinnes are not alike, (as the *Stoicks* affirme:) but, some are more mischievous, and more repugnant, than others, to *God* himselfe, and to our *salvation*, and to the *good* of *others*; and are more incompatible with justice, and charity, than others are: as Idolatry, perjury, &c.

§.19. *Of the malignity of the sinnes against the Gospell, above those committed against the Law.*

Sinnes against the Gospell worse than against the Law.

The *sinnes* that are done immediately against the *Gospell*, are more *dangerous* and *worse* than those that are committed immediatly against the *Law*, whereof I will give *three reasons*.

Reasons.

1. *First*, for their *nature*; they are of a higher straine than the sinnes of the *Law*, as the *Gospell* is more eminent, than the Law, which is intimated, *Heb.* 10.28, 29.

2. *Secondly*, these sinnes against the *Gospell* are done, with more opposition against more abundant meanes and grace, by those that now live in the *Church*, than the sins of the *Law*: as *Paul* manifests to us, 2 *Cor.* 3.8.

3. *Thirdly*, the sinnes against the *Gospell* are committed with farre more inevitable destruction, than the sinnes against the *Law*: for, if a man doe sinne against the *Law* he hath the *Gospell* as a City of *refuge* to flee to, to save him from the killing and damnation of the *Law*: but if a man doe sinne (as aforesaid) against the *Gospell*, there remaines no further meanes, or hope of safety, but a fearefull

fearefull expectation of eternall deſtruction, by his own wilfull procurement; murdering his owne ſoule.

Obſerve. *From* the conſideration of the aforeſaid ſins of *Commiſſion*, againſt the *Law* and the *Goſpell*; with their deadly *effects*, we may *obſerve*,

1. Sin coſts deare. *Firſt*, that there is nothing that coſts ſo *deare* as ſin: it ſelfe is a thing of nought, but wonderfully deare to buy and poſſeſſe: and therefore before we meddle with it, we ſhould conſider the price of it; whether we be willing to die eternally for it; otherwiſe abſtaine from it.

2. To have our wills brings deſtruction. *Secondly*, we may ſee, that we cannot have our own wills in ſinfull courſes, but with the deſtruction of our ſoules: our folly is ſeene in undoing our ſelves by our owne workes and wayes; ſo that a mans courſe of finning, and following of his luſts, is indeed but a courſe of Gods heavy ſpirituall judgements upon him; wherein he is rather to be pittied, as miſerable; than to be envyed as formidable: *God* will have his will in mans deſtruction; when man will not let *God* have his will in his Commandements.

§. 20. *The improvement of the knowledge of ſpirituall ſelf-murder.*

Vſes. The *Vſes* of the knowledge of the aforeſaid *ſpirituall ſelf-murder* are ſpecially *Foure*.

1. Sin is a courſe of ſelf-murder. *Firſt*, It ſerves to *informe* our *judgement*, what to think and eſteeme of the ſinfull and careleſſe courſes of many, that live wilfully and impenitently tranſgreſſing both *Law* and *Goſpell*: namely, that the ſame is a vile courſe of *ſelf-murder* of their own ſoules; for, by thoſe courſes onely, men doe periſh: and in thoſe courſes none eſcape deſtruction as one ſayes, *Vitium eſt non ens, & receſſus ab ente, & vivus interitus ipſius eſſe: & virtus eſt vita ipſius eſſe. Vice is a non-ens, and a departure from entity, and a living deſtruction of beeing it ſelfe: whereas vertue is the* Picol.

 life

life of being. For, although such men intend not directly to destroy their owne soules; but to *indulgere genio*, and live in self-content and pleasure; yet the courses that they directly intend & prosecute, being such as, of themselves, destroy the soule, which thing they know and are warned of, they are no lesse *self-murderers* of their soules, than they that (intending to prevent, or ease themselves of some present evill,) doe cut their own throats; by a lesser evill (as they thinke) preventing a greater: and therefore, such are infamous *self-murderers*; and cannot at the day of judgement be excused therefrom, by charging the blame of their destruction upon any others:
Numb. 13.36. *And*, especially such persons as live under the light and profession of the Gospell, in such sinfull courses and transgressions, are most guilty; and shall be most deepely damned in hell; having least to plead in excuse for themselves; and therefore our *Saviour* sayes that it shall be easier at the *day of judgement*, for *Tyre* and *Sidon*, *than for such. Mat.* 11.22.

Use 2. Spirituall self-murder is most hainous and damnable. The soule killed.

The second use of the point is, to shew us that this *spirituall self-murder*, is farre greater and worser, than men ordinarily thinke it to be, which is apparent in *three* respects.

First, In regard of the thing killed; which in *spirituall self-murder*, is the *soule* of man, that is much more excellent than the body; both for the *nature* of it, that cannot be valued with earthly things; and also for the *use* thereof *rationall*, and *spirituall*, whereby man excells all other earthly creatures: and, by the murdering thereof, he dejects himselfe, in state beneath them all, in misery and contemptiblenesse.

2. The body with the soul killed.

Secondly, for that they that kill their owne *soules*, doe consequently thereby also kill their owne *bodies*; because the *body* partakes in estate with the *soule*[a], and so are *both cast into hell: Mat.* 10.28. the *nobler* part drawes the *other* into *identity* of condition.

[a] *Rev.* 20.15.

Thirdly,

Thirdly, it is the *worst* of *murders*, in regard of the *quality* of the *death* it selfe: this *murder* of the soule is *spirituall* and eternall, not onely depriving a mans self of spirituall good: but also subjecting him to all misery of *sense* and *smart*; that the *devill* himself, the capitall enemy of mankinde cannot doe, nor desire worse to man, than (in this case) he doth to himself. *Murder* of the *body*, although it be vile and odious; yet, of it self it is but a *privation* from temporary good, leaving the body without sense or feeling of evill, and at the last day the *body* shall be raised againe to life, in the union of it with its owne *soule*, and *therefore* of all *self-murderers* the *self-soul-murderer* should be most miserable. 3. The quality of this kinde of self-murder.

The third use is, that as all men by *naturall instinct* do desire to be saved, and to escape *hell* and damnation, we should be carefull to *use* the *meanes*, and to walke in the way, whereby wee may attaine to life, and avoide destruction: for both are diversly entailed unto, and depend upon severall contrary courses, and appertaine to men of contrary lives and qualifications, without the which they cannot have the same. Although that many men doe divide the *end* from the *meanes*, supposing that, notwithstanding their unregenerate estate, and wicked lives, they shall escape destruction; and that, although they neither love, nor practise goodnesse, they shall bee saved and doe well enough: and so flattering and self-beguiling themselves in their owne courses, they run securely, and precipitate themselves into perdition: *and therefore*, I conclude with *Solomon*, *Let thine eyes looke right on, and let thine eye-lids looke straight before thee: ponder the path of thy feete, and let all thy wayes be established: turne not to the right hand nor to the left: remove thy foote from evill.* [b] *Use* 3. Endeavour to be saved, and preserved from soul-destruction.

[b] *Prov.*4.25.

The fourth use is, to direct us how we may rightly *judge* of our *selves*, and of our spirituall *estates*, and future ends, by the courses that we take. If the same bee deadly *Use* 4. Our courses in this life foreshew our estates what they shall be in the world to come.

deadly wayes of sin that we doe embrace and persist in, then must we die: and as those courses are of our owne voluntary choise, so cannot we blame any, but cry out of our selves and our owne wayes, as did the *Prophet, Woe unto us that we have sinned. Lament.* 5. 16. that so in time we may labour to prevent our destruction by speedy repentance.

Againe, if our *wayes* and *state* be good, and such as life is promised unto, wee may have assurance and comfort: that upon our perseverance, we shall have happinesse and life eternall.

So that we need not pleade uncertainty and ignorance of whether we are going to *heaven* or *hell*; or whether in the state or course we live in, we shall be saved, or damned; seeing that the *Scripture* makes it manifest what shall be the reward and event of every man; according to the *state* and *course* he lives and dyes in: that we need *neither* put off the knowledge, *nor* the blame, *or* cause of whether we shall be saved or damned, upon our *prædestination*; when wee doe determine the same in the accomplishment thereof, by our owne courses.

CHAP. 9.

Of bodily self-murder in speciall.

§. 1. *How bodily self-murder is defined and differenced.*

NOw we are to prosecute the *second* branch of *self-murder*; which is called *bodily self-murder*; and is thus defined.

Bodily self-murder is the killing of a mans owne body, in destroying of his naturall life; by himself, his owne voluntary meanes, or procurement.

This

This kind of *self-murder* is *differenced* from *spirituall self-murder*, by *two* things. *First*, by the *object* that is killed; in *this* the *soule* and spirituall life is destroyed: in *that*, the *body* or mans naturall life is undone.

Secondly, they *differ* in the *meanes* and *manner* of killing of them; the *soule*, or spirituall life is slaine, by *spirituall* and *morall* meanes; the *body*, by *naturall*, or bodily self-willed waies.

§. 2. *Of Mans body and its works.*

Touching the *body* of man, in this case, we are to consider *three things*.

First, that it is an *essentiall* part, and not onely an *integrall* part, constituting the *person* of man; without which he cannot be a man, *personally* considered: and therefore, by killing of his *body*, he destroyes his *person*, that it ceases from being, or subsisting in this world. Considerations. 1.

Secondly, the *body* of man is the *organ* or instrument, whereby the *soule* works *organically*: and *therefore*, hee that kills his owne *body* destroyes all those works, that the *soule* was to worke in it; and which it cannot doe, without it. 2.

The morall-organicall works of mans *soule* in the *body*, are of *three* sorts. *First*, such as immediatly intend, and concerne the advancement of the *glory* of *God*, in this life; where, the living, and not the dead, do praise him. The soules morall workes in the body. 1.

Secondly, such works as are serviceable for the *morall* and *spirituall* good of the *person* himselfe; which is to bee attained and procured by life; before we can come to enjoy it by death. 2.

Thirdly, such works as promote the good of the *Church* and *Common-wealth*; of both which every Christian is a member; and can, onely by his life, and not after death, benefit the same: so that, by killing himselfe, 3.

a man wrongs *God*, *himselfe*, the *Church* and *Common-wealth*; in bereaving them of that service and good, which they all might have by his life.

3. Considera-tion.

The *third* thing here *considerable* in mans body is, that it, with the soule, makes the *person*; and so, in that respect, is the subject, or seate of Gods *Image*, and *therefore*, a man, in killing of his owne *body*, not only dishonours, but also, in a sort, doth what in him lieth, to kill *God* himselfe; as he is *similitudinarily* in him, and incurres the horrible crime of *Læsa majestatis divinæ*; or treason against the sacred *Majesty* of *God*.

Observ. The body suffers by, and for the soule.

So then, the *body*, which is the soules instrument, or servant; and is no way culpable, or nocent, but by partnership with, and inserviceablenesse to the *soule*, is ill rewarded, and indignely suffers, by its owne *master*, abusing it to sinne, and subjecting it to misery and punishment: who is not content to weare it out; but, after his owne lust, breakes and spoyles it; whereof hee cannot turne one *haire* to *be white, or black*: hee spares his soule, in its sinnes, which he should mortifie; and, in a sinfull course, kills his body, which he should spare.

Life is unsure.

Naturall life is both a blessing of it selfe; and also is a meanes of blessing *God* and others, in this world; and whereby wee may attaine to everlasting blessednesse hereafter; of all which, a man deprives himselfe, by thus killing of himselfe: which cannot be done, but against the light and reluctancie of nature in all men; whereby, the *actors* declare themselves to bee unnaturall and barbarous *monsters*. *Naturall* life, that is a tenant at will in man, is most uncertaine, and soone thrust out at doores; when it is not secure from him that owes it. Man is unworthy of this life, that is no more thankfull for it, neither more values it, nor makes better use of it; but after his wastefull expence of it, in sinfull courses, desperately destroyes it.

God in his Word, never appointed, nor commended any

any *meanes* for a man to kill himſelfe by; becauſe, where *God* appoints not the *end*, he appoints not the meanes to attaine it; yet, man wants not meanes to doe it, by perverting his power, and skill to that *end*; and abuſing other things, contrary to the uſe for which *God* made them, when he purpoſes to doe ſuch an act; ſo, abuſing both himſelfe, and all other things, to his owne ruine.

The body is but a *paſſive ſubject*, in reſpect of the *ſoule*, to whoſe power and will it is obnoxious: and *therefore*, it is the more ſubject to ſuffer; and it is the more inexcuſable ſinne, to miſuſe it; ſeeing, it neither deſerves to be ill intreated at his hand, that owes it; nor yet hath it power to reſiſt, or defend it ſelfe, againſt the invaſions of him, to whom it is committed to preſerve it. In this *bodily ſelf-murder*, not onely doth the *ſoule* turne *enemy* to the body; but it, moreover, makes an unnaturall *mutinie* againſt, and amongſt the members; raiſing, by faction, a partie for it ſelfe; ſo cauſing the hand to ſtab the body, and the parts to be inſtruments to undoe the whole: and thus, by *inteſtine* oppoſition, a man ſubverts and pulls downe upon his owne head the *tabernacle* of his owne body; (as *Samſon* did the houſe wherein he was) whereby he cruſhes and undoeth himſelfe ordinarily, in body and ſoule.

The body is paſſive.

§. 3. *Of the degrees of ſelf-murder and proneneſſe of men to it.*

This ſelf-murder of the body is either *inchoate*, and begun, only in *purpoſes*, and *courſes* tending to the effecting thereof in time; if it be not ſeaſonably prevented: *or elſe* it is *conſummate*, in the full *accompliſhment* thereof. No man falls into the higheſt extremities of evill, but by *degrees*; the leaſt whereof makes way for, and drawes on the greateſt.

The degrees of ſelf-murder.

Cauſes of proneneſſe to ſelf-bodily murder.

The *cauſes* why men often are prone to the ſelf-murdering of their *bodies*, are *two*.

1. 2.

Firſt, the *meanneſſe* of it, in compariſon of the *ſoule*, for *nature* and *durance*; it being but earthly and fraile; whereby it muſt naturally die. *Secondly*, in regard that by it the *ſoule* is ſubjected to manifold ſufferings, here in this life, and is hindered from that eaſe and advancement, that freed out of the body, it might have.

Anſwer to 1.

But, touching the *firſt*, it ſhould make us the more tender over *it*, chary to uſe it; and to conſider that, by ſelf-murderouſly deſtroying our bodies, wee do contaminate and defile our ſoules; whereby wee make them far more vile, than any carion can be: ſeeing, ſinne is the onely *excrement* and *morall* defilement, for which *God* deteſts and abhorres men, as loathſome.

Anſwer to 2.

For anſwer to the *ſecond*, it is to be *obſerved*, that, by ſelf-murder of the body, a man is ſo farre from bettering of himſelfe; that thereby he deprives himſelfe of happineſſe; and ſubjects himſelfe to that wofull miſery; which, otherwiſe, living he might eſcape: and *therefore*, our bodies, and naturall lives are to be reſpected and cheriſhed; not onely, for their worth; but alſo, for their *uſe*; for w[ch] *God* hath given them to us. So that we are not to force a *divorce* of thoſe things, that *God* hath coupled ſo neere together; nor to thruſt away, or reject that which *God* requires us not then, and that way to lay downe.

CHAP. 10.

Of the kindes of bodily ſelf-murder.

§. 1. *Direct and indirect ſelf-murder defined.*

1. Direct ſelf-murder.

THe *kindes* of *bodily ſelf-murder*, are *two*: *Direct* and *Indirect*. *Self-murder* is not ſuch a *generall*, as in the

the *Schooles* is called *Genus univocum*, ſo predicated of them both, as equally communicating it ſelf to both thoſe *ſpecies*, or ſpecialls under it; but is *genus analogum ab uno*; or *commune genus* καθ' ἓν; or πρὸς ἓν. for that the ſame doth properly and primarily belong to *direct ſelf-murder*.

Direct bodily ſelf-murder is the killing of a mans bodie or naturall life by himſelf, or his owne meanes, adviſedly, wittingly, and willingly; intending and effecting his owne death.

Indirect ſelf-murder of the body is, when a man adviſedly, wittingly, and willingly intends, and doth that, which he knowes may be of it ſelf, the meanes of the deſtruction of his naturall life: Although he doth not purpoſely intend to kill himſelf thereby. Or, it is the killing of a mans owne body, by unlawfull, either morall, or naturall meanes of his owne uſing, without intending of his death thereby. 2. Indirect ſelf-murder.

§. 2. *Of the differences between direct and indirect ſelf-murder.*

The proper *differences* between *direct* and *indirect ſelf-murderers*, conſiſts ſpecially in *three* things. 1. They differ in their ends.

Firſt, in the *ends*, directly and immediately intended by the *ſelf-murderers* of both kindes, in their ſeverall *acts*: the *end* that is immediately intended in *direct ſelf-murder*, is *death* it ſelf of their bodies that kill themſelves; although not for it ſelf, but in reſpect of ſome benefit conceited to be had thereby; which is their *ultimate end*, whereunto death is in the *murderers* intention, *ſubordinate*: as for a man to kill himſelf, that he may be out of trouble.

The end that in *indirect ſelf-murder* is immediately aimed at, is the attainment of ſome good, *reall*, or *apparent* in, or by the meanes that an indirect *ſelf murderer* doth uſe; without any reſpect, or expectation of *death* thereupon ensuing : as in surfeiting by drunkennesse, or gluttony.

2. In their meanes.

Secondly, they *differ* in the *meanes* that are used by them, for accomplishing those *ends* ; in *direct* self-murder, the *meanes* abused to that *effect* and *end*, are not proper of themselves, nor by Gods appointment ; but are perverted by him that kills himself thereby ; as knives, or the like : for *God* never appointed *meanes* for any man lawfully to use for effecting that which he would never have men to doe : a *direct self-murderer* uses not the *meanes* for any pleasure he hath in them; but for the consequent *effects* that he intends by them.

In indirect self-murder, the meanes and course used are such, as doe properly kill in the end ; if that they bee persisted in, as *drunkennesse*, and the like : although they have in them a shew of present good, which gives the users of them a kinde of delight and contentment in them; whereof they shall be disappointed; when, in the end, they shall, in stead thereof, finde *death*; which they least expected, and most abhorred; and would resist the same, if it were inferred, or offered to them by others.

3. In the good aimed at.

Thirdly, *direct* and *indirect* self-murder doe *differ* in the *good* that is aimed at by them; and in the *time* wherein they looke to enjoy *it*. A *direct self-murderer* doth fancy his *good* intended by him, in his act of self-murder, not to be in the *meanes* that he uses to kill himself; *but* in, or by *death* ; in his *freedome* from *evill*, or *enjoying* of *good* : the time of his reaping of which benefit he conceives to be, after that he is dead and gone.

An indirect self-murderer conceits the *good* that hee aymes at, by his course, to bee, and rest in the very meanes themselves that he uses; therein expecting the present enjoyment thereof, before, and not after his death; the cogitations, and inflicting whereof hee abhorres, although he doe prosecute with eager delight, the courses that doe hasten and bring his death.

§. 3. *How*

§. 3. *How indirect self-murder is greater, in some respects, than direct.*

It is demanded, whether *direct*, or *indirect self-murder* be the greater sinne? *I answer,* if we consider the *freenesse* of the *will*, with lesse inforcement, and with more delight, prosecuting those deadly courses of *indirect self-murder*; there can be, in that respect, lesse said to excuse it; than for *direct self-murder. An indirect self-murderer* is at last, (in respect of the mortall *meanes* he uses, and persists in, untill the *effect* be accomplished,) as sure of *death*, which he abhorres; as a *direct self-murderer* is of the same, that he desires, and indeavours for, and longs after.

Which of them is the greater sinne?

Answer. In some respects, Indirect self-murder.

1. For freenesse of willing.

Againe, an *indirect self-murderer* is more hardly diverted from his unlawfull dangerous course, than, at first, a *direct self-murderer. Because*, this man may be sooner convinced of the vilenesse of his purposed fact; in excuse whereof he hath so little to say; and also, the danger of it is more apparent, and ghastfull to the mind, that advisedly in cold blood considers of it.

2. Obstinatenesse.

The other is taken up, with looking upon the present contentment in the meanes that he uses; not considering death and danger, thereupon attending and insuing; but self-deceives himselfe, with excuses, and colourable pretenses; and so doth wink (as it were) that he may not see the blow of *death*, that he is giving himselfe, with his owne hands.

Of direct self murder the *cause*, or occasion is ordinarily from discontentment, and sorrow; but, of *Indirect self-murder* the *cause* commonly is *pleasure* and delight; of these *two motives*, *pleasure* is the strongest; and their motion most violent, and indivertible, that are led by it; because, it moves with *nature*, and not against it; and hath *will*

Dolores ferre facilius est, qu im a voluptatibus abstinere: Arist. 3. Eth. c. 12.

will in men more propense that way; which by *griefe* is rather forced, than seconded.

§. 4. *How absolutly direct self-murder is the greatest.*

Direct self-murder is the greater sinne, and why.

Notwithstanding, Direct self-murder is the farre more grievous sin, in *three respects.*

1. End intended.

First, in *respect* of the *direct* intention of the *will*; and of its immediate *object* of murder of a mans *selfe:* whereby, it partakes, more properly and fully, of the *nature* of *self-murder*, than *indirect self-murder* doth. For, what is under a common *Genus*, or *generall*, directly partakes more of the *nature* of that *Genus*, than that which is under it but by *reduction*; or *indirectly*. So then, although *direct*, and *indirect self-murder* be both *self-murder*; yet they are not *equall self-murder*; but the former is the greater.

Etiamsi æquè, non tamen æqualiter.

2. The consequences of their acts.

Secondly, for the *consequences* of the acts of them both, *direct self-murder* brings more certaine, and sudden inevitable destruction, than *indirect*; which in this *latter* may better be prevented, by having time of repentance, than it can be in the *former*; and *death* in *this* is an *accidentall effect*, besides the intention of the *agent*, and nature of the meanes; which in the former is *per se*, and of the nature of the *action* so purposely ordered to that end.

3. Company of other sinnes.

Thirdly, direct self-murder hath more, and greater sinnes complicated in it, than *indirect* hath, both by *extension*, in kindes, and number, against God, others, and our selves; and also for *intension*, in *degrees*; by *reason* of *circumstances* of the party doing the same, against the light and reluctancie of nature, with direct intention to kill himselfe.

§. 5. *Of*

§.5. *Of the degrees of ſinne, and how to eſcape the greateſt, and its end.*

The *uſes* of this doctrine, of the diſtinction of *ſelf-murder* into *direct* and *indirect*; and of the differences betweene them; are ſpecially *two*. *Vſes.*

Firſt, to teach us that, there are *differences* and *degrees* in the ſame *kindes* of ſinnes; ſome being more grievous, than other ſome. So that although we be not guilty of ſinne in the ſame degree; yet we may be in the ſame kinde; as appeares by the *Iewes* convicted in their conſciences, of uncleanneſſe; although they were not taken in the *act*; as the *Woman* was, *Iohn* 8.9. 1. Degrees of ſin.

And therefore, to eſcape falling into the higheſt *degrees* of ſinne, wee ſhould be carefull to avoide, and to be free of the ſame generall *kindes* of ſinne; *both* as they are unformed and confuſed, in originall corruption; as in their *ſeminall Chaos*; and alſo, as they are formed in their diſtinct habits; ſo improperly called, becauſe, after the manner of *habits*, they *either* are in the place of true *habits*, *or* unite themſelves in, and with *them*; that they may both brooke one common name: and ſo we ſhould labour to be cleare of ſinne; both habitually, and actually. How to eſcape great ſins.

Wee ſhould not bee *conceited*, and bleſſe our ſelves ſo much, becauſe we are not fallen into the *fowleſt degrees* of ſinne; as we ſhould be *humble*, and penitently confeſſe our guiltineſſe in the *kindes* thereof; the difference herein being betweene us and others, but in *magis* and *minus*, in *greater and leſſer*: where the leaſt degree makes way, and diſpoſes us for the greateſt; and makes us liable to the ſame *kinde* of puniſhment, although not to the ſame meaſure of it. *Obſerve.*

The ſecond uſe ſerves to *inſtruct* us that men doe come to the ſame diſmall *ends*, as *Saul* and others did, by ſeverall courſes, being guilty of their owne deaths in The ſame end ſeverall waies attained.

Comparison.

diverse manners; as men may come into the same prison, at and by severall doores. For, although a man can draw a right, or straight line betwixt the same points but one way; yet he may draw crooked lines many waies, and they all be terminated in the same points.

Therefore, as a man would beware of any evill end, so should he shunne all the courses, that may lead, or bring him to it. For, it is no benefit to a man in misery to consider, how, and by what sinfull course hee came thither; so long as he is in that woefull *state*. Wee see many men come and end their daies together, upon the same *Gallowes*, but by severall courses, and differing crimes; some for *pettie treason*; some for *wilfull murder*; some for *burglary*; some for *pettie larceny*; and yet, to him that is hanged for the lesser offence, it is small ease and comfort, because he suffers not for a greater; so long as it is for any that he dies.

Chap. 11.

Of Indirect self-murder of the body.

§. 1. *Why Indirect self-murder is first treated of.*

Indirect self-murder is handled first;

Although that by *logicall method*, I should treat first of *Direct self-murder*; *because*, that which is directly under a *Genus*, or *generall* head, should bee handled before that, which is but indirectly under it, for the neerenesse thereof unto the same; and for the light that it may afford, for the better understanding of the other: yet, for all that, I will heere begin with *indirect self-murder* for *three causes*.

Reasons.

1. Imitation of nature.

First, because I will herein imitate *nature*, which proceeds frō things lesse perfect, to things more perfect: because

because *perfectiō* is her *ultimate end. Indirect self-murder* is lesse perfect *self-murder* than *direct self-murder*; because, the *Genus* of *self-murder* agrees more properly, and primarily to *direct self-murder*, than to *indirect*.

Secondly, *indirect self-murder* is ordinarily, both the *way*, and the *cause* of *direct self-murder*: and therefore, may be fitly treated of *first*; the rather because, *direct self-murder* never goeth before *indirect*; but, *this* goeth often before, and without *that*. 2. Precedency in execution.

Thirdly, because my intention is to insist specially upon *direct self-murder*, and by meanes of it onely doe I speake of *indirect self-murder*, *therefore*, I purpose first to dispatch it, as an accessary to the *other*; which I principally intend, as my last end in this treatise, therewithall to conclude the same. 3. End intended.

§. 2. *Of Indirect self-murder by omission.*

Having shewed what *indirect self-murder* is, and how it is differenced from *direct self-murder*, I will now declare how men doe fall into the same; which is done *two waies*. *First*, by *omission*. Secondly, by *commission*. How indirect self-murder is performed.

By omission a man may indirectly *murder himselfe*, being the *deficient* cause of the preservation of his *life*; *two* waies: either in a *physicall* naturall manner; or in a *morall* meritorious course. 1. By omission.

§. 3. *Of indirect self-murder, by omission physically wrought.*

First *physically*, and after a naturall manner, a man may *indirectly murder* himselfe, divers waies: as Wayes how.

First, a man may *indirectly murder* himselfe, by way of *omission*; if out of *sullennesse*, *griefe*, or *nigardize*; or by undiscreet *punishment* of his body, he shall stubbornly and foolishly refuse to eate, or drinke; in that *measure*, or 1. Physically, diverse waies. 1. Neglect of food.

or *kinde* that is requisite for his preservation, by abstinency, and sparing, either starving himselfe to death; or breeding in himselfe and contracting that which kills him: somewhat like hereunto was the practise of *Ahab*, 1 *King*. 21. 4. who because *Naboth* would not let him have his *vineyard*, *heavie and displeased, layd him downe upon his bed; and turned away his face, and would eat no bread*: the contrary whereof *Paul* commanded *Timothy*.

1 *Tim*.5.23.

A Caveat.

Yet, to avoid this danger, men may not *Gormandize*, or excessively pamper themselves, *indulgendo Genio*; but may, and ought at set times to *fast*; both for *civill*, and *divine* ends; with respect to the good both of *soule* and *body*.

2. Contempt of Physick.

Secondly, in this kinde of *omission*, a man may *indirectly murder* himselfe; by wilfull *contempt* of the lawfull *use* of *Physick*, or *Chirurgery*; *either* to cure, *or* prevent apparent mortall diseases or griefes; *or*, when he will not be ordered, by the wholesome direction of the *skilfull* in their calling; *or*, doth not depend upon *God*, for a blessing upon the meanes; who, by his over-ruling *providence*, *directs* the course, and *blesses* the meanes.

A Caveat.

Yet, men must herein be *carefull* that they slavishly enthrall not themselves to the *meanes*; *nor* anxiously perplexe themselves, *if* they cannot have them; *or*, that the successe answers not their expectation: because, the *Lord* disposes things so, as he also may effect his worke and will, often by crossing ours.

Neglect of prevention of dangers.

Thirdly, a man may incurre *indirect self-murder*, by *regardlesnesse* of preserving himself against mortall *dangers*; from without himself; as, in not seeking to *God* for reconciliation, by humiliation, and repentance; in some imminent judgements that threaten from *God* our destruction; that we may bee preserved either from them, or in them: *Or as*, when wee are in danger of invasion by enemies, for a man then regardlesly to shut his eyes from foreseeing the same, that it may suddenly surprise him;

him; *or*, that he should not prepare himself, and do his utmost endeavours in his owne defence, to save his life; if by resisting it may be done; or otherwise to provide for himselfe by *flight*; or other prudent *diversion*, or preventing of the *evill*; that he may not carelesly suffer his *life* to be lost. *So* then, the *cowardise* of men in extremities by *Sea* or land, that will not doe their utmost endeavours, for their owne preservation; as likewise the *griplenesse* of those that to spare their goods, indanger the losse of their lives, for want of *military* furniture and meanes to make opposition; are much to be blamed for this course of *indirect self-murder*.

But yet, touching this point, men should be wary that they *neither* be so carefull to preserve their *lives*, that they should spare to venture them where they ought; and may comfortably spend and lay them downe: *nor yet*, have their eyes and confidence so upon earthly *meanes*, of humane strength and provision; that they should forget, or neglect to seeke to *God*, and to depend upon him, for safety and victorious successe. A caveat.

Fourthly, of *indirect self-murder* a man may be guilty, by not avoiding and fleeing from *persons* and *places* destinated to destruction; which are under a curse; *or*, in a course of mortall judgements; when we are not necessarily tyed by duty, or calling, to commerce and bee with them: as is apparent by *Lots* forsaking of *Sodome*; and by the command of *Moses* to the *Israelites*, to depart from the tents of *Corah*, *Dathan and Abiram*; and by that divine commandement, charging all the *godly* to come out of *Babylon*; *that they might not be partakers of her sins*; *and that they might not receive of her plagues*. 4. Not avoiding dangerous persons & places. *Gen.* 19. *Numb.* 17.26. *Rev.* 18. 4.

And therefore, such as out of unwarrantable *presumption*, or *carnall security*, avoid not *persons*, and *places* infected with the pestilence; or subjected to perdition; when their presence is unnecessary, & not to be justified, and pernicious to themselves; they must be cast upon the inditement of *indirect self-murder*; if by the aforesaid *meanes*, they doe miscary.

§.4. Of indirect self-murder by omission morally wrought.

By way of *deficiency*, or *omission* of *indirect self-murder*, a man may be guilty by a *morall* meritorious default; *two* wayes:

2. Morally.

1. By neglect of good life.

First, by his wilfull *neglect* or *contempt* to live and walke in the wayes of *godlinesse*, and obedience to gods *affirmative* commandements; whereunto the *promises* of *life* and *protection* are annexed [a], and which we may certainly expect; so long as we keepe our selves within compasse of *morall* obedience to the *Law* and *Gospell*; and within the limits and precincts of our speciall *callings*; so that if therein, or therefore, we should lose our lives, we shall be free of the imputation of *self-murder* any way, in that respect.

[a] *Gal.*3.12.

2. Neglect of prayer, &c.

Secondly, in meritorious *morall* manner, a man may miscary, and be indirectly guilty of his own death; by wilfull omission and neglect of commending himselfe in *constant and ordinary prayer to God*; for *divine* preservation and safety of his *life*, against all evills and dangers, which may hurt him; and over which, and over *him*, *God* hath a soveraigne power and command. *And* also, by his *unbeliefe*, and not trusting in *God* in all estates, for preservation; under whose wings he may securely rest, a man may be justly deserted, and given over to perish and sinke; as *Peter* when he doubted, was in danger of *drowning*. [b]

Unbeliefe.

[b] *Mat.*14.30,31

Whence it proceeds.

This neglect of thus depending upon *God*, ariseth *either* from *self-confidence* in mans owne power and meanes; whereupon he rests as secure: *or* else, from *Atheisticall* conceits of the *providence* of *God*; as if he were *regardlesse* of humane affaires, and that all things did fall out

out by *chance* and *fortune*; because they doe see all things in this world fall out alike to all men: which being more exactly considered, manifests rather the free and *soveraigne* powerfull *providence* of *God* over-ruling all things.

Yet, this *divine preservation*, by *faith* and *prayer* to *God*, excludes not, but includes the conscionable use of lawfull meanes, and walking in appointed courses; without which we can expect safety no more, than *Paul* and his *company* could, if they did let the *mariners* forsake the *Ship*: [a] if a man by the aforesaid neglect of *prayer* and dependance upon *God*, doe not perish; it is Gods speciall worke, reserving him *either* for *repentance* and amendment of his life; *or* for some *worse end*, and heavier judgement.

A caveat.

a *Acts* 27. 31.

From this degree of *indirect self-murder*, by omission of meanes, wee may *observe* that when *God* gives *meanes* of life; if we use them not to that end, we tempt *God*, to follow our owne wills; while we will not follow his: and if we use the meanes, with *trusting* in them, then we make *gods* of the meanes; and *therefore*, in that respect, it is just with *God* to disappoint us of our expectation, and to condemne us of *indirect self-murder*, upon our miscarying, in not using the *meanes*.

Observe.

Neglect of meanes is tempting of God.

For, all *meanes*, as they are *meanes*, have relation to the *end*; why, and whereunto they are appointed: and so, in their *use* to that *end* consists their perfection; without which they were uselesse and needlesse: *and therefore*, by the *omission* of the use of the *meanes* of life, which men would enjoy, they either tempt *God* to doe things otherwise than he hath ordained; or else, they doe shew themselves regardlesse of *God*, preferring their owne wills above his, expecting to have their owne purposes without him; whereby many men deceive themselves.

§. 5. *A*

§. 5. *A question resolved about standers mute at tryall.*

About mutes refusing to undergoe the ordinary legall triall for their lives.

To this branch of *indirect self-murder* by *omission* belongs the *case* about *mutes*, who are persons standing legally indited and arraigned for some capitall crimes, that doe wilfully and obstinately decline and refuse either to confesse themselves *guilty* of the same, or to submit themselves to be tryed by *God* and the *Country*; notwithstanding that they certainly know that for their stubborne *mutenesse*, they shall in fearefull manner bee *pressed* to death; in which respect they are indirect *self-murderers*; although that they are thereunto moved especially by foure seeming *reasons*.

Their reasons.

1. First, because that by that way they would save their estates, (if they have any) from being confiscate to the King, that their heires may enjoy the same.

2. Secondly, that so they may escape the death that is most ignominious in their eyes, and infamous in the world to their memories, friends, and posterities, whereunto they foresee they should be subject, if so be they should undergoe an ordinary tryall.

3. Thirdly, that it may not be said that they suffered and dyed for so odious and shamefull crimes and *facts* as they are accused of, and indited for.

4. Fourthly, that they may not be cast, condemned, or suffer by the meanes, wills, and hands of such prosecutors, *witnesses*, *Iury*, or *Iudges* as they take to be their capitall enemies; they choose to die by that course of their owne election wherein their adversaries can least (as they thinke) have their will of them.

They should die, and why.

But whatever be their reasons of standing *mute* in that case, it is most just that therefore they should bee put to death in most terrible and ignominious manner; for *two reasons*.

First,

First, because of the intollerable wrong that thereby they doe to *authority* and *justice*; tending to the overthrow of the same, by refusing to subject their lives to the triall and judgement thereof; and by their deaths (as it may be truly interpreted) depriving their highest *Soveraignes* on earth both of the commendation of *Iust*, and also of opportunity of shewing mercy, and giving pardon to delinquents: and so not submitting to the judicature, they actually declare themselves to be rebellious *outlawes*, for which they are justly to die. 1.

Secondly, because such persons, by declining so just a way of trial by *God* and their *Peeres*, doe (in iust construction) declare themselves to bee guilty of the facts and crimes whereof they are indited; and for which they ought to die, but seeke to crosse the law in the proper kindes of punishment due for the same. 2.

And that they are guilty of their owne deaths by a grosse course of *indirect self-murder*, is evident by foure reasons.

Mutes are self-murderers.

Reasons.

First, because such an *one* wilfully and obstinately reiects that lawfull and ordinary course of *triall*, whereby it is possible that he might escape with his life; either by not being found *guilty*; or else by *replevin*, or pardon from the *execution*; and chooses that illegall course of standing *mute*, whereby, and for which hee certainly knowes he shall die: and as certaine it is that so dying, he is an indirect *self-murderer*; in regard that he casts away his life wilfully by that course, which was in his owne power most lawfully to have avoyded. 1.

Secondly, by choise of that course of standing *mute*, when he is called to a lawfull tryall, he dies not only for that contumacy against *authority* and *law*; but also thereby he unnaturally witnesses, and gives verdict against himselfe to be guilty of the originall fact or crime for which he is indited, and ought to die if it can bee proved and found against him; which thing hee (by his *mutenesse*), 2.

doing, in that respect hee justly perishes by his owne meanes, and is indirectly a *self-murderer*: for no innocent would decline so just and lawfull a tryall, by *God* and his *Peeres*, when he knowes that by so refusing hee shall surely die.

3. Thirdly, it is apparent that such a body is indirectly a *self-murderer*; because of the *morall* nature of their course of standing *mute*; which is most wicked and unlawfull, both by *Gods* law and *mans*: For, by the law of *God* and *nature*, every man is bound to plead and doe the best he can by all lawfull meanes to prolong, or preserve his life; but *standers mute* in case of triall upon their lives, doe not so, but utterly neglect the use of lawfull meanes to prolong, or save their lives; and therefore are of this kinde of *self-murderers*.

By *mans law*, for a person arraigned to stand *mute*, is most unlawfull, because it crosses the execution of Justice, and is justly punished by a most terrible kinde of death, by *pressing*. Man hath not an allowed choise given him by law, either to submit to *triall*, or to be *mute*, as he shall please: for if the choise were lawfull, why then should hee bee punished for doing that which hee may lawfully choose, which could not be done by the magistrate without great injustice?

4. Fourthly, that such *mutes* are *indirect self-murderers*, is evident by the voluntary disposition of their wills in the free *choise* of that mortall course, and by the proper *nature* of their death, and by the *meritorious cause* and reason of it; all proceeding from themselves in *active* manner. Whereas, touching their deaths, and course of inflicting thereof, they should *passively* and obediently submit to *God* and lawfull *authority* to live, or die as they please, where no lawfull choise is given in mortall courses, there no man can choose that which is unlawfull without being an *indirect self-murderer*, as it is in this case.

The

The motives whereupon any persons doe stand *mute*, refusing to be tryed in an ordinary lawfull manner, are altogether insufficient to justifie their practise.

Answer to their motives.

For answer to the *first*, it is certaine that we should do nothing that is unlawfull to save our worldly *estates* for our *heires*: but this course is unlawfull; *Ergo.*

To be more carefull to provide for the safety of their worldly goods, than of their soules, is wretchednesse and desperate folly; which all those doe which by unlawfull meanes would preserve their estates. Such *mutes* are so farre from being worthy of having their estates preserved by this course, that therefore they should the rather lose them, and themselves be the more cruelly and ignominiously entreated, for being guilty of two horrible crimes; first, that whereof they are indited, and for which they refuse to answer to be legally tryed; the second is their contumacious rejecting of all just and legall courses of tryall, and active obedient subjection to authority, requiring their submission.

Touching their *second* and *third motives* of standing *mute*, with respect onely to the matter of their worldly *credit*, the same is meere folly; because by this course they doe farre more discredit and make themselves infamous; in regard that *ipso facto* they make themselves guilty of a double crime; both of that whereof they are indited, and also of contumacy against *authority* and *law*; and the death of *pressing* that they suffer, is the just reward of their obstinate *mutenesse*, besides all their other demerits: it is chiefly the morall *manner* of dying that is comfortable and honourable, wherein such *mutes* are wanting.

Their *fourth motive*, which is from *feare*, proud *impaciencie* of suffering uninstly, or inimically by others, in the course of ordinary legall triall, is most *vaine*: for why should we wrong our selves, that we may escape being wronged, or insulted over by others? this was the practise of *Saul*, to kill himselfe that he might prevent being insulted over and mocked by the *uncircumcised Philistims*: the matter of the greatest triumph to our enemies over us, is to give them a victory by our owne hands, both over our bodies and mindes; as such *mutes* doe, to their eternall destruction.

Such *mutes* are not onely guilty of their owne deaths; but also, by that course they subiect themselves to everlasting damnation both in *soule* and *body*: both because they die impenitently and wilfully in a sinfull way of their owne obstinate procurement and choise: and also doe cast away their soules in departing this world in uncharitable manner, without either confession or clearing of themselves in lawfull manner, of the crimes for which they are indited and arraigned: and so perish as *outlaws* against both *God* and *humane authority*; whose fact is equivalent to *direct self-murder*, by wittingly and willingly doing that unlawfull act, which they know will inevitably subiect them to death, without hope of escape.

§. 6. *About malefactors arraigned for crimes; how they are to answer to the question Guilty or not guilty.*

Question 2. A second *question* considerable about the foresaid *subject* is touching *malefactors*, indited and arraigned at the barre of *Iustice*, before a lawfull *magistrate*, to be tryed upon their lives for some capitall crimes that they have done; as *petty treason*, *burglary*, *murder*, or the like, touching their lives; whether, when they hold up their hands at the *barre*, and are in legall manner asked the *question* whether *they be guilty*, or *not guilty* of such a fact whereof they are indited; and which indeed they themselves know they have done: whether (I say) are they

they bound in conscience, and may they answer affirmatively that they are *guilty*: without any danger of being indirectly guilty of *self-murder*?

Answer. They that confesse themselves to be guilty are indirect self-murderers.

For resolution of this *question* I answer, that when a man is accused of such a capitall crime, and is therefore brought to a legall triall, whereunto he is subjected for finding, or not finding him to be *guilty* of that fact, upon the verdict of which enquiry, *Law* and *Authority* is satisfied, and determines their proceeding with the party; for him, upon that question, whether he *be guilty*, or *not guilty*; before the triall, to confesse himselfe to be *guilty*; so, by his owne onely witnesse and verdict casting himselfe upon the losse of his life, hee may in a strict construction, and in some sort be accompted culpable of *indirect self-murder*.

Exception.

Except it be in *case* to save *innocents*, from suffering wrongfully, for his fault, or that it be for greater good of the *State*, of the *Church*, or of his owne *Soule*; when the fact can no otherwise be knowne, or proved against him, but by his owne confession.

Touching a voluntary and full *confession* after conviction and condemnation I know none that is not of opinion, that it is necessary for the salvation of the malefactors soule, although his body do perish as *Achan* did, *Joshua* 7.20.

That such an affirmative answer of *guilty*, to that *question*, makes the *answerer*, I say in some sort, indirectly guilty of *self-murder* (although they are not the worst men, morally considered, that doe so;) I will make it plaine.

Reasons. 1.

First, a *malefactor*, by such an affirmative answer, anticipates, and deprives himselfe of that legall triall, whereby it were possible for him to have escaped, and not to have beene found guilty of that capitall fact, for which he is indited; and therefore, by dying upon his owne onely confession, witnesse and verdict; which hee

 needed

needed not to have done, he is guilty of indirect *self-murder.*

Now, for a man that hath, in danger of life, lawfull choise of two waies; the one most certainely mortall, the other more doubtfully deadly; if hee choose, and perish by the former, he is indirectly a *self-murderer*; because, he willingly rejected the latter and safer, whereby he might have lived : thus it is in this case of answering *guilty*, before the triall.

2. *Nemo tenetur prodere seipsum; quisq; tenetur defendere seipsum. Unusquisq; præsupponitur esse bonus, donec probetur esse malus.*

Secondly, it is a naturall *axiome, that no man is bound to betray himself:* and *that every one is tied to defend himselfe.* A Traytour (saies D[r]. *Kellet* Miscel.li.1.p.164.) *may without sin plead not guilty; that is, not proved guilty at your barre; where, every one is presupposed to be good,* untill he is proved to be bad. *I am not guilty so farre, that I am bound to accuse my selfe : and this is* (saies hee) *the allowed generall acceptation of that usance.*

For further manifestation hereof, it is to be considered, that the *question* and *answer* is made in a humane *civill Court,* wherein hee is demanded, not whether in *Conscience,* but whether in *Law* he be *guilty*; whereby he is bound to confesse no more against his life, than can be legally proved against him; specially seeing he answers not upon *oath*, or *adjuration*; which binds the *examinate,* or *prisoner* at the *barre,* in conscience, upon obligation of *religion*, to depose the truth concerning himselfe, knowne onely to that deponent; and according to whose owne testimony hee is to be acquited, or condemned; but, this being most unreasonable, to make a man witnesse, Jurie, and Judge in his owne cause; about and for things secret, to bring him to publick judicature and censure, it is not in use among us.

Of answering upon oath about crimes concerning a mans selfe.

The seeming contrary practise in this *Kingdome*, is (as I take it) onely in *Courts* of *Conscience*, having more spirituall power; to bee used specially for the good of mens soules, without blood-shedding, or danger of their lives;

lives; who are not required upon oath to depose of criminall matters concerning themselves; but where there are first *promoters* and *accusers* offering to prove the same: in which case, for the better informing and resolving of the Court, from the conscience of the *accused*; in favour of whom, it is originally allowed, from the supreme governour and Judge of that Judicature, that hee may answer his knowledge upon his *oath* to the articles of his accusation; not with legall intention, by that course, to make him unnaturally to accuse or condemne himselfe, where none others can, or are about to doe the same; but for answere in his owne defence touching the things that he is accused of; thereby, either to make his innocency to appeare, if he be blamelesse; or otherwise, by his owne confession of his faults, for the good of the *Church*, and his soules health to discover the danger, and shew his ingenuity that hee may repent, amend, and find favour.

Objection 1.

It may be objected, that such a *malefactor* is bound, in this case, to answere, according to his owne conscience and knowledge, that he is *guilty*: because, if he answer *not guilty*, when he is indeed *guilty*, he *lies*: which is unlawfull for him to doe.

Answer 1.

Cont. Marc. 6. lib. 4. *Justa & digna praescriptio est in omni quaestione, ad propositum interrogationis pertinere debere sensum responsionis: aliud consulenti, aliud respondere, dementis est. Sensus responsionis non est ad aliud dirigendus quam ad propositum interrogationis.*

To this I reply; first, that the *malefactors* answer is to be made according to the intention of the *Law*, and of the *Judge* that moves the *question*: according as *Tertullian* saith; *it is a just and worthy rule, that in every question the answer should bee applied to the same sense and purpose, to which the interrogation is made.*

To answer of one thing, when he is asked another, is the part of a mad man.

Againe, the sense of the answer is not to be directed to any other thing, than that which was propounded in the interrogation.

Now, the *Judge* propounding, according to *Law*, this question to the *prisoner* at the *barre*, *art thou guilty*, or *or not guilty of this felony*, or the like; intends not that he should answer, from his onely conscience, *guilty*; which is unnaturall and suspitious, for him to give witnesse and virdict against himselfe, to the taking away of his owne life; but that he should answer *not guilty*, in law, at the barre whereof hee stands arraigned, that so, for finding of him *guilty* of that whereof hee is indited, hee may legally bee put upon the triall of *God* and the *Countrey*.

For the *question* being propounded in a *disjunctive* proposition, *art thou guilty, or art thou not guilty?* both gives a free choise which of them to answer, and also puts in minde, and poynts rather to the latter, as more naturall and equall, than to insist upon the former.

It is a free and lawfull election offered, in mercy and favour to the *prisoner*, from the *King* by the *Iudge*, for the indicted person to choose which he will; whether voluntarily to confesse the *fact*, or rather to put himselfe upon the triall of *God* and the *Countrey* for the same.

His negative answer of *not guilty*, is but his choise and imbracing of the latter triall; which is most agreeable to *nature*, to the Law, and the Kings favour and mercy, in this case; which he can no otherwise have, but by first pleading to the *inditement, not guilty*; And so, his *answer* and *plea* of *not guilty* is no lye, although hee have done the fact, whereof he pleads he is *not guilty*, and for triall thereof puts himselfe upon *God* and the *Country*.

Objection 2. If it be againe *objected* that seeing the *Law* that makes this disjunctive question, accepts of the *prisoners* affirmative answer; and thereupon condemnes and executes him; (as *David* did with the *Amalekite*, upon his confession that he had slaine *Saul*, 2 *Sam.* 1. 16.) it seemes to be lawfull and requisite for all *malefactors* to answer to the *question* affirmatively; touching the things that in conscience they are guilty of.

Answer. I answer, it is lawfull and fit for *Magistrates* to use many

many meanes to winde out the truth of facts from delinquents, which *malefactors* are not bound, upon such questions or inquisition, to reveale against their owne lives:in regard, that every one severally is to order their practise and course, according to the rules proper and pertinent to their owne conditions and callings.

The *Law* indeed accepts of the malefactors answer of, *Guilty*; and accordingly proceeds to condemne and execute him; because, by his confession, giving testimony and verdict against himselfe,he cuts of, prevents and excludes himselfe from triall by others, whereby he might be either cleared, or condemned; in regard,that it is justly supposed that none other can know a man and his actions so well as himselfe doth : and therefore, the *Law* for ease,certainty,& other politick respects,doth permit and accept of such an affirmative answer, but neither commands,nor commends it : because, the Law takes notice of things, and censures them *politically*, and not *theologically* considered.

Thirdly, it may perhaps be here *replied*, that when a man (besides his owne knowledge of his *capitall fact*) hath, upon *examination* before a *Iustice*, confessed the *fact* under his hand, which is produced against him at the *Triall*,how can he plead *negatively* to the *inditement*, *Not guilty*, without *lying* either in the *former*, or in the *latter*;seeing of *cōtradictiōs* of necessity one must be false? Objection 3.

I *answer*, that for such an one to answer at the *Barre*,*Not guilty*,is not a *lie*,nor properly a contradiction to his former *confession*; or to his owne knowledge ; neither is that *negative plea* any concealement of the *truth*, from being then and there knowne, by such lawfull meanes, as by *Law*, and the *Iudge*, is intended for discovery of the same, which is by other evidence than a mans owne *confession*. Answer.

For clearing of the truth whereof, it is to be observed that the *question* made to him touching his *fact*, is propounded to him, and hee charged with the *fact*, in his *Inditement*, in such a *nature* and *forme* of *Law termes*, as it may be he properly understands not; as whether he be *guilty* of that *treason*, *felony*, *burglary*, or the like? in which respect, or *Law notion*, put upon his *fact*, his life is questioned, and in danger to bee taken away. And therefore when the *question* requires an *answer* touching his *fact*, as it is *vested* in that *forme*, or *Law terme* and *notion*, he *lies* not, nor *contradicts* himselfe in answering *negatively*, *Not guilty*.

For, although hee knowes, and hath elsewhere confessed himselfe to bee *guilty* of the *fact*, *materially* considered in the substance of it; yet he may be ignorant (as most men are) whether that *fact* of his, *formally* considered, is, or may be found to be *treason*, *felony*, *burglary*, or the like, as by the *inditement* it is charged upon him; and in which respect he is to suffer *death* for it, if he do answer *affirmatively*. And although he should certainly know that his *fact* were such, in *construction* and *termes* of *Law*, as, by his *Inditement*, the same is charged upon him; yet is he not to answer *affirmatively*: because, not he, but the present *impannelled Iury*, are the competent and lawfull *Iudges* to find, or not to find it to be such, in that *forme*, and Law *quality*.

And therefore, hee is bound in *conscience* to answer *negatively*, *Not guilty* of such a *fact* under that *forme*, or *terme* and *Law notion*; whereby, and wherefore his life, in that respect, may be taken away.

And so, by pleading *not guilty*, hee *lies* not, nor contradicts himselfe; but thereby takes the allowed benefit of putting it to a *legall triall*, whether his *fact* shall bee found against him in that *sense* and *forme*, as, in those *Law termes*, he is charged with the same in his *inditement*; and in which respect onely he can be put to death for it: which course if hee should not use of answering *Not guilty*; but that he should stand *mute*, or answer affirmatively *Guilty*, he should be *indirectly* a *self-murderer*: as hath beene shewed.

But then, it may be further replied, when such a *malefactor* shall (after his pleading to the *Inditement*, *not guilty*,) bee publickly examined by the *Judge* about his *fact*, considered in the *substance* of it, without the vesture of such *termes*, *or Law notions* put upon it; how can he answer *negatively*, against his conscience, and former *confession* before a Justice. *Repli.*

I answer, first, the *Judges questions* to such an one, at publick triall, (after his *negative plea* to the *bill* of *Inditement*,) are ministred in favour of the party arraigned; both that he may, upon better advisement, *traverse* his former *confession*, by his *negative* answer, contrary to the which *confession* hee is allowed at the *barre* to plead *not guilty*. And also, that hee may not bee cast, or condemned, upon any evidence, or verdit of others against him; before he bee heard answer for himselfe, what hee can say for the *negative* in his owne defence, against the *affirmative* evidence, or sentence produced against him: where it is to be considered that, the *primary* intention and expectation of the *Judge* in his *questions* at *triall* is, that, by the *prisoners* answers, hee may the better decerne the *truth*, or *falshood* of the *evidence* of others against him, and how himselfe may proceed in accepting of the *verdit*, and in giving judgement according to *justice*, and not thereby to wring *affirmative answers* from the arraigned, against their owne lives; when others cannot touch them; which is contrary to the *Law* of *nature*, and of *God*. *Answer.*

Secondly, it is alwaies to be observed by every *malefactor* that in his answers hee doe not, to save his life make any *lie*, neither *directly*, nor yet by *equivocation*, or *mentall reservation*: and also, that he doe not so confesse the *truth* against his owne life, that he should thereby make himselfe *guilty* of *indirect self-murder*.

Both which *evils* hee may avoid by the *medium* or middle course, either of *traverse*, and *demurrer* delaying and putting off the *Judge* and *Jury* from himselfe, to informe themselves by other evidences than his owne: or else by *silence* (after his generall *negative plea* of *not guilty*,) replying nothing to such *questions*, as the answers thereof may intangle him, either in a *lie*, or in *indirect self-murder*, after which manner of answering nothing, our *blessed Saviour* behaved himself before *Pilate*, *John* 19. 9.

Although that such *silence*, or not answering directly may be construed to be an acknowledgement of the *fact*, that he is indited for; yet thereby he shall not be *active*, but onely *passive* in being found guilty, and so condemned to die; whereby he shall be free of *indirect self-murder*, in that respect.

The *confession* of a *malefactor*, upon examination before a *Justice*, when the same is against his owne life, may bee construed to have beene either rashly and unwarrantably done by the *Examinate*; against which therefore he is allowed at his *Triall* to *plead not guilty*: or else that hee did the same upon some motives and reasons of *conscience*, for the good and salvation of his *soule*: which are things properly belonging to another *Court*.

And therefore, in humane *Courts* of *Assize*, the *questions* and *answers* (in this case) reach not so farre as to rack, or discover the *conscience* of a man, to the taking away of his owne life, by his owne *confession*, which the *Law* of *nature* and of *God* binds a man to preserve.

Although a *capitall malefactor* is bound in conscience not to *lie* in his answers, yet he is not bound to reveale all the truth he knowes against himselfe; specially where hee is not tied by some speciall *divine* bond so to doe.

A *negative* answer at *triall* is as strong to save a man, as his former *affirmative* in confession before a *Justice* can be to condemne him; except either he publickly at his

his triall acknowledge the same; or that there be some other proofe, or evidence against him.

And therefore I conclude, that it is not necessary in conscience that whatsoever truth such a man (in this case) hath once confessed, that he should every where, and at all times, upon *interrogatories* to be answered at will, confesse the same with perill of his life; but that hee may be *silent*, or forbeare to answer otherwise than he is bound by the *lawes* of the *Court* where he answers.

For, if another be bound to keepe close a mans *confession* made to him of his secret faults, that man is not compellable to disclose the same of himselfe, specially against his owne life; when he cannot doe the same without being guilty of indirect *self-murder*; as in this *case* I have shewed by the rules of *divinity* and right *reason*, for resolving of weak consciences in this point; not intermedling to argue and determine the same by the rules of the *Common-law* of this *Kingdome*, which is impertinent to my *profession*, and beyond my understanding; and therefore I leave that worke to the *learned* of that most *Honourable profession*; to whose cognizance this subject (legally considered) doth appertaine.

§. 7. *Of indirect self-murder by commission.*

The second meanes of *indirect self-murder* is by a course of *commission*, or of doing things, unlawfully tending to bring a man to his death; which is a degree grosser than the former, and consists in divers *branches*. The second degree of indirect self-murder is by commission, in divers branches.

First, by *abusing* lawfull things, in transgressing due *moderation* in their *use*; for *time*, *measure*, and *manner*; falling into *extreames*, either of *defect*, or of *excesse*, or of *unseasonablenesse*: which is done *two* wayes. *First*, in things both respecting the *body*, and in the *acts* about them: as in *eating* to gluttony, and *drinking* to drunkennesse; using *labour* and *recreations* to surfeiting: and also in 1. Abuse of lawfull things. 1. As meate, drinke, &c.

in things respecting the *minde*; as in the overstraining, and
2. Distemperature of the minde. surcharging of the *thoughts*, *fancy*, and *understanding*; in the immoderate distemperature of the *affections*, and *passions* of the minde, suffocating or wasting the *spirits* by excesse of *choller*, *griefe*, *fretfulnesse*, and the like; which being let loose, and extended beyond the bankes of their due *moderation*, doe often prove mortall, and meanes of *indirect self-murder*, when they are willingly and indulgently entertained, and given way to: It is a hard thing for a man to *use meanes*, and not to *abuse* them; which causes many a mans *table* to become a *snare* to him, and a *trap*[a], and shortens his time upon earth.

[a] *Psal.*69.22.

2. Self-mutilation. *Secondly*, indirectly, a man may be guilty of self-murder, by needlesse *mutilating* of himselfe, and *cutting* off any of his *members*, (as *Origen* did) to the hurt and danger of his life; which, by the preservation of such a *member*, might have beene in more safety; *for*, lifes perfection is in the perfection of the whole body. *Notwithstanding*, for the safety of the whole, a man may lawfully and necessarily cut off a member; which cannot be preserved without manifest danger of thereby losing his life; *but*, neither to *punish* a sin past, nor to *prevent* a sin to come, may a man destroy or cut off any of his *members*, whereby he may be lesse able to doe the offices and duties for which *God* hath given him the same; *seeing* that both for chastisement, and prevention of sin, *God* hath appointed other *morall* meanes, which wee are to use, and therein to depend upon *God* for the successe; for not in mans forced disability to *act* sin, but in the renovation of the heart consists true *sanctification*: that of pulling out the *right eye*, and of *cutting off* the *right hand*, *Mat.*5.29, 30. is meant of *morall* mortification, whereby those members are made uselesse, and as if *they were not*, to any unlawfull use.

Note.

§.8. Of

§. 8. *Of Indirect self-murder of commission by unwarrantable practise of Physick, &c.*

Thirdly, a man may be guilty of *indirect self-murder*, by practising of *Physick*, or *Chirurgery* unskilfully, immoderately, or dangerously upon himselfe; *either* above his strength, or knowledge; killing himselfe by his unwarrantable endeavours to cure himselfe: *or* else, by leaving those that they know to be skilfull, carefull, and have lawfull calling to practise; to put themselves into their hands, whom they neither know to have *skill*, nor *calling* to undertake such cures; *or*, are such as be desperate *attempters*, with small regard of mens lives in their *practise*: if a man know the same, and doth wilfully choose and commit himselfe, specially in *difficult cases*, into the hands of such, he can look for no good successe, and must be self-guilty of the mortall effects thereupon following: but of this see more in the abuses of taking of Physick, *Chap.* 4. §. 6. 3. Unwarrantable practise of Physick.

§. 9. *Of indirect self-murder by unthriftinesse, &c.*

Fourthly, this *indirect self-murder* is committed by wilfull *unthriftinesse* and prodigality, whereby a man provides not, but mispends the meanes of his livelihood, and so subjects himselfe and his to the perill of *famine*, contrary to the light of *nature*, and *Scripture*. 4. Vnthriftinesse. *Deut.* 2. 19. *Prov.* 27. 27.

Yet we are herein to be wary *that* for prevention of want of livelihood; we fall not into covetousnesse, and carking cares; *or* that we follow the world with neglect of better things; *or* that we should spare more than is fitting; and shut up the *bowells* of *compassion*, with the overthrow of *liberality*, and workes of *charity* and *piety*. *A Caveat.*

§. 10. Of

§. 10. *Of indirect self-murder of commission wrought by desperate hazard in 6. Cases.*

5. Desperate hazzard.

Fifthly, indirect self-murder is committed by those that cast themselves into *desperate hazard* of losse of their lives; by undiscreetly and rashly venturing into deadly dangers; without lawfull *calling*, and above their strength to escape: where there is no necessity for greater good of others, or gods glory requiring the same: which falls out specially in *sixe cases.*

The first Case, of Braves and Gallants.

Case 1. Concerning Braves.

First, when any doe out of a *bravery*, and gallantry of spirit, goe needlesly with a charge of money, or of mens persons, or errands; *either* in the night, through a place haunted and beset with murderous robbers; *or*, at any time through knowne *ambushments*, and strong *troupes* of enemies, above the passengers strength to resist, or escape; whereby, if they fall, they are guilty of this *indirect self-murder.*

Concerning purchase and rescue.

Case 2.

Secondly, when any doe, out of over-great *affection* to worldly *goods*, make desperate *attempts*, with the apparent perill of their lives, *either* to *get* goods; either by violent taking them from others, as theeves and spoilers doe; *or*, by *labour* in their callings above that which with their health they are able to endure: *or* else, by their *desperate* adventuring to save, or recover their goods out of *fire*, or *water*; or from, and out of the hands of their *enemies*; with the casting away of their owne lives; above all meanes and strength that in this case they have to save them; in such undertakings beyond

yond all warrantable calling: within neither of these two cases are we to restraine, or bound the *divine-heroicke* enterprises of such as by *supernaturall* instinct, or power, doe undertake transcendent enterprises, above the allowance of ordinary rules: as *David* to kil *Goliah* [a], and *Ionathan* and his *Armour-bearer* to invade a whole *Garrison* of the *Philistims* [b]. *Such* men must have both a *calling*, by *divine* inward *instinct, motion,* and *qualification*; and also, a strong well grounded *faith,* in assurance of Gods assistance: as the *Scripture* tells us, how such, *through faith subdued Kingdomes, escaped the edge of the sword, out of weakenesse were made strong, waxed valiant in fight, turned to flight the armies of the Aliens*; *Heb.* 11. 33, 34. *Exception.*

[a] 1 *Sam.* 17. 32.

[b] 1 *Sam.* 14. 6.

Concerning some souldiers.

Case 3.

Thirdly, when *self-conceited,* wilfull, *foole-hardy men* will *fight* against their *enemies,* upon desperate *disadvantages*; and imminent perill of death; when they are neither *forced* to it by unavoidable *necessity*; nor are warranted by command of such *superiours* as either have absolute power over them of *life* and *death*; *or* can assure them, or give them the *victory,* [c] (as *God* often did to the *Israelites,* fighting by his command, or approbation upon strange disadvantages) yea, when they cannot probably come off with the safety of their lives; then that is a course of *indirect self-murder.*

[c] *Numb.* 14. 40. *Usq; ad finem.*

Concerning Mariners.

Case 4.

The fourth Case is of those that trade by *Sea,* who often runne into mortall and desperate *adventures*, out of eagernesse to make their *voyages*; either putting to *Sea* in such *weather,* and *seasons* as is like to endanger all; *or* putting for the *Port,* upon desperate *hazards* of miscary-

ing

ing by *stormes*, *sands*, or *rocks*, *or* running presumptuously into the danger of *Pyrates*; or other mortall ingagement by *Sea*, *either* through wilfull negligence, or through self-*confidence* of skill, or power more than they have, so tempting *God*.

Observe.

The true *occasion* of which miscariages of men by *Sea*, is often given by *Merchants* upon the *Land*; who praise and respect men for *fortunate* and *valiant* according to the successe, and the event of their courses, without respect to the due *rules* of the managing the same; which makes many a man come short home, by adventuring to please their *Merchants*, contrary to the *rules* of *art* and *wisdome*.

--careat successibus opto, Quisquis ab eventu facta probanda putat.

Note.

In this case I would *advise* men, rather to looke to do what they may warrantably justifie; and may therein have peace in their consciences, although the successe answer not their desire; than to endeavour contrary to wisdome and art, to please their *owners* and *Merchants* by such courses of desperate and unwarrantable adventures: as (if *they* or their *charge* miscary therein,) will over-cloud them with just blame & ignominie, and will bereave them of that comfort in their consciences, *which* should cheere and uphold them under their crosses; a course of *accidentall* good successe, and a course of *direct* ill successe, are not so to be compared together; that for the *former* a man should venture upon the *latter*; with the guilt of *self-murder* to be imputed to him, if therein he doe perish.

Concerning Duells.

Case 5.

The fifth Case of *desperate adventure*, is of those that undertake *Duells*; or doe give, or accept *challenges* of single *combats*, upon their owne *private* motion, for private *revenge*; or for supposed maintenance of impeached *honour*; who, if they perish in the attempt, or by

meanes

meanes of the conflict, are guilty of more than *indirect self-murder*: *because*, that course so unwarrantably, and needlesly undertaken, is commonly where the wronged may have better redresse, with lesse adventure of life; and those *Duellers*, or single *combattants* doe, by such challenges, shew themselves to be *lawlesse* contemners of *authority*; whose allowance they have not (as they ought) for such a triall by *battle* to make the same just; but by *usurpation* they make themselves *Kings*, (in contempt and prejudice of lawfull *authority*) in erecting a *tribunall* for *Iustice*, of their owne making, in their own case; where themselves alone are *Parties*, *Iurie*, *Witnesse*, *Judge* and *Sheriffe*: whereas it is the *prerogative* of *Kings* to make warre and peace, and independently to execute justice under God.

Duellers what they be.

It also argueth in them, both great *folly*, and *impotency* of minde, so lightly to adventure or give away their *lives*; a price so far exceeding the worth of the purchase that they contend for, and which they may have decided farre better, without any such desperate danger; and also it proclaimes their *pusillanimity* and *weaknesse*, in that they cannot beare *crosses* and *injuries*. *And finally*, it makes their cause apparently unjust; when they passe by, or neglect a peaceable triall by equall *justice* and reason; and doe put it to be decided by bodily strength, and chance of *warre*; in a course more beseeming *beasts* than *men*. *It* seemes that *such men* doe account themselves and their lives little worth, and that they are weary of living; who so rashly expose the same by *thrasonicall provocations* and *darings*, to be taken away and destroyed in such a manner; wherein, having abandoned the command of *reason*, they become *beasts*; and becomming *slaves* to their vilest *passions of fury*, *madnesse*, *cruelty*, and the like, (whereby they are overcome, who would in that *course* overcome others) *Duellers* degenerate into incarnate *devills*: And while they thus contend to gain or maintaine reputation of *Honour* and *Valour* by this most dishonourable and base brutish course of impetuous *self-revenge* by *Duells*; they justly lose that for which they contend, and otherwise might have had.

Concerning desperate attempts upon daring and wagering.

Case 6.
1. About daring.

The sixt *case* of desperate *hazzard* and *adventure*, whereby men may *indirectly* be *self-murderers*, is in the point of *provocation* by others, for proofe of their *courage* and *valour*, challenging them to *dare* to attempt the effecting of some deadly enterprise beyond all warrantable calling, or lawfull meanes safely and lawfully to accomplish the same: as, for a man needlesly to conflict with a *Lyon*, to run over *rocks*; to provoke, or assault *Adversaries* too potent for him to resist, or offend, with safety of his life; or, upon such daring to doe some capitall act or mischiefe, whereby he is most like to perish; and not thereby without just imputation to himselfe of guiltinesse of his owne *death*, in regard of the unlawfulnesse of that his course, wherein hee cannot warrantably looke for any blessing, or protection from *God*: neither doe such unjustifiable *daring practises* argue any true *fortitude* and *valour*, but onely bewraie temerarious *audaciousnesse*; which is, in *excesse*, contrary to *fortitude*: because, true *valour* is seene in couragiously undertaking and accomplishing dangerous performances upon advised *reason*, by *lawfull courses*, to just and necessary *ends*; but *rash audaciousnesse* in daring to doe unwarrantable attempts is manifest, by the unreasonablenesse and unnecessarinesse thereof, undertaken upon unadvised *passion*, and foole-hardy *presumption*; with *arrogancy* in the manner of accomplishing, and *folly* in the end of it.

A truly *valorous* man manifests his *fortitude* by his unconquera-

unconquerablenesse upon any provocation of *daring*, to doe any thing that is not fit and warrantable for him to undertake upon good grounds and reason; that if hee bee crossed, or perish in atchieving it, hee may have honour and peace, and no way be guilty of his owne death: So that, although *daring audaciousnesse* exceeds true *fortitude* in unwarrantably adventuring beyond *it*; yet it comes short of valorous *fortitude* in the *grounds*, and *manner* of enterprising, and of consequent *effects* and honour of it.

A *valorous* man is his owne *master*, in disposing of himselfe and his actions about dangerous enterprises, according to his owne minde, sound reason, and advised resolution. Whereas, an *audacious man* is but as a servant to others, by whose will and *daring* provocations he orders himself and his actions, as *they* list, at their pleasure, and for their service; that he must needs doe whatsoever desperate attempts they will *dare* him to doe, even to the perill of the losse of his life, without any lawfull reason and calling.

To this case also belongs desperate undertakings with danger of life upon *wagers*; as for a man, either upon a *naked contract* for a certaine summe, or upon *assumpsit* of ten for one, or the like, to be paid to him when he shall have performed some desperate hazardous enterprise agreed upon, for him in that consideration onely to undertake and attempt the same with the danger of the losse of his life: as to walke under the water; to crosse the *Ocean* in a Wherry: in a few dayes to goe backward, or blindfold a long journey in a dangerous way, or some such unreasonable, needlesse, dangerous, mad, and idle vaine-glorious prancks, with adventure and losse of life; whereby such are *indirectly* self-murderers; and those that lay such wagers with them, are accessary to their death, thereby hireing and provoking them to a mortall course of *self-destruction*. For, such a course is no war- 2. Wagering.

rantable way and calling of Gods appointment, thereby to adventure, or get goods; and therefore, no blessing can be therein, nor thereby expected; it is a needlesse tempting of God to commit themselves to such a mortall course which they may well avoyd, and can looke for no protection in it, nor comfort of the action wherein they perish; being guilty of their owne death therein. Such desperate enterprises, upon *wagering*, whereby a man may lose his life, proceede either from covetousnesse, to be rich; or from necessity, to live: but by unlawfull meanes never destinated of *God* to that end, neither of them can comfortably be expected nor endeavoured: it seemes that such men either value their lives to be little worth, or apprehend their present condition to be most miserable; that they preferre the uncertaine attaining of a little lucre and worldly goods before them, and had rather die than live as they are; and therefore goe to seeke up *death*, where they can find him, to make an end of their dayes, by this desperate and last shift that they doe use, when otherwise they cannot live. That man is neere driven, that cannot subsist but by courses of selfe-ruine: and he is very destitute of good parts and of vertuous actions, that despaires of better fame and repute in the world; than he can procure by such needlesse vaine undertakings and accomplishments; which are but the pastime of fooles, and the ludibrie and scorne of the wise, and uncomfortable vanity and sinne of the performers.

§.11. *Of indirect self-murder committed by covenant and society with persons destinate to destruction.*

6 Branch of indirect self-murder by commission.

The sixt branch of *indirect self-murder* by *commission*, is, by wilfull contracting, and keeping *society* with those,

those, that are under a *curse*, and apparent danger of destruction; whereby all such *are* most probably like to share with them, that have neere communion with them; which falls out specially in *three cases*.

First, when a man unwarrantably enters a *league*, or *bond* of neere amity and society with *persons*, *Princes*, or *States* worthy of, and (as it were) marked out to destruction; as *Iehoram* did contract and keepe with *Ahaziah* [a], whereby hee involved and inwrapped himselfe into the same *ruine* with him. Which barres not *conclusions* for *commerce* of trade; and also, for intercourse of *correspondency* with them, at such a distance and degree, whereby hurt from them may be avoyded, and *use* made of them for warrantable advantage; as the *Scripture* requires, that wee should have *peace* with all men, if it be possible [b].

Case 1. Of leagues.

[a] 2 *King*. 9. 27.

[b] *Heb*. 12. 14.

The second case of *indirect self-murdring society* is, when a man takes up *armes*, or puts himselfe into *military* service, or joynes with others in *warre*, offensive, or defensive; *either* to hinder, or oppresse equity and truth; *or*, in opposition of *Gods Church*, to prejudice, or oppresse the *Gospell* and true *religion*; by this *latter* fighting against and provoking God; and by the *former*, irritating mankind justly to destroy such, as goe about to overthrow *Gods Kingdome*, and humane justice, on earth; *without* which the *world* cannot subsist; in which course of *Combination*, or *society*, whosoever perishes is guilty of *indirect self-murder*, by death of his owne unwarrantable procurement.

Case 2. Concerning warre.

Although warre bee lawfull, yet it is a violent course of *justice*, the decision whereof is hereby cast upon the *omnipotent Lord God*, for him to determine the same, as he pleases, by victory, or vanquishment. *And therefore*, none should dare voluntarily to engage himselfe, in that course, upon his life, where hee knowes *that* just and powerfull *Iudge* to bee party for the truth against him; lest

lest he perish by this *indirect self-murder*; whereas, to bee safe therefrom, wee should ever bee *party* on *Gods* side.

Crosse event of warre.

Reasons.

That the *event* falls out contrary, so that the *Abetters* in a good cause do often fall, and the *propugners* of an evill do prosper; it comes to passe by Gods speciall wise *providence*, for *three causes*.

1. *First*, to chastise some sinnes, or to exercise some vertues in the vanquished.

2. *Secondly*, to make men more loath to fall to warre and blood-shed, upon presumption of their strength and cause, but rather, with some losse, to make peaceable composition.

3. *Thirdly*, that *God* may shew and exercise his absolute *soveraignty* over the world; disposing humane things as he pleases, in the demolishing and translating of *Empyres* and *dominion*, by the ruines of *one* making way for the building of *another*; that it may be apparent, that by him *Kings Raigne*; and that as many *Principalities* and *Empires* are raised, and stand upon the foundation of *invasion, latrocinies, rapines*, and *blood*; so shall they answer for the same, and bee shaken to peeces, by a divine hand of *Iustice*; as wee may see expressed by the *dashing* of the *Image* to peeces, by that small *stone* out of the divine hand of *God, Daniel* 2.33.

Case 3. Presuming into infectious places and company.

The third case of *indirect self-murdering society* is, when men do wilfully presume, without necessity, or warrantable calling, into deadly infectious places and companies; wherein, or by which *meanes* if they miscarry or perish, they are guilty of their owne death, in a higher degree of *indirect self-murder*; as also, are those that doe, without a warrantable calling, put themselves into such places, or imployments, as doe procure or hasten their deaths.

§.12. *Of*

§.12. *Of indirect self-murder by doing that, which naturally procures that which kills the doer.*

Seventhly; if a man doe, willingly and wittingly, any such unlawfull act, as proves the *cause*, or *occasion* of that, which by *Gods providence* in just judgement, kills him, or takes away his life; he *indirectly* murders himselfe: as a *drunken man*, that falls into a ditch or a pit, and is drowned; breakes his neck off his horse; dies by surfeits, or the like: he is in this *degree*, guilty of his owne death: *for the cause of the cause is the cause of the effect*: such a mans *precedent* unlawfull course, or disposition, is so farre from excusing the *consequent effect*; that in a sort it doubles his sin: a man that kills another, when he is drunk, is not excused; but hanged when he is sober.

7. *Branch.*

Causa causæ est causa causati.

§.13. *Of indirect self-murder by doing of capitall crimes against humane Lawes and authority.*

Eightly, men doe commit *indirect self-murder*, by their breaking out into *capitall* courses and crimes; in transgressing and violating capitall good humane *Lawes*, the *penalty* whereof is *death*, whereby they bring themselves under the *sword* of *Iustice*, thereby to lose their lives; as do *Traitors*, and rebellious persons against the *King, State*, or *Kingdome*: *spoylers* of other mens lives, or *goods*; as *murderers*, *Pirates*, *Robbers*, and the like: which is a thing both just and expedient in reason, that for preserving & upholding of the whole *body* publick; or the more *noble parts* thereof, *inferiour* and rotten members should suffer *amputation*; who, by their owne vile practises, have subjected themselves to the *penall* censure of death: by their misdeserving courses, being *indirectly self-murderers*; *their blood being upon themselves*, and not upon the *Magistrate*, by whose hands they justly fall

8. *Branch.*
Capital crimes.

fall, as is apparent; *Levit.* 20. 9. where the *blood* of him that was put to death, for cursing his *Father*, is said to be *upon himselfe*: and 2 *Sam.* 1. 16. touching him that *David* killed, for saying that hee had *slaine Saul*, he said that his *blood was upon his head*: as also, 1 *King.* 2. 32, 37. touching *Ioab*, for his murder; and *Shimei*, for his railing; it is said that their *blood* was upon their owne heads; for that they were the wilfull meritorious cause, although not the immediate *instruments* of their owne deaths.

And so thus, all men that die by the merits of their owne actions, *morally*, or *civilly* considered, are *murderers* of their owne naturall lives and bodies, as man may truly be said to be the overthrower of the *salvation* of his owne soule, by the merits of his owne sins.

§. 14. *Of indirect self-murder by wilfull transgression of Gods Lawes.*

9. *Branch.* Transgression against Gods Law.

Ninthly, men *indirectly murder* their owne *bodies*, by wilfully and impenitently walking in a course of *transgression of Gods Law*; in such *kinds* and *degrees*, as are accompanied with fearefull *threatnings* of death and destruction, to bee inflicted, not onely upon the *soules*, but also upon the *bodies* of such transgressours, by fearefull *judgments*, even in this life, as we see it was done to *Pharaoh*: which is performed *two waies*.

1. Kills after a naturall manner.

First, in a *physicall*, or *naturall* manner, by the very *nature* and act of some sinnes themselves immediatly wasting; filling the body with diseases, and at last killing it: as, by *drunkennesse* and *gluttony*, distempring and surfeiting the body; according as *Salomon* saies, that *to those that tarrie long at the Wine, and that do goe to seeke mixt Wine, is woe, sorrow, contentious babling, wounds without cause, and rednesse of the eyes*, *Prov.* 23. 29, 30.

Also, by *whoredome*, and bodily uncleannesse, the strength

strength is wasted, as *the Apostle shewes how such doe sin against their owne bodies*, 1. *Cor*. 6. 18. and *Solomon* tells us that *the house of a strange woman inclines to death*, *Prov*.2.18. and by her, *a mans flesh and body is consumed*, *Prov*.5.11. and, *the adultresse hunteth after the pretious life*.

And also, by the immoderatenesse of the *passions* of the minde, in giving way and liberty to them, to break out, and have dominion over us; wherby the *vitall spirits* are suffocated, or wasted: as, by excesse of *choler*, *fretfulnes* or *griefe*, or the like; extinguishing the life of man; as, a *fire* is put out, by oppressing it with water; or, by wastefully burning up suddenly the fewell of the maintenance of it: therefore, it is needfull, that we suffer no commotion to be raised in our *passions* and *affections*, but upon just cause and ground, and that then therein we do keepe due moderation, by the command of *reason*; and by the possessing and taking of them up, with divine and heavenly *objects* and imployment; about things concerning a better life: it is a very dangerous, and costly *contentment* that a man hath, by giving immoderate scope to his unruly *affections* and *passions*; with the consumption of his owne life thereby, in this course of *indirect self-murder*. Of Passions. *Note*.

Secondly, men by their self-willed sinfull courses, are *indirect self-murderers* of their *bodies efficiently*; in a *moral* manner, and by way of *merit*, according to the *justice* of *God*, threatning and punishing disobedient prophanenesse and wickednesse from heaven; not onely inwrapping transgressors into publick *generall judgements* with others; but also, by inflicting *particular* personall destruction upon them; as *God* did upon *Corah*, *Dathan*, and *Abiram* [a], and upon some, for their unworthy and prophane receiving of the *Sacrament* of the *Lords Supper*, did die [b], by their owne meritorious procurement: and, wee are taught in the *Proverbs*, [c] *that sinners do lay waite for their owne blood*, and, *eate the fruit of their owne* 2. A morall meritorious manner of self-killing.

[a] *Numb*. 16.38.

[b] 1 *Cor*.11.30.

[c] *Prov*.1.8 31, 32.

way: and that the *turning away of the simple shall slay him*. In the *Prophet Ezekiel*, *Robbers*, *adulterers*, and *usurers*,[d] are threatned with death; and there it is said, that *their blood shall be upon their owne heads*; which intimates that they are guilty of their own deaths. *And* againe, *secure persons*, not repenting after admonition, are threatned with *death*; and that their *blood shall be upon their owne heads*.[e] Yea, all the damned in *hell*, whose *bodies* with their *soules* shall be subject to the *second death* by meanes of their owne sins; are, and shall be guilty of their own deaths, both of *soule* and *body*; and so are *self-murderers* also of their bodies, at least *indirectly*.

d *Ezek*. 18. 13.

e *Ezek*. 33. 4, 5.

In Adam, and by his first sin, all men naturally are self-murderers.

Moreover Adam, and all mankinde in him lapsed, are *indirectly self-murderers*, by *merit* of that first *transgression*; for, and through which, *death* entred into the world: according to the testimony of the *Apostle*; who saith, that *by one man sin entred into the world, and death by sin: so death passed upon all men, for that all have sinned*. *Rom*. 5. 12. So that no man can blame any for his death, in regard of *originall merit* and *desert*, but himselfe. *Now*, that this *death* of our selves, may not be imputed to our selves, that we should stand guilty before *God* of this *indirect self-murder*; we must labour to get our pardon from *God* in *Christ*, for the comfort of our consciences, and for our security from the *avenger of blood*, upon our reconciliation with our *God*; and bee carefull that we live not wilfully and impenitently in any knowne sinne; without which care, all stand guilty before *God* of this sinne of *self-murder*, and shall suffer for it.

Observe. The world is full of self-murderers.

From hence we may *observe*, that there are many more *self-murderers* than the world takes notice of, or that do thinke themselves to be such; yea, the world is full of them; whose sinnes are more haynous than they conceive, and specially against themselves most pernicious: *and therefore*, it is no marvell that one man endeavours the

the ruine and destruction of another; when we see how desperately and eagerly they doe the same against themselves: For, who can expect better respect and usage from any man, than he gives to himselfe; or is in him to performe? Some difference there is in the *affection* and *intention* of betternesse to himselfe; but his *reall* performances are to himselfe worst.

Thus having declared what *indirect self-murder* is, and how it is diversly procured and committed; now I will shew certaine exempt cases; which, although in the *materiality* of the *facts* they differ not from *indirect self-murder*; yet, in the *formality* of their *acting*, are much discrepant.

§. 15. *Of certaine exempt Cases.*

Three cases there are, wherein men are warrantably to expose their bodies to the apparent danger of death; without perill of *self-murder*, or just blame of guiltinesse of their owne deaths. Exempt cases.

First, when a man hath a lawfull *calling*, generall, or particular; which, without danger of losse of his life, in discharging thereof, he cannot execute; then is he to adventure his life, that he may *doe* his *duty*, (which otherwise cannot be performed) committing himselfe to *Gods* protection, and disposall. *As Peter* did in comming downe out of the *Ship* to walke upon the *Sea*, when *Christ* commanded him [a]: and as *Sampson*, in execution of his office of *Iudge* against his enemies, pulled downe the *house*, whereby hee with them did perish, [b] and is commended among the *faithfull*: *Heb.* 11. 32. whom *Bacchiarius*, an ancient *Author*, calls a *Martyr*: of which *David a Mauden* gives the reason—*quia illæ quæ ad Martyrium requiruntur conditiones in ipso reperiuntur*: *the things requisite for Martyrdome were found in him*, being a person reconciled to *God*; and dying for Gods *glo-*

1. By calling.

[a] *Mat.* 14.29.

[b] *Judges* 16. *Bacchiarius ad Januarium. In fine obitus sui sub Martyrii passione*— *David a Mauden in præceptum* 6. *discurs. decim.*

ry, and in defence of the *truth*, and by a warrantable *calling* of *divine instinct*, and supernaturall ability. *And* we see, that when God did call *Moses* to come up into the mount, there to die; he obeyed, and went willingly and wittingly unto his owne death. *Deut.* 34.

By this *rule*, *souldiers* and *servants* taking wages, or otherwise bound to fight for their lives, or at the command of their *superiours*, are bound (as *Manden* sayes) *ex justitia*, by the *law* of *justice*, to expose their lives to death, in discharge of their *duty*; to obey and protect their *superiours*.

Reasons of incouragement.

The reasons of incouragement to undertake such mortall *adventures*, are specially *two*. *First*, our *knowledge* and *assurance* that *God*, whom herein wee are to respect and obey, *originally*, or secondarily commanding us, will either protect us in our wayes and undertakings; *or* will so dispose of us, as shall be best for us; with comfort, and honour, in, and after our death: in which respect, both *Plato pro Socrate*; and also *Aristotle* affirme, that *honesta mors turpi vita est praferenda*: *An honourable death is to be preferred before a shamefull life.*

Knowledge.

2. Benefit of death.

Secondly, the *feare* of the losse of our lives should bee no *remora*, or hinderance to our dutifull performances: *because* our deaths in this manner, may be the *medium*, or *meanes* to the *end*, that is better than our *lives*: *Wee* see, that if a thing destinated to a certaine *end*, doe at any time crosse or hinder the attaining of that *end*; in that respect it is to be deemed *evill*, and to be rejected: as our *Saviour* commands, that *if our eye cause us to offend, then pull it out*; *and in like case to cut off our hand, or foote*. *Mat.* 5. 30. which is done by mortification and grace, making them as uselesse to any scandalous courses, as if they were cut off in semblable manner, as men throw away their *armour* to save their lives by flight in a hot pursuit of their enemies, and as men at *Sea* throw their *goods* into the water to save themselves.

§. 16. *A particular question about souldiers flying, resolved.*

A question may be here moved, whether it be in *conscience lawfull* for any *souldier*, out of feare of death, upon his owne apprehensions, to flee and runne away to save his life, before a signall, command, or example bee given him by his *Commander* so to doe? *About souldiers, a case of conscience.* ***Question.***

I answer, for the *fact* it is true, nothing is more frequently done in *warre*, than so to runne away in disorderly manner; *because feare* bereaves men of their use and command of reason; *and* also *self-love* makes every man more carefull of his owne *particular*, than of the *publike*; things that are neerest doe most affect; extremities of dangers convert all a mans thoughts, to thinke how then to preserve himselfe. *But*, for the *morall lawfulnesse* of that course it appeares not to me; *yea rather*, I conceive that although present *death* stood ready before them to swallow them up; they are not to turne their backs, to leave their stations, and runne away without due *order*, *signall*, or example of their *Commanders*. *Because* such *desertion* of their *Commanders* and *fellowes* in distresse, is a betraying of them into their enemies hands. *Againe*, the greatest destruction and ruine of an Army, comes by *disorderly flight*; wherein every man is objected to the *enemies* execution: *Whereas*, by resolution and couragious resisting to death, many victories are gotten, with the preservation of the body of an Army. *Finally*, if the *publike* doe miscary, our *particular* cannot bee safe; but those that escape may (in regard of their after-miseries) wish that they had fallen in the army, by the sword of their enemies. ***Answer.*** *Souldiers are to stand.*

We are bound to attribute so much to the wisdome, and valour of our *Commanders*; that *they will not* cast away the lives of their men, but upon apparent possibilities

ties of *victory* or *preservation*, by opposition; although we see it not. *The helps* to enable us to this high courage of performing of *duty*, are *two* : *First*, *Faith*; both for the goodnesse of our *estate* in *Christ* to Godward; wherby we may be assured of everlasting life and glory, when we die : *and also*, for the lawfulnesse of *our calling* and *imployment* in that service, wherein death attaches us; that we may as comfortably there end our dayes, as if we dyed upon our beds; being perswaded of our future happy condition; and that our *death* in that manner is more *usefull* to men, and more *acceptable* to *God*, than our lives.

Helps so to do. 1. Faith.

Secondly, undaunted *resolution* to be *obedient* in doing our duties; considering that *obedience is better than sacrifice*, although in doing thereof wee doe perish. *For*, for to enjoy vertue and union with *God*, (which consists in obedience to Gods will,) is better than life without them.

2. Resolution.

§. 17. *The second exempt case about venturing of life, which is upon urgent necessity.*

The second Case, Necessity: in three points.

The second Case wherein we may wittingly and willingly, without danger of *self-murder*, adventure the losse of our lives, is a present, urgent, and unavoidable *necessity*, for a certaine greater more *eligible good* : which falls out in *three points*. *First*, not only when with an *uncertaine* danger of our owne lives, wee seeke to redeeme the *certaine* destruction of our neighbours; as to cast our selves into the water, being skilfull to swimme, to save him from assured drowning, who hath no other meanes of safety : *or*, to cast our selves into desperate dangers for rescue of our *wives*, *children*, or *friends*, from out of the *fire*; or out of the hands of our *enemies*; as did *Abraham* for *Lot* [a], and *David* for his *wives* [b]; or to minister to the necessities of our *sick* houshold, that they perish

1. Vncertaine death, for certaine good.

[a] *Gen.*14.14.
[b] 1 *Sam.*30.

perish not in neglect; wee ought to venture our lives with them in their infectious diseases. *But* further also, to save *another* from certainly perishing, sometimes men may object themselves to certaine death; as if the person be a publicke *Magistrate*, or *Prince*, or evidently of more use and worth in *Church* or *Common-wealth* than our selves, we may exchange our selves to passe for him, as the Scripture intimates, with commendation; *that peradventure for a good man some would even dare to die*. *Rom. 6.7.* and the peoples esteeme of *David* was, that he was *worth ten thousand of them*; and therefore, would not let him adventure himselfe; where, *if halfe of them should die, the enemies would not care for them.* *2 Sam.18.3.* *this* respect and preferment of *eminency* and *vertue* is not only from *love* of themselves, but also from love of that *publike body*, to which those persons by their lives may be beneficiall.

Certaine death for Superiours.

Also, a man may, for preservation of his deare *friend*, put himselfe upon assured death; as our *Saviour* implies, by way of commending the same; when he sayes, *Greater love hath no man than this, that a man lay downe his life for his friends.* Therefore, this degree of *love* hee may have, and was practised by divers, as betweene *Nisus* and *Euryalus*, *Damon* and *Pythias*, *Pylades* and *Orestes*.

For a friend.

Ambros. lib.3. officiorum c.12. de duobus Pythagoraeis.

Virgil.—me me adsum qui feci, in me convertite ferrum.

The thing that may seeme to withstand the *lawfulnesse* of this practice, is that generall rule of *loving our neighbours as our selves*, and not otherwise. *But* this is easily *answered*; *first*, by the right understanding of the *rule*; *as our selves*; which notes, not the *degree* or measure of our love; for then must we *love* all men alike, if the rule of the measure be *one* : for, *quæ conveniunt in uno tertio, conveniunt inter se* : *they that agree in any one third thing, doe agree within themselves* : *but*, that we are to love all men alike, is absurd, and against the practice of our *Saviour Christ*, who loved *Iohn* above the rest of the *Apostles*; then [*as our selves*] notes the *sincerity* of our love:

Object.

Answ.

1.

It is required that our love be sincere.

love: for as the *Apostle* tells us; *No man ever yet hated his owne flesh, Ephes.* 5. 29. *So then*, here is commanded *first*, that we should love our neighbours; *secondly*, that for the quality of this love, it should be in truth; and as we would that others should love us: which doth not exclude such a *superlative degree* of *love*, as may expresse it selfe by a mans dying for his friend; as if it were an unlawfull excesse.

2. To dye for a friend may bee self-love, and lawfull.

Secondly, this doubt may be resolved, by the true interpretation of such a mans *act*: *because*, in that *degree* of love so expressed for his *friend*, he loves *himselfe*, both by the consummation and earthly *perfection* of the vertue of *friendship* in him; which in some sort *beatifies* the *subject* wherein it is; and also thereby he gaines to himselfe the *honour* to be counted more *worthy* of a *friend*, than a friend was of him: & *lovers* are said to live rather in *those* that they doe love, than in *themselves*; so that without such *friends* their lives would be but a languishing dying. With mee in this point, accords *Cardinall Folet* upon [a] *Iohn* 15. 13. and *David à Mauden* in his *tenth discourse* upon the *sixt Commandement*, is peremptory; and sayes, that * *Certum est licitum esse vitam suam certo periculo exponere, pro servanda amici vita temporali, ex motivo honestatis & amicitiæ: quandoquidem honestas virtutis majus bonum sit, quàm vita propria corporalis: It is certaine that it is lawfull for a man to expose his life to certaine danger, for to preserve the temporall life of his friend, upon the motive of honesty and friendship; seeing the honesty of vertue is a greater good, than his owne corporall life.*

Amicus est alter ego.

[a] *Idem ibid.*

* *Id non facit ex amore vitæ alterius--sed ex amore virtutis amicitiæ, & ad aliorum exemplum: quod dum facit, se plus quã amicum diligit.*

From hence he sayes, that the Doctors affirme that it is lawfull to doe service to a friend that is sick of the pestilence,

Licitum esse aiunt Doctores amico peste laboranti inservire, cum æquè certo periculo mortis, & in communi naufragio tabulam socio cedere; unde si duo amici simul naufragium fecissent, iisq; residua esset tabula, cujus subsidio alteruter ex illis tantum posset salvari, posset quidem alter eã non uti, ut sibi eam amicus assumeret, cujus saluti consultum cupit. In hoc tamen eventu cavendum est, ne quis per positivam aliquam actionem directè neci suæ cooperetur; hoc enim illicitum est. Discurs. 10 *in præcept.* 6. *numer.* 3. 5. **Ema: Sa:** *in vocabulo vita.*

with

with equally certaine danger of death; and in a common shipwrack to yeeld a board to a fellow companion: as if two friends have suffered shipwrack together, and that there were a board remaining to them; by the help whereof only one of them could be saved; the one of them may forbeare to make use of the same, that his friend, whose safety he desires, may take it to himselfe. Notwithstanding, in this case heed must be taken that no man doe directly, by any positive action cooperate to his owne death: for, that is unlawfull. *Emanuel Sa* in his *Aphorismes* affirmes as much.

§. 18. *Of the second point, which is concerning certaine death for certaine more publike good.*

The second point concerning present urgent *necessity*, wherein a man may adventure the losse of his life for a greater good, without any danger of *self-murder*, is when by the *losse* of *one*, or of a *few* lives, *many* more are *preserved*: for, *bonum commune est præferendum proprio: the publike good is to be preferred before our owne private*; which argueth the greater *charity* for *extension* of it abroad: *and* as we are not made every one for himselfe onely; but for the *good* one of another: *So* should wee endeavour the same by life and death: as the *Apostle* commands that we should not looke *every man on his owne things, but every man also on the things of others. Phil.* 2.4.

The second point.

Certaine death for greater publike good.

In the *publike* good, the good of every *particular* is comprehended; and therefore, the *members*, severally considered, are to expose themselves to suffer for the good and preservation of the *Whole*. *Thomas* of *Aquine* sayes well, that *Charitas communia propriis anteponit*: [a] *Charity preferres the publike before the private*: In this also *David a Mauden* is cleare, when he sayes, in his

[a] *Tho:* 2. 2. *quæst.* 26. *artic.* 4. *ad* 3.

 aforenamed

aforenamed *discourse* : *Laudabiliter facit, qui pro bono publico se periculo exponit* : *Sicut enim in naturalibus pars una corporis, rectè periculo exponitur pro servando toto corpore; ita & in politicis, particulare Reipub. membrum pro servanda tota Republica* : *That man doth commendably, that exposes himselfe to danger for the publike good* : *as even in naturall things, one part of the body is rightly exposed to save the whole body; so also in things politique, a particular member of the common-wealth is to be exposed for to save the whole. And* therefore the *Prophet David* upon this ground, accompanied with a speciall *instinct* and *motion* of the *Spirit*, for the generall good of his *nation*, undertooke with the perill of his life; a dangerous combate against the *Gyant Goliah.*[b] *Caiaphas* did tell a truth, when he said, *that it was better that one man should die for the people, than that the whole Nation should perish.*[c] *Eleazar* is commended, *Qui se in mortem dedit, ut populum suum liberaret* : *Who gave himselfe, that he might deliver his people*, sayes *Mauden.* Examples of this practice are frequent among the *Heathen*, and by them celebrated with greate praise : As *Codrus* the *Athenian King*, (if I be not mistaken) who thrust himselfe into death among his enemies, that hee might procure victory to his people, according to the *Oracle.* Also of *Curtius* the *Romane* it is said; that *Se pro Republica præcipitavit in hiatum terræ* : *for preservation of the common-wealth hee did throw himselfe into a gulfe of the earth* : But of this kinde many might be alleadged. *Vpon* this ground it is, that the keeping of a *Passe*; the defending of a *Town*, or *Fort*, or the making of a *Stand* to check the pursuing enemy, may be committed to a few, against an unresistable multitude of enemies : which charge and service those few are not to decline, nor disert and quitt; although they doe foresee that in that service they must all die upon the place; when it is apparent, that by the losse of the lives of those few, after that brave manner, the lives of many others are preserved,

[b] 1 *Sam.*17.

[c] *John* 11.50.

preserved, with a more generall publike good of that *body* and *State* whereof they are members: So *Sampson-like*, doing more good by their thus dying, than they ever did, or could, by otherwise living.

§. 19. Of certaine questions resolved.

To this point belongs the decision of divers *questions*. As, *first*, if a man have *killed* another, and escaped; for revenge whereof the *kindred* and *friends* of the slaine, in their pursuit of the *manslayer* for justice, doe fall upon his *kindred* and *friends* that favour or entertaine him; whereby may follow the effusion of much innocent blood, where there is not sufficient power and authority to order and protect men against such outrages; *then* is such a *manslayer* bound in conscience to put himselfe betweene his *friends* and such harme, and to offer himselfe a *sacrifice* to appease wrath; and to prevent a more generall bloodshed, mortality, and deadly *feud*; Whereby, for his sake, many of his dearest *friends* might perish. It is better that one should die for preserving of many, than that many should die for preserving *one* of no more worth and use than any *one* of the other: which is apparent by *Ioabs* demand in his pursuit of *Sheba*, at *Abel* of *Bethmaachah*, requiring him to bee delivered up to him, upon promise that he would depart from the City; which was done accordingly. [a]

Questions 1. About a manslayer, for whose sake his friends are pursued to death.

[a] 2 *Sam*.20.21.

§. 20. About a man under deadly displeasure of Superiours.

Secondly, if a man be fallen so farre under the displeasure of his *Prince*, or *State*, (although unjustly, and undeservedly) that they pursue him with that eagernesse to death, that for his sake and life, a storme of destruction is like to light upon, and consume his dearest and nearest

Question 2.

friends ; then ought he, for their safety, to put himselfe into the hands of implacable authority ; to bee thereby heaved, as *Ionas* [a], into the high grown *sea* of *Superiours* displeasure; that the same may cease from the raging thereof. Which practise and care seemes to have beene used by our *Saviour Christ*, when he said, *if you seeke me, let these go their way* [b]: to make a party, if hee were able to resist; were to make an innocent man guilty of rebellion, and the meanes of more generall ruine.

[a] *Jonah* 2.15.

[b] *Iohn* 18.8.

An objection.

If it be replied, that *self-love* is against this course; and that the preservation of *justice* is to be preferred above many mens lives; and that such yeelding doth condemne the *sufferer*, as guilty, and encourages the persecutors in their injustice :

Answer.

1. About love.

I answer, that the *love* of the *whole*, or more generall body, or *principaller* parts thereof, is to be preferred before the *love* of any *particular*, or inferiour member of the body ; as is cleared by what is spoken already.

2. About Justice. 1. In generall.

To the *second* I reply ; that, of *justice* in generall, it is true, that it is to be preferred before the *bodies* and lives of many men; *because*, neither *trade*, humane *society*, nor the *world* can consist without it : and *therefore* it is, that, for maintenance therof, *Kingdome* is justly armed against *Kingdome* ; to reduce, and keepe those to *justice*, that, otherwise transgressing the same, would confound all in *tyrannie*, or *anarchy*.

2. In particular.

But, the case is not so in particular execution of *justice*, about every *individuall* person; when, by seeking, or preserving of *Iustice* in particulars, wee open a way for greater *injustice*; using a *medicine* worse than the *disease*. But our *Saviour Christ* fully cleares this point, in the fift of *Mathew*, when he saies, *Yee have heard that it hath beene said, an eye for an eye, and a tooth for a tooth : but I say unto you, that yee resist not evill : but, whosoever shall smite thee on the right Cheeke, turne to him the other also. And if any man sue thee at the Law, and take away thy*

thy Coate, let him have thy Cloake also : and whosoever shall compell thee to goe a mile, goe with him twaine [a]. For, no man is so farre bound to contend for *justice*, in his owne particular, but that he may, upon good reasons forbeare, or dispense with his owne right; whereby he incurres onely an evill of *damage*, and not of *sin*.

[a] Mat.5.38, 39,40.41.

Thirdly, this yeelding is not a making of the innocent *sufferer* to be guilty; nor of the *nocent* wrong doer to be just; or more obstinately to persist in his unjust courses; no more than the not applying of medicines to the disease called *Noli me tangere*, doth foment it, when the medling with it, would inrage it and make it worse. This course of yeelding to suffer wrongs, makes way and place for *passive obedience*; and for *God*, the great and righteous *Judge* of the world, to do *justice*, even upon the *highest*; and to worke his owne glorious works, with redresse of all such evills, as neither by right nor might can bee by man reformed: in which course of suffering wrong, wee have the *Martyrs* for examples to follow.

3. Of yeelding to suffer.

§.21. *Touching the voluntary appearance of Felons at liberty upon baile, to free their baile.*

A third question reducible to this point is, whether a man that, for some capitall crime, is under bond of his owne *promise*; or upon some penall summe of money; or upon *bond* of a *friend* for him, of *body* for *body*, for his personall appearing at the *Assizes*; ought thereupon to appeare, when he certainely foresees that there he shall be cast, and die: as put the case it be for *battery*, or *wounding* of a man *mortally*; who dies thereupon, after such bond given.

Third question. Touching the voluntary appearing of Felons to receive justice.

I answer, if the *bond* for his *appearance* bee his owne *promise*, hee ought in conscience to appeare; because, *Gods* Word and Law bindes us to keepe our *promises*; if

Answer. When they ought.

if the same be not to doe sin; although the same may bee *damogeable* to us [a]; but if so bee that his bond for appearance, be a *penall summe* of money, onely by *sureties*; then, *all that a man hath, he will give for his life*: so that, in this case, I see not that he is bound in conscience to appeare, where he foresees his owne death; when the *Magistrate* hath accepted a *penall summe* for *fiduciary caution*, in stead of his personall imprisonment, or other assurance for his appearance; and so may shift himselfe, for his safety, to some place, as a *City* of *refuge*, to keep himselfe from the hands of the *avenger of blood*. *But*, if hee bee at liberty, upon his friends bond, of body for body, for appearance, then ought hee in conscience to appeare, although hee certainely foresee that there hee shall die; that he may free his *friend*, by his meanes, and for his sake, so ingaged; both, in respect of the *Law* of *friendship*; and in regard of the *cause*, that is not his *friends*, but his owne, that by his meanes, and for him, an innocent man do not perish: which were his grievous sinne.

[a] *Psal.* 15.

When againe they ought.

§. 22. *What a guilty person ought to do to free the innocent.*

Fourth question. Concerning an innocent mans suffering by misprision or error, in stead of the nocent: and what the guilty ought in that case to doe.

A fourth question that belongeth to this point, may be this; if a *burglary* or a *murder* be committed, and an innocent man be attached, arraigned, found guilty, and, upon presumptions, be condemned for it to die, the true *fellon* not being knowne; as it fell out, where a certaine *young man*, a Suiter to a Maid, was taken, cast, and condemned to death, and suffered for the murder, and death of that maide, with whom he was late in company, after the rest of the family were in bed, and she the next morning found murdered; which fact was done by a *Villaine* that was hid about the house; and not by the *young man-suiter*, as the *Fellon* afterward confessed.

Whether

Whether is not the true *actor* of such a fact bound in conscience to discover himselfe and confesse; that hee may save the life of an *innocent*, that for his sinne he may not die?

I answer, that hee is bound in conscience so to doe: for, otherwise he is guilty, both by his fact, and silence, of the death of such an innocent man so suffering, whom he might and ought to rescue; now, it is certaine, that no man is to doe, or omit *that* which, by the doing, or omission thereof, either *multiplies*, or *aggravates* his sin; to his owne worse, and eternall condemnation: *againe*, he is bound not to *suffer* other men to sinne, either by rashnesse, or malice, in the *witnesses* or *jurie*, when it is in his power to prevent it, by true information; as, in this case he may: *yet*, I thinke he is to do it, with as great *circumspection*, for *safety* of his owne life, as he can; being sure that he leave not the truth undiscovered; nor suffer the innocent to perish, through his *feare* or *neglect*.

Answer. The nocent ought to discover himselfe. And how.

§.23. *About a mans voluntary revealing to the Magistrate, his own secret capitall crimes.*

A fift question, hitherto belonging to bee resolved, is; if a man have committed a *capitall crime*, as *murder*, *Polygamy*, or the like, which was done so *long* agoe, or so *farre* off, or so *secretly* that none knowes, or will accuse him thereof; and is so *troubled* in *conscience* about it, that upon his private *confession* to *Divines* thereof, and their counsell and consolations ministred to him, he hath no rest nor comfort; but in revenge upon himselfe, is strongly tempted to destroy himselfe, by his owne hands; and cannot prevaile against his resolutions of doing it; whether then is he to accuse himselfe of the crime, and to put himselfe into the hands of *Justice* to suffer for it.

Fift question. About secret capitall crimes.

Answer. When and how the delinquent is to reveale his crimes, that are capitall.

In this case, I think, such an one ought so to do: both for the easing of his *conscience*, that no otherwise can have rest; that thereupon others may be affraid to venture upon sinne, with presumption of secrecy; when they shall see the force of *conscience* compelling men to blaze their owne crimes and shame. *And also*, for preventing of *self-murder*, by submission to the *sword* of *Iustice*, and to the mercy of the *Magistrate*; who perhaps will hardly, in such a case, condemne a man, upon his owne *inditement* and *witnesse*; where there is no other that doth the same; and when the *act* seemes to be unreasonable, that any man should seeke his death; where none accuseth: *and* if he were, in this case, condemned, it is most like that the *supreme Magistrate* would save such a one by *pardon*, or *replevin*; for the usefulnesse of his life in time to come: for, the *sword* of *Iustice* cuts men off, not onely for *punishment* of mischiefe done; but also specially for *prevention* of evill to come.

The barre removed.

The barre, that may hinder such a man from taking this course, may bee the *feare* of immortall *shame* and disgrace, that he thinks he should never be able to indure, if hee should live, and the *Magistrate* not put him to death, after this publick accusation of himselfe. *But* to that it is easily answered, that the *comfort*, and *ease* of the *conscience* would bee such, upon that course, and the opinion and respect of the godly and wise, concerning him; that all *that feared shame* and disgrace would vanish in the ayre, and he be the better approved.

§. 24. *A sixt question, about burning or sinking of a Ship in sea fight.*

A Sea case.

For conclusion of this point, I will propound a *sea case*: to wit, whether it be lawfull for a *Captaine*, or *Master* of a *Ship*, being overcharched with enemies in a *Sea fight*,

fight, rather to *fire*, or *sink* his *Ship*, with himselfe and his company to perish in her, than to yeild and bee at the mercy of his enemies?

Touching a Sea fight.

I answer, if the *Ship* do belong to the *King*, and is in service for the *State*, and committed to her Commanders with charge rather to *burne*, or *sink* her, than to yeeld: then are *they* to follow their *Commission* in obedience to their *Superiours*: alwaies being carefull that they neither directly *burne* nor *sink* the ship, with themselves in her; but as the same may be done by the invading *enemies*, or *accidentally* by themselves in their owne defence; as by *blowing up* the *Ship*, with intention to destroy their enemies: although they do see that they cannot doe the same, without the death of themselves thereby; as *Sampson* did.

Answer. Touching Ships Royall. When to sustaine untill the ship be burnt or sunk without danger of self-murder.

Furthermore, such a *Commander* may himselfe *burne*, or *sink* such a *Ship* so committed to him, when he is no longer able to keepe her out of his *enemies* hands; for that, he is to deprive the enemies of all the strength hee can: provided that he, and the remnant of his Company, do forsake her, and shift for their lives otherwise; as they best can; that they may not bee guilty of *selfe-murder*.

When a man himselfe may burne or sink his owne ship without danger of self-murder. A proviso.

But, if a *Captaine*, or *Master* have Command of such a *Ship*, without such peremptory charge; then is he no further bound in *conscience* touching *yeelding*, *keeping*, *sinking*, or *burning* of her, in such a desperate case; than such a *Captaine*, or *Master* that Commands at, or by his owne discretion; according to the *Lawes*, and *Customes* of the Sea, the *determination* whereof is touched in the next.

But, if so be that the *Ship* be a *merchant-man*, and is commanded by her *Captaine*, or *Master* at his owne discretion, according to the *Lawes* and *Customes* of the *Sea*; if so be that he be so oppressed in fight with his enemies, that he is not able to make longer resistance, or to escape; and

Touching a Merchant man whē to sustaine untill she be burnt, or sunk without danger of self-murder.

and shall certainely foreknow, that, if *he*, his *Ship*, and *Company* do fall into the hands of their enemies, their adversaries will thereby be so encouraged and strengthned, that the *Nation*, or *State*, to which such a ship did belong, shall suffer much more harme, and damage, by the imployment of her, her Company, and goods against the same; than if so be that such a *Ship* should have perished in the *Sea*, with all her *company* and *goods*: *or*, if so be that such a *Commander* do foresee, that his yeelding will bring him, and his men, to a captivity, or death more tedious, than what by resistance they can suffer; then ought such a *Commander* to choose the best of the *two evils of damage*, and rather die in resisting, induring the *Ship* to be sunk, or fired by his enemies; or to doe it himselfe, alwaies being carefull, in such a case, for preservation of their lives, as long as they can, by quitting her, and shifting as they can in the *Sea*, at the mercy of their enemies, and of the waters; when Gods providence unevitably casts them into their hands. *In* such a desperate pinch, to blow up the *Ship*, whereby they foresee that themselves also must perish; is no more unlawfull, than *Sampsons* pulling downe the house upon his enemies and himselfe, so long as their intention is not to kill *themselves*, but their *enemies*, in their owne just defence; which (in this case) they cannot doe without killing themselves *accidentally*. *But*, if there bee not so great danger and losse like to ensue, by their enemies taking such a *Ship*, as by perishing in resisting; then is such a *Commander* to yeeld, that he may not bee guilty of *indirect self-murder*: as hath beene said about fighting beyond our *warrant*, or upon desperate *disadvantages*, and that he may save himselfe and his Company, for further service of *God*, his *Countrey*, and *friends*.

A proviso.

When to yeeld.

§. 25. Of

§. 25. *Of adventuring about saving of soules.*

The third point concerning the *second case*, about present urgent *necessity*, wherein a man may adventure the losse of his life for a greater good, without any danger of *self-murder*; is, when the *necessity*, and *opportunity* of *saving mens soules* requires the adventuring of the losse of a mans naturall life to doe it; which may fall out in *two Cases*. The third point, saving of soules.

First, if a man be *sick* of some *pestilent infectious* mortall disease; and labours not only under the feare, and pangs of death; *But* also lyes oppressed with the horror of a *troubled conscience*, like to be swallowed up in utter despaire; languishing and longing for meanes and comfort of *salvation*; then may the *Minister*, within whose charge such a one is; *or*, in his default some *other*, either *Minister*, or *private Christian*; upon outward *calling* from the *party*, or by Gods *providence* inviting him; finding withall an inward *motion* and inclination of the *spirit* to take the opportunity to save a soule; then (I say) may one of these adventure into such infectious *places*, and to such infected *persons*, out of love and zeale to save a soul in danger of perishing: so they indanger no other lives than their owne, by so adventuring. *Case* 1. Of adventuring to infectious persons.

The grounds of which *adventure* are; *first*, *confidence* of Gods protection in that warrantable pious imployment, so farre as God sees good. Grounds of adventuring. 1.

Secondly, *comfort*, that (if in that service a man doe die) he had a lawfull *calling*; and his *adventure* was for saving that which is better than many lives, & for which the deare *Son* of *God* did die upon the crosse. 2.

Yet, men are herein to be observant, that they *tempt not God* by their rash presumption, or self-confidence, needlesly, or beyond their due bounds, thrusting themselves into such *dangers*; but that they doe use as great *A Caveat.*

 caution,

caution, and as good *preservatives* as they can; with earnest *prayer* to *God*, to give him successe and safety; that if they doe *die* by meanes of such dangerous enterprises, their *conscience* may not justly accuse them, that they were wilfully negligent of their own lives;and so thereby accessary to their owne deaths.

Case 2. Of adventuring among heathens to preach the Gospell.

Secondly, in such times, and places where the publike *preaching* of the *truth* necessary to salvation is wholly wanting; or powerfully suppressed; and grosse *ignorance*, or damnable *error*, and *heresies* prevailes; as among the *heathens*, and grosse *Idolaters*; then, and there is any *Christian man*, that hath a warrantable *calling* and opportunity to teach others the *truth*, and to warne them of *errors*, although they cannot doe the same without danger of persecution and death; this course we finde warranted not onely by the practise of the *Apostles*; who ceased not to preach *Christ*, both publikely, and from house to house, although they were otherwise charged, and therefore threatned and persecuted to death: [a] *But* even others more private Christians did so, as *Aquila* and *Priscilla*, and those that were scattered from *Ierusalem*: [b] whose labours God greatly blessed, to the advancement of the *Church*: Of such examples *Ecclesiasticall histories* are full, in times of the primitive persecutions; as *Theodoret* reports *hist. lib.* 1. *cap.* 23. of two yong men called *Ædesius* and *Frumentius*, who while they were *lay* men did teach among the *Indians*. [a]

And of *Christian Merchants Socrates* affirmes, that they did instruct some of the *Indians* in the principles of *religion*; [b] *also Theodoret* makes mention *hist. l.*1.*c.*24. of a certaine captive *Christian* woman, who did convert the *nation* of the *Iberians* to the *Faith*: [c] with whose report consents *Sozomen*, *lib.* 2. *cap.* 6. speaking of the conversion of the *Iberians*, he sayes, that the same was, that

[a] *Acts* 20.20.

b *Acts* 5.28,29. *Acts* 18.16. *Acts* 8.4.

[a] *Quoniam in vero Dei cultu educati erant mercatores, qui eò commeabant, cohortati sunt, ut in unum congregati divina ministeria obirent.*

b *Christiani illi quosdam ex Indis fidei principiis instituentes.*

c *Mulier quędam capta in bello, Iberes ad veritatem traduxit.*

that *that Nation* did leave their ancient *religion*, upon the perswasion of a captive woman.[d]

And Socrates speaking of the *King* and *Queene* of *Iberia* converted by the *woman*, hee sayes that both the *King* and *Queene* did preach *Christ*; *He* to the men, and *Shee* to the women: [e] Extraordinary things and accidents, are not bounded and regulated by ordinary rules: and so much doth *God* himselfe require us to doe in many places, that the soules of our brethren may not perish for lack of his saving truth, which all are bound to maintaine.

d *Fama est hanc Iberiam, suasu mulieris Christianæ captivæ patriam & avitam religionem deseruisse.*

e *Utriq; Christū prædicant: Rex viris: Regina mulieribus.*

Deut.6.7.
Colos.3.16.

§. 26. *Of adventuring for salvation and religion.*

The third generall case. About religion.

The third generall case, wherein men may expose their lives to death without any danger of indirect *self-murder*, is in the cause of *religion*; for maintenance of the *truth*; for advancing of Gods *glory*; and for the conversion, and confirmation of others, both in profession and practise; although the same should cost us our *lives*: *as* we see was done by *Daniel* and his three *companions*.[a] Whereunto wee are bound by that love, that we owe both to *God*, and our *Neighbour*. According to which, *David à Mauden* sayes well, that *Ex charitate tenetur quis fidem profiteri cum periculo vitæ, quando honor Dei id exigit, aut externa confessio necessaria est ad aliquorum conversionem ad fidem, vel in eadem vacillantium confirmationem; seu quando credit minus firmos in fide, eam facilè vel bonorum temporalium amore, vel vitæ conservandæ causa negaturos*: that is, *A man is bound by charity to professe his faith with danger of his life, when the glory of God requires the same, or when our outward confession is necessary, for the conversion of some to the faith; or to confirme those that waver in it, or when a man beleeves that the weake in faith will easily out of love of temporall goods, or*

a *Daniel* 6.10. and 3.17.

David à Mau-precept.6.discurs.10.

or to preserve their lives, deny the faith. This adventuring of our lives for religion, consists of *foure points* or members.

§. 27. *Of the first case or point, which is about defence of religion.*

Members of it.

1.

Defence of the truth.

First, in the *defence* of the truth and religion, both by *speaking* and *writing* for it; when the same is reproached, impugned, and slandered, with endeavouring to overthrow it; although that such a course of patrociny were capitall to the undertakers: for which, we have a luculent warrant and example, in the practise of *Hester* in the like case; [b] and in the practise of *Iustin Martyr* against the *Heathen*, upon no lesse danger; yet, herein it were to be wished, that men would rather content themselves to prove and commend what they hold to bee the truth, and fit for godly edifying, than for to multiply unprofitable *controversies*, and to alienate *affections*; by bitter disgracefull imputations, and railing confutations of the errors of others.

[b] *Hest.* 4.14,16.

And also we are to defend the *truth* and *religion*, by objecting our selves with perill of our lives, to resist by force & armes, the unjust invasion of *hostility*; endeavouring to roote out the *professors* of the same, only for the truths sake, when the enemies doe endeavour quite to extirpate the truth of *God*: *Although* that force and armes, in hostile invasion, is not to bee used to propagate and spread the truth, and to reforme errours and abuses in religion; which is to be done by teaching and perswasions, to draw, and not to force the conscience about divine things.

Note.

Moderation of warre for religion.

Yet, in just defence a man may oppose himselfe with force and armes against forraigne, or usurping, unjust invaders, that violently would thrust him out of his *possession* of the truth; *because* the course taken against him is most *tyrannically unjust*, in usurping to domineere over mens

mens consciences, which are subject onely to *God*: *and* if for spreading of *religion*, and rooting out of *errors*, it were lawfull to make hostile invasion; then might the whole *world* be in a flaming fire of warre; every *nation* and *people* one against another; according as they differ in *opinions* and *customes* about *religion*; seeing that every one thinkes his owne *religion* best, and condemnes, and dislikes all others. *And againe*, of all the *goods* a man hath, true *religion* is the chiefe; and doth most neerely concerne him, to keepe it above his life; and it is the choisest and most necessary thing that he can provide, preserve, and commend to his *posterity*: *So that*, if there be any thing of worth in this world, for which he ought to *contend* to death, [a] it must be the true *religion*; that, through his neglect or fearefulnesse, he suffer it not violently by force of forraigne armes to be opprest, and himselfe and his to be tyrannically thrust out of his just *possession* of it; without which to be, were better not to bee; when, therefore, he shall bee forcibly inthralled and subjected to that, which he is perswaded is erroneous and hereticall, and the bane of his soule.

[a] *Jud.* 3.

§.28. *About the publike confession, or profession of the truth.*

The second member of the *case*, wherein a man ought to expose his life to death, in cause of *religion*; is in point of *confession* of the *Gospell* and true religion, with danger of our lives for the same: which is to bee done, both when wee are called to declare our *faith* and opinion about the truth; so that then we are neither to dissemble nor deny it; but are commanded to make *profession* of it. 1 *Pet*.3.15. as was practised by *Iohn* the *Baptist*, *Iohn* 1. 20. and so by all the blessed *Martyrs*. 1.

The second member about confession of the truth.

And also, when we doe see that our concealement of our *profession* may prejudice the truth, dishonour *God*, 2.

 strengthen

strengthen and confirme the adversaries; or may discourage and offend the *weake* Christians, whereby they may droope, or fall; then, no feare of death should cause a man to forbeare to declare himselfe in point of *religion*; *lest* that of our *Saviour Christ* be verified upon him, *He that loveth his life shall lose it.* [a] Whereas contrariwise, *He that hateth his life in this world*, (or as it is in *Matthew*, *loseth it for Christs sake* [b]) *shall keep it unto life eternall.*

[a] *John* 12.25.

[b] *Mat.*10.39.

By failing in this point, many a man *slanders* himselfe, causing the *people* of *God* to thinke worse of him than he is indeed; and deprives himselfe of much *honour*, and comfort that he might have, by exposing himselfe to all hazzards, for Gods cause; to whom, that in the fifth of the *Judges*, concerning *Ruben*, may be applyed; that *for the divisions of Reuben there were great thoughts of heart: why abodest thou among the sheepfolds, to heare the bleatings of the flocks?* [c] *And* againe, that concerning *Meroz*; *Curse ye Meroz, saith the Angel of the Lord, curse yee bitterly the inhabitants thereof, because they came not to the help of the Lord against the mighty.* Whereas contrariwise, in the same cause, it is said with commendation, *Zebulon* and *Napthalie* were *a people that jeoparded their lives unto death.*

[c] *Judges* 5.15, 16. 23.18.

§.29. *Touching not omission of necessary duties commanded of God in any perill of life for the same.*

The third member is about omission of duty.

The third member of the *case*, wherein a man ought to expose his life to death in cause of *religion*, is, when he is *charged* and bidden by any humane command, or *authority*, upon threatning paine of death, to forbeare doing of that which *God commands* him to doe; whether the same be *personall* duties of generall obedience to *Gods* lawes,

lawes, that are proper to all men; *or officiall*, respecting some conditions of men in their speciall places and relations; as *officers* and the like, if they have the same in charge immediately from *God*, without dispensation; then, a man is not upon any *humane* prohibition to omit doing of such duties; which he is bound by immediate authority from *God* to performe; [a] as *honouring of our parents*, and all the other *affirmatives* of Gods *morall Commandements*; which no man can release or dispense withall, to discharge a man before *God*, for his omission of them. 1. *Personall.* [a] *Dan.*6.10.

Also, for *officiall* duties, which are so proper to mens particular *places* and *relations* wherein they are; that without performance of those duties, these *relations* and *places* would be marred; a man is not to omit them upon any threatning and danger, so long as he stands in such *relation*, or *place*; *because*, both the *places* and *duties* belonging to them, are of divine, and not humane ordination and dependance; *as* the *places* and *duties* of *parents*, *children*, *husbands*, *wives*, *masters*, *servants*, *magistrates*, *subjects*, &c. who are not upon any humane command, or danger, to omit their *duties* to those, to whom they owe them upon divine bond; which is so plaine, that it is professed of the *Pope*, that he cannot, nor will not absolve *subjects* from their *allegiance*, and *obedience* due to their *Princes*; [b] but only from *obedience* to such as *by heresie*, *contumacy*, or the like, are fallen from their *places* of *Kingly authority* which they had; being unworthy of it, and of the *duties* and *respects* due to the same. 2. *Officiall.* 1. Of divine institution. [b] *Bellar. in dialogismo adversus Borclaium, c.*31.

But it is to be observed, that for those *places* and their *duties*, which are wholly of *humane* ordination; as *offices* of *State* or *Common-wealth*, they are to bee executed or suspended by the *superiour authority*; although our endeavours are not to concurre in it, mainly and clearely to crosse the morall rules of *equity* and *religion*. 2. Of humane institution.

Also, for *callings* that are fundamentally of divine ordination;

dination; the manner of execution whereof depends upon the rules of *Gods* direction in his *Word*: as is the *Ministry* of the *Gospell*; so long as the *persons* that exercise that function, have their *calling* thereunto by men who are the *Church* of *God*; by the same power they may be discharged and put out of place; or, while they are in it, be suspended from liberty of exercising their publike office and ministry: for the same *power* that makes, may unmake; and the *affirmative* Commandements of *God* doe not binde *ad semper*, to the doing of them alwayes; specially when the *intermission* only, or restraint of exercise of those *duties* is intended by the deprivers, or suspenders; *so long* as there is sufficient provision by others to perform the same without so great dãge to the *Church*, as might arise to the same, by the *Ministers* doing of the duties of his *calling*, contrary to the said *authority*: then such a *deprivation*, or *suspension*, (although it were unjust) is to be obeyed; and for a man in that case, to suffer for his disobedience to the sãme, he can have no comfort nor just incouragement; except such restraint were so generall, that there were not men enough in *places* to discharge the duties of that function; without which a true *Church* cannot subsist; so as therein, and by the doctrine thereof, men may be saved: *then*, in that case of extreame necessity, such a deprived or suspended *Minister*, by the rule of *charity*, which warrants *lay-men* to help to uphold the truth and *Church*, is bound to doe the *duties* of his *calling*, notwithstanding any such former restraint, or danger of disobedience to it: *because*, the power of the *Church* is but *ministeriall*; under, and according to *God*; rather *declarative*, than *Soveraigne*; *therefore*, what she doth, tyes not men here on earth to obey it, to the destruction, but to the edification of the *Church*, or at least to prevent a greater mischiefe; *And also*, because the true *Church* may doe no such acts of deprivation, or suspension, whereby to intend or effect the destruction

Of obedience to suspension, and deprivation.

Exception against suspension and deprivation of ministers by the Church of Rome.

destruction of the *Church*; and *therefore* (in that case) transgressing of such restraints is no disobedience to the *Church*, but rather an obeying the intent of the same; as in times of persecution we have plentifull *examples*, specially of the *Church* of the *Iewes* against the *Christians*.

Yet, herein is to be observed, that such performance of *duties* in that case, after restraint, bee done in meeke patient manner, without tumults or forcible opposition of *authority*; submitting with *passive* obedience, where they cannot lawfully performe *active*. *A Caveat.*

This extends not to warrant any *schisme*, or *heresie*, that esteem themselves only to be the *true Church*; as did the *Donatists* and others; to oppose (out of feare of their owne ruine) the proceedings and restraints of the more *Orthodoxe*, and generall *body* of a sound *Church*, (whose authority doth preponderate and oversway her apostating members) so long as by the doctrine publikely taught in her, men may be saved, and built up.

§. 30. *Against commission of evill upon any humane command, or threats.*

The fourth member of the case, wherein a man ought to expose his life to death, in causes concerning religion; is, when a man is desired, commanded, or threatned to *doe any sinne* forbidden by *Gods word*; that then hee doe it not, although he therefore doe die; as *Iosephs* practise manifests in resisting his whorish *mistris*,[a] and the three *children*, that would not upon the *Kings* command worship the golden *Image* to save their lives, *Daniel* 3. 18. *Because* it is better for us to die, than deliberately and wilfully to sinne against *God*: as the *woman* with her seaven *sonnes* did choose, 2 *Mach*. 7. according to S. *Augustines* judgement, who sayes, that if it be propounded to a man, *Vt aut mali aliquid faciat, aut mali aliquid patiatur, eligat non facere mala, quam non pati mala*, [b] *that either*

Fourth member about commission of evill upon humane command.

[a] Gen. 39. 12.

[b] Epist. 204.

either he should doe some evill, or suffer some calamity; then let him choose rather not to doe evill, than not to suffer evill.

Observe. How we are to abhorre sin.

For, we are ever to doe that which may most neerely unite us to *God* our chiefe good; and to shunne what may divide us from *him*; which nothing can doe but our sinnes; specially those that consist in the transgression of the *negative Commandements*, and are most opposite to *God*, and incompatible with him; *and* therefore those lawes doe binde *ad semper*, to the alwayes observing of them; and cannot be *dispensed* withall, seeing *God* is unchangeable. *The* evill of sinne should be more terrible to us than death it selfe; not onely for that it is the cause of death, and imbitters it; *but* also because it deprives us of a greater good, of our *spirituall* life, that farre exceeds the *naturall*. The *beatificall object* that sinne deprives us of, is the infinite blessed *God*, from whom to be separated is worse than death it self; and in that respect, rather than we should sinne, we should choose to suffer death, which is a glorious kinde of *Martyrdome*, and a meanes of advancement to happinesse, for the power and practise of the truth laying downe our lives; which is a more undoubted signe of grace and salvation, than is the suffering of many, for holding the truth in opinion and profession. *Wee* should choose rather not to *bee*, than not to bee happy; *for*, the originall, and end of our being is better than our being it selfe; in regard that our happinesse is not of, and in our selves; but in and from another, who is both our beginning and end.

§. 31. *Of the kindes of sinnes of commission to be avoyded.*

Evils of sin to be avoided.

These sinfull evills, that wee ought thus carefully to avoid and forbeare to death, are of *two* sorts.

I. Against the law of nature.

First, those that be *directly* and absolutely forbidden by by the Law of *nature*, as fundamentally unlawfull, at all times, and in all cases, for the contrariety that they have against the nature of *God*, and against the inbred principles of reason and conscience: of which no question can be made, but that wee are alwaies utterly to shun them, notwithstanding any *humane command*, or *inforcement* that may be to the contrary: *because*, no *human power* can dissolve the obligation of those ingrafted Commandements of *God*, and *nature*, that we may be discharged in conscience from keeping of them, which would overthrow both divinity and humanity: neither can any free us from the punishment of the transgression of them; both because, *equity* and *Law* requires that, *the soule that sins, shall die*; and, also for that, there is no power matchable with *Gods*, and *natures*, to protect, or free us, by force from *their vengeance*. *Innata Lex. Rom. 2. 15.*

Secondly, the *sins* that wee are to shun, and not wittingly and willingly to do, upon any threats, or worldly danger, or for any profit, are those that are forbidden by the *positive Law* and revealed *will* of *God*; the violating whereof doth wrong the *soveraignty* and *honor* of *God*; who is the absolute and onely independant *King* of all the world; and his *will* the supreame unerring *rule* of our *obedience* throughout our lives; our transgression whereof is a breach of that *loyalty*, and due subjection, which wee owe to *that* our highest *Lord*. To whose *positive Law conformity* is more properly *obedience* to God, than *conformity* to the *Law* of *nature* is, by it selfe considered. Because, the *ground* of our conformity to the Law of *nature*, is *naturall inclination* and *Reason*, equally binding *Heathens* aswell as *Christians*. But, the ground of our conformity to the *positive Law* of *God*, is principally the soveraigne *Authority* and *Will* of God himselfe; which kinde of *obedience* is that which is properly of the *Church* and her members to *God*; and proceeds from faith, love, feare, &c. *Evangelicall*, or *Theologicall* graces. 2. Against the positive Law of God.

From

From which *obedience* to *God* no *wight* can absolve, or excuse us, that we may lawfully and safely subject our selves to feare, to please, or to obey any other, in opposition, or contraty to *him* and his *will*.

Reasons. 1. Because, there is none above *God*, whose will may be preferred, or equalled to his, to whom all is subordinate, in *nature*, *state* and imployment.

2. Neither is any man *Lord* over the *Conscience*, either to bind, or discharge it, contrary to the *Law*, or *will* of *God*, that we should dare, upon any motive of *humane will*, *profit*, or *penalty*, wilfully to transgresse the same.

3. *God* is our *ultimate*, or last *end*, that we are to aime at; that we may both *enjoy*, and *please* him, in whom consists our *happinesse*.

4. All promises of blessings are made to the doers of Gods will; and all threatnings of judgements to the transgressors of the same [a]: which *reward* no *humane* power can hinder, or frustrate. And therefore, wee cannot dispense with our selves, upon any humane pretence or motive, to do any thing contrary to Gods word and positive Law; although for not transgressing the same we should incurre death.

[a] *Rom.* 2. v. 6, 7, 8, 9, 10.

§. 32. *Of indifferent things, how they become sinfull.*

Indifferents accidentally evill.

But, in *subject ô indifferente*, in things that are of themselves but *indifferent* (whose use is neither directly nor absolutely commanded nor forbidden by Gods word, as are kinds of *meate*, *drinke*, *apparrell*, and the like, and for which we ought not to command to death) the using, or not using of them becomes sinfull onely *accidentally*, *either* by reason of externall *circumstances*, about the *action*, or *omission* of them; *or* of some *erroneous qualities* in the *agents*, or *omitters*; and not from the intrinsecall *nature* of the things, *or morall* disposition of the *action*,

action, or *omission* absolutely considered, without respect of *circumstances* and Law. *For* touching the *use* of *indifferent* things, onely mans *individuall* voluntary actions about them, specially proceeding from *deliberate* judgment, are morally either *good* or *evill*; well done or ill done; *because*, they are accompanied, and indowed with such *actionall circumstances*, as do so affect and qualifie them, that they are no more indifferent; either *Physically* to be done, or not done; (*for, Vnumquodq; dum est, necessario est, Every thing when it is, it is necessarily*, and then cannot be otherwise than it is;) or *morally*, because, if the same were otherwise than it is, it must necessarily be either better or worse than it is. For, no action can stand equally morally affected with differing circumstances; and at the same time, to be done, or not to bee done, cannot be equally morally *indifferent*. For, *Thomas Aquinas* saies, *That it falls out that an action may be indifferent, secundum speciem, in the generall kind of it : qui tamen est bonus vel malus in individuo consideratus, which notwithstanding is either good or evill, considered in its individuall subject and act. Whereof hee gives the reason, quia actus moralis non solum habet bonitatem ex objecto, à quo habet speciem; sed etiam ex circumstantiis : because, a morall action hath its goodnesse, not onely from its object, by which it is specified for kinde, but also from circumstances*; of which every *individuall act* of necessity hath some, whereby it is drawne to be good or bad, *Ad minus ex parte intentionis finis, at least in respect of the end intended: And therefore*, he concludes properly, *necesse est omnem actum hominis à deliberativa ratione procedentem in individuo consideratum, bonum esse vel malum : it is of necessity, that every act of man proceeding from deliberate reason, and considered in its individuall performance and*

The individual acts of things indifferent, are not indifferent when they are done.

Not Physically.

Nor morally.

Tho. *prima secundæ, quæst.* 18. *artic.* 9. *Cum enim rationis sit ordinare, actus à ratione deliberativa procedens, si non sit ad debitũ finẽ ordinatus; ex hoc ipso repugnat rationi, et habet rationem mali; si vero ordinetur ad debitũ finẽ, convenit ad eum ordine rationis unde habet rationem boni.* Ex Filliucio To.2.p.3. *Patet actiones humanas, quatenus à ratione, & volũtate diriguntur, dici morales, hoc est dignas laude vel vituperatione, ex* Arist. Ethic. c.13. *actio homini propria est voluntaria, & libera & adeo digna laude aut vituperatione.* Tho. 1.2. q.1. art.1. Azor. l.1.c.1.

subject, is good or evill: For, seeing the *will* of man rightly ordered is subject to right *reason* and divine *Law*, then all actions proceeding from it, as it is so guided in all performances, are *morally* good or bad: and as all things are destinated to an *ultimate end* of Gods *glory*, and to other particular subordinate *ends* of effecting any *good*; so is their *use* subject to proportionable *rules* and *Lawes*, for ordering the same thereby, that they may attaine their *end* intended: and in that respect, when they are done; they are *morally* either well or ill done, according to that proportion, or disproportion that their use then hath to their due *ends* and rules; and to be a fit and effectuall *meanes* of accomplishing the same: or contrariewise.

Conclusion. *So* now, wee have seene how that, for to prevent suffering, and death, we are not wittingly and willingly to doe evill of sin (in any case) specially, or any thing directly against Gods Law. *And therefore*, doe conclude with *David à Mauden*, touching the aforesaid *three* generall *cases*; wherein a man suffering to death is exempted from indirect *self-murder, pro bono publico fide, religione Catholica, aliisq; de causis bonis & honestis vitam propriam periculo exponere, non solum laudabile, sed etiam interdum necessarium est: For a man to expose his owne life to danger for the publike good; for his faith, for the true religion, and for other good and honest causes; it is not onely commendable, but also sometimes necessary.*

§. 33. *Of the properties of an indirect selfe-murderer.*

An indirect self-murderer hath *two* bad *properties*.

The first property. Folly. *First*, hee is *foolish* in advisedly and wilfully using mortall meanes, and fatall to himselfe; and yet thinks not thereby to die, but to live more happily; as *Eve*, in eating of the forbidden *fruit*, that was the meanes of death,

death, did conceit to attaine thereby to a more excellent *life*, as if a man should looke to gather *grapes* of *thornes*; and good & comfort of deadly courses. Which proceeds from the stupid *unbeleefe* of man, who would rather make *God* a lyer, than he will be diverted from his desperate courses, or will beleeve more, than hee comprehends, or conceives, by his *senses*, *being as the horse or mule, which have no understanding: whose mouth must be kept in with bit and bridle*: as the *Prophet* tells us, *Psal.* 32.9. — Frō unbeleefe.

Secondly, an *indirect self-murderer* is *wicked*; for, knowing both his course, and the event thereof to bee evill, opposite both to the will of *God*, and to his owne future good, he doth wilfully continue in, and prosecute it still, which is damnable impiety. — The second property, Wicked.

Which flowes from the *self-contentment*, that men take in their owne sinfull waies; and from their *misconstruction* and abuse of the long *patience* of *God*, not executing his threatned judgements speedily upon such as themselves are [a]: which takes away from them all remorse for their evill courses, and all care of reformation to be better. — The ground of it self-content.

[a] *Eccles.* 8.11.

§. 34. *Observations from indirect self-murder.*

The uses of the former doctrine about indirect self-murder, are specially *three*. — *Uses.*

First, it serves for our *instruction*; that we may see that many men are deceived in their self-pleasing courses; whereby they promise to themselves much comfort and good; but indeed reape death and destruction, by their own meanes and procurements: according to the *Proverb*, *There is a way which seemeth right unto a man, but the end thereof are the waies of death* [b]: *as* is apparent, by the course of our first *parents Adam* and *Eve*; destroying themselves, and us in them, by following their own — 1. Men self-deceived.

[b] *Prov.* 14.12.

wits and wills, without obedience to their Maker.

Causes of self-deceit.

The true *causes* of this deceit and errour of man in this point, are *foure.*

1. Vnbeliefe.

First, *unbeliefe* of Gods threatnings, while men trust to *lying vanities*, upon groundlesse presumptions, and erroneous carnall principles, and misinformations, and misconstructions; willing to bee perswaded, and to beleeve that which stands best with their liking and sinfull condition; so corrupting their understanding to give a false verdict against the truth of God, to their owne destruction.

2. Self-conceit.

Secondly, men are self-beguiled, by *self-conceit* of the goodnesse of their unsound estates, and by being taken up with *contentment* in the present seeming good of their self-pleasing sinfull courses: for that they did never throughly see, and apprehend the miserable badnesse of their owne wretched estates, nor did truly see, and taste the excellency and sweetnesse of a better.

3. Prosperity of the wicked.

Thirdly, men are here self-deceived, by resting upon the present visible dealing of *God* with many as bad, or worse than themselves, whom they see still to *prosper* in their ill courses: *Because judgement is not speedily executed, therefore their hearts are set to doe evill*; being perswaded that it shall bee as well with them, as others of their owne ranke, that they see flourish and doe well enough, as they thinke.

4. Shifting the blame.

Fourthly, men deceive themselves, by shifting off the *blame* of their ill courses from themselves, to other concurring, or accessary *causes* of their evill wayes; as *Adam* did to *Eve*: as if they were freed by the temptations or partnership of others with them in evill. But the condemnation of *accessaries* doth condemne, and not cleare the *principals*.

Predestination is blamelesse.

But, they that to cleare, or encourage themselves in their naughty courses, shift off the blame thereof to Gods *Predestination*, are impudently impious; by both making *God*

God the *author* of sin, and *also* by traducing his *justice*, for unjustly punishing them; that, by their owne verdict, are blamelesse: *But God Predestinates* no man to an *end*, without respect of *meanes*, whose use is within the compasse of a mans power, and wherein he himselfe is a voluntary *agent*; *so that* predestination offers no force to any mans *will*: and *therefore* a man living in a sinfull course, of his owne choosing and liking, cannot blame *God*, or his *Predestination*; seeing that God both gives him sufficient meanes, and invitation to come out of that sinfull state. So men that runne into evill courses, are by their own meanes darkened in their judgements, and doe wilfully put out their owne eyes of their understandings, that they may fearelesly goe on to their own ruine, in their owne wayes of destruction. Who is so blinde as he that will not see? *Observe.* Men self-binded.

Many mens *estates* are found by themselves, in the end, to be farre worse, and more desperate than they expected; and this also many come not to see untill it is too late, and past all hope of amendment, or recovery; which by carefulnesse and good heed taking in time, might have been prevented. Deceived.

The second use is for *admonition*; that wee doe well consider our courses what they be, and whither they tend; that we may not dare to venture upon that, which may make us accessary to our owne destruction: It is dishonourable and uncomfortable for a man to suffer by his owne deservings, or procurement. And *therefore*, we are to observe how the *Apostle Peter* advises us, *That none of us doe suffer as an evill doer*, 1 *Pet* 4. 15. *Use* 2. Consideration of our courses.

If we be entred upon an unwarrantable course, then are we to breake off, and to make hast to returne by true repentance, and to walk in the way that leades to life. And *therefore*, I conclude with the *Prophet*, *Cast away from you all your transgressions, whereby ye have transgressed, and make you a new heart, and a new spirit; for why* Repent and reforme.

will ye die ô house of Israel? For, I have no pleasure in the death of him that dyeth, saith the Lord God: wherefore turne your selves, and live yee. Ezek. 18. 31, 32.

That we may doe so, we must beware of self-conceitednesse and obstinacy, in our owne self-will'd wayes; and be carefull to listen to good counsell, and advertisement; and to consider the latter end, and not the present contentment, and faining *flattery* of evill courses.

Use 3. Men sin against themselves.

The third use is an *intimation*; to shew unto those that doe desperately or carelesly venture upon courses tending to their owne self-destruction; that they are not only guilty of sinnes against *God*, and their *Neighbours* immediately; but even also against *themselves*, in *self-murder*, a crime of the vilest nature; for which they shall be arraigned before *God*, and suffer; their owne wrongs being revenged upon themselves, and their own unjust and unnaturall suffering at their owne hands, being punished upon themselves by the hand of *God*.

Observe 1. Ill courses are most harmfull to the doers of them.

Where it is *observable*, that man being both the wrong-doer, and wrong-sufferer in the same act by himselfe, doth justly suffer by the hand of *God*, for wronging his creature, and for breaking his Law, in mans self-respect, and usage of himselfe. The *consideration* of which terrible end of such courses, redounding to the destruction of the doers, should affright men from them.

Observe 2.

Where it is also remarkable, that a man cannot wrong *God* or *others*, but by ruinating *himselfe* therewithall; and so all ill courses doe prove a punishment to the *doers* of them: and *therefore*, if there were any true love in such persons to themselves, they would abandon all such courses as tend to the ruine and perdition of the entertainers, or proceeders in the same.

CHAP.

CHAP. 12.

Of direct bodily self-murder.

§. 1. What it is.

NOw it followes that we treate of *direct self-murder*; and *first*, shew what it is: *Direct bodily self-murder is an advised, witting and willing intention, and effectuall endeavour of a man, by his owne hands, or meanes, to take away or destroy his owne life, whereby he doth indeed kill himselfe.*

In which *description* wee are to *observe two* things: *First*, the *generall*, and then the *specificall* nature of *direct self-murder*.

Touching the genericall, or generall *nature* of *direct self-murder*, which is as the *matter* of it; we are to consider, *first*, that it is a *morall act* proceeding from mans *will*; and *therefore* is good, or bad; and so wee are to bee the more carefull how we doe purpose, or performe it. Generall nature of it. 1. A morall act.

Secondly, we are to observe touching that action, the *object* thereof, about which it is exercised: and that is the naturall *life* of man, who hath no such other precious worldly thing: and *therefore*, we should be very wary how we venture to deale therewith. 2. The object of it, Life.

Thirdly, the *subject* of this *action* is a mans *selfe*; by whom, and upon whom the same is done; and so is both the *active* and *passive subject* of the same act; and so it doth neerely concerne a man, that he may well consider, both what he doth, and suffers in that case; seeing he may bee guilty of a double blame, if he doth both *doe*, and *suffer* that which he ought not by his owne hands. 3. The subject of it, Mans selfe.

Fourthly,

4. The end of it, To destroy.

Fourthly, the *end* of this *action* is remarkable; that it is not to cherish and preserve, but to destroy and take away a mans owne life: *It* is the *end* that makes or marres even a good action, and increases the maliciousnesse of an evill. And *therefore* it concernes us much, in all our actions, to consider well their *ends*, whether the same be *good* or *evill*.

The specificall nature of it.

The *specificall* nature of *direct self-murder*, is that which is the true *forme* of it; whereby it is properly and directly *self-murder*. This *specificall* nature of it is *remota & proxima*, *remote and next*.

Remote.

The *remote* nature of *direct self-murder* consists in *two* things.

1. Restraint of the act it selfe.

First, in the restraint, or limitation of the *act* of killing, for *agent* and *patient*; for choise and application of the meanes to a mans owne *selfe*; who thereby reflects and returnes upon himselfe, in an *act* of the greatest hostility and cruelty that can be in the world, to destroy himselfe and his owne life, by his owne meanes; so becomming his owne *Burrio* and executioner.

2. The Agent, understanding what he doth.

Secondly, the *remote nature* of *direct self-murder* consists in the *disposition* of the *agent*, *both* in his *understanding*, and *will*; in respect of his understanding, the *actour* of it doth the same advisedly, and wittingly.

Advisedly.

Advisedly he doth it; when after premeditation in his minde of killing of *himselfe*, *and* after approbation of the *fact* in his judgement, he resolves upon his unwarrantable *motives* to doe it; *and* devises and plots the meanes and manner how to doe it, after deliberation, and conflict with himselfe betweene opposite *reasons*: *and* when withall the *understanding* works and prevailes upon the *will*, to draw the same to concurre in the resolution to doe it, and to command and imploy the body in consent with both the understanding and the will, to execute their pleasure to its owne destruction, as is manifest in the practise of *Abitophel* [a] and *Judas*. [b] Then it is an advised

[a] 2 *Sam.* 17.23.
[b] *Mat.* 27.5.

vised act, done by a man in such advised manner, and so cannot be excused by ignorance, or inconsiderate haste; *but* is done with the fullest careere of morall motion, and with the greatest ingagement of the whole man, in an action of the highest nature of self-mischiefe.

Note.

The *vilest actions* are often done upon greatest advisement, and deliberation; which makes them the worse, and more odious. *Mans wisdome is madnesse when he is left to himselfe*; and a depraved judgement perverts the will, and leads a man into many vile practises; seeing the *will* followes the last *determination* of the *practicall understanding*. If the light of understanding that is in man be darknesse, how great then is that darknesse?

Wittingly.

Wittingly, a man doth take away his owne life, when at the very time of doing the *act*, hee knowes both that he is doing such an *act*, materially considered; and also, that the same *act*, for the *nature* and *forme* of it, tends directly to his own destruction, and is wicked and unlawfull to be done, and yet for all that doth not desist; whereby man that is a *rationall creature*, able to judge of his owne actions, is self-condemned in his own conscience, while he is about, and in doing the *act* it selfe.

Willingly.

The *disposition* of the *agent*, or *actour* in *direct self-murder* in respect of his *will*, is that he doth it *willingly*; as to *hang*, or *stab*, or *poyson* himselfe, or the like. For *violence* or inforcement cannot be done to the *will*, in its *act* of *willing*, which necessarily must be *free*; either *absolutely*, or *conditionally*.

Willingnesse.

This *willingnesse* in a man to kill himselfe, is *twofold*.

1. Antecedent.

First, that which is *antecedent* before the *fact*; whereby he wills *not only* that he were dead; but *also* wills that such a murderous *act* should be done by himselfe, upon himselfe, to take away his owne *life*; which by a contrary *act*, and change of his will might be prevented; as it is said of *Ahitophel*, that he came sober to destroy himselfe, as *Cæsar* came sober to ruinate the common wealth.

Ahitophel *accessit sobrius ad perdendum seipsum, ut* Cæsar *ad perdendam Rempub:*

Concomitant.

Secondly, he hath a willingnesse *concomitant* at the *act* doing; so that when it is in his power to suspend his act, and not to doe it, yet he wills and doth it indeed: which is so much the more grievous, by how much the more it hath of *wilfulnesse*; as will is both the originall fountaine of sin, and is so essentiall to it, that *absolutely* against, or without mans will he hath no actuall sin, neither can have any.

The proximate or neerest nature of direct self-murder.

The next, or neerest *specificall nature* of *direct self-murder* consists of *two subordinate branches.*

1. Mans intention.

First, in the immediate *intention* of a man; which is to kill himselfe, and doth conclude the joynt *act* therein both of his *judgement* and *will*; because such an *intention* is grounded upon, and proceeds from advisement and deliberation, and doth also respect the *fact* that he minds to doe, *sub ratione finis*; *under consideration of an end*; and so, in his judgement, *good*: and *therefore* it includes his will, desiring and endeavouring that it may be done; and so to him such a fact falls not out by *accident*, or unexpected, or not intended; but it is the thing he aymes at.

2. The bodies imployment.

The second branch of the neerest *specificall nature* of *direct self murder* is, the *actuall* imployment of the body and the strength thereof, upon direction of the *understanding*, and command of the *will*, fully to accomplish his intention, and effect the killing of a mans *selfe* by his owne hands, or meanes, whereby it is perfected and consummated, with self-perdition, in a wicked conspiracy of self-destruction, by *soul* and *body* against themselves. Wherein is to be *observed* and condemned both the wretched abuse of the *authority* and power of mans *understanding* and *will*, directing and commanding the inferiour faculties and body to doe that which tends directly to destruction both of their parts, and whole: *and also* we may see herein a patterne of unwarrantable *obedience*, in the bodies yeelding to doe that which is unlawfull, and ruinates it selfe; the *superiority* of the understanding

Observe Abuse of power, and of obedience.

derstanding and will frees not the body from blame; for then why should it suffer with the soule for that *act?* But the sin is the greater, by how much the further it extends to involve partizans, or *accessaries*, and makes many guilty of the same crime; who are to be condemned, not only for the *fact* done by them, but also for violating the rights and duties of their places, in *unlawfully* commanding, and obeying in that which is *evill*, contrary to an *higher* rule.

§. 2. *Of the imaginary good conceited to bee in self-murder.*

It may be *objected*, that for a man *advisedly*, *wittingly*, and *willingly* to propound to himselfe, and to ayme at that for his *end*, that is his destruction, is against nature; *because* the *end* is, or ought ever to be the *perfection* of the thing that desires it, and endeavours to have it; and *good* only is desirable, and to be sought after; which may content us in the enjoying thereof: and *therefore*, the *conclusion* may seeme to be good, that no man can *advisedly*, *wittingly*, and *willingly* purpose and endeavour to kill himselfe. *Object.* Evill cannot be an end.

Whereunto may be answered; although *death* bee the immediate *end* intended, and sought in *direct self-murder*; yet it is not the *ultimate*, or last *end*; *neither*, is it sought for at any time for it selfe, but *accidentally*, and for another thing, which is good; for obtaining whereof, a *self-murderer* would use that as a *meanes*. As *Physick* is immediately desired and taken, not for it selfe; but for health thereby, which is the patients *ultimate end* in taking of medicines: & *therefore*, one sayes, *Mors ut malum non est optabilis, nec optatur per se, sed gratiâ alteri⁹: Death, as it is an evill thing, is not desirable; neither is it of it selfe desired, but in respect of some other thing; and so is desired per consequutionem, & non per se; by consequution, and* *Answ.* Death is not the ultimate end. *Comparison.*

not of it ſelfe; *for*, death is never deſired by a *naturall appetite*, as oppoſite to that appetite or deſire that followes reaſon, either right or depraved: *becauſe nature* is *materiatum quid*, *ſome materiated thing belonging to the perſon*, in reſpect both of *matter* and *forme*, ſoule and body, ſo long as they are united; and *therefore* ever deſires the good and preſervation of the perſon, in that union.

The imaginary good of ſelf-murder.

The good ultimately intended, and conceited to bee obtained by *ſelf-murder*, is *twofold*.

1. Freedome from evill.

Firſt, *freedome* from greater *evill felt*, or *feared*; *reall*, or but *imaginary*; which in a *ſelf-murderers* opinion is no other way avoidable: and they *deſpaire* to be able to beare it; (meaſuring themſelves by themſelves) ſo as if they cannot ſhake off the yoke, then will they violently diſſolve themſelves.

Cauſes.

1. Conceited badneſſe of eſtate.

The true *cauſes* hereof, are *firſt*, the *ſelf-murderers* conceit, that his preſent, or feared *condition* is worſe than any other that can betide him; or that he can ſhift into by death.

2. Want of meanes.

Secondly, his *want* of having, or foreſeeing *meanes* of prevention, or deliverance from the evils that he deſpaires to be able to beare; cauſes him to fall upon this wicked damnable courſe of ridding himſelfe from them.

3. Impatience.

Thirdly, diſobedient *impatiency*, that will not let a man in all things ſubmit to bee ordered by *God*; and an evill heart of *unbeliefe*, that hinders him from truſting and depending upon *God*, for ſupportation and deliverance.

Note.

1. By meanes of his reaſon man ſuffers.

Man, by meanes of his underſtanding and reaſon, is ſubject to many more miſeries and troubles, than any *brüite beaſts*; becauſe he *fancies* many imaginary calamities to himſelfe, from poſſibilities in reaſon, that doe as much ſometimes affect and trouble the minde, as if they were reall, although they never be inflicted.

And preſent troubles men doe aggravate in their

eſteeme

esteeme and opinion, for measure and extent, beyond that which they are in truth and sense, so making them needlesly the more importable.

And troubles, future and past, man, by his *imagination*, makes present, by helpe of his *memory* and *feare*, overcharging himselfe with the burden of more, than ever *God* did lay upon him at once. 2. By meanes of memory.

And finally, in his minde he is capable, by meanes of reason, of manifold *spirituall* afflictions, farre exceeding those that are upon the body, and whereof no *irrationall* creature is capable. Spirituall afflictions.

And yet, of all these *troubles*, the greatest part is *imaginary*, of mans owne needlesse, and voluntary contracting, by meanes of his abused *reason*, and doe worke most *reall* and *desperate effects*, even to *self-murder*. Imagination.

Although that *self-murder* be no fit, or appropriated meanes to preserve, or deliver a man from misery, or troubles, yet, a *self-murderer* doth use it; deeming, according to the *Philosophers, that a lesser evill, compared with a worse, obtaines the place of good*; and is to be desired for good [a], which is onely to be understood of the evill of *punishment*, and not of the evill of *sin*: for, for to avoid all punishment we are to doe no sin; which to doe, were a greater *punishment*, and would draw punishment more abundantly upon the doers of the same: in evils of sinne there is no choise, or lawfull *election*, where all is forbidden.

[a] Arist. *ad* Nicom. lib.5.c.6. Picol.grad.pol. *Minus malum comparatū cum deteriore obtinet locū boni, & pro bono optabile est.*

The second imaginary *good*, conceited to be had by *self-murder*, is the *advancement* of a mans selfe thereby to more *good*, or to a better *estate* than he hath at present; either to an *estate* really better, as to absolute *good* in heavenly happinesse; or to fancied, or comparative *good*, in comparison of greater evill, in the *self-murderers* apprehension, that he may be in an estate lesse miserable, (as he thinks) than that is which he feeles or feares: which in that respect he esteemes to be better than the present. 2. Advancement to good.

In these regards *self-murderers* are willing to exchange their lives by death; but of evill properly there comes no good. For, men gather not *grapes* of *thornes*, neither will any expect it, that is not spiritually mad.

Oh miserable state of life that is more tedious to a man than death!

A blessing may become a judgment.

Thus the greatest earthly blessing may become, in mans sense and opinion, a grievous judgement: *For, God* can make a man a terror to himself, and to all his friends; so that in that respect, he may brooke the name of *Magor Missabib*, as did *Pashur, Ier.* 20. 3,4. when a man leaves God, or is left of him, who is the blessed *object* and fountaine of all true contentment and solid comfort.

Observe. The misery of the damned in hell.

Whereby, wee may see in part the miserable state of the *damned* in *hell*, whose living there is a *second death*, farre exceeding the first in misery; there is a death of *dissolution*, and a death of *torment*; the *former* brings the *subject* to an end, the *latter* brings the *subject* of it to all miseries: they that are in this *latter* shall wish for the former, and shall not finde it; whereby we may in some sort see *two* things:

1. For measure.

First, the *measure* of hells misery upon a man in it; being even as if a man, in his perfect strength and senses, were struggling, and in the very pinch, and agonie of the last and fiercest *act* of death, labouring under the unspeakeable horror, and unsupportable, and untolerable paine of it, and in *kinde* and *degree* much more; as a man, in that death of *hell*, shall bee made more capable, and spiritually sensible of misery, than he is here; and whereas, here a man can die but by one mortall paine, there shall the damned be under all paines and mortall miseries in their extremities, to the utmost measure and degree, that those damned *wretches* are capable of, with exact spirituall sense and feeling of the same; besides their woe, for want of that infinite happinesse in heaven, whereof they are deprived.

Secondly,

Secondly, wee may see here, the *everlastingnesse* and endlesse continuance of that death in *hell*, which shall be as long as the damned shall have *being*, which shall be ever; that they may be capable of suffering, to the utmost of their capacity; *so* that, their *being* gives neither ease nor comfort; but they shall ever be in the same extremity of death, for evermore; without any relaxation, or abatement; which fills them with utter *desperation*, and unexpressible woe. For, they have all that can make any creature miserable, *viz.* in *hell*, they have both *life* and *death*; *by* their living there, they are capable of, and doe suffer the punishment of *sensible* misery; and by that death, they have punishment of damage, in *deprivation* of all comfortable *good*; and so, whatsoever wee can be, in the absence of *good*, and in presence of *evill*, they have the same.

2. The durance of it.

Note.

§. 3. *Concerning the wills object, and faultinesse.*

That we may further understand how a man can will his owne death, wee are to observe that the *will* never chooses to doe a thing *sub ratione mali*, as it is *evill*; but wills a thing that is either in it selfe *good*, or apparently *such* in our apprehension; *or* else, it chooses a thing that in it selfe is *evill*, but is *comparatively* good, in respect of another *evill*, which in our judgement or sense is greater or worser: *and* so no man chooses *death* for it selfe, but in respect of some conceited *good* imagined to be had by it, and not otherwise: *or*, to have a lesser *evill* for a greater, by that exchange: as *Saul*, who, that hee might escape the *mocking* of the heathen, killed himselfe[a]: so that, no man is *absolutely* willing, in the *act* of *selfe-murder*, but *conditionally because*, he uses it not for it self, but as a meanes for a further end and good.

Object of the will is good.

[a] 1 *Sam.*31.4.

Will hath ever good for the *object* of it: but of this *good* there is a *double triplicity: First, bonum animi, corporis*

The kinds of good.

&

& fortunæ : Good of the minde, of the body, and of wealth and preferment. *Secondly*, there is *Bonum utile, jucundum & honestum : Good profitable, pleasant, and honest : Of* these *goods*, the *will* doth not ever respect *bonum honestum*, or *morale, vertuous or morall good*, but often makes choise of *profit*, or *pleasure*, as the greater *good*, before the other : and still *bonum*, or *good*, is the *object* of the *will*.

Note.

From hence it is evident, that the error of the *will* is not all, nor ever from the mis-information of the *judgement*, but that the *will* is in it selfe very *faulty*, in *three respects*.

Wils faultines.
1.
It obeyes not the sound understanding.

First, in that it doth not ever listen unto, nor obey the true and good directions of the *understanding*, but rejects them, or inclines against them, according to that old saying, *Video meliora proboq́, Deteriora sequor : I see and approve better things, but follow the worser*, the bounds of the understanding and will are not of equall extent.

2.
It submits to the affections.

Secondly, the fault of the *will* is, that it submits it selfe to receive information, and direction from the *affections, passions*, and *senses*, following the same without *reasons* precedent triall and approbation, whereby it inverts the course of nature, rebells against its Soveraigne, and subjects its selfe to her servants, and labours so to enthrall the *understanding* to the same.

3.
Corrupted by innated pravity.

Thridly, *will* is corrupted by *innated pravity*, whereby it is more inclinable to erroneous directions, than to true ; *readier* to move to vice, than to vertue ; and by meanes of that pravity, either inbred in it selfe, or *acquired*, by impressions from inferiour faculties and senses, it labours to deceive and corrupt the *minde* and *understanding*, that the same may determine and give direction according to *wills* owne disposition; whereby it comes to passe, that the *will* ever followes the last determination of the *practicall understanding*, and yet is not, therefore, blamelesse; *For*, sinne is *vitium suppositi*, *the*

the vice of the person; and *therefore*, is in all the parts and faculties of the same, especially in the *will*, which is the *primus motor*, the *first mover in all practicall actions*, which are sinfull, but as they are voluntary.

The motions of mans *will* are very diverse, and often contrary. *For*, although *will* in man is answerable to instinct in *irrationall creatures*; and to *naturall* inclinations in *insensibles*; yet it moves much more variously, *both*, as man is compounded of many more various things; whereof every one conferres to his motion *naturall* and morall; according to its *nature*: and *also*, as *man*, and his *will* is *passively* affected, and wrought upon, by *motives* within and without, *and* as his *reason* directs, and perswades variously, according to occasions, *whereupon* it followes, that *man* is the most *uncertaine*, and unstable creature in the world, most restlesse, and tossed, as the *Sea*, with tempests and stormes in his will, distracting him in his resolutions, and performances: *una eurusque notusque ruunt, creberque procellis Affricus*, as the East, the South, and West windes of contrary thoughts, making their incursions at once upon him, *whereby*, he is sometime driven, and cast away upon the deadly rock of *direct self-murder*, with the furious impetuosity of his owne self-perverted judgement, will, and affections.

Will variable.

Note.

§. 4. *Observations from the knowledge of direct self-murder.*

The uses of this knowledge of *direct bodily-self-murder*, what it is; are specially *three*. *Vses.* 1.

First, it serves to *informe* our understanding, in *two* points. Information of judgement.

1. *First*, touching the execrable horriblenesse of the fact of this *self-murder*: which is seene in *three degrees*. Horriblenesse of self-murder. Degrees of it.

First, in that it is an *unjust* taking away of the life of

1.

a man, contrary to Gods Commandement, *Gen.* 9.5. and to the sixt Commandement of the *Law*, which makes it to be murder.

2. *Secondly*, in that it is the so taking away of a mans *owne life*, which is most neere and deare to him, which makes the fact to be *self-murder*, and is directly opposite to the Law of *nature*.

3. *Thirdly*, in that it is a fact done by a mans selfe upon himselfe, *advisedly*, *wittingly* and *willingly*, which makes it to be *direct self-murder*, intended to the highest degree of that kinde; being complicated with, and compounded of many pernicious *ingredients*, raising it to the highest pitch of poysonfull disposition: *which* both aggravates the sinne of *self-murder*, to a transcendency of wretched badnesse; and also shewes the horrible malice and cunning of *Satan*, that was a murderer from the *beginning* [a], in indeavouring mans destruction by mans selfe, in such a damnable manner and degree of sinning, as the *devill* himselfe, without mans owne help, cannot possibly effect, both to the destruction of Gods *Image* in him, and also to the certaine damnation of the *self-murderers* soule, which by that fact, the *devill* labours to gaine to himselfe, to make man partner with him in his torments; and out of malice against *God*, to disgrace and deface his *Image*.

The greatnesse of self-murder.

[a] Ioh.8.44.

2. Mans perversnesse.

The second point, wherein the former doctrine serves to informe our understanding, is concerning the *perversnesse* of the nature of man, and the excessive exorbitancy of his courses; whereby he is subject, and breakes out to kill himselfe; which practise of *self-murder* all other creatures doe abhorre, by the instinct of *nature*: *and* so we see, that the most *noble* creatures are obnoxious and subject to commit the greatest errors, by their abuse of their most eminent parts; whereby they doe abase and deject themselves into a miserable estate, as farre beneath other creatures, by violating the *Law* of *nature*, as ever

God

God had advanced them above them; as is apparent, by the fall of the *devils*: for, the grievousnesse of sin is to be measured, not onely by the *matter*, and *act* of it, *but* also, by the *quality* of the *doers* of it, and by the *circumstances* of doing thereof.

The second use is, to *admonish* us, that we are not onely to be carefull, how we behave our selves, in things concerning *God*, and our *neighbours*; *but also how we behave our selves towards our selves, and in our owne affaires and goods: because*, our *love* to our *selves*, is the *rule* of our *love* to our neighbours; *whom we are to love, as our selves* [a], *and to whom wee are to doe, as we would be done to by them* [b]: and therefore, it behooves the *rule* to bee straight; otherwise, all things measured by it must be crooked: and so from him that carelesly failes towards himselfe, no right performances can be done by him to any other: *qui sibi nequam, cui bonus? to whom can he be good, that is nought to himselfe?* — *Vse 2. How to behave our selves to our selves.* — [a] *Levit.19.18.* [b] *Mat.7.12.*

And therefore, seeing wee often prove our owne greatest enemies, and doe as much evill to our selves, as the *devill* himselfe can desire, and more than he by himselfe, or by any other meanes, is able to effect, or bring to passe upon us; it is requisite and needfull that wee bee affraid of our *selves*, and that we neither trust our selves, nor trust to our selves; but that we be carefull, and doe watch over our selves, neither giving way to our owne opinions, nor purposes, before wee doe examine them, and finde them conformable to the truth: all things are to be suspected that come from an *Enemy. Timeo Danaos & dona ferentes*: and a man hath no such dangerous enemie to *himself* as *himself*, because of his neerenesse to himselfe, of his advantages of prevailing against himselfe, and of his deceitfull cunning to beguile himselfe; so exercising all hostilitie and mischiefe upon himself, under pretence and colour of love and friendship to himselfe, he is self-betrayed, and self-destroyed. — *Vse 3. A man is to feare, and watch himself.*

Use 3. To discerne things that differ.

The third use of the former doctrine of *self-murder* is, that thereby wee may *discriminate*, and know diverse cases that are very like this *self-murder*, and yet properly are not *direct self-murder*; nor the *doers* thereof thereby perishing, *self-murderers:* the which exempt cases are of *foure sorts.*

Exempt cases.

§. 5. *Of certaine exempt cases.*

1. Men without reason, are not self-murderers.

The first is, when a man, destitute of *understanding*, or of the *use* of *reason*, kills himselfe, as a *child* without discretion, a naturall *foole*, a mad man in his mad fits, one in his sleepe; *or* in such fits or sicknesse as is accompanied with a *delirium* or phrensey, as, in a *calenture*; the same is not in them properly *self-murder : because*, understanding in them is *deficient*, or *passively* depraved, and not *actively* and wilfully done by themselves: *so* that they cannot judge *morally*, nor sometimes naturally, of their owne actions; *neither* are able rightly to direct them, in a *state* of that impotency of understanding: *neither* is such an *act* in such persons to be deemed willing, or an *act* of the *will*, so long as reason is wanting, without which it is not possible for a mans *will rationally* to move.

Reasons why.

And therefore, in such prancks, and mad acts, the *will* whereby they are done, is but *brutus impetus*, *a brute motion or violence*, which motion is not from the understanding so much, as from accidents, making a man not to be himselfe: *and* such a man in doing such an *act*, whereby he kills himselfe, intends not the same upon knowledge, to the end to kill himselfe; *and therefore*, neither in the *Courts* of earth, nor heaven, are such persons condemned as *self murderers*, for killing themselves, because, they are not properly so much *agents*, as *sufferers*; both in the *act* doing; and also in the *effect*, or death thereupon ensuing.

The

The second exempt case herein is, when a man kills himselfe *ignorantly*, not knowing what he doth; *or* not knowing the mortall *nature* of the meanes, whereby he doth it. *As* he that eates *poyson*, the nature whereof he knowes not; *or* when a man doth kill himselfe out of a rash precipitancy, and sudden unpremeditate pang, and fit of forcible *passion*, or temptation, tempestuously raised by others; making violent impressions upon him, suppressing *reason*, and captivating the *will* to doe that, which otherwise hee abhorres; *and* for which, in the *Court* of *heaven*, he is not properly a *direct self murderer*; because such a *fact* before *God*, is but a kinde of *chance-medly*; when it proceeds not out of advised judgement and will; but that the doer thereof is therein *quoad principium motus, for the originall of his motion* in that *act*, more *passive* than *active*; as a *Ship* that may be overset in a storme, and as persons *possessed* by uncleane *spirits*; that by their meanes did cast themselves into the *fire*, and *water* [a]; wherein, if they had perished, they had not beene *self-murderers*, when they were not in their owne power; nor was it an *act* of their owne *free judgement* and *will*.

Case 2. About self-killing ignorantly

Comparison.

[a] *Marke* 9.22.

The third case is, when a man kills himselfe by *mischance*, or *misadventure*, in his doing of an *act* of *lawfull* imployment, without any intent to take away his owne life. *As* a man in his attempt to save another out of the fire, or water, is by his act drowned, or burnt to death himselfe; *or* if a man be killed by the breaking of a peece of his owne shooting off at another marke, or the like: *This* is an *act* of *God* in his speciall *providence*, taking away the life of a man, *Exod.* 21.13. and is not an act of *self-murder*; *because* the *actors* end and intention is not to kill himselfe, but to doe a lawfull duty; neither doth that act of his, in regard of that mortall effect of it, proceed from his judgement and will, but to him is meerely *casuall*, and contrary to his expectation and desire; and so in that

Case 3. Killing by mischance.

respect he is meerely *passive*, and so *formaliter*, and in truth not a *self-murderer*.

Case 4.

Self-killing in discharge of ones calling.

The fourth exempt case is, when a man in discharge of his *calling*, doth wittingly, and willingly such an act, whereby hee knowes hee must die; as did *Samson*, of whom *Augustine* sayes, that *Spiritus latenter hoc jusserat, the spirit did secretly command it*; in this case such an one is not a *direct self-murderer*; *because* hee intends not primarily his owne death, but the discharge of his necessary *duty*, otherwise not feasable. *And* this *death* is not from an act of his owne meere *judgement* and will, but from *Gods*; in obedience whereunto he layes downe his life.

Case 5.

About phrenticks.

The *fift exempt case* is, of *phrentick persons*, of whom when it shall happen any to kill himselfe in his fit of *phrensie*, he cannot *justly* be said to be a *direct self-murderer*; (nor yet an indirect self-murderer, where his *phrensie* is not contracted by his own fault) because of his defect of the use of his understanding in his *act* of *self-killing*, whereof then he knowes not the *morall* nature, neither properly can he be said to be a voluntary *agent* therein; because then he hath not a *will determined* by any *act* of the *practicall understanding*; but doth it only by a *bruit passion*, or unreasonable internall *impulsion*, equivalent to *inforcement*, from *negation*, or their faultlesse defect of power of sufficient opposition: which is evident by that which they are habitually to the contrary, manifested when they have any *Lucide intervalls*; or when they were, or are in their sound mindes, alwayes abhorring such a fact. *Of this see more*, *Cap.* 15. §. 22. and *Cap.* 18. §. 2.

CHAP.

Chap. 13.

Of direct self-murderers.

§. 1. *Practise and habit gives denomination.*

A *Self-murderer* hath *denomination* from his fact of *self-murder*; whereby it staines him with an ill and odious *name*: *although* a man properly is not to be named from one single *act*, but from an *habituall* disposition, and continued *practise*; yet here one *act* gives the *name*, *because* it proceeds from that which is in a man by way of *habit*; and is an *act* that in regard of the extinguishment of its subject, can be done but once by one body; *but* if they should live againe in the same state, *yet* upon the same motives and disposition would againe and againe doe the same; as we see by the practise of those that after restraint, or disappointment of effecting their purpose therein, doe not cease still to attempt the same untill it be done, and therefore such a fact is equivalent to a constant practise: *if* any body be impatient and ashamed of the imputation of the name of any notorious *vice*, then should he be most carefull to avoide the thing, in respect whereof, the same is due unto him: *He* that hath the *principall* must have the *appurtenances*, the name of any crime must goe with the thing to which it belongs; the odious repute of the name shewes the vilenesse of the vice, which is farre more to be abhorred than the *nickname* of, or from it. *But*, men are commonly like witlesse *children*, more affraid of shadowes than substance; as children are gastered with mentioning of *Goblins* and *bugbeares*; so many men are startled with the disgracefull

One act of self-murder gives denomination to those that do it, and why.

Observe

Comparison.

disgracefull names of vice imputed unto them, who are not at all affraid of the vices which they entertaine, and for which the names of the same are due to them, who doe deserve to brooke the name of the *master* whom they serve, and of the *trade* which they practise. Why should any man serve such a *master*, or exercise such a *trade* whereof he is ashamed, and would not brooke their names?

§. 2. *How it is by Scripture apparent that many men doe murder themselves.*

That some men doe murder themselves is apparent.

That many do *murder* and destroy themselves by their acting of that horrible unnaturall fact and sin upon their owne bodies, is apparent *three* wayes.

1. By the Scriptures.

First, by the *Scriptures* of the *old* and *new Testament*; in the old *Testament* we reade of *Saul*, and of his *armour-bearer*, that they killed themselves. 1 *Sam.* 31. Of *Abimelech* that did the same by his owne command. *Iudges* 9. 54. Also of *Abitophel*, that he hanged himselfe. 2 *Sam.* 17. 23. Of *Zimri*, that hee burnt himselfe to death. 1 *King.* 16. 18.

In the *new Testament* we reade of *Iudas*, that, though he were one of *Christs disciples*, hanged himselfe. *Mat.* 27. 5.

Which intimates,

That the *Scripture* witnesseth so much, it intimates to us *three* things.

1. The certainty of such facts.

First, it evidences to us the *certainty* of such facts; *because* the *Scripture* is infallibly true, aswell in matter of *history* as of *doctrine*: *It* records them not for imitation, but for condemnation: *which* is plaine, if wee consider how ungratious the persons were that did it; *the* manner of the *Scriptures* propounding, and relating of the same, with dislike of it; *and* the doctrine elsewhere in Gods *word*, and sound reason condemning of it.

2.

Secondly, the *Scriptures* recording of such facts, shews the

the *antiquity* of this vile sin; which doth not justifie, but demonstrate the inveterate maliciousnesse of it, rooted and strengthened by age; whose continuation from age to age brings forth every yeare new crops. The antiquity of self-murder.

Thirdly, it manifests that even this horrible sinne hath fallen out, and still doth fall out in the *Church* of *God*, among the visible members thereof, and by *professors* of the truth. 3. It falls out in the Church.

Which points out unto us, that what sins soever fall out elsewhere, may, and doe fall out sometimes within the *visible Church*.[a] *Observe.* [a] 1 *Cor.* 10.13.

It is not therefore to be said, that the *doctrine*, or *profession* of the truth is the cause of the same, or of any such horrible facts breaking out in the *Church*, where the *Gospell* is professed and practised: neither is the *Word*, nor *Gods worship*, nor true *Professors* to be upbraided, nor condemned for such things, as are not by them caused, nor approved; but are condemned, reproved, and punished. The truth is blamelesse.

The causes why such horrible *facts* fall out sometimes in the *Church*, among professors; are *two*. Horible crimes fall out in the Church. *Causes.*

First, the raging malice of the *devill*, specially against the *Church*, and *Professors* of the truth; whereby he endeavours *two* things: *First*, to scandalize and disgrace the truth, that so he may keep off others from embraceing of it, incense them against it, and harden them in their owne wicked self-pleasing wayes. *Woe to the world because of offences*.[b] 1. The devills malice. 1. To scandall the truth. [b] *Mat.* 18.7.

Secondly, hee endeavours thereby to blemish the *Church*, and to disturbe the comfort and growth of godly *professors*, and to sift and try them to fall; that by such reproachfull crimes *God* may be dishonoured. 2. To blemish the Church.

The second cause of those notorious facts within the *Church*, is the *rage of mans corruption*, when it prevailes, and gets head and vent against the damme and opposition of grace and truth, restraining and mortifying of it; 2. Rage of mans corruption upon opposition.

 which

which then is irritated and rages the more furiously, when it gets advantage, and breakes out; as *waters* fed with continuall springs, when they overswell the banks that shut them up, doe impetuously and unresistably beare all downe before them, where they breake out.

Comparison.

Sinfull and grosse wicked *facts* breaking out in the *Church*, and among *professors* of *religion*, are more scandalous, and more condemned, because they reproach religion, and subject the truth to blasphemy.

Why grosse sins are most offensive in professors.

§. 3. *Self-murderers are apparent by history.*

The second way whereby it is seene that divers *persons* doe *murder* themselves, is *humane histories*, both *Heathen* and *Christian*, *Civill*, and *Ecclesiasticall*, which are full of such wofull examples: as *Livie* tells us of *Lucretia*; others of *Cleopatra*, *Cato Vticensis*, *Empedocles*, *Cleombrotus*, *Ostorius*, *Pomponius Atticus*, *Tullius Marcellinus*, *Cleanthes*, *Dido*, and many others; and *Baldwin* reports, that *Inter Turcas Barbarasq; gentes Indiæ sunt qui se in gratiam suorum dominorum à muris aut turribus præcipitant, in signum summæ submissionis & observantiæ: Among the Turkes and barbarous nations of the Indies, there are some that in favour of their masters, doe throw themselves headlong from walls and towers, in signe of the highest submission and respect.*

The second way of discovery of self-murderers. Histories. 1. Heathen.

But, it may seem very strange that *Heathens*, in whom nature was so prevalent with humane *reason*, should kill themselves, having so little hope of a better life, and all their comfort bounded within this present world.

Heathens did murder themselves.

That they did it is apparent, whereof *three reasons* may be assigned.

Reasons.

First, their want of *grace* and faith in *Christ* to comfort and content their mindes, and to strengthen and enable them patiently to suffer adversities; *and* their *want* of *wills* to be in every state and thing obedient to *God*; who

1. Want of grace in Christ.

who leaving them to themselves, they sunke under the power of their owne temptations. So wretched is mans state out of *Christ*.

Secondly, many *Heathens* killed themselves out of an affectation of *honour* and *immortality*; *either* by *fame* on earth; *or* by *happinesse* in a better place after death, whereof some of them had an obscure glimpse; to which, they knew no better speedier way, than by this kinde of death; which proceeded from their *ignorance* of a better course, to bring them to what they desired; and from want of foresight of *destruction* in the end of that meanes which they used. So unhappy a thing it is to be without divine direction. 2.

Thirdly, of the *Heathens* that knew no better *good* than what they had in this world, and aymed at no higher end in all their proceedings, than their owne *good*; divers of them being in *calamitous conditions*, without hope of other freedome, and under despaire of ability to endure as was fit; by this course of *self-murder* laboured to free themselves from these evills, after which they looked for no more. This is the wisdome of flesh and blood, of corrupt nature and carnall reason, such as was taught by the *Stoicks*, who were the best morall *Philosophers* among the heathen. 3. Freedome from evills.

Where wee are to *observe*, that it is no wonder that such did fall into such notorious enormities, so long as they thought the same lawfull and fit to bee done; and wanted both that *illumination* in the truth, and also the power of *grace* in *Christ*; which now *God* hath bestowed upon *Christians*. *Observe* They thought self-murder to be lawfull.

But, it is more to bee marvelled at, that *Christians*, who have meanes of more abundant knowledge and grace, should dare willingly to run into the same flagitious and capitall courses of the *Heathen*; being *Christians* in profession, *but heathens* in manners and practise. *Whereas* the consideration of the parties murdering themselves being *Heathens*, should deterre *Christians* from such vile facts, that they may not be worse than *heathens* in their practise, from whom they are so far divided in *profession*.

Self-murdering Christians are heathens.

But Christians that kill themselves upon the same reasons that the *heathen* doe, doe thereby declare, that in this point they have nothing of *Christians*, but the name, and otherwise are *heathens*; and in that respect are justly to be debarred *Christian buriall*.

2. Ecclesiasticall histories.

Wee also finde the like examples in *Ecclesiasticall* and Christian *histories*; as in *Eusebius* his *history, lib*. 8. *cap*. 6. Where he sayes, *Quo tempore famâ est viros & mulieres etiam divina & inexplicabili alacritate suâ sponte in rogum insiluisse: In the which time (of persecution) the same is, that both men and women did of their owne accord leape into the fire, with divine and unutterable cheerefulnesse*: and *Ambrose*, and others, doe note divers *professors* to have done the like; as *Pelagia*, *Apollonia*, and many others.

Ambros. lib. 3. *de virginibus.*

Observe.

Which shewes to us, that as all *mankinde* are sprung from the same roote, and are infected with the same disease; so are we all lyable to commit the same sins, if the *Lord* doe not renew and keepe us. *So* that wee need not so much to think it strange, a member of the *visible Church* kills himselfe; as to admire the gratious goodnesse of *God* in keeping of us, that very many doe not the same, in *regard* both of our owne wicked naturall disposition, and outward temptations; whereby what betydes men, may betyde all men in the same case.

All are sick of the same disease

Observe. To depend upon God.

Here we are to *observe*, that those examples of *self-murder*, recorded within the *Church*, are not registred for imitation, but for *caution*; that all *Christians* may be stirred up the more carefully to cleave to *God*, and thank him for their preservation, even from this horrible act of *self-murder*, whereinto many professing Christianity have fallen.

§. 4. Self-

§. 4. *Self-murderers knowne by experience.*

Thirdly, that many do murder themselves, it is cleare by wofull *experience* in all places and ages; notwithstanding, that they may be terrified frō the same, *both* by the fearefull *examples* of manifold *wreckes* of that kinde; *and also* by the *doctrine* of the truth condemning that vile practise; *besides* manifold other restraints, and ignominious censures of that odious course: against all which, such breakings out doe shew the continued rage and power of *Satan* against *Mankinde*; and manifest mans madnesse and perversenesse still in all places, furiously running upon this most horrible and dismall sinne. *Whereby* men doe most ignominiously shut up the period of their lives, with the losse of their good names, and with the destruction of their soules for ever; depriving their posterity of their estates, and uncomfortably overshadowing them with the shamefull disgrace, and ill example of their execrable fact of *self-murder*.

The third way of discovery of self-murderers. Experience.

Hurt of self-murder.

The uses of this point are specially *two*.

Vses.

First, it serves to teach us to be *observant* of the daily occurrences that fall out from time to time; *that* thereby wee may grow, by *sense* in *experimentall knowledge*, both of facts done, and *also* of the nature and causes of the same; whereby we may be *wise*, not only for to direct our owne course aright; *but* also may be able prudently to advise others, and to give a right estimate of things that fall out, and make a holy use of them. *So* that the longer we live, and the world stands, we should bee the wiser and better, in regard of the helps that we have to know *Gods will*; both by his Word and workes, that we may not be carelesly secure of the most haynous crimes: *but*, without *grace* and *Gods protection*, neither *doctrine*, nor *example* is sufficient to withstand mens impetuous wilfull running upon destruction.

1. To be observant of occurrences.

Note.

The lamentable *spectacles* of manifold executions, for *murders,* and robberies; we may thinke might affright all men from committing the like crimes, which we see it doth not. *So* as the multitude of *Shipwracks* terrifies not men from going to Sea, neither doe *examples* of frequent miscariages, by *self-murder,* prevaile with graceless men, to hinder them from the like *facts;* who doe thereby rather harden themselves to attempt and perpetrate the same.

Comparison.

Self-murderers not deterred from the fact.

Use 2.

Beware of self-muder.

The second use of this point is, to admonish us to *abhorre,* and *beware* of this odious sin of *self-murder,* which runnes through all times, and sorts of people: *although* we may seeme to be out of danger of it, in regard of the present distance and opposition betweene us and it, yet are we not to be over-secure. For, the sins which at first we seeme to loath, afterwards by degrees, through negligence, or venturing upon the causes and occasions thereof, men doe embrace, and commit; as we see by the example of *Hazael,* 2 *Kings* 8. 13.

Motions of self-murder most hardly shaken off.

And of all sinnes, even the *motions,* and setled *purposes* of *self-murder,* are most hardly shaken off; *because* all unnaturall and hideous sins breaking impetuously through the strongest hedges and pales of opposition, and outragiously overflowing the bankes of all resistance, both of *nature* and *grace,* have nothing left of sufficient force to withstand them, but that they rage in that high and transcendent degree without shame or restraint, as they list: the most *grosse* and unnaturall sinnes are ever done by desperately wicked men, with the least remorse of conscience, and with the greatest shamelessenesse and obstinacy of will, and indivertiblenesse of indeavours.

Note.

The use of examples.

Touching the use of the *examples* of *self-murderers, Augustine* sayes well, *Non quærimus utrum factum, sed utrum faciendum. Sana ratio exemplis anteponenda est: We enquire not whether self-murder hath beene done, but whether it ought to have been done. Sound reason is to be preferred before examples.*

CHAP.

CHAP. 14.

Of the usuall means and furtherances of self-murdering.

§. 1. *Of the meanes of self-murdering.*

About the fact of *Self-murder*, we are to consider the *meanes* thereunto used; and the *application*, and *method* thereof, by *self-murderers*. 1. Meanes.

Meanes there are none proper, of lawfull ordination, for to doe *evill*; *because* that, the same ought not at all to be done: *but*, man *either* abuses *good*, *or* devises ill *meanes* of his owne invention, to doe naughtinesse and mischiefe withall. None lawfull for that use.

The *meanes* abused by *self-murderers* to kill themselves, are of *two* sorts. Meanes abused.

First, such as be *destinated* and appropriated by *God* for the good, and preservation of mans life: as, *water*, *fire*, *swords* are, and the like; which a *self-murderer* perverts, to *drowne*, *burne*, *stab himselfe* to death, &c. 1. Good.

The second kinde of *meanes* of *self-murder* be those, that be *evill* and sinfull; in themselves fitter to destroy, than to save; such as, *eating*, and *drinking* of *poyson*; throwing ones selfe over *rocks*, (as did the *Circumcellians*,) or, *out of windowes*; or, from off *high places* and *turrets*, with intent to kill themselves; as the *devill* would have had our *Saviour Christ* to have done [a]; *going unwarrantably into the mouth of destruction*, *with purpose to be slaine*, *commanding others to doe it*; as *Abimelech* did, *Judg*. 9. 54. *hanging* ones selfe, as *Judas*, and *Abitophel* did; *fretting*, *or starving ones selfe purposely to death*, as *Pomponius Atticus* did; *or*, *in mortall sicknesse*, *or wounds*, *rejecting* 2. Evill.

[a] *Mat*. 4. 6.

rejecting the helps of cure by Physick, or other meanes; and disordering ones selfe purposely, that they may thereby die, and the like: so that, for this vile act men are inabled by all the furniture and power of *hell,* and what their owne wit can invent or abuse for that end.

Observ. It is hard to do good: easie to doe evill.

From hence wee may *observe*; *First*, that whereas, when wee are to do *good*, wee are hardly drawne to it, and do excuse our backwardnesse, by pretence of *disability*, and want of *meanes*; and by alledging of *impediments* and letts, as *Moses* did [a]: the *sluggard* pretends that a *Lion* is in the way [b]: *But*, when wee are about to do *evill*, we make no such *objections*, but finde abundance of *helps*, with opportunities, and great frowardnesse, and readinesse to doe the same.

[a] *Exod.*4.10,13.
[b] *Prov.*26.13.

Causes 1. Mans disposition.

The causes hereof are specially *two*; *First, internall*, in mans owne *will*, and *disposition*, far more prone to evill, than to good: where *will* and *inclination* are to a thing, they will find *meanes*.

2. The devill, and evils easinesse.

Secondly, there is an *externall* cause hereof; to witt, the *devill*, who doth powerfully instigate, and help to do mischiefe, according to mens tempers, and the outward occasion: *and* the work of doing *evill* is farre more easie, than of doing *good*; *because* of the *entitie* that is in goodnesse, and the *non entity* that is in evill; *goodnesse* is an *effect* of *power*, and *evill* is more properly an *effect* of *impotency: to* pull downe is more easie than to build up; to erre, than to go aright.

Observe.2. Self-murderers are guilty of abuse of Gods Creatures.

Secondly, we may here *observe*, that he that is a *self-murderer* is guilty, *not* onely of the vile act of *self-murder*, but also of the *abuse* of Gods good creatures, *and* of his owne abilities, in perverting the same to that unnaturall end, contrary to *Gods* ordination, whereby they are, in this respect, *subject to vanity* [c]: *so* that, a *self-murderer*, erects a counterwork of *creation*, and *use* of things against *God*, while he gives *being* to *self-murder*, against both *nature* and *religion*; *so* setting up his owne works

[c] *Rom.*8.20.

works of evill, against Gods that are good; and disposing of *Gods* good *works*, to his owne vile ends, contrary to Gods *will* and ordination: whereby it is apparent, that such wicked *persons* are factiously-rebellious against *God*, and disturbers of the peace and tranquillity of all the *frame* of *nature* and *grace*, contrary to the *Lawes* and *ordinances* of God. *Sinne* is in the world, as pestilentiall humors in the body, which disorder and indanger all where they are. *Note.*

§. 2. *Of the application of the meanes of self-killing.*

For application of the aforesaid *meanes* to the wicked act of *self-murder*; there are *three* things considerable. 2. *Application.*

First, the *self-murderers premeditation*, and determination of the *end*, which is his owne *death* to be effected by himselfe; so setting limits to his owne daies, as if he were his owne absolute *Master*; and that he were so unhappy, that his life were worse than death, which death all other *creatures* do abhorre; *and* that he were so desperate and forlorne, for want of present mercy, or future hope; and that he were so forsaken of *all*, that he can finde none to rid him out of his life and misery, but that he must kill himselfe; *so* hastening himselfe, by a most wofull exchange, into a farre greater misery, by so doing, than ever it was possible for him to suffer in this world, by living, although that therein he should live for ever, under the most exquisite torments, that here he can be capable of. In it 3. things considerable. 1. Predestination and determination of the end.

The second thing considerable, in the *application* of the meanes to the acting of *self-murder*, is the *election* and choise of the particular *meanes* to effect the same: all *self-murderers* do not choose to die, by the same *meanes*; *For*, then the way of so dying would be unvariably one and the same, in them all. 2. Election of meanes.

Wherein a self-murderer observes three things.

In election of meanes to kill himselfe, a *self-murderer* observes specially *three* things.

1. Such as best agree with his temper.

First, he is carefull to make choise of such *meanes*, as do best fit, and agree with his *naturall temper* and *sexe*; *and* are least formidable, and terrible to his *fancie*, or *sense*, in the execution, *such* as are *familiar* to him by daily *use*; *or* such as in his judgement, or sense, are least horrible, or painfull; as *Cleopatra*, that chose to kill her selfe by *Aspes*, making her die sleeping.

2. Such as be readiest.

Secondly, a *self-murderer* makes choise of such *meanes* to kill himselfe, that are *readiest* at hand, and *easiest* for him to have, according to his *sexe*, *calling*, *occasions*, or *imployment*.

3. Most certaine to effect death.

Thirdly, he chooses to use those *meanes*, which, in his opinion, are most *certaine* to effect that end, most easily, speedily, and unperceivedly from the knowledge of others, that he may not be crost of his designe and aime, nor be long in paine.

Observe. 1. It is easie to do evill.

Here we may *observe*, that there is variety, and choise of *meanes*, to doe any one *evill*, or *sinne*: which shewes with what facility and ease we may sinne, and perish; and with what difficulty and hardnesse wee may doe good, and bee saved; which cannot bee done by such multiplicity of meanes, and waies: a *right line* can bee drawne but one way, and the truth is simple, and not manifold.

2. The folly and madnesse of self-murderers.

Secondly, here appeares the folly and madnesse of those, that are so circumspect and carefull about choise of the *meanes*, whereby they would die, and are so regardlesse of the *morall maner* how they die, and of their consequent condition, that will follow upon such a death: every grosse and notorious sin is ever committed with a spice of *madnesse* accompanying the same; *because*, it is done against the *dictat* of sound *reason*, and of true *religion*; and *therefore*, such men are so frequently in the *Proverbs* called *fooles*; in respect not onely of the

Observe.

thing

thing they doe, but also in regard, both of the reasons of their proceedings, and also of the fruit and end of their courses: touching whom it may be said, that they *have sowne the wind, and they shall reap the whirlewinde*, as sayes the *Prophet* [a].

[a] *Hosea* 8.7.

§. 3. *Of the method of self-murderers.*

The method and maner of execution of self-murder.

The *method* and *manner*, that a *self-murderer* observes in execution of *self-murder*, consists in *three branches*.

1. He observes opportunities.

First, he watches and hunts after all *opportunities*; and affects retired *solitarinesse*, that he may without hinderance kill himselfe.

2. Secrecy.

Secondly, hee affects *secrecie*, and expedition to accomplish that vile act; upon performing whereof all his indeavours and power being bent; and being deserted and left of *God*, and his good *Angels*; and the *devill* instigating and helping him; and all *meanes* fitly concurring for that execution, the *self-murderers* successe, and atchievement herein is quick and great, beyond expectation: *except* the Lord be minded here to punish such an one with paine, as well as in the life to come.

3. Obstinacy.

Thirdly, a *self-murderer* is *constant*, or rather *obstinate*, in his resolution and indeavours to kill himselfe, contrary to all good counsell, letts, and impediments objected to hinder him from the same; *in* so much, that if such *self-murderers*, at any time, be crossed of their opportunities, and disappointed in their attempts of killing themselves; *or*, that they be hindered, or do but hurt, and not forthwith kill themselves; they are sorry for their disappointment, and do continue more desperately their resolutions, and indeavours, untill it be done by them: *the medicine* doth here irritate the disease, which is a deplored and desperate case: so that they must perish, if the Lord God do not mercifully step in to pull them, by repentance, out of that fire of destructi-

 on;

on; *or*, by some other over-ruling meanes prevent it, that by living they may be saved.

Observe. It is dangerous to give way to Satan, in this point, wherein he is hardly resisted.

Here wee may learne how dangerous and pernicious a thing it is to give way to *Satan*, or to our owne exorbitant thoughts, in this or in any such ill, or unnaturall motions to sinne; *For*, by entertainment thereof, we are taught from hell to be pregnant, ingenious, industrious, diligent, and obstinately desperate to commit the same; in the meane time, being restlesse untill it be done: the execution, or performance whereof is most hardly prevented, where the doing of it is peremptorily resolved, and all our indeavours set to accomplish it; the reasons hereof are *two*.

Reason 1. Against knowledge and resistance.

First, in regard that it is concluded, and resolved upon, and attempted with the overthrow, or contempt of so great *knowledge*, and *resistance*, naturall and divine; *against* which when such purposes prevaile, there is nothing left to withstand the performing of the same; but that such outragious corruption, having broken over the banks that impaled it, may rage and range, without resistance, as it list.

2. The danger of self-murder not knowne by experience.

Secondly, the performance of *self murder*, resolved upon, is hardly prevented; *because*, the true danger and evill thereof, in the full extent, and latitude thereof, is not knowne by *experience* to the living; *for*, of those that die so by their owne hands, none doe returne to tell tales how it fares with them afterwards: *except* we credit the report of *Virgill*, who affirmes from *Æneas* his observation, in his fained descent into hell, who there did see *self-murderers* in a very low *region*, and miserable *estate*; that would now full gladly indure poverty, and all hard travell, and miseries in this world, so as they might be in it againe, out of their present miseries.

Virgil.

— *Quàm vellent æthere in alto,*
Nunc & pauperiem, & duros perferre labores!

Self-

Self-murder is such an act, as a man can doe but once in all, *because* it concludes and finishes his *life*; so as hee can have no more time either to get *experimentall* knowledge of it, what it is; or yet to be able by repentance, to reforme it; seeing it is not in mans power to quicken, and give himselfe life againe, that hee may use it better than he hath done. *And therefore* in this respect *self-murder* is the most dangerous and worst sinne that a man can commit: *for* after other sinnes, how hainous soever, a man may have time, and meanes of repentance and salvation; *but* after this he can have none.

CHAP. 15.

The self-murderers motives to kill themselues.

§. 1. *Men by abused reason sin worst.*

ALthough that the crime of *self-murder* be naturally most horrible; yet men only of all creatures do venture upon it, and doe it: *the noblest* creatures are subject to commit the foulest errors, as *men* and *Angels*; and of men, the inlightned only can sinne that mortall sin against the *holy Ghost*: *for*, they that are able to doe most good, by perverting of their abilities, are able to doe most mischiefe. *David* in that respect was more affraid of *Abitophel* [a] than of all the rest that were against him.

The noblest creatures faile most.

[a] 2 *Sam*.15.31.

But, that man may doe this horrible fact of *self-murder* more boldly and securely, without being over-ruled by the check of his conscience; he abuses his *reason* to encourage him to doe that, the uglinesse, and unnaturalnesse whereof might otherwise deterre and astonish him from it.

Reason abused

For, all such grosse facts, condemned by the light of *nature*, and apparent *reason*, man doth vaile and maske under specious pretexts, before hee dares venture to enterprise the doing of them in cold blood; and likewise he obscures the contrary vertuous courses, by aspersions of *titles*, and *names* of disgrace; labouring, if it were possible, to make vertue vice, and vice vertue; condemning the generation of the *righteous*, and justifying the *wicked*; turning *hell* into *heaven*, and *heaven* into *hell*: *because* the *majesty* and *glory* of the *truth* is such, that none dares to looke it on the open face, and revile and smite it; but, as they first attire and maske it under the habit and name of vice; as the wicked *Iewes* did first blind-fold our blessed *Saviour*, and then stroke him on the face. [a]

[a] *Luke* 22.64.

So farre doth man abuse his reason, whereby hee excells beasts; that thereby he doth make himselfe worse than the worst of beasts, of whom none will kill themselves in any case.

No reason for self-murder.

For a man to murder himselfe there is no *reason* indeed: *for* although he doth it not but (as hee thinkes) upon good reason; yet, this *reason* of his is neither from the *nature* of that action, as if it were in it selfe a lawfull duty to be done; *nor* yet is it *reason elicite*, or drawn out from inbred *principles* and *motives* in *nature*, or from other light acquired by the truth of *God*: *because* there can be no good *reason* against the *Word* and *Law* of *God*, who is the Lord of *nature*. *For reason* is never repugnant, or contradictory to it selfe; *neither* is any thing opposite to *reason* in any thing, but in unreasonablenesse; *as* nothing is opposite to truth, but error.

And for *nature* in man, it cannot naturally yeeld any reason from it selfe, why it should destroy it selfe, *because* it is monstrous that *one* should be *two*; and that *division* should be in *unity*, and that instead of good, it should attract to it selfe evill.

But all the pretense of *reason* that a *self-murderer* can have

have to kill himselfe, is onely from *externall motives*, which are without a mans selfe; whereupon, and from whence *self-murderers* doe impertinently conclude, and endeavour to kill themselves.

But there is no true *cause* or *reason* why any man should doe evill; no not for the greatest good, should we doe the least sinne: *because* there is no evill so great as is sinne; in respect *both* of the *nature* thereof, whereby it is most contrary to *God*, who is the greatest and chiefest *good*; and *also*, in regard of the *merits* and *effects* thereof; procuring and imbittering all *evill* to those that sin. For of *evill* properly comes nothing but evill; as of nought and nought comes nothing but nought; the effect cannot exceed in goodnesse the nature and vertue of its cause.

No true cause of evill.

§. 2. *Of motives in generall to self-murder, there can be none warrantably sufficient.*

Neither is there indeed any *externall motive* sufficient of it selfe, to induce and perswade a man to kill himself, by any true *reason* that can be in, or from the *motive* to doe such an act, without respect of a *conceit* of *good* ensuing upon the act of *self-murder*, to the *self-murderer*.

Externall motives to self-murder.

But, in regard that these motives worke not upon all to doe that act of *self-murder*; it is from the *disposition*, and *qualities* of the *persons* that are therewith affected, and wrought upon to doe the same, and not properly from the *motives* themselves: for then all men, by the same *motives*, should doe the same act of *self-murder*.

The motives are divers that doe diversly move divers persons to kill themselves: for, all *self-murderers* do not kill themselves upon the same occasions; some are not affected with one *motive*, that are affected with another to doe that fact. *For*, *arguments* are weake, or strong to severall persons, as they are of deep or shallow *judgement*;

Divers.

Arguments how weak and strong.

ment; *or*, as they stand differently affected, and possessed with *prejudices* sutable to their humours, designes, and ends: *Whereby* to *some*, weake *arguments* are strong, and strong are weake; and by *few* are they apprehended according to their due worth; which is the *cause* of much unreconcileable opposition, and division in the world, and of the building of weighty *conclusions* upon weake *premises* and foundations, *and* of indivertible *resolutions* and *practises*, founded more upon passionate wilfulnesse, than upon judicious reasons: *as* we see about the *objects* of bodily sight, the which is represented, and conceived by us to be according to the disposition of the *medium*, or *meane*; and of the *organ* or eye whereby wee see them.

Comparison.

Note.

Which shewes how needfull it is for matter of *reason* and *judgement*, that wee looke upon the same as it is, without all distemperature, and prejudices in our mindes.

§. 3. *Concerning perverted Judgement, by Laws and Custome.*

The first motive to self-murder, is error of judgement.

These external motives of self-murder I will, for *memory*, and *method*, reduce into *eight* rankes.

The first whereof is *errour of judgement*; when men thinke, and beleeve, upon *deceitfull* grounds, that they ought, or may lawfully kill themselves, *either absolutely* when they list; *or* in some *cases*, when they see it requisite in regard of some circumstances.

Grounds of it:

The unsound *grounds* of this perverted judgement are *foure*.

1. Lawes and Customes.

In India.

First, *Lawes* and *Customes* in some places seeming to require and warrant people in some cases to kill themselves. As among the *Heathens* and *Indians*; where by *custome* or *law*, *servants* and *wives*, in testimony of love to their *Masters* and *Husbands*, were wont to cast themselves

ſelves into the fire to bee burnt, with the corps of their dead *maſters* and *husbands* : *but* the true *cauſe* of that *Law* was, to reſtraine the frequent *poyſoning* of maſters and husbands, by their ſervants and wives; *and* that *law* and *cuſtome* was practiſed to avoide ſuſpition, and ignominie that they lived in, if they did not ſo kill themſelves. *Plutarch* reports of the *Virgins* of *Lemnos*, that cuſtomarily they hanged themſelves, upon no other knowne cauſe, but *cuſtome*; and from that vile practiſe could not be reſtrained, untill the ſame was puniſhed by drawing of their bodies naked through the ſtreets, after that they were dead; by *ſenſible ignominie* reforming a bad and odious *cuſtome*. *Alſo* among the *Turkes*, *ſervants* in teſtimony of their *obedience*, at their living maſters command doe throw themſelves over rocks, or into rivers, or the like; as *Baldwin* [a] the *Caſuiſt* reports: but it is moſt like that they doe it to prevent a greater miſery if they ſhould diſobey. *But*, they that did ſo were thought to doe well, and were therefore commended; and the parties themſelves did verily thinke, that either they did but their duties, or that which was beſt for them to doe; which if they did not, then were they evill thought of, and evill intreated.

In Lemnos.

In Turkie.

[a] *Lib.3.cap.4. Caſ.13.circa melancholicos.*

Thus farre doe *law* and *cuſtome* prevaile againſt the light of *nature* among the *Heathen*; becauſe they knew no higher *rule* to examine and try their *lawes* by, and therefore ſubmit to *humane ordinances* abſolutely, bee they good or bad.

The prevailing of lawes and cuſtomes againſt nature.

Cuſtome, which is another *nature*, maketh it familiar, and to ſeeme lawfull, and commendable in the judgement of *ſenſe*, that in the judgement of right *reaſon* is moſt abominable. *Cuſtome* is a *tyrant*, captivating both *judgement* and *practiſe* to her lore; *becauſe*, what by generall practiſe ſeemes to have the approbation of all, is deemed beſt, and moſt reaſonable, for peaceable conformity both in *opinion*, and practiſe; from which to be ſingular, is odious.

The judgement of the learned hath the force of a Law.

That also which in this case obtains the *force* of a *law*, is the *judgement* of the *learned*, & the practise of *persons* in esteem, commended by *posterity* for the same. *As* among the *Philosophers*, the *Stoicks* did in some cases both direct, commend, and practise *self-murder*; which *historians* and *Poëts* magnifie, in their high praises of *Lucretia*, *Cato*, and others for the same. The high esteeme of the *persons* of men of that opinion, and of the *practisers* of that *act*; and ambition of like praises, for the like thing; hath forcibly driven many men, contrary to their owne minde, to cast themselves away, upon this infernall rock.

The error of this ground.

It is contrary to religion and reason.

Note.

The *deceitfulnesse* of this ground is, that it is meerely *humane*, against *divinity*, *and* that more is attributed to it, and built upon it than it can beare. *For*, all *lawes*, *customes*, *opinions*, and *practises* of men are to be regulated and ordered by sound *reason*, according to *Gods word*; and are subordinate to the same, and thereby to be tryed and examined: *So* that no *law*, or *custome*; no *opinions*, or *practise* of any men is to be imbraced, and obeyed; when the same is manifestly impious, or against *Gods Law*, and right *reason*. *As* we see by the practise of the *Apostles*, *Acts* 4. 19. *For that* (in such cases) in conforming to man, we cannot be excused before *God*, for transgressing his *will*. An *inferiour* hath no power over the right of his *superiour*, to dispense therewith.

Observe to examine.

In judgement of discretion therefore, customes, laws, opinions, and practises of men are to be examined by *reason* and *Gods word*. *Try all things*, *follow that which is good*, 1 *Thess*. 5. 21. *because* whatsoever is humane, may be, as it is humane, erroneous; proceeding from men subject to be deceived, and erre.

Caveat against vaine praise.

To conclude this point, I would intreate all men, specially *Scholars*, and men of sublimated brave *spirits*, to beware of the *encomiasticall* discourses of *heathen authors*; either encouraging to *self-murder*, or commending *self-murderers*: that neither the poyson of that opinion,

nor

nor the example of that vile practise, in eminent and famous persons, may insensibly corrupt and seduce us to dare to enterprise the like upon our selves: for, by the praise of *self-murderers*, and by *amorous discourses*, the *heathen writers* have done much hurt in the *Christian Church*; besides the example and dregges of their Idolatry, from which the *Christian* world is not yet well purged: but among us, where there is no *law*, nor approved *custome*, *doctrine*, nor *practise* of *self-murdering*; we are not in like danger, as *heathens*, to erre in our judgements upon this ground; seeing wee have sufficient meanes of knowledge, and restraint to the contrary. *Observe.*

§. 4. *Of misunderstood Scripture perverting the Iudgement; and the remedy thereof.*

The second ground of a deceived *judgement* in this point, is *misunderstanding* of the *Scriptures*. As our *Saviour* told the *Sadduces*, *That they did erre not knowing the Scriptures.* [a]

The second ground of errors in judgements is misunderstood Scripture.

[a] *Mat.22.29.*

Whereof wee have *Origen* for an example; who gelt himselfe upon his misconceiving the speech of our *Saviour*, saying, *There be Eunuches which have made themselves Eunuchs for the kingdom of heavēs sake, Mat.*19.12.

Martinius [b] *Professor* at *Breme* in *Germany*, tells of those that he cals *Patriciani*, (who held that the substance of mans flesh was made not by *God*, but by the *devill*,) that they held it lawful to kil thēselves, to be rid of their *bodies*; from which they supposed that all sin did come.

[b] *Christiana pietas, lib.2. de homicidio.*

Baldwin [c] the *Casuist* speakes of a certaine *Hermit*, that threw himselfe into a well, to drowne himselfe, out of the abundance of his devotion that he had to mortifie himselfe; upon the mistake of the meaning of *Col.*3.5. in like manner did *Baals priests*, in the heat of their devotion, cut themselves. 1 *Kings* 18.

[c] *Cas.lib.3.c.4. Cas.13.circa melancholicos.*

The *Circumcellions* among the *Donatists* did count it

Gloriæ sibi putabant, si seipsos ex petris precipitarent; in igne n conjicerent, vel alia ratione neci traderent.

an honour to them, if they did throw down themselves off rocks, cast themselves into the fire, or by any other meanes kill themselves.

Augustine speaking of them in his booke of *heresies*, written to *Quod-vult-Deus*; sayes, that in a mad cruelty they did not spare themselves; for they used to kill themselves by divers kindes of deathes; chiefly by water, fire, and throwing themselves downe headlong from high places [a]: their grounds of so doing were abused *Scripture*. Such as, that *the flesh is to be mortified*; and *he that hates his life shall finde it*.

Augustine sayes, that *there were specially two vile and usuall deaths of them who doe kill themselves; the halter, and steep headlong places: Self-murder both Iudas and the Donatists have learned from the same master. Iudas to doe it by the halter; the Donatists by steep headlong places.* [b]

[a] *Non sibi insana feritate parcẽdo; nam per mortes varias, maximè præcipitiorum & aquarum, & ignium seipsos necare consueverũt.*

[b] *Duæ sunt maximè viles atq; usitatæ mortes eorum qui seipsos interimunt; laqueus & præcipitium; spontaneas mortes ab uno magistro utriq; didicerunt; Judas laqueum, Donatistæ precipitium.*

Causes of mis-understanding Scripture.

The causes, or *meanes* of mis-understanding the *Scripture*, are specially *three*.

1. False teachers, and undiscreete

First, *false teachers*, who under pretence of their *learning* and *authority*, seduce and beguile the simple, by specious pretexts, obtruding error for truth, or intermingling falsehood with verity, *or* obscuring or corrupting the truth from the simplicity thereof. *And* also, *undiscreet teachers* are a meanes to men of mis-understanding the *Scriptures*, by their neglect, or transgressing the true *genuine* scope and meaning of their *texts*, in their preaching, *diffused* into the latitude of common places, multiplyed according to the number of the words.

Metamorphosed preaching.

And likewise, those *teachers* that expresse the *truth* in *termes*, and *phrases* proper to *heretickes*, or *schismaticks*, (teaching things wherein we differ from them in sense and meaning) doe not only make themselves to be suspected

ſuſpected of error; *but* alſo they open a way for entertainment of errors from others. *And* alſo they that do *diſguiſe* the ancient *truth*, into new fangled *habit* of *method* and *expreſſions*; (whereby, it may ſeeme to be ſome other more tranſcendent thing, than it is, and do with curioſity, dangerouſly mince and marre the truth, contrary to that which is warrantably revealed, whereby the way to peace is rather loſt than found:) they unſetle men from their former faith about the truth, and incline them to embrace erroneous innovations, about opinions, whereby their judgments are miſ-informed, or made doubtfull what to hold, or ſtick to, being ſhaken by this courſe; which is ſutable to the *practiſe* of ſome ore-curious *Schoolmen*, who did degenerate from the plaine ſimplicity of the *Fathers*, in handling and publiſhing of the *truth*, which thoſe *Sophiſters* corrupted and perverted, by ſuch foraine *Philoſophicall termes* and perplexed *diſtinctions*, and *method*, as both obſcured and did weare out of uſe, and reſpect, the plaine ancient *truth*; and alſo, laid grounds, and gave occaſions for, and raiſed manifold *errors*, which filled the *Church* with *contention*, *ſchiſmes* and *hereſies*, which overthrew *peace*, *ſincerity*, and the *power* of *godlineſſe*. The Schoolmen.

Secondly, wee are often deceived by the weakeneſſe of our owne *intellectuals*, and ſhallow capacities, *as* were the *Capernaits* about eating of *Chriſts* body [a]: when we limit and interpret the *Scriptures*, according to our reaſon and ſenſe, and not by themſelves, as wee ought; with the helpe of the meanes in the Church, that God hath given us. 2. Shallow capacities. [a] *Iohn* 6.52.

Thirdly, our miſunderſtanding of the *Scripture* proceeds from the ſtrength of our headſtrong *affections*, ſelf-willed *reſolutions*, and from our *ambition* after vaine glory; whereby wee wring and wreſt the ſenſe and meaning of the *Scriptures*, to make them favour, and ſpeake what we fancie and hold: *So* not taking the *ſenſe* 3. Headſtrong affections.

 contained

contained in the *Scripture*; but imposing our *sense* upon the Scripture, as best pleases us, to maintaine our owne opinions, or to purchase the vaine glory of extraordinary learning among shallow braind or prejudicate persons, whom nothing pleases, but that which is strange, or new, or suits and agrees with their humours and ends.

Note.

The higher that this *ground* of error of judgement is, the more obstinate are the *resolutions* that are built upon the same: *Because*, such *conclusions* are, to the deceived, matters of conscience, founded (as they think) upon divine *authority*; farre above the countermand of any humane reason, or argument and testimony of truth; dissenting from their tenets and opinions.

Observe. Abused Scripture harmefull. [a] *Rom.* 1.16.

From hence we may *observe*, that, although *God* hath graciously given us his holy *Scriptures*, to be the powerfull meanes of *life* [a], yet many men do abuse, and make the same the meanes of their owne destruction; as *Peter* speakes of the unlearned and unstable, *who did wrest the Epistles* of *Paul*, *as they did also the other Scriptures, unto their owne destruction* [b]: *and* so the Commandement that was ordained to life, is found to bee unto death to them, *Rom.* 7. 10. as the *Gospell*, *that is the savour of life to life to those that are saved*, *is the savour of death to death to those that perish* [c]. Nothing doth so much hurt, when it is abused, as that which may do most good, when it is rightly used.

[b] 2 *Pet.* 3. 16.

[c] 2 *Cor.* 2. 16.

There is no *heresie*, or *practise*, or *opinion* so vile in the *Christian* world, that pretends not, and abuses not *Scripture*, or something in it, or from it, in defence or excuse of the same; *and*, upon that ground chiefly, prevailes upon mens consciences, and holds them captivated in their errors, and ill courses: and so men do turne the sweetest *Manna* into the bitterest *gall* of *Aspes*, to their owne perdition. *As* a man by managing a sword by its handle, may defend himselfe thereby; *so*, by taking, and using it by the point, or edges, mischiefes himselfe by the

Comparison.

the same. *Therefore*, wee need take heed how wee use the sword of the *Word*.

For prevention of error of judgement, from this ground of abused *Scripture*, wee are to be carefull, that we be not moved with the letter of the *Scripture*, without its proper *sense* agreeable to the truth; contrary to which, the abused *letter* of the *Scripture* is no warrant for us to beleeve, or do any thing; as wee see by our *Saviour Christs* replie to *Satan*, who, in tempting of him, alledged *Scriptures*, after his manner, to perswade him to doe evill.

Prevention of this error, by not following the letter against the true meaning of the Scripture.

[a] *Mat* 4.6.

Our faith and *practise* should be founded upon sound knowledge; otherwise, all our building will fall, that is reared up upon a rotten foundation; and wee shall commit *two* faults at once, one in error of our judgment, *another* in our unwarrantable practise, according to the same.

Observe.

Therefore, that we may not wrest the *Scripture* from its true *sense*, to our meaning that wee shall please to give it; or that wee should take it in a carnall, or grosse sense contrary to its owne interpretation, we are to observe *foure rules*, or helps, that wee may rightly understand the *Scripture*.

Rules or meanes of knowledge of the Scripture.

First, it is needfull that we be indowed with *humility* of spirit, that denying our owne selves and carnall reason, wee may submit to take such *fence* and meaning of the *Scripture*, as it of it selfe affords, with the assistance of the helps of the Church; and not to impose upon it any sense of our owne making; *or*, to wrythe, or wrest it to favour our conceits, or purposes: but that, laying aside all ambition of over-ruling the *Scripture*, to force it to patronize and countenance any new fangled humorous opinions, or old errors of ours, for our vaine ostentation or sinfull profit; we are humbly to conforme all our opinions and courses to the *Scriptures*, and not to bring the *Scriptures* into subjection to our *opinions* and *practise*:

1 Humility.

God

God will guide the meeke in judgement: and the meeke will he teach his wayes, saies *David, Psal.* 25.9.

2. Holinesse.

The second meanes, whereby we may be able rightly to understand the *Scriptures*; is *holinesse* of heart and conversation, as our *Saviour* tells us, that *if any man will do his will, he shall know of his doctrine, whether it be of God, John* 7.17. *For*, as the *Philosopher* saies, *Every evill body is an ignorant, and* persons prepossessed with error and vice, labour to interpret all *Scripture* in favour of the same. *Whereas*, godly people indowed with a new *divine nature*, as *Peter* tels us [a], are thereby inclined so to expound the *Scripture*, as best agrees with the truth, and grace of God in them, who are divinely illightned, whereby they are able to *try things that differ* [b], *Phil.* 1. 10. When others are *blinde*, and *cannot see a farre off*, 2 *Pet.* 1.9.

Omnis malus est ignorans. Arist. Ethic. l.3.

[a] 2 Pet. 1.4.

[b] δοκιμάζειν τὰ διαφέροντα.

3. Prayer.

The third meanes, to help us rightly to understand the *Scriptures*, is *Prayer* to *God*; that he would both reveale, and manifest to us his truth; and also, would give us grace rightly to conceive it in our minds and hearts, as the *Prophet David* praies, *Teach me good judgment, and knowledge, Psal.* 119.66. that so we may be taught of *God* [c]. *For*, the matter of the *Scripture* is, in many points, so supernaturall and high; and wee so dull and grosse in conceiving such truths, that as flesh and blood cannot reveale them to us; neither can the naturall man receive the things of the Spirit of God [d], without divine help, procured by *prayer*.

[c] θεοδίδακτοι. 1 *Thes.* 4.9.

[d] 1 *Cor.* 2 14.

4. The Spirit of God.

The fourth meanes of rightly understanding the Scripture is, the *Spirit of God*, in and by our use of hearing, and reading, and conferring; illightning our mindes, and perswading our consciences of the truth, according to the promise of our *Saviour* touching the holy *Spirit*, whom he said he would send, and that when this *Spirit* of truth is come, he would guide us into all truth, which he manifests to us by a *twofold light*.

Twofold light of the Spirit.

First

First, that which accompanies the *Word* and truth it selfe, whereby it makes it selfe conspicuous to all that have eyes to see it, even as the *Sun* manifests it selfe, by its owne light and splendour, to the world. 1. In the Word. Comparison.

The second kind of light, whereby the Spirit manifests the truth of the Scripture to us, is that *light*, that hee endowes our minds withall; whereby we are enabled, and made capable to see and apprehend the former light of truth in the Word: *as a blind man*, that can see nothing, before that he hath both an inward faculty of sight restored to him, and also an externall light to make the *object* visible. So then, none can truly, nor fully understand the truth of the *Scriptures*, but by the same *Spirit* that gave them. *For*, as the *Apostle* saith, *The things of God knoweth no man, but the Spirit of God*[a]: and *therefore*, it is said, that *the spirituall man discerneth all things*: by this Spirit, a mans judgement is conformable to the truth contained in the Scriptures, and sound doctrine of the Church. 2. In our mindes. Comparison.

[a] 1 Cor.2.11.15

Touching the mistake and abuse of *Scripture*, for the vile fact of *self-murder*, *Augustine* gives this admonition: *Take heed to thy selfe, that it may not slily creep upon thee, to have a mind to kill thy selfe; by so understanding these words of Scripture; That thou oughtest to hate thy life, in this world. For, from thence some malignant and perverse men, and most cruell and wretched murderers against themselves, do throw themselves into the fire, do choake themselves in the waters, and by headlong downfalls do crush themselves, and perish*[b].

Our Saviour Christ told *Peter*, that *others should gird, and carry him whither he would not*[c]; whereby hee intimates, that *Peter* should not will to gird and destroy himselfe.

Also, the same *Augustine* calls such *self-murderers*

[b] *Vide ne tibi subrepat, ut teipsum velis interimere, sic intelligendo, quod debes odisse in hoc mundo animam tuam: hinc enim quidam maligni & perversi homines & in seipsos crudeliores, &c.* August. Tract. in Ioan. 51.

[c] *John* 21.18.

Ee the

the *devils martyrs*, when he answers to *Petilian* the *Donatist*, saying, *These your confessors, when they throw themselves headlong from steepe places, to whom doe they conserate martyrdome? whether do they it to Christ, who rejected the devill when hee suggested the doing of such things? or do they it not rather to the devill himselfe; who did suggest to Christ such things for him to do? Wee doe not honor those by the name of Martyrs, who have hanged themselves.*

Confessores illi vestri, quando seipsos præcipitãt, cui dicant Martyrium? utrum Christo qui talia suggerentem diabolum repulit, an potius ipsi diabolo qui talia Christo suggessit? Non veneramur nomine Martyrum eos, qui sibi collum ligaverunt. August. contra lit. Petil. l. 2. c. 49.

The *Scripture*, rightly understood, is the best promptuary, and antidote against *self-murder*, both by meanes of the light of it, shewing us the unlawfulnesse and vilenesse of that fact, and also by the power thereof, or of the Spirit therein, disswading, and vehemently withdrawing of us there-from: to whose advice and motions so long as we obediently listen, we are safe from *self-murder*.

§. 5. *Of misconstrued decree and destiny, to the perverting of judgement.*

The third ground of a deceived judgement, Conceit of decree and destiny.

The third ground of a deceived judgement, which occasions *self-murder*, is the *self-murderers* strong apprehension that it is the unalterable *decree of God*, and his owne unevitable *fortune* for him so to die, by his owne hands; as *Tertullian* speakes of some: *which* conceit arises from two *originals*.

Dinumerant in semetipsos mentis malæ impetus, vel fato vel astris imputant. Tertul. Apolog. c. 1.

Originall of it. 1. Impostures. *Note.*

First, from the *oracles* or impostures of *Magitians* and *fortune-tellers*, that declare to those who unwarrantably seeke to them for knowledge and resolution of future contingent things, specially touching their death, that so they shall die and perish. Which is the just reward of such unlawfull curiosity, that so they may thereby be punished; *either* by doing of the deed, *or* by continuall torment of feare that they shall doe it. *God* never conceales any thing from us, but that, whereof the ignorance is better for us, than the knowledge.

It

It was *curiosity* after this kind of knowledge, that made *Eve* willing to learne of the *devill*, being her *schoolemaster* [a], that, whereby she was a meanes to undoe her selfe,and all mankinde. *We* see, by the practise of *Saul* in killing himselfe, how dangerous a thing it is to advise with *witches* [b], *soothsayers, magitians, Astrologers*, or any of that black rabble: upon affectation of curious and secret knowledge,from those persons,a man shall but play the Gnat about the candle, delighting in the light thereof,untill it be at last burnt up with the heat thereof: as many a man may grieve that he hath so little knowledge of profitable things; so many may grieve that they have so much unprofitable, and needlesse knowledge. *People* are ignorant of necessary things,because they bend their minds so much to know unnecessary things: but was it ever knowne that the *devill* did give advice that was good, both for *matter* and *end?*

[a] *Gen.3.5,6.*

[b] 1 *Sam.28.7.*

Observ.

Necessaria nescimus, quia non necessaria discimus.

The second originall of the strong conceit of *self-murder* in the minde, is deep *impressions* in the thoughts of man, that it is the unalterable, and unresistable *decree* of *God*, that he must kill himselfe: which proceeds from *satans* cunning suggestions,slily darting in,and fomenting the same perswasion: *and* withall, where the *self-murderers* thoughts and mind are ever taken up with, and running upon the same, *and* are under such continuall powerfull temptations to kill himselfe, that hee thinks he cannot resist,then falls he to resolve,and to endeavour to do it; as,being perswaded that it is his *fatall destiny* so to die. *And therefore,* what such think must be done at last, they deeme it best to doe it as soone as they can; *both* that they may be out of the torment of the thoughts of it; and also, may finish out of the way, what is *Gods will* that they must doe: as *Iudas* did, who went quickly to betray his *Master* [c]. *Men* of this perswasion and practise do thinke, that if they do that onely, which is agreeable to Gods decree,and secret wil,they are blame-

2. Conceit that it is Gods decree.

[c] *Iohn*13.27.30.

They thinke that they sinne not.

 lesse;

Their error. lesse; but they are in a greater errour.

Reasons.

1. Absurdity of it. *For first*, by that argument, no man in the world should be culpable of any sin for any thing that hee doth, how flagitious soever it were; *and* so both God and man should be blameable for unjust dealing, in punishing any man for any thing that he doth; be it *murder*, *treason*, *theft*, or any like thing; and in vaine were all lawes, divine and humane, requiring the doing of that good, or forbidding that evill; if justly a man may not be rewarded for the former, nor condemned for the latter.

Observe. *For*, there is nothing that possibly can fall out, or come to passe contrary to *Gods* eternall *decree*, in regard both of Gods prescience & fore-knowledge of all things; and also in respect of his power, and wise providence; from, and by which is the whole motion of all creatures, and their abilitie in all manner of actions. Which is further apparent by the testimony of the *Apostles*, in their confession to *God*, saying, *Of a truth, against thy holy childe Iesus, whom thou hast annointed, both Herod, and Pontius Pilate, with the Gentiles, and the people of Israel were gathered together for to doe whatsoever thy hand and thy Counsell determined before to be done* [a]. *Will* any man *therefore* say, that neither *Iudas*, nor any of those were blameable for betraying and putting our blessed *Saviour* so cruelly and spitefully to death?

[a] *Acts* 4. 27, 28.

If Gods decrees were sufficient to warrant men to doe evill; then, *either* there could bee no sinne in the world, whatsoever men doe; *or else*, *God* must be the author of sinne, and the onely sinner; which is a thing most blasphemous to thinke.

2. Ignorance. *The second reason* that manifests the *error* of those who thinke themselves warranted to doe whatsoever God hath decreed, is both their *ignorance* of what God hath decreed; (which for the most part he keepes so secret, that it is not certainly known, but by the event and effect what it is; *and* in this case the *Scripture* sayes, that *the*

secret

secret things belong unto the Lord our God, but those things which are revealed belong unto us, and to our children for ever; that we may do all the words of this Law.) *And also,* it is their *ignorance* of the *use* of *Gods decree*, which is properly his owne will whereby, and according to which, he in wise and in soveraigne manner orders all things according to his owne good pleasure. *But* it is not that which he would have alwayes to bee our *will*, and according to which we should order our wills and practise; *for* which he hath given us his revealed *word* and law; which is to be, in all practicall things, the measure of our *wills* and wayes. *And therefore*, so long as *Gods* word forbids *self-murder*, we are not to dare, upon pretence of destiny, or Gods decree, to entertaine thoughts to attempt it. *Gods* secret decrees containe no *formall commandements* to us what we should doe; *nor* put any reall *influxe* to incline us to sin, nor subject us to *compulsory* necessity of sinning, contrary to our owne *wills*, or to the meanes, and Commandements that we have against the same.

Deut. 29. 29.

Gods secret will is the rule of his owne actions.

Gods revealed will is the rule of our actions.

So then, it is certaine that our fulfilling of the *secret will* and *decree* of *God* by our wretched courses, and the accidentall good that may come to others thereby, cannot excuse us from damnation, for running a course contrary to the revealed wil of Gods Commandements, and to the meanes whereby we are to order our practise in obedience to God.

Observe.

It is not in the power of the most wretched and malicious men in the world to crosse, but must fulfill the secret *decree* of *God*, *neither* is any man commended or saved for fulfilling that *decree* which no man can disappoint: *But* all men are commended, or condemned for those courses and meanes which they use, according as the same is commanded or forbidden in the Word; whereby the severall *decrees* of *God* for mans salvation, or destruction, are voluntarily accomplished by men themselves.

No man is saved for fulfilling the will of Gods decree, which no man can overthrow.

Note. Mans care should be to live well. *Non ita inter vos vixi, ut pudeat me vivere; nec timeo mori, quoniam Dominum bonum habemus.*

Mans only care in all estates, should be to live well, in conformity to Gods revealed will and word; not being solicitous so much for our deaths, which after a good life can never be ill. *We* serve not such a *master* as will not be carefull of our good; *in* which regard, worthy is that speech of dying S. *Ambrose* recorded by *Paulinus* in his life, *I have not so lived in the world, that I am ashamed to live; neither am I affraid to die, because wee have a good Lord.*

Where wee have no commandement we should be passive about our deaths.

Although that *God* is active, and workes in all things about us, and that we are to cooperate with him in all things where hee gives us a commandement to worke; yet in those workes of God, where wee have no commandement of his to worke with him; as in and about our deaths, there we are only to be *passive.*

Observe.

Three things we are to observe from this point of *deceit* of the *judgement.*

1. Men are strong to beleeve errors.

First, we may here see, that people that are *weakest* in faith, and most diffident to beleeve *Gods word*, and saving truth, upon the credit and authority of *God* himselfe; are often strongest and most confident in *beliefe of errors* upon any seeming ground; as *Solomon* saith, *The simple beleeveth every word*[a]; *The reason* hereof is plaine; *because* such persons are overswayed by *prejudices*, and strength of passion so farre, that they rather suspect and reject *Gods* sacred and infallible *truth*, than their owne *fancies*, and *Satans* suggestions. When men *leave the truth, they become both superstitious, and vainely credulous.*

[a] *Prov.* 14. 15.

Note.

They therefore that beleeve *God*, and in *God*, are freed from many errours, and much needlesse feare.

2. Disobedients to God, are forward to obey the devill.

Secondly, we may from hence *observe*, that many persons that are most disobedient to *Gods* lawes, by keeping whereof they might live; are most forward to obey *Satan* and their owne lusts, to their owne destruction. *For* a man cannot serve both these contrary *masters* at once.[b] Such people like well to have *God* to be their *friend*, but they

[b] *Mat.* 6. 24.

they care not for having him to be their *master*, but would live as they list; but when they forsake him, they are unhappy in their choise; when they can serve none other but to their owne ruine.

Thirdly, from hence we may see, that *many men are willing to doe evill, but are loth to beare the burden of the blame thereof*: and therefore they turne it upon *God*, and would make him a party with them against himself; in breaking of his owne lawes. 3. Men to excuse themselves blame God.

Men that would not have their courses framed by the right rule of *Gods* truth, labour to frame all *reason* and *divinity* by their owne crooked fancies and courses; *whereby* they doe, as farre as they can, deturb, and cast downe God from his *throne*, and advance themselves unto the same, by their perverting the order established by him; and by making themselves *gods*, to live by their owne wills, as the *supreme* rule of all their actions. *Which* shewes to us, how needfull it is for us to labour for *self-deniall*, and that wee may resigne our selves wholly to *God*, to bee ordered and disposed wholly by him in all things as he pleases; which is the onely meanes of our preservation from sin and damnation.

§. 6. *Of conceited good by self-murder, perverting the judgement.*

The fourth, and last *ground* of a mistaken understanding, which causes or occasions *self-murder*, is both the *conceit* of *good* that comes by that fact, and also *ignorance* of the *illnesse* of that action. Apprehension of the presence of God, and of absence of evill, perswades the minde of the lawfulnesse of the thing, and makes the conscience bold to undertake the performance of it. The fourth ground of error in judgement, is conceit of benefit.

Of the goodnesse that a *self-murderer* conceives to be in killing of himselfe, I have spoken already in the explication of the definition of *self-murder*. Good conceived. Cap.12.§.2.

Touching

How apparent good affects the understanding.

Touching which, I will onely now observe how *bonum*, or *good*, that properly is the *object* of the *will*, *or* of the *soule*, in its *elections* and *actions*, can affect the understanding; when it is but apparent good, and contrary to truth.

1. By the wills working upon it from the senses.

To cleare this, it is to be marked; *first*, that the *will* receiving impressions from the *senses*, doth often (by ascending) worke upon the *understanding*, and drawes it; as formerly we have heard.

2. Goodnesse and truth are equally the object of the understanding.

Secondly, whereas *bonum* and *verum*, *good* and *truth*, in a *metaphysicall notion*, are the same, and convertible, confineable to no one *Category*; (as neither are any of the *properties* or *attributes* of the *Godhead*) they are likewise equally the *object* of the *understanding*, as of the *will*: which in the soule, doe not differ *essentially*; but are only the divers powers, offices, and workes of the same *soule*, about its severall *objects*; which doe give the occasion of the distinction of those things which in themselves are *one*: and so where ever *bonum*, *good*, is presented to the minde; there also it offers it selfe to the same, as *verum*, *true*. Whereby the understanding is deceived, when the *object* thereof is not that which it is supposed by it to be; which makes a man no lesse bold to doe it, than if it were indeed true.

Of self-murder the illnesse unknowne, incourages a man to commit it.

What blindes men.

1. Sinne.

[a] 2 Pet.1.9.

2. Consequent of sinne.

The ignorance of the *illnesse* of this sinne of *self-murder* incourages men to commit it; when they doe not judge of it by the morall rules whereby it is forbidden and censured. The thing that hides the *vilenesse* of sin from sinners, is even the sin it selfe. As the *Apostle Peter* speakes of such, *That they are blinde, and cannot see afarre off* [a]. Men are first blinded that they may the more boldly sin; as *Samson* was, that he might be led about to grinde. *There* is a *subsequent* blindnesse that followes upon sinning, whereby the oftner that sin is committed, the lesse evill it seemes to be to the doers thereof; in respect both of the sinfulnesse and punishment thereof; *in* which regard,

regard, the *Prophet* sayes, that *Ephraim was like a silly dove*, *Hosea* 7.11. And *Augustine* affirmes, that *darknesse followes those that transgresse the Law*[a]. *The former* ignorance proceeds from *love* and affection to sinne; *the latter* from the *habit* and *custome* of sinning. *The ignorance* of the *illnesse* of the sinne of *self-murder* proceeds from it selfe; *which* in the motions and resolutions of it, blindes the understanding *two wayes*.

[a] *Obumbratio sequitur eos qui legem transgrediuntur.*

Self-murder blindes the minde.

1. Privatively.

First privatively, by drawing away of the minde from advised and serious consideration of the truth about that sin, whereby the vilenesse of it might be seene: and by declining the thoughts from all arguments, reasons, and censures, whereby a man may be kept from doing of it; *So* that when he comes to the *act*, he sees nothing, or but little to hinder him from doing of it.

2. Positively.

Secondly, this sinne blindes the understanding *positively*; *both* by setting the *minde* aworke, as it presents it selfe to it, to wrest the *Scripture*, and to finde out *reasons* that may make the fact *eligible*; as *Eve* did about eating of the forbidden fruit, *Gen*. 3. 6. *And* also it makes the *will*, by the command that it hath got over it, to labour upon the *understanding*, to coyne arguments to justifie the evill fact of *self murder*, against future reproach and punishment; which vile and odious crime it is now in consultation to doe.

Thus doth it *labour* upon the *understanding*, as *Balak* did upon *Balaam*, that by change of his *stations* he might finde a place to *curse Gods people*[b]. *It* is the property of the greatest and most wilfull sinners, to labour to seeme to be least guilty, and pretend the most excuses to justifie themselves; as did *Saul*[c], *Simeon* and *Levi*[d]; and the *harlot* in the Proverbs[e]: If hypocrite-like they cannot hide their sinnes, then they labour to defend them; making, if it were possible, vice to be vertue, and vertue to be vice.

[b] *Numb.* 23.

Observ.

[c] 1 *Sam*.15.20, 21.

[d] *Gen* 34. 31.

[e] *Prov*.30 20.

Note.

Men self-blinded.

Thus doe men blinde themselves by wilfulnesse in ill courses;

courses; *and* also *God* in just judgement doth the same, by giving those over that will not entertaine the truth with the love of it, to be deluded with error and folly; and to beleeve it; as the *Apostle* shewes, 2 *Thess.* 2. 11. and as God commanded the *Prophet* to preach to the people, that *they should heare, but not understand* [a]. *Whereupon,* such men are wise in their owne eyes, and doe thinke their owne wayes best.

[a] *Esay* 6. 9.

If the *judgement* be subdued to the sinne, then men doe runne unresistably to the *fact*. *But* all such *reasons* are nothing but *error*, that are used to prove an *error*; which at last, upon these *delusions*, the minde conceits to bee a *truth*: the truth is in some sort hidden to those that perish.

Note.

Observe.

Wee are here to *observe two things* for our instruction in this point.

1. Ignorance makes way for destruction.

First, that ignorance and error opens the way to destruction, when men are loth to know the true *nature* of their sinnes, the *judgements* due to them, and to take notice of the *meanes* whereby they both may be prevented.

2. Our care to obey the truth.

Secondly, our care should be to know, and obey the truth, by the help of the *Word*, and directions of approved *teachers*; that we may not be self-deceived, through the neglect of *meanes* of knowledge; which makes our sins the greater.

Not to be self-conceited.

And therefore we are to *observe*, that we be not *self-conceited* of our owne wit, and opinions, that we should trust to the same, specially in our *passions*. *And* wee are also to be carefull that we affect not *odde straines*, nor adventure to do great things, upon new and weakly grounded *opinions*; which is, as if a man at *Sea* upon life and death, should dare to ride out a storme by a weak halsser, or small roape; the which, if it breake, will lay him dead on shore. *Therefore* in matters of such importance upon life and death, men should open themselves to, and advise with those that are godly and wise; *both* about what they

Comparison.

they are to do; and also upon what grounds and reasons, that they may not be deceived.

But this is *remarkable*, that ever the worse the thing is that is to be done, and the weaker the reasons of doing of the same are, the lother the doers thereof are to reveale the same; lest they should bee crossed of their purpose, or *shamed* for their weaknesse and enterprise so disclosed. *Note.*

§. 7. *Concerning afflictions upon the body, occasioning self-murder.*

The second generall motive occasioning *self-murder*, is *immoderate affectation of freedome from evill of punishment that sinfull man is liable unto*; for bearing of which, he hath neither comfort, nor strength, as he apprehends. Second generall motive of self-murder. Calamities.

These evills are, either *reall* and true, *or* but *fancied* and conceited; and are either present, *or* feared; *and* are such as a *self-murderer* despaires, either to be able of himselfe to beare, *or* that *God* will uphold him in them, *or* will deliver him from them: *and therefore* hee resolves not to endure them; but out of obstinacy of minde and will, purposes to remove himselfe by *self-murder*, from that which hee cannot remove from himselfe. *As* wee see in part by the pettish humour of *Ionah*, *Ion.*4.8. The sorts of them.

These evills whereby men take occasion to kill themselves, are of *three* sorts. Three sorts of them.

First, they are those that are upon their *bodies*; which doe also much affect their *soules*, *because* of their neere union together; whereby they doe make one *person*, and doe *so sympathise* together, that what is proper to the one nature in matter of action, or passion, is deemed to bee common to the other, in regard of the unity of the person consisting of them both: *Whereupon* it is, that the sufferings of the *body* doe drive the *soule* into strange *passions* and undertakings, on the bodies behalfe. 1. Vpon the body.

Evills upon the body are threefold.

These evills upon the body occasioning *self-murder*, are of *three kindes.*

1. Inbred diseases

Non est vivere, sed valere vita.

Better eye out, than alwayes aking.

First, they are *inbred diseases*, and torments of continuall grievous painfulnesse; being in the judgement of *sense* importable; both for intensive greatnesse, and also for extensive multitude, or unintermitted continuance: as may be the *gout, stone, strangury, racking aches, furious fevers*, incurable *gangreenes*, and the like desperately raging, or noysome diseases; from which to be rid, as from an irksome, long, and painfull death, many doe make choise to kill themselves; dispatching that by a voluntary short death, which they see will otherwise cost them a tedious and long death. *As* did *Pomponius Atticus, Tullius Marcellinus*, and other like, *starve* themselves to death, thereby to cure such desperate griefes.

2. Inflicted torments.

Secondly, the *evills* upon the body that often occasion *self-murder*, are, *either sense* of inflicted *torments*, or of ignominy by man; greater, and more shamefull than they can, or will endure: *Or else* they are such, as they horribly feare shall be inflicted upon them if they doe live, and are strongly perswaded that they shall not be able to endure the same; but that they shall, if they live, disgrace both themselves and their cause, by their sinking under the burden, or by their unseemly manner of behaviour in their troubles; and therefore divers, to prevent the *latter*, and to be delivered out of the *former*, have murderously killed themselves:

Joseph de bello Judaico lib. 7. cap. 28.

As *Josephus* reports of *Eleazar* and his *companions*, who killed themselves *that they might not bee punished by the Romanes, but might escape from their tyranny; that their wives might die undefiled, and their children not taste of servile captivity.* Alleadging (but unjustly) *that it was misery to live, and not to die*: because *death freeth our soules from prison unto their most pure and proper place, where never after they shall be touched with calamities.*

Upon which motive it was, that the *Stoick Seneca* said; that

that for our readie dispatch, *every veine of our body, is a way to liberty* [a]; meaning, by bleeding to death: *and* upon this reason it was that *Saul* killed himselfe [b]; *and* whereupon also the *Iaylor* would have done the like [c]; *so* farre doth the forerunners and feare of death prevaile with some, that the same makes them to cast themselves headlong into that, which they would most shun.

[a] *Quamcunque venam nostri corporis esse viam ad libertatem.*
[b] 1 *Sam.* 31.4.
[c] *Acts* 16.27.

Note.

Thirdly, the *evils* on the body, whereupon some people doe precipitate themselves into the jawes of *self-murder*, are *want of necessaries of livelyhood, being without meanes, or hope of supply thereof*; whereby they, and theirs depending upon them, are pinched with famishing hunger, starved with piercing cold, vexed with intolerable *oppression* and neglect, *that makes a wise man mad, Eccles.* 7.7.

3. Want of necessaries for the body.

Which fills them with painfull smart, for their owne particular; oppresses them with sorrow and griefe, to behold the miseries, and to heare the ruefull complaints, and lamentations of those they dearely love, as of their *Wives, Children*, and neerest *friends*, walking as living and forlorne ghosts upon the earth: which possesses them with comfortlesse and hopelesse desperation, especially when they consider what plenty they have had; and what others their *inferiours* still have; whose bowells of compassion they finde shut up against them and theirs.

An image of which estate we may see in the *Lamentations* of *Ieremie* [d], *Mine eyes do faile with teares, my bowels are troubled, my liver is powred upon the earth, for the destruction of the daughter of my people; because the children and the sucklings swouned in the streets of the City; they say to their Mothers, where is corne and wine?* When they *swouned, as the wounded in the streets of the City*, when *their soule was powred out in their mothers bosome*: the *tongue of the sucking child, cleaving to the roofe of his mouth for thirst: the young children aske bread,* and

[d] *Lam.* 2.11, 14.

b *Chap.* 2.20. *and no man breaketh it unto them* [b] : *By* which necessity it came to passe, that *women did eate their fruit, and children of a span long: the hands of the pitifull women have sodden their owne children, they were their meate, in the destruction of the daughter of my people* [c] : *according* both to the threatnings of the breach of the Law [d], and also to practise in besieged *townes* [e].

c *Cap.* 4.10.
d *Deut.*28.53.
e 2 *King.* 6.29.

f *Lam.*4.9.

In which regard it is said, *that they that be slaine with the sword, are better than they that be slaine with hunger* [f].

Therefore, diverse persons, that they may prevent what they, or theirs may uncomfortably doe, or suffer, in such felt, or feared distresse, doe, with their owne hands, kill their *Wives*, or *Children*, and then *themselves*; that they may not feele, or behold a greater evill upon them, as they suppose; *the* death, that they cannot indure to see, or suffer inflicted by other meanes, they unnaturally and wickedly, out of *cruell mercy*, inflict themselves. *So* hard a thing it is to indure to see a cruell *act* done, over it is for ones selfe to do it; *evils* are ever more discernable by, and terrible to us, when they are in others, than in our selves.

Note.

§. 8. *Of crosses upon mans outward estate, occasioning self-murder.*

2. Calamities upon mens externall good things.

1. Upon their estates.

The second kind of *evils*, that give men occasion to *murder* themselves, are those that are upon mens outward worldy *estates:* when either, having beene rich, or well to live, they fall to decay, and goe backward: *or* when, having meanes, and carefully toyling, and using their indeavours to live, and grow in the world, they are incountred with crosses and losses, or their goods are imbesiled, or wasted, by wife, husband, children, or servants; that still they go behind-hand, and run into debt; *having* neither meanes, nor hopes, to live, and keepe their charge, in fashion, as they would, and were wont

wont; *nor* yet, to pay every man his owne: *or*, when ſome rich man, by the fall of the price of corne, or failing of his croppe, is diſappointed of his gaped-for gaine; the *former*, becauſe, he cannot be but poore, as he would not; and the *latter*, becauſe, he cannot be rich, ſo as he would; both of them reſolve to kill themſelves, to help themſelves by a mad kinde of remedy: *the one*, becauſe he cannot have as much as he would, takes a courſe to loſe all that he hath: *the other*, becauſe he hath ſo little, takes a way to have nothing at all: and both of them caſt away their lives, for that, which ſhould be but their ſervant. *Note.*

The true *ground* and *cauſes* of this wicked practiſe, is both exceſſive covetouſneſſe, and high *eſteeme* and *love* of the world, which ſome doe make their *god*, and prize it above their lives: *and alſo pride* of heart; whereby ſome will not ſtoope, to be content with that eſtate, that *God* would have them to be in; and *therefore*, becauſe they cannot bee, and live in ſtate as *they* would, they will not live at all; but rather deſtroy themſelves; and ſo, by going about thus to free themſelves from their preſent, or feared eſtate, that they diſlike, they madly caſt themſelves into a worſe: *ſo bad* is our *exchange*, when wee forſake the *will* of God to follow our owne.

The true cauſes of ſelf-murder upon croſſes in eſtate. 1. Covetouſnes. 2. Pride. *Note.*

§.9. *Of diſhonour cauſing ſelf-murder.*

Secondly, the calamities which are upon that which externally belongs to men: which occaſions men to *murder* themſelves, are thoſe diſaſters that concerne their worldly *honours*; *as*, *diſappointment* of their expected *dignities*, and high reſpects and favour with eminent *perſonages*: *or*, the degrading and diſplacing of them, from their preferments, and honourable degrees of advancement with *Princes*, or *people*: *or*, the *over-clouding* of

2. Calamities upõ their honours.

of them with the contempt, and disdaine of those of whose favour they are ambitious; *and* when with all, dejected from their aspiring greatnesse, or hopes, they shall see their *inferiours*, and enemies exalted and preferred before them; as *Haman* did see *Mordecai*: then are their thoughts and resolutions impatiently set to kill themselves, as not able to live in such an *eclypse* of *honour*. *Of* this, *vaine ambition* is the onely *cause*; as it was in *Abitophel*, and *Zimri*; *but*, ô how vaine and wretched is that man, whose happinesse is not in himselfe, but in other unstable creatures; that, by change of their favour, can every houre make him miserable, when they list! *And*, ô how weake and fraile are they, whom a frowne, a harsh speech, *or* one remove in Courtly favour, can kill, or cause them to kill themselves! *Who* would thinke that these men were in their right wits, or cared for any *honor*; who, by *self-murder*, make themselves everlastingly miserable and *infamous* in the highest degree of *ignominy*, even to the overshadowing and disgracing of their innocent posterity? *Mans* ambition to be higher than *God* would have him, brings him to *shame*.

The true cause of self murder upon this motive. Ambition.

§. 10. *Of disasters upon friends, occasioning self-murder.*

3. Calamities upon their friends.

Thirdly, the *evils* that are upon that, which externally belongs to men, whereby divers times some are occasioned to *murder* themselves, are those that concerne their neerest, and dearest *friends*, as their *wives*, *children*, *kindred*, *masters*, familiars, and the like: and that falls out in *two cases*.

In two cases.

1. By suffering, or doing evill.

First, when such *friends* either do, or suffer some woefull or shamefull things, while they do live; which makes them, in their opinion that love them, miserable, as are the flagitious *lives*, and *practises* of *wife*, *children*, *kindred*,

kindred, or the like; *or*, their ignominious and cruell sufferings, redounding to the extreame griefe, or disgrace of those, to whom they so neerely belong; which they cannot, nor will not indure, but do kill themselves, that they may not live to see it, or heare of the same.

Secondly, when such *friends* doe die, or are taken away from them; whereby they thinke themselves miserable, in the losse of their company, and of the benefit that they had by them: *and therefore*, they are so affected, that, in the *former case*, they will not abide to live in this world with them; *nor* in the *latter case*, will live in this world without them; but will needs kill themselves, in the *former* case, to be rid from them; and in the *latter*, that they may not be without them. *So* that, such mens *friends* may seeme, in these *two* differing respects, to make them miserable, the one by their presence, and the other by their absence: *and* so, the *cause* of their comfort, is made the meanes of their woe, by their owne folly; who will live, not by the life that is in themselves, but by that, which is in others: and do set their hearts more on such *friends*, than on *God*, in so much that if they cannot enjoy their *friends*, as they desire, they will not enjoy themselves; as *Sauls Armour-bearer*, who killed himselfe that hee might not out-live his *Master* [a].

2. By being bereaved of them.

Observe.

[a] 1 *Sam.* 31.5.

§.11. *Of trouble of conscience, occasioning self-murder.*

The third kind of *evill*, whereupon men take occasion to kill themselves, is that which is upon their *minds*, as in the immediate *subject* thereof, which the neerer it is, the more intollerably it doth affect: all other sufferings being as whippings upon the coats, but this as upon the naked skin; and more intollerable than death, which some men choose, and voluntarily inflict, with their own hands,

3. Inward upon the mind.

hands, upon themselves, that thereby they may be freed from the trouble of their minds.

Foure sorts of troubles of mind.

This *trouble* of the *minde* is of *foure* sorts.

1. Trouble of conscience for sinne.

First, extreame griefe of minde and trouble of conscience, in respect of *sin: which*, by the guiltinesse thereof, and by the terror of the expected punishment thereof; distresses, and overcharges the wounded *conscience, when* withall a man apprehends himselfe to bee wholly destitute of true *grace*, and deserted and forsaken of *God*; given over to a reprobate sense; *whereby* he cannot rest, but is comfortlesse, and at last, is swallowed up of utter desperation; living as if he were continually in *hell*, sensibly feeling, as he thinks, the flames and tortures of the damned, in his conscience: *For* ease out of which estate, men many times kill themselves, hoping to mend themselves by change; although it bee but, as skipping out of the frying-pan into the fire.

Grounds of this trouble of mind.

The grounds of which perplexities of the mind, about sinne, are *three*.

1. Greatnesse of sin and its punishment.

First, a mans thorow apprehension of the *greatnesse* and *deformity* of his *sinne*, and of the fearefull *judgements* due to him for the same: which affrights the conscience, and drives it to runne into any course, to hide it selfe from the same.

2. Emptinesse of grace, &c.

Secondly, the *soules emptinesse* of *repentance*, and *grace*; *and* the possession and dominion that noysome *lusts*, disorderly affections, and fearefull temptations have of the same, whereby, it seemes to be a cage of uncleane *spirits*, *from* which when a man can no other wayes be rid, then resolves hee to kill himselfe, to free himselfe from that horror of minde, that he is not able to indure.

3. Conceit of time of grace to be past.

Thirdly, when the *soule* conceives that its time of *grace* is *past*, *and* that it is too late to repent, and get grace; against which when men find themselves hardned and shut up; then, falling under desperation, they resolve to destroy their owne lives; that seeing they have no hope

hope that they shall be better by living, they may not thereby make their estates worse, by what they may indure, both in this life, and in the life to come.

We may here *observe* how men are *deceived* by sinne, which promiseth, at first, all contentment and happinesse to the *clients* and entertainers thereof; but, in conclusion, paies them with destruction, and shuts up their dayes, and life, with a *tragicall conclusion*. *None* are more faithfull drudges to any *Master*, than sinners are to sin; and none are so ill rewarded by their *Masters*, for their service, as they.

Observ. 1. Men deceived by sinne.

Note.

Againe, from hence it is remarkable, that so long as men, in distresse of conscience for their sinne, looke not out off, or beyond themselves, for ease and comfort, they cannot but sinke under their owne burden. *For*, our blessed *Saviour* directs us to a better course, in this case, when he sayes, *Come unto me, all yee that labour, and are heavie laden, and I will give you rest*[a].

2. No ease of conscience frō our selves.

[a] *Mat.* 11.28.

§.12. *Of discontentment of minde.*

The second sort of the *troubles* of mind, which occasions *self-murder*, is mens excessive *discontentment*; for being crossed, *or* disappointed of their desires, or wills; in which respect it was that *Ieremy* did wish his own death[b], at least, was weary of his life.

The second sort of trouble of minde is discontentmēt.

[b] *Ier.* 20.17.

This discontentment of minde arises from *two causes*. *First*, from want of that good, true or seeming, which we desire, or expect. *Secondly*, from suffering of that *evill* which we would not.

1. Grounds of it.

This discontentment of minde is *twofold*.

2. Kinds of discontentment.

First, that which ariseth from the crossing, or disappointment of the *will* of mens *affections* and *lusts*; *as* those that immoderately affect and love to have and enjoy others of the other sexe, and are deeply overset in carnall,

1. From disappointment of mens passiōs and affections.

 or

or conjugall *love*, which is an unruly *passion*, and being disappointed, occasions people therefore to kill themselves: a *wife* kills her selfe because her *husband* crosses her will; *that* either he will not doe as she would have him; *or* that he will not let her have her will to goe, and doe as she list; *or* is displeased with her match: which proceeds from hatred to her husband, whom she envies the enjoying of her, and so I might instance in many like particulars: but it is most unreasonable, that because a body cannot have their love or will, that therefore such an one should revenge the same upon himselfe, by an act of the greatest hatred and hostility in the world: and that one should rather choose to kill himselfe, than to live after a repulse in suite of love; or to see another brooke what they impotently affected to enjoy.

The second kinde of discōtentment crossing the will of reason in three particulars.

Secondly, discontentment of minde is that which proceeds from the *crossing*, or frustrating of the *will* of sound and naturall *reason*, in *three particulars*.

1. Concerning a mans selfe. Iustice.

First, in things concerning a mans self; as if he cannot have *equity* and *justice* done him; hee in discontentment therefore kills himselfe: *or* as a *childe*, because his *parents* will not give him fit maintenance, as they are able, nor dispose of him or her, as they might and ought, murders himselfe.

2. Concerning a mans family. [a] *Gen* 27.46.

Secondly, in things concerning a mans *family* or *friends*; as *Rebeccah* was weary of her life, because of her *daughters* in law [a]; *and as* if *parents* should, for their being crossed of their wills in and about their *children*, kill themselves.

3. Concerning Church or Common-wealth. *Qui non poterat ferre dominatum Cæsaris.* Filli.

Thirdly, in things concerning the generall body of *Church* or *Common-wealth*, whereof a man is a member; *as* if for the ill government or miscariage of either, or of both of them, he should kill himselfe, as did *Cato Uticensis*. *But* all this may bee uneffectuall to move a man, or woman to kill themselves, if they would deny their owne *wills*, and submit themselves wholy to Gods; who suffers,

suffers, and orders all these *evills*, and brings good out of them. *And* if they would consider that not by *dying*, but by *living*, things are reformed; and by *self-murder* disorders are increased; and judgements provoked and deserved; and not prevented nor amended.

§. 13. *Of shame and confusion.*

The third kinde of troubles of minde that sometimes occasions *self-murder*, is *shame* and *confusion*; *either* for what a man hath ignominiously done, or suffered; or is certainly like to do or suffer; whereby he falls under contempt, scorne, and importable disgrace with those whose respect he overvalues: *and* so apprehending himselfe to bee dejected, and used more indignly and unworthily than he thinkes he hath deserved, or can indure, he resolves to kill himselfe, to free him from the same; *or* at least from the sense of it. As did *Lucretia*, who having beene ravished by *Tarquinius* stabd her selfe to avoide the shame of it: of whom *Augustine* sayes, that *being sick and impatient of the villany committed against her, she killed her selfe*: The Romane Lady *ambitious of praise, was ashamed of another mans filthinesse committed against her, and therefore, that she might not be thought to have willingly suffered that abuse, she destroyed her selfe.* And *Ovid* sayes of her; that,

Third kinde of troubles of minde. Shame.

Fœdi in se commissi sceleris ægra atq; impatiens se peremit, turpitudinis alienæ in se commissæ Romana mulier laudis avida, ne putaretur libenter passa.

> *Succubuit famæ victa puella metu.*
> *The Damosell fell overcome with feare of shame.*

Also Curtius makes mention in his ninth *booke*, of one *Dioxippus* of *Athens*; that when he was falsly accused to have stollen a cup from *Alexanders* table, hee was so ashamed to be so disgraced by the imputation of theft, that he presently went out and hanged himselfe, for to prevent or get out of insupportable confusion and ignominy:

miny: *So* intollerable a thing is *shame* to some, specially of the noblest natures; that they thinke the same worse than death; and that they had rather not to *bee*, than to live in *shame*, it confounds the judgement, and drives into desperate shifts *and practises* to be rid of it: *shame* will both make a man doe evill and sin; when the contrary goodnesse and vertuous courses procure contempt and disgrace with men; *and* also it is a punishment of sin in the end [a], upon which it doth ever attend, as true honour doth upon well-doing [b]: according as *Iob* sayes, *That the haters of God shall be clothed with shame*, *Iob* 8. *ult.* *and* the *Psalmist* imprecates *shame* upon his enemies, as one of the greatest judgements: *Psal.* 35. 4. 26. *Of* earthly creatures only *man* is capable of *glory*, and of all blessings, glory is counted the chiefe, wherein also man doth *analogically* partake with *God*. *So* contrarily no earthly creature but man, is capable of *shame*, or greatly affected withall, whereunto he is subject in regard of his understanding and reason; *and* of all punishments, this shame is the greatest, which immediately affects the soule in a high degree, for being abased either by our owne practises, or in the esteeme or usage of others.

Effects of shame.

[a] *Rom.* 6. 21.
[b] *Rom.* 2. 7.

Man only capable of shame.

There are *two kindes* of *shame*; *first*, that which is *good* and godly; *and* is *both* that which goes before sinne, and restraines men from daring to doe evill; *and also* that which followes after sinne, whereby they are driven, or moved to repentance for their sinnes past, wherof they are ashamed [c]. *So* that to be shamelesse and impudent, opens the way for such to rush into any wickednesse, and hardens their hearts from repentance.

Kindes of shame.
1.
Good shame.

[c] *Rom.* 6. 21.
Note.

Secondly, there is an *ungodly* and wicked *shame*: *and* that is *first*, when a man is *ashamed to doe good*, or to reforme his life; *which* falls out when goodnesse is in common disgrace with the world, which he labours to please and to curry favour withall; *or* when wickednesse is habituated in him by a long continued practise; *and* he is a stranger

2.
Vngodly shame
1.
ashamed to do good.

ſtranger to vertue and goodneſſe: he is then aſhamed to attempt to doe that which to him is ſtrange, and at which he is unskilfull, and for which he feares he ſhall be mocked by his former companions. Hee is a weake man whom a puffe of a winde, diſgracefull words and flouts, keepes or beates back from goodneſſe: and yet there is nothing generally more powerfull with moſt people to effect the ſame, than this *hobgoblin* of worldly *diſgrace*.

Secondly, wicked *ſhame* is that, which is the *ſhame of confuſion*, proper to the wicked, and is their portion in *hell*; whereby they are ſwallowed up of deſperation, and which makes them ſeeke and endeavour their owne utter deſtruction, ſometimes in this life by *ſelf-murder*: and ever in *hell*, wiſhing and deſiring that they were quite extinct; raging with, and againſt themſelves, for being the meritorious cauſe of that their owne damnation: *ſo* that beſides all other torments, themſelves are againſt themſelves. *Here* we may *obſerve* how men are lyable and ſubject to *ſhame* for evill, and that *ſhame* is one of the greateſt puniſhments that can betide man, and is a moſt forcible *motive* to good, or evill. *Therefore* our care ſhould be to keepe it within its due bounds, by fearing to ſinne, or to continue in ſinne, but that we doe alwayes walke in warrantable courſes: to be ſhamefully intreated for well-doing, is moſt honourable [a], and matter of rejoycing.

2. Shame of confuſion.

Obſerve.

Evill brings ſhame.

[a] 2 *Theſſ.* 2. *Job* 31. 35, 36.

That ſhame ſhould move a man to kill himſelfe, is a mad and unreaſonable practiſe; *becauſe* it is the way to bring a man into farre greater *ſhame*, and everlaſting and unrecoverable diſgrace: *and* ſo to thinke to free himſelfe from *ſhame*, by running into a courſe of greater *ſhame*; is, as if a man to cure his head-ache ſhould knock out his braines.

Self-murder cannot cure ſhame.

§. 14. *Of*

§. 14. *Of feare occasioning self-murder.*

Fourth kinde of the mindes trouble. Feare. Occasioned,

The fourth kinde of the mindes *trouble*, that may occasion *self-murder*, is servile and excessive *feare*; wherewith a man may be surprised and possessed, either from the
1. present evills that he suffers, which he conceives are beyond his strength to beare, and out of which hee sees no meanes of delivery, to be freed so soone as he would, but
2. by killing himselfe: *or else*, from apprehension of inevitable miseries; that as he foresees in their *causes*, will fall upon himselfe, or upon his; which he conceives he is not able to avoide, nor yet to beare with any comfort: and *therefore*, to escape what feare hath made more certaine and terrible by *fancy*, than it is in it selfe, self-murder is often resolved upon, as the back-doore of evasion. *Panicke feare* makes men flee before their owne shadowes, and at the noise of their enemies, as did the *Aramites*, or *Syrians*. If men would absolutely submit in all things to *Gods will*, and trust in his promises and power, they might be secure in all estates.

Note.

2 *Kings* 7.6,7.

But, when they are guided by their owne wisdome and wills, then are they most in danger of miscarying: and when as they thinke to saile by their owne compasse most securely, then doe they runne into the greatest dangers.

Observ. How feare makes bold.

It is *observable* here how *feare*, (the mother of cowardize) makes men *daring* and bold, wittingly and willingly to run into the jawes of farre more horrible dangers and mischiefes, than those be, from which feare makes them to flee; *as*, for a *man*, or a *woman* to dare to kill themselves, that never durst in anger draw blood of any other body; *and* that those, who out of feare, least others should abuse their bodies, would, to prevent the same, kill themselves; as we read of many in the *histories* of the *Church*.

And

And so, men taking their owne wayes, without advising with God, runne into the mischiefe that they would shunne; which shewes that mans wisdome is folly, and his courses without God, madnesse. Note.

§. 15. *Of the true causes of self-murder in afflictions.*

Although these things in this second generall motive doe commonly beare the blame of *self-murder* in this case; *because* they are most sensible and apparent: yet there are other *foure things* more secret and latent, which are indeed the true *causes* of the same. The true causes of self-murder upon this motive of mans sufferings.

The first cause is, mans *unbeliefe*; *whereby* he neither beleeves in *God*; from whom, and by whom hee might have power in *Christ* to stand fast in all estates: *nor* yet doth he firmely beleeve and credit *God* in the *Scriptures*, to entertaine and cleave to the direction of his Word, and to rest upon his promises, and to be perswaded of the gracious intent and nature of *Gods* dealing with his in afflictions, and of the blessed end thereof: *but, as by faith we live*, so by *unbeliefe* wee die; *Iehosaphats* drooping heart in his distresse, was revived and upheld when his eyes were towards God, and hee depended upon him. *Peter* when he doubted, he sunke. O you *self murderers* of little faith, why doe you doubt in your troubles? *why* doe you not (as *David*) rebuke your owne soules, and say every one of you: *Why art thou cast down ô my soul, and why art thou disquieted within me? hope thou in God, for I shall yet praise him, who is the health of my countenance, and my God.* [a] 1. Vnbeliefe. Remedy. Our eyes to God.

[a] *Psal* 42.11.

The second true *cause* of *self-murder*, upon the motive of evill of punishment, or calamities of affliction, is unruly *impatiency*, and *pusillanimity*; when a man apprehends himselfe to be overburdened with miseries, beyond the meanes that he sees of deliverance out of the same, 2. Impatiency.

 and

and beyond the strength that he hath in himselfe, with any comfort to beare it, conceiving his afflictions to bee excessive above his strength, or deserving; *or*, that they are all from God in his wrath; which because he thinkes he cannot beare, nor shake them off, hee labours to rid himselfe from by killing himselfe.

The hurt of impatiency. *Impatiency* makes all evills the more intolerable to be borne; *because* it hinders the minde from submitting to the burthen, and troubles it, by seeking subterfuges of evasion, or opportunities to shake off the yoke.

Who be most impatient. *To impatiency* some are more strongly inclined than others; *either* by naturall temper of excessive *choler*; *or* else by the deep apprehension of understanding and sense of the *objects* of discontentment; whereunto *melancholick* persons are most incident.

Remedies of impatiency. *In* this case, to help men against this *impatiency*, they should consider:

1. *First*, that they have no good, but great hurt thereby; both to their bodies, and their mindes.

2. *Secondly*, their afflictions come from *God*, and are ordered by him, who is our wise, powerfull, and loving father for our good.

3. *Thirdly*, the same is the portion of others that are better than we, and doe endure more than we doe.

4. *Fourthly*, our sufferings are lesse than our deservings.

5. *Fifthly*, God turnes them to be blessings to his owne people, they are momentany and light: wherein *God* assists those that in them trust in him, that they may comfortably above humane strength beare the same.

6. *Sixthly*, in the end they shall be recompensed with a farre greater and eternall weight of glory [a]. *So* that a man shall lose no more by his *passive*, than by his *active* obedience; yea, his gaine and reward shall be greater; as is the honour of *Martyrs* above *Confessors*.

[a] 2 *Cor.* 4. 17.

3. Pride. *The third true cause of self-murder*, upon *afflictions*, is stubborne *Pride*; that will not let a man in whom it is, buckle

buckle to be willingly in that estate of adversity, wherein God would have him to bee: but will rather make him venture breaking of the mast, than to let him lower his sailes in a storme.

Est factum hominum superborum & pusillanimorum mortem sibi inferentium. David à Mauden.

This pride proceeds from an overweining conceit, either of our owne *worth*, for deservings; *or* of our owne *wisdome*, for intelligence and prudence; *whereby* we conceive that the estate that we would have is more due and fit for us, than that wherein wee are: *Whereupon* wee preferre our owne wills before *Gods*; and accordingly to have our wills, we are apt to use the meanes of our own fond devising, how unlawfull soever they bee; even to *self-murder*.

Whence pride proceeds.

The best remedy against this *pride* is, *first*, a thorow knowledge by the *Word*, of a mans selfe; how unworthy and unsufficient he is; and the apprehension of *Gods* mercifull affection and dealing towards him; having his eye cast ever upon the *promises* of *God* to support him.

Remedies against pride. 1. Knowledge of a mans selfe.

Secondly, pride is overthrowne by mans *self-deniall*; when he doth in all things so farre resigne himselfe to *God*; that he denies his owne wisdome, will, and wayes; submitting himselfe to be disposed of by Gods will, and obediently conforming himselfe thereunto, as *David* did, 2 *Sam.* 15.26. *God resists the proud, and exalts the humble.*

2. Self-deniall.

The fourth cause of *self-murder* upon crosses and afflictions, is *pusillanimity*, or weaknesse of minde; *whereby* some are not able to indure to live to brooke, or suffer some kinde of wrongs done to them indeed, or as they conceive: as *husbands* and *wives* under extremity of *Iealousie*, or certainty of knowledge, that their *conjugall consorts* doe give their *loves*, and make their bodies common to others. *And* as passionate *suters*, and persons deeply *inamoured*, and over-ingaged in their affections to those, whom they ambitiously and over-eagerly seeke or presume to enjoy: who see, or conceit themselves to

4. Pusillanimity.

be repudiated, neglected, or forsaken by their *wel-beloved*; after past promises, or strong hopes, or immoderate desires of enjoying them; of both which sorts of people divers doe choose rather to die by their owne hands, than that they will indure to live rejected, and to see others to enjoy that, which they would as their lives possesse alone to themselves.

Vnreasonablenesse of the fact of self-murder in this case.

But, this is most unreasonable and impious, that any *one*, for another bodies fault, should do a worse themselves; and that hee, or shee, in recompense of such a wrong done to them, should doe themselves a far greater injury in their owne unrecoverable self-destruction: *passion prevailing makes mad*; and *weaknesse makes men doe the greatest acts of impotency*. If wee in *Christ* enjoy our good *God*, and if withall we possesse the peace of our *consciences* in well-doing, and be our selves taken up about heavenly things, and holy imployments; then is it not in the hand of any creature to make us miserable, or weary of our lives; the comfort whereof depends not upon any earthly wight: our repudiating, desertion, and wrong by those here on earth, that should least faile us, should make us cleave the more close to *God*, and to live here as possessing none of these things, 1 *Cor.*7.29, 30, 31. that for our want of them, or suffering by them, we may care the lesse, considering what little assurance we have of them at any time, which at all times are accompanied with dislikes.

§. 16. *Of afflictions unwarrantablenesse to kill ones selfe.*

Insufficiency of this motive of crosses for a man to kill himselfe.

The insufficiency of this ground of *affliction* to warrant any man to murder himselfe, is apparent, by *foure* things. *First*, by the consideration of the *nature* of the things that men by *self-murder* would rid themselves from, which are *afflictions*; *and therefore* in that respect not properly

1. Afflictions are not simply evill.

properly *evill*, much lesse so bad as *self-murder*, which is the course men take to free themselves from the former: *It* is certainely madnesse for any body, wittingly and willingly, to cast themselves into a greater *evill*, that they may free themselves from a lesser.

For a man to get out of trouble by *making a stollen escape, he encreases his deserved punishment: wee must not breake prison, but wait Gods leisure.*

Non enim pœna vitatur furtiva discessione, sed crescit.

Secondly, if a man consider what hee parts from, namely, his life, to bee freed from troubles; he may see the folly of such a course of *self-murder*, upon this *motive*. *For*, the goods of nature, and of the world, are farre inferiour to a mans selfe, and to the worth of his life; *because*, in them consists not a mans chiefe happinesse; *and therefore*, for the same should not a man kill himself. The *Philosopher* sayes that *Poverty is not horrible, or to bee feared, neither death, neither any thing at all besides sinne* [a].

2. Death is worse than afflictiōs.

Donum vitæ majus est ijs omnibus: Filli.

[a] Arist. *asserit nec paupertatem esse horribilem, aut pertinvescendam, nec mortem, nec omnino quicquam præter culpam.*

Therefore, why should a man kill himselfe for that, whereof he should not be afraid? *and* why should hee make so bad an exchange, in giving away his life for ease from that, which cannot, by its presence, make miserable: and for to precipitate himselfe into endlesse misery?

Thirdly, if a self-murderer did consider how he is *deceived*, in his expectation of being eased, or delivered from troubles, by killing himselfe, when thereby he casts himselfe into infinite greater miseries, hee might see what little force this *motive* hath in it to worke, and justifie this effect: *Seeing*, life is more proper and effectuall, than such a death, to procure happinesse. *Although* that *self-murder* be a quick way of dispatch, and of putting out all feeling of bodily paine, it is not therefore better, when the exchange is for the worse; ease and expedition in doing self-murder is no argument of commendation; seeing evill of sin is most easily performed,

3. A self-murderer is deceived.

Vltimū malorum hujus vitæ, & maximè terribile est mors; et iccirco inferre sibi mortē, ad alias hujus vitæ miserias evadendas, est majus malum assumere ad minoris mali vitationem. Tho.2.2.q.64. Art.5.

formed, as the *Apostle* shewes *Rom.* 7. 21. *Heb.* 12. 1. *Because*, it is not an act of power, but of impotency.

Peter Martyr wonders at the *Stoicks*, that place happy life *in vertue*; and doe hold that *adversity* is not evill, that they should, to free themselves from troubles, kill themselves; and sayes, *What kind of happinesse is that, which death doth perfit? if life be happie, then should wee labour to abide therein: what happinesse is that which may be overcome by those things that are not evill* [a]? *For* persecution, our *Saviour* bids us flee from it, or patiently to endure it; and no where allowes that we should kill our selves to prevent, or escape it: *our* blessed *Saviour*, although he were to lay downe his life, yet would not kill himselfe, for accomplishment of that worke, that necessarily was to be done.

Ludovicus Vives cites out of *Plutarch*, and he out of *Menander*, *That it is not the part of a good and valiant man to say, I will not suffer this, but to say, I will not doe this* [b].

4. He resists Gods will.

Fourthly, he that kills himselfe, for to free himselfe thereby out of troubles and afflictions; resists the *will* of *God*, by shaking off that burden, which *God* hath laid upon him to beare, during his good pleasure, to which all are subject. *And* thereunto the Son of God submitted himselfe, when he said to *Peter*, *The cup that my Father hath given me, shall I not drinke it* [c]? *And* therefore, we are bound, in this case, to fulfill the *will* of *God*, by *passive* obedience, when we cannot doe the contrary without offending *God*, neither did the *Saints* of *God* use self-murder, to free themselves out of troubles; whereof we have neither precept, nor commendable example.

§. 17. *Of certaine uses about afflicted persons.*

Observe.

The uses or observations *observable* from this motive generally considered, are *two*.

First,

[a] *Quaenam est faelicitas quae morte est perficienda? Si vita est beata, in ea est manendum: quae est faelicitas quae vinci potest ab ijs quae non sunt mala?*

[b] *Non est boni et fortis viri dicere hoc non patiar, sed hoc non faciã.*

[c] *Iohn* 18. 11.

First, we are here to *observe*, that persons in trouble and adversity are under a double burden; *both* of their afflictions, which they suffer, *and* also of strong temptations; wherby thereupon *Satan* assaults them: both which the persons in distresse doe commonly aggravate; so making their estates more tedious and unsupportable, than otherwise they would be; *in* which condition men should beware of hard uncharitable conclusions against themselves; *either* in *censuring* themselves to be reprobates, forsaken of *God*, or the like: *or* in determining rashly of, or against themselves, what they will doe with themselves, or to themselves in that case; otherwise than they have warrant from *God*. *Againe*, in that estate, they should take heed of over-close *concealement* of their troubles, from those that may advise, and help them to beare their burdens: concealed griefe is most dangerous to sink a man; but vent gives ease, and procures help.

Afflicted persons are doubly burdened.

Note.

Beware of censuring.

Beware of concealement.

Finally, of persons in adversity others are to be *observant*, how they doe; and to be helpfull to them, by their countenance, counsell, and aide of assistance, from themselves, and by their intercession, from others: that so, that may be easily borne, that is borne by many.

Be observant and helpfull.

The second use, or observation from the point is, that people in distresse do *fit* themselves, and so *order* their course and behaviour, as is most pertinent, and best becomming their present estate, that they may not be overcome by it.

2. How men are to order themselves in afflictions.

1.

First, by their care to *live by faith* [a], and not by sense: *and* that they may ride by the *anchor* of *hope*, *cast upward within the vaile* [b].

[a] *Habak*.2.4.
b *Heb*.6.19.

2.

Secondly, by humbly *submitting* themselves under the mighty hand of *God*, with *passive* obedience; *rather* cutting our *masts* of *self-will, and pride* by the board, than to hazard being over-set, by a high saile, in the storme of troubles.

3.

Thirdly, they should labour *to possesse themselves in patience*,

patience; that they may stand fast, and overcome by suffering.

4. *Fourthly*, they should endeavour to be chearefull under the crosse.

5. *Fifthly*, they should not be *carefull* of future events, so long as they walke in a good course, but commend themselves by prayer to *God*, and rest confidently upon him, being imployed and taken up with meditation of the gratious promises and dealing of *God* towards those that depend upon him. *By neglect* of which course the *Devill* prevailes much against people in that estate; even sometimes to *self-murder*.

[a] *Phil.*4.6. *Mat.*6.25.

§. 18. *Concerning anger and revenge.*

The third generall motive of self-murder. Anger and revenge.

The *third* generall *motive* of *self-murder* is the rage of *Anger*, and the unsatiable desire of *revenge*: which are most furious *passiõs*, that most spoile, and are least subject to the command of *reason*, or *religion*; and can most hardly be supprest, or kept within any due compasse: which, when they cannot ease themselves, by vent upon others, will reflect upon the *subject* wherein they are, to destroy the same.

Kinds of it.

This *anger* and *revenge* is of *two sorts*.

1. Against a mans selfe.

First, that which is directly against a mans *owne selfe*: and that is *either*, for what he hath done; *or else*, for what he presently is. *Sometimes* men fall into that degree of *anger* and *revenge* against themselves, for what they are, or have done, or beene, that nothing will content them, but murdring of themselves; *as*, for some hainous crime, or flagitious course of life; whereby they finde themselves, upon sight and sense hereof, subjected *either* to importable shame and punishment; *or* to intolerable griefe of conscience: *as* those, that are guilty of some horrible capitall crimes done against their consciences, such as *wilfull murder*, spitefull *blasphemie* against

Propter peccata admissa: For sinnes done.

gainst *God*, and the like; *in* regard of the former, wee see how *Iudas* hanged himselfe: *and* the more secret that such crimes have beene kept, and secure from the stroke of humane justice; the more is man armed and bent with self murder to destroy himselfe, whom *divine justice will not suffer to live.*

Againe, for the present, when a man labours in a continuall conflict against the execrable *viciousnesse* of his nature, *and* against the horrible *motions* of his minde and inclinations of his heart, with much uncomfortable molestation and trouble, without hope of overcomming the same, finding the same more and more to prevaile against him; so that hee concludes; that, if he doe live, hee shall be quite overcome by it, and caried headlong to all evill, to his greater shame, and eternall ruine; *which* that hee may prevent, or bee revenged upon his wretched flesh and corruption; out of his furious zeale, he by the instigation of *Satan*, murders himselfe: and so upon pretence of destroying sinne, hee destroyes himselfe, in and by the most horrible sinne of *self-murder.* Viciousnesse of nature and wicked motions.

Touching this killing of a mans selfe in griefe and revenge, for his sinnes committed, *Alphonsus à Castro adversus hæreses, de Martyrio hæresi secunda*; sayes it *is an heresie, which teaches that those that kill themselves for their sinne, ought to be called Martyres; because, they doe punish in themselves that, for which they grieve that they have committed it.* The *Author* of which *heresie* he sayes was *Petilian* the Donatist, against whom S^t^. *Augustine* wrote: which name of *heresie* it may well brooke, if we consider the damnable danger of it, specially accompanied with obstinacy in opinion, against the judgement and advice of the *Church.* Heresie. *Hæresis est quæ docet eos qui se pro peccato interimunt debere Martyres nuncupari, pro eò quod puniunt in se, quod dolent commisisse.*

Than to bee counted an *heretick* nothing was more odious; because, the same excludes a man both from the Communion and priviledges of the *Church* on earth, and also from the fruition of glory in Heaven: to which

 for

for *punishment*, *self-murder* is equivalent; and if in any case, it bee held obstinately in opinion to bee lawfull, it is directly and formally an *heresie*: because, the contrary is, according to truth, determined by the *Church*, as a point concerning salvation.

Twofold revenge upon ones selfe for sinne.

There is a *twofold revenge* upon ones self, for sin: a *good* and a *bad*.

1. Good. In three things.

The *good* is that whereof the *Apostle* speakes, 2 *Cor.* 7. 11. *Behold what revenge*; which flowes from *griefe* for offending *God*: *and* consists in *three things*.

1. Mortifying humiliation.

First, godly *revenge* upon ones *selfe*, for their sinnes, is in our *chastising* of our selves, and afflicting of our soules before *God*, in penitent manner, in mortifying humiliation; subduing our bodies by discipline, abstinence, &c. whereby, through *Christ* both the *guilt*, and *love* of sinne is extinguished in us; *and* also the power of the corruption of it is killed.

2. Curbing our lusts.

Secondly, it is in the restraining and *curbing* of our owne *lusts* and *wills*, to subdue them wholly to the will of *God*; which cannot bee done without both much trouble and paines, and dislike to the old man of nature.

Cutting off the meanes of sin.

And also, it is in the *stinting*, or depriving of our selves of the use of those things, by which the flesh hath, or doth take occasion to sin against *God*: *as*, delights and pleasures, or things above necessity, when wee abuse them, *which is as to pluck out the right eye, or to cut off the right hand*.

3. Strictnesse.

Thirdly, it is in a more strict tasking of our selves to *religious observances*, to holy duties, and good life; and to opportunities, and offices of doing good to our selves and others: so cutting our selves short of that liberty, whereby wee are apt to breake out to dishonour God; and so bringing our selves under the yoake of more severe spirituall subjection and discipline to *God*, wee shall subdue and mortifie our *old man* of sinne: in which three points lyes the *revenge* here allowed.

The

The second kind of *revenge* upon ones selfe for sinne, is that which is *bad: and* it is either a wilfull *debiliating* of ones selfe to good; *or* killing of ones selfe, for his *sin*, by excessive *griefe:* against which wee have already spoken, in some sort : *or else* this *revenge* is in laying violent hands upon ones selfe purposely to *mutilate*, or kill himselfe, out of indignation for his sinne.

The second kind of revenge upon ones self. Bad.

The causes hereof are specially *two*.

Causes.

1. *First*, *desperation*, in regard of the horriblenesse and grievousnesse of the sinnes, whereof a man is guilty, and by which hee is confounded in his conscience: and for that, withall hee conceives and perswades himselfe that God will never be mercifull to him to pardon him.

Desperation.

2. *Secondly*, affectation & indeavour to *ease* ones troubled and restlesse *conscience*, for some unnaturall cruelties, and crying crimes; by satisfaction of *Iustice*, according to his demerits; makes himself to destroy himself: but of this case we have spoken before.

Ease of conscience.

This *revenge* upon ones selfe in this manner, upon this *cause*, is many wayes *faulty*.

The faultinesse of this revenge.

1. *First*, *because*, of the opinion of expiation of sinne thereby, which nothing can doe away, or can quiet the conscience, but onely the *blood* of our blessed *Saviour Christ*.

2. *Secondly*, *because sinne* cannot be done away by *sin*, and such as is worse than the former; *no more* than fire can be quenched by addition of more fire to it: the punishment of sinne belongs to *God* and his *Vicegerents*, whose lawes are violated.

3. *Thirdly*, no man is a competent *judge* over himselfe, in this case, either to cleare, or to condemne himselfe. *Because*, it is impossible that he should bee both *Superiour* and *inferiour* to himselfe; or that he should not be partially inclined in his affection to himself, either in love or hatred.

Non est quis idoneus judex in se, in propria causa. Nemo habet in se authoritatē, cū non sit seipso superior. Filli.

4. *Fourthly*, not by killing our selves, which deprives us

of the necessary time of repentance; but by *repentance*, and *faith* in *Christ*, our past sinnes are to be done away, how grievous soever they be: *by* living according to the will of *God*, and not by dying by our owne hands; our sinnes are reformed, *and God* glorified. *God* sayes, that *he wills not the death of a sinner, Ezek.* 18. why then should *we will it?*

Sibi adimit necessariũ pœnitẽtiæ tẽpus. Tho. 2. 2. q. 64. Art 5.

5. For peace of conscience, what is to be done in this case.

Fiftly, for peace of *conscience*, in that case, *God* hath appointed other meanes: as

1. *First*, *humiliation* and repentance before *God*.

2. *Secondly*, *confession* to *godly Ministers*, for advice and comfort.

3. *Thirdly*, if the former will not do, then are we to put our selves to open shame for private faults, by publick penance in the *Church*; *or* to put our selves into the hands of the *Magistrates*, to suffer for our crimes, by the civill sword.

Second kind of revenge. Against others.

The second kinde of revenge is intended *against others*, by ones killing of himselfe: *when* he is implacably offended by others, from whom he can neither have satisfaction, nor reformation of his grievances; *and when* his death by his owne hands may redound to the hurt, or disgrace, as he thinks, of those that have wronged him.

Who in this respect are most subject to self-murder.

Which practise of *self-murder*, upon this motive, is most incident to persons of the weakest *sexe*, and worst disposition and condition; such as be *women*, and *servants*, and *men sympathizing* with them in qualities; as a *Wife* that, because shee cannot have her will of, or with her *Husband*, kils her selfe, to the intent to disgrace him, with the reproach of being the occasion of that fact; to grieve and vexe him, and to deprive him of all benefit and comfort that he might have by her life, and to hurt him by all the evill, that can betide him by her death.

The unreasonablenesse of the practise.

Which is a mad course, for one to pull out both their owne eyes, to the end that another may lose one of his: *Such* persons doe die in implacable malice, and are certainely

tainely damned by their owne act and manner of concluding their life.

There is a good and *lawfull revenge* to bee exercised upon those that wroug us; which is in killing that *evill* in them, whereby they offend God and us; *by* instructing and reforming them, by holy admonitions and example; *and* also in killing their enmity, with preservation of their persons, by our *love* and good dealing towards them; making them our friends, both in affection and behaviour; whereby our enemies are destroyed, and our selves benefited.

A good revenge.

Touching killing a mans selfe in *revenge* for his sins, S. *Augustine* sayes, that *We affirme that no man ought for his sinnes past to kill himselfe; for which hee hath rather need of his life, that by repentance they may be healed*: And condemnes the same, *when we may by living performe profitable repentance before God*: And further sayes, *that we doe justly abhorre the fact of Iudas, seeing when hee hanged himselfe, he did rather increase, than expiate the fact of his flagitious treason; because damnably despairing of the mercy of God, he left no place of saving repentance to himselfe; he ended this life being guilty of his own death; for although he was slaine for his owne vile fact, yet it was by another vile fact of his owne.* And so it is apparent, that for *sinne* past, or for *revenge*, no man can murder himselfe warrantably.

Hoc asserimus — neminem propter sua peccata preterita, propter quę magis hac vita opus est, ut possit pœnitendo sanari, cum fructuosam agere possumus pœnitentiam apud Deum. Judæ factum meritò detestamur, cùm se laqueo suspendit, sceleratæ illius traditionis auxisse potiùs quam expiâsse commissum: quoniam Dei misericordiam desperando exitiabiliter, penitus nullum sibi salubris pœnitentiæ locum reliquit, suæ mortis reus finivit hanc vitam, quia, licet propter suum scelus, alio scelere suo occisus est.

§. 19. *Concerning prevention of sin to come.*

The fourth generall *motive* of men to *self-murder*, is *prevention* of sin to come; which a man conceives will inevitably be effected to Gods dishonour, and his owne disgrace,

The fourth generall motive to self-murder: Prevention of sinne.

disgrace, if he doe still live; and may by his death be prevented: and *therefore* doth he hasten and inflict the same with his owne hands.

Those sins for which hee would kill himselfe to prevent them, are of *two sorts.*

1. The sins of others.

First, they are the *sinnes* of *others*, for which a man would kill himselfe; *either* that he may not see them to his griefe, *or* that he may not be the *object*, or subject of other mens committing of them. *As* those *women* that to avoide *ravishment*, and of being deflowred, did kill themselves. Of whom *Eusebius* makes mention in his *history, booke* 8. *cap.* 12. and also *Ambrose* in his *third booke* of *Virgins*; and *Augustine* in his *first booke of the City of God.* Also Hierome writing to *Gerontia*, makes mention of the wife of *Hasdrubal*, who tooke her children in her hands, and did throw her selfe headlong into the fire, that she might not suffer *ravishment.*[a]

[a] *Hasdrubalis uxor apprehensis utrâq; manu liberis in subvectū se præcipitavit incendium, ne pudicitiæ damna sentiret.*

This motive is insufficient.

That this is a very insufficient *motive* for a man to kill himselfe, *Augustine* makes manifest, *de Civit. lib.* 1. *c.* 17. when he sayes, *aliena non sunt nostra peccata, other mens sinnes are not ours. Vertue* and sinne is properly in the heart, out of which they flow, and are not in the body without the mindes consent; where we are but the *passive object*, and involuntary sufferers; *and* therefore, such sinne is not ours, but the *agents* thereof, *except* the sufferer doe yeeld consent to it.

Nisi quis consentiat, non inquinatur corpus nisi de consensu mentis. Dict. Luciæ.

If God, that hates sinne much more than we can, and can easily restraine or destroy sinners, doth notwithstanding *endure with much long suffering the vessels of wrath fitted to destruction*[b]; *Why* should not we suffer what wee cannot amend, leaving the same to *God* the righteous Iudge? *Wee* must not labour to prevent another mans sin, by doing a worse of our owne: *For* so wee shall fall into that, with destruction to our selves, which we oppose in others. Wee may comfortably beleeve, that if wee doe what wee can to resist the yeelding to another mans

[b] *Rom* 9.22.

Non debet in se committere crimen maximum, ut vitet minus crimen alienum. Tho. 2.2. q. 64. art. 5.

mans sinne, *God* will either keep us from consenting, or will graciously pardon it. After that by prayer, advise, resistance and flight, we have done what we can that the same may not be committed.

The second sort of sins, for prevention whereof some people would kill themselves, *are a mans owne sins*, that he is confident he shall doe, to his owne great *shame* and hurt, to Gods great *dishonour, and* to the disgrace of his *friends* and *cause*, if he doe live. 2. A mans owne sinnes.

Which he conceives will unavoidably come to passe, in regard of his extreame inward *frailty*, or prevalent vicious inclination of his owne heart, and of outward force of *attempts* and *temptations*; wherewith he is perswaded he shall be powerfully assaulted, beyond all ability that he hath to withstand the same; *and therefore*, to prevent such a fall, he resolves to kill himselfe, and so destroyes himselfe wilfully by a most certaine and damnable sinne, to prevent an uncertaine and lesser sinne; as it is written of *Apolonia*, who did cast her selfe into the *fire*, and so killed her selfe, that she might not be forced to *worship Idolls*. His grounds of feare that he shall doe them.

Chemnitius reports out of *Lira*, that there were *Hebrewes*, that did teach that it was not only *lawfull*, but that it was also *meritorious* for a man to kill himselfe, in *two cases*.

First, that his life may not be a scorne, to the contempt of *God*. 1. *Ne in contemptū Dei vita ludibrio habeatur.*

Secondly, if a man should be affraid lest he should *fall away* from the *truth*, through the greatnesse of his torments. To which S. *Augustine* writing against *Gaudentius lib*. 2. *cap*. 12. addes a *third* from the *Donatists*; to wit, *feare* of falling away in *persecution*, because of the infirmity of the flesh. 2. *Si timeas ne magnitudine tormentorum deficias.*

The *weaknesse* and insufficiency of this *motive*, for any body thereupon to kill themselves, is apparent by *five reasons*. Insufficiency of this motive. *Reasons.*

First,

1\.
Future evill is but contingent

First, the motive is from uncertaine *future* things; which as they are in *Gods* power to dispose as he lists, so are we to leave them to him; and not for preventing thereof, to attempt any thing certainly evill without *divine* warrant; whereby wee may hasten what we feare, or something worse.

2\.
Self-killing is no lawfull meanes, but otheis to prevent sin.

Secondly, God never appointed *self-murder* to be used for this, or any other end: but for remedy, hath appointed us to walke unvariably and constantly in the way and course appointed by him, and to rely upon his promises, 1 *Cor.* 10. 13. *Who will not suffer us to be tempted above our power: God shewes his power in our weaknesse.* 2 *Cor.* 1. 2, 9.

3\.
Self-murder is evill.

Thirdly, we *must not doe evill that good may come* [a]: *self-murder* is *evill*, and therefore for no good is to bee done. If we would die to avoide sin, why should we so hainously sin, wherby we may die for ever, with perpetuall ignominy? [b]

[a] *Rom.* 3. 8.

[b] *Ac si dicat, jam nunc peccemus, ne postea forte peccemus; jam nunc perpetremus homicidium, ne postea forte incidamus in Adulterium. Nonne si tantum damnatur iniquitas, ut in innocentia, sed potius peccata eligantur; satius est incertum pro futuro adulterium; quam certū de præsenti homicidiū? nonne satius est flagitium committere, quod pœnitendo sanetur, quā tale facinus; ubi locus salubris pœnitentiæ non relinquitur.* Aug. de Civ. Dei lib. 1. cap. 25.

4\.

Fourthly, if to prevent sinnes any man might lawfully kill himselfe, then all men and women in the world might kill themselves: *because*, so long as wee live wee doe sinne; and are lyable to grosse falls many times. *But* if all might upon that reason kill themselves, if their heart would serve them, then all mankinde might presently be extinct, and the *Church* of *God* on earth be abolished; and so the continuance and number of the same should depend upon the will of men themselves, rather than upon the will of *God*: which were a thing most absurd and impious.

5\.

Fifthly, to prevent sin, wee are commanded to *feare God*,

God, and to walke with him in all our wayes; for no man falls into any grosse evill that observes that course; seeing *sinne is a transgression of the law* : *and* therefore, by transgressing of the law cannot be avoided, but is run into, and increased.

From hence we are to *observe,* that *no holy end or effect is to be accomplished by ill or unlawfull meanes.* For *God,* that destinates the end, is al-sufficient to give good meanes, and to make them powerfull to performe what he would have to be done; that wee need not goe to bee beholding to the *devill* for his help to doe Gods worke, about which hee and his wicked meanes are never imployed but they spoile it. *And therefore,* as the worke we doe is good, and as we would have good come of it; we must be carefull to use only good meanes, that we may looke for a blessing from *God* upon them.

Observe. Evill is not to be done to accomplish goodnesse.

Againe, we must not measure and judge an action to be good, only by the good *end* and *intention* of the doers thereof in their act of doing the same : for *Saul* offered sacrifice[a], and *Paul* persecuted the *Church*[b]; both of them with a good intention; *and* yet for all that their actions were evill. *Because,* to make an action good, there are many other things necessary than the good intention of the doers of it: it is sufficient to make an action morally evill, if it be defective in any thing requisite for to make it good; but to be good it must be every way perfect.

Actions are not good onely from intention

[a] 1 *Sam.*13.12.
[b] *Acts* 22.4.

§. 20. *Concerning ambition.*

The fifth generall *motive* of *self-murderers* to kill themselves, is *Ambition*; either to keep, or get a greater good by killing themselves, than they can have or enjoy by living any longer, as they thinke; which profitable exchange makes them thinke it both lawfull and expedient to kill themselves. *This* good is of *two* kindes, whereof

The fifth generall motive, Ambition.

Kinds of good aimed at by ambition.

man is ambitious to death, and for which some kill themselves.

1.
Glory and praise.
Ethnici tanquam insignem fortitudinẽ celebrārũt.

First, it is worldly *glory* and *praise*, which they think to purchase to themselves, by the very acting and doing of *self-murder*, touching which, the *heathen* hath commended such for their *fortitude*; specially when they did it to preserve their personall liberties, from falling under subjection to their enemies, as did *Cato*: to whom I may apply that of *Brutus*, that it *was the love of his countrey, and excessive ambition of praise that made him to kill himselfe.*

Amor patriæ, laudumq; immensa cupido.

And when they did the same, lest they should either suffer, or doe any thing, as they thought, more disgracefull. *Vaine-glory*, and popular praise is so powerfull a *motive*, that for the same it is said that *Empedocles* killed himselfe.

2.
A better life after death.
Ad assequendam gloriam æternam

The second good, for ambition whereof, some kill themselves that they may hasten to attaine the same, is another and *better life* after death; as did *Cleombrotus*, who upon reading in *Plato* of another more happy life after this, which cannot bee attained but by death, did precipitate himselfe into the mouth of death; and so killed himselfe, as *Cicero* in the *first booke* of his *Tusculan questions* makes report.

In such esteeme was that life even with naturall men, that they did willingly run into death, that they might enjoy that whereof they had but a small glimpse, and little assurance. *Which* may condemne many *Christians*, who have greater knowledge, and better evidences for the same, and doe so sightly regard it, that for it they will not forsake their pleasures and lusts, nor will doe duties of easier performance according to Gods appointment, to have it. *Men* would willingly be *saved* and go to *heaven*, but

but by their owne wayes and courses, and not by *Gods*; *although* their owne bee more tedious and chargeable than his; so farre is man wedded to his self-will, and so ready to doe what himselfe devises.

Men are not so much deceived in the *ends* that they project to themselves; (which commonly are good, but especially the last) as they are self-beguiled in the *meanes* and wayes that they use of their self-devising and pleasing, to attaine their ends: whereupon it comes to passe, that so many are frustrated of their desires and expectation. *For good ends*, which be *morally* and *beatifically* such, are never got but by good meanes of *Gods* owne appointment; whereabouts man is to deny his own will, and only to follow *Gods*; who never disappoints us thereby of good successe, according to our hearts desire in the attainement of our last *end*.

Note. Men are more deceived in the meanes, than in the ends.

The insufficiency of the former *motive* of *praise* and *fortitude*, justly to cause a man to kill himselfe, is apparent by that which *Augustine* sayes of *Cato*, that it *was not fortitude, but a softnesse that made him kill himselfe, because he was not able to beare adversity* [a]; *and* did it out of impatiency at *Cæsars empire*; but being impatiently self-willed, would not submit to *Gods* providence: he sayes, *his fact was great, but not good* [b]: *and* further affirmes, that *it is pusillanimity not to be able to suffer*; which is a thing whereunto the weakest, as *women*, are most apt; *both* for want of *strength* to endure to suffer; *and also* for want of *wisdome* to make choise of that which indeed is best for them; *for* as the *Philosopher* saith, *no man kills himselfe, nisi depravata ratione* [c], *but by depravation of his reason*; and so is (as it were) a *mad man*, that is worse than a beast.

Insufficiency of the former motive touching the first branch.

[a] *Non fortitudo, sed moll ties; non potuit ferre res adversas:*

[b] *Magnum potius factum quam bene, Fortiter ille facit qui miser esse potest;* Sene. Epist. 59. *Imbecillis est & ignavus qui propter dolorem moritur.* Arist. 3. Nicomach. cap. 7.

Molles sunt qui amoris gratia vel paupertatis sibi mortem consciscunt: non posse pati, non est vera fortitudo, sed magis quædam mollities animi, non valentis mala pœnalia sustinere: Tho. 2. 2. q 64. art. 5.

c & Arist. Eth. lib. 3. cap. 8.

Praise is got by well-doing.

The true way and meanes for a man to gaine true *honour* and *praise*, is *well-doing*, according to the will and commandements of *God*, (as the *Apostle* sayes) *Glory, honour, and peace to every man that worketh good*[a]; which extends it selfe to all eternity; in the presence, and with the commendation of *God*, his holy *angels*, and of all Gods people: *whereas*, of *evill doing* there comes nothing but *shame*, and confusion eternall: *for* even to bee commended by vaine and wicked persons for doing good, casts some suspition, or aspersion upon the commended; much more is it disgracefull to be praised by such for evill doing; which is the matter of mans shame; and *therefore* upon that motive not to be done.

a *Rom.* 2.10.

About the second branch, the insufficiency of the motive from a better life kill ones selfe.

For the second branch of the aforesaid *motive*: *viz.* about a better life, the insufficiency thereof to make a man undertake to kill himselfe, thereby the sooner to come to eternity, is evident by *foure particulars*.

1. Self-murder is not the way to heaven.

First, *self-murder* being a most grievous sin, it cannot be the *way* to *heaven* and life; *but* to *hell* and death. *The* Saints of *God* that did most long for this eternall life of happinesse, and to whom their naturall lives were not deare, for them to spend them to attaine it; did not therfore kill themselves to have it, which they knew was the way to lose it[b], *as* we see by the practise of the *Apo*: *Paul*, who although he had a desire to depart, and to bee with *Christ*, which he deemed to be best[c], yet would he not kil himself, upon pretence the sooner to have his desire; *Who*, if that had beene a *way* to it, would not have omitted it. *Also old Simeon*, having seene *Christ*, and being desirous to be translated into a better life, did not kill himselfe to effect it; but said, *Lord now lettest thou thy servant depart in peace*[d]. If self-killing were a lawfull meanes the sooner to have life eternall, why should not all *Gods* dearest *servants* have used it; who were to omit no lawfull course to advance themselves to that estate?

b *Reos suæ mortis melior post mortem vita non suscipit.* August.
c *Phil.* 1.23.

d *Luke* 2.29.

Secondly,

Secondly, we are to waite our appointed time of God, and not to stint, or cut it short, as we list; *as* we see was the practise of *Iob*, who said, *All the daies of my appointed time will I waite, till my change come* [a]; wee are not our owne *Masters*, and therefore, may not leave our stations when we list.

Wee are to wait Gods appointed time for heaven.

a *Iob*.14.14.

Thirdly, wee should not affect and flie upon the reward, before that wee have done all the service for the same appointed us of *God*; in the spending of our *lives* to that *period* determined by him; *our* day must bee at an end, before we can receive our *pennie*, *Mat*.20.8. the which day we must not precipitate, by making the light of our lives to set at noone, or before its due time, by a self-murdring hand: *He that beleeves makes not haste*; the promises are attained by patient waiting, which is a part of our obedience best pleasing to God; delay brings increase of glory.

3. We are to do all our service before we have the reward.

Fourthly, wee have a certaine, and comfortable enjoying of *eternall life* begun here in this world, *by grace*, in faith, holy life, and communion with *God*: as the *Apostle* tels us, that the *Kingdome of God is in righteousnesse, peace, and joy of the holy Ghost* [b]: without which in this life, wee shall never inherit the Kingdome of God in the life to come; *and* if we have this, in this life, then may wee well waite for the accomplishment of it in the life to come; when we have such possession, assurance and comfort of it here.

4. Eternall life is here begun.

b *Rom*.14.17.

Here we may *observe*, that *Satan* will abuse the *hope* of *advancement*, to make man venture upon the doing of any sin; as he did *Eve*: *by* this *baite*, more mischiefe hath beene done, and more soules hooked into *hell*, than by any one other meanes in the world. *And* hereby it is that *ambitious* men, and persons of *parts*, and of aspiring spirits, do most frequently perish.

Observ. Hope of advancement abused to evill.

Note. The present estate of the godly is best for that present.

We are to consider that, the *present estate* wherein we are, by Gods appointment and will, is the estate of our

 best

best advancement for the present; beyond which, for us, by our self-willed courses, to transgresse; is but the way for us to come downe and catch a fall.

§. 21. *Of the motions of the Devill, to self-murder.*

The sixt generall motive to self-murder. *Impulsus diaboli.* The instigation of the devill.

The sixt generall *motive,* whereupon *self-murderers* do kill themselves, is the *strong impulse, powerfull motions, and command of the Devill,* who is himselfe a *murderer,* and also moves man to practise it; *both* upon others, *and* upon himselfe; *thereby* to dishonour God, in the destruction of his *Image,* and in the contempt and breach of his *Law: and* that by the same he may destroy *mankind,* overthrow the works of *God, and* fill the world with confusion: hee attempted it against *Christ* himselfe [a]; *he* caused the Swine to drowne themselves [b]; *he* endeavoured to have made the possessed *child* to have killed it self. *Mar.9.22.*

[a] *Mat.4.*
[b] *Mat.8.*

Whence the devill hath his power.

That the *devill* hath such power sometime over *man,* proceeds from the *leave* and permission of *God,* without which hee can do nothing: *and also* it is from his *spirituall nature,* whereby hee is naturally *superiour* to man, and can strangely affect him; *that* hee so farre prevailes over him sometimes, that hee can make him kill himselfe.

How thereby self-murder is effected.

This infernall command, or powerfull inclination of *self-murder* is given, or wrought by *Satan two wayes.*

1. In visible apparition.

First, in some visible *apparition* of the *devill,* speaking to, and perswading a man to kill himselfe. *Which* hee doth *either outwardly* in some bodily shape, as he spake to *Eve,* and to our *Saviour Christ: or else inwardly* to the *fancie,* whereby a man thinks that he heares, or sees the *devill,* or some other, that can be none else but hee, bidding, or perswading him to *stab* himselfe, or to fling himselfe

1. Outwardly.
2. Inwardly.

selfe into the *water*; *or* out of a *window*, or the like, to kill himselfe thereby.

The persons thus *haunted* by *Satan*, are either notorious wretches, mancipated to the *devils* service, and guilty of horrible *crying* crimes; *or else* they are persons extreamly *melancholick*, *fearefull*, or discontented, whose tempers, and imaginations give the *devill* advantage this way to worke upon them.

Persons haunted.

1. Wicked.

2. Melancholick.

Secondly, the devill doth powerfully move a man to kill himselfe, in manner *equivalent* to a commandement, by *internall suggestions*, and raising of such inward powerfull *motions* of self-killing in the minde, as can hardly be put out, or withstood: in *regard* of the deepe and firme impression of them in man, and of the intimate entertainement and commanding possession that they have in him, by meanes of his corruption conspiring with *Satan*, to mans owne destruction.

2. Satans powerful motions in the minde.

The grounds that *Satan* works upon, after this manner, to prevaile with man to kill himselfe, are *three*.

Satans grounds of working to prevaile.

First, he takes advantage of all other *motives* to *self-murder*, both furthering and powerfully intending all occasions to that effect; *perverting* the *judgement*, and *kindling pride*, or *impatiencie*, as is apparent by his dealing with *Iob*, whose afflictions he both procured, and poysoned, with the leaven of his intermingled malitiousnesse.

1. The advantage of all other motives.

And also, hee workes and injects into the minds of men, upon those crosse occasions, such self-killing *resolutions*, as puts them upon that vile *act*; in a mans sufferings and distractions the *devill* is most busie to worke his owne ends thereby, who subtilly intermingles himselfe in all *stormes* of troubles, against man.

He injects resolutions of self-killing.

The second ground, whereby *Satan* prevailes with man to kill himselfe, is mans wretched *prophanenesse* and *idlenesse*: *for*, a heart emptie of goodnesse, and filled with wickednesse, is a fit receptacle for *Satan*, *especially* when such

2. Prophanenesse and idlenesse.

such an one is not taken up with holy thoughts, and with good and warrantable imployment, in some calling, then is there roome, and fit time, for the *devill* to cast in his firie temptations, to take possession of such a man, and forcibly to incline him to what horrible evils he list, even to *self-destruction.*

3. Peoples fit temper and disposition.

The third ground whereupon *Satan* overswaies men to kill themselves, is the speciall *temper* and *disposition* of people, whereby they are, in differing manner, capable of severall *impressions*; this *disposition* or *temper* is either

1. Naturall.

naturall, as *melancholick*, *fearefull*, *proud*, *ambitious*, or the like; *which* kind of persons are naturally aptest to resolve upon, and attempt dismall acts of *self-murder*, upon the *devils* suggestion, in the fits and pangs of their distemperature.

2. Morall.

Or else, the temper most capable to receive the *impressions* of *self-murder* from *Satan*, is *morall*: *as* in *people* surcharged with the bondage and horror of their sinnes; and with the feare of the punishment due for them: which the *devill* aggravates to such a man, to drive him to *desperation*; and obscures, or overshadowes the *grace* and *mercy* of *God* from him; *and* so perplexes a distressed *conscience* with conceit of unpardonablenesse of his sins, from apprehension of the excessive *greatnesse* of the same; of the *kind* of them, as if they were against the *holy Ghost*, and from conceit that either the time of *grace* to him is past; *or* that *God* will never pardon him, although he should seeke to him for forgivenesse: then such an one resolves, by the *devils* perswasion, to kill himselfe, that he may prevent the making of his *estate* worse, than presently it is, and to ease himselfe of the present distresse of conscience that he is in.

How these motiōs be known to be frō Satan.

That we may know whether this self-murderous *impulsion*, and strong *motion* be from the *devill*, we are to observe *three things*.

1. *First*, if the motion of self-murder, so raised, or injected

jected be such; as upon the first sight thereof, *nature* in a man abhorres it, and *reason* and *grace* withstands, with a continuall strife and conflict against it; then the same is of *Satan*. By natures and reasons abhorring of them.

Secondly, if the forciblenesse of the *motion* to *self-murder*, for effecting the act, be not so much, from the apparent *occasions*, as from secret *impelling power*, then, the same is from *Satan*; *because*, the thing whereunto a man is moved is *evill*, and *therefore*, cannot be from *God*, or any good *principle*. 2. When they are from some secret impelling power.

That the *devill* may make a man to murder himselfe, he both *hides* the uglinesse of the sinne, and the greatnes of the danger; *and also*, he makes a false representation of great, or pleasing good by it to man, more than he can have by living. Satans deceitfull craft.

The *insufficiency* of this *motive* from *Satan*, to warrant a man to kill himselfe, is apparent by *two things*. Insufficiency of this motive from Satan to kill ones selfe.

First, we ought neither to beleeve the *devill* who is a *lyar*, nor to *obey* him; but to resist him, and give him no place[a]. For, *God* is our Lord whom we are to respect, and not *Satan*: *and* whatsoever *motions* doe come from the *devill*, we are the more to abhorre them, because they come from him. 1. Beleeve him not. [a] *Jam.*4.7. *Ephes.*4.27.

Secondly, such a vile *motion* is contrary to right *reason*, and *Gods will*; *both*, *because* it flowes originally from *Satan*; and *also* is grounded, neither upon *reason* nor *religion*, but upon fond conceits and self-will: a *reasonable* man, and Christian, should do nothing advisedly, neither warrantably can doe any thing, but according to sound *reason* and *religion*. 2. Contrarie to reason and religion.

Wee are to *observe*, from this generall *motive* of *self-murder*, the danger that men are in by the *devill*, who indeavours the destruction both of soule and body: *and* of the body hee desires the over-throw specially by a mans owne hands: *because*, thereby he also ruinates the soule, in its horrible act of transgression by *self-murder*; *Observe.* Men are in danger by the Devill.

which is the thing that hee specially aimes at.

And therefore, wee need to observe diligently the *Apostle Peters* direction, to be *sober* and *vigilant*, because *our adversary the devill, as a roaring Lion walketh about seeking whom he may devoure*[b]. *And also*, wee should be carefull to cleave to *God* by faith, in beleeving in him through *Christ*, and to depend alwaies upon him by prayer, who is the *preserver* of men: *and* so we shall be safe, walking in the waies of *Gods* appointment, and adhering to the direction of his word.

[b] 1 Pet. 5 8.

Note.

§. 22. *Of Phrensie occasioning self-killing.*

The seventh generall motive of self-murder. Phrensie.

The *seventh motive* occasioning *self-killing*, is *phrentick distemperatures*; which are either *voluntarily* contracted and entertained, as in violent *passions* of *love*, *anger*, and the like; whereby some kill themselves: *or else* they are *involuntary*, and such as a man is but *passively* affected with, and subject to; whereby a man being deprived of the *use* of *reason*, doth most unreasonable actions, as to kill himselfe, or his dearest friends; led onely by a *brute passion*, without reason, or understanding.

1. Voluntary. *Ira furor brevis est.*

2. Involuntary.

Kinds of it. 1. Naturall.

This involuntary phrentick distemperature is either *naturall*, or *spirituall*:

1. Fooles.

Naturall, is *first* in persons from their birth, *wanting the use of reason*, and disposed to mad prancks, by a *depraved* disposition, or deficiency; as *fooles*, having instead of *reason* a spice of *phrensie*, when passion is provoked in them, not sticking to do themselves mischiefe.

2. Mad men.

Secondly, it is in *mad men* and *lunaticks*, who are inclined to do unreasonable harmefull acts, without any respect of good to themselves, in that which they do.

3. Melancholick persons.

Thirdly, it is in extreame *melancholick persons*; who are possessed with *direfull apprehensions*, and oppressed with uncomfortable sadnesse, and are driven into fearefull resolutions, sometimes of self-murder: upon deepe

impressions

impressions in them of heavie things and terrible, flowing from their owne fancies, and strong imaginations, which often, never comes to passe.

The *distemperature* of *spirituall phrensie* in a man, which occasions *self-murder*, is that which deprives a man of the *use* of *spirituall reason* and *divinity*, that hee hath in him, and inclines him to do acts contrary to *grace* and *naturall reason*. 2. Spirituall.

This kinde of distemperature arises from *two grounds* especially. The grounds of spirituall phrensie.

First, from an *abused* or *perverted judgement*, *either* upon *mistaken principles*, from conceit of the motion of *Gods Spirit*; *or* by *over-clouding* of a mans *minde*, by mad *error*, *raging passions*, *furious preposterous zeale*; and by the foggie mists of *misprisions* and *horrors*, overspreading mans *understanding* and conscience, whereby a man becomes spiritually *phrentick*; which is a kind of learning that makes mad [a]. All wilfull sin is a spice of *spirituall*, or *morall madnesse*, *in* which respect *David* confessed of himselfe, *that he was as a beast before God* [b]. 1. Abused judgement.

[a] *Act.* 16.24.
Note.
[b] *Psal.* 73.22.

The second cause of *spirituall phrensie*, that occasions *self-murder*, is inextricable perplexity of distresse of *conscience*, proceeding from want of all sensible feeling of *grace*, of the *favour* of *God*, of *comfort*, or *hope*, and from apprehension of Gods heavie *displeasure*, and of fearefull subjection to eternall *damnation* and misery: *in* which estate a man hath not the use of those parts of *understanding* and *grace*, which he hath in him; *but* is like a *ship* in a storme driven, without command of sailes, or rudder, to destruction. 2. Distresse of conscience.

This motive, although it be powerfull sometimes to the effecting of *self-killing*, warrants not an act done both against *reason* and *religion*: where the foresaid *phrensie* is by default contracted, *or*, in the time of the *lucide intervals* thereof, if a man do kill himselfe, he is directly and *formally* a *self-murderer*. Some kind of phrensie excuses not, and some doth excuse a self-killer, from the imputation of self-murder.

Observe. Phrensie is calamitous, and to be prayed against.

We are to *observe* from hence, how *dangerous* and calamitous a thing it is to be subject to such *phrentick distempers : and therefore,* wee are to labour and pray for a *sound minde*, and that we may be able *wisely* to *use* those parts of *understanding* and *religion* that wee have for our owne good, and the good of others; that having our right wits and senses, we may not doe those prankes, or so live as may prove that we are fitter for *Bedlam*, or to be begged for *fooles*, than to be reputed reasonable or wise men.

§. 23. *Of examples of self-murder.*

The last generall motive to self-murder. Examples.

The eighth and last generall *motive*, whereupon *self-murderers* doe kill themselves, is frequent *examples* both of *heathens* and *Christians*, who have done the same, and are celebrated, and famous in *histories*, of whom we neither see, nor heare of further evill befallen them. *It is* certaine, that *examples* of commendable persons, and such as we love, is a strong *motive* to draw men to the like practise.

Note.

But it is to be *observed*, that they are *neither* the *best* men, nor the *wisest*, that are led by *examples*, as by their *supreme rule*, without respect of more warrantable direction and reason: but of this see more afterward, *Cap.* 17. §. 7. *arg.* 17. *and cap.* 18. §. 4.

De bello Judaico lib. 7, cap. 28.

Iosephus reports how *Eleazar* by this *motive* encouraged himselfe and others to kill themselves : in these words. *Let us see the example of the wiser sort* (as hee calls them) *of the Indians, who* (he said) *being just men, did tolerate this life as a necessary office of nature for a certaine time, though against their wills; yet did they hasten to unloose the soule bound in this mortall body, though not urged thereunto by any calamity, or necessity; but only for desire of immortality.*

But this *motive* from *examples* of *self-murder* is unsufsufficient to warrant the same, because they are contrary to sound *reason* and *religion*, against which no example is to be followed: and such examples are the practise not of the best, but of the worst disposed of men, who are not to be imitated, specially in that which is evill; and none are warrantably commended in *histories*, nor famous in the *Church*, because, and in respect that they killed themselves, but for some precedent *vertues*, and pious disposition in their lives. For all men who are guided in their judgement by sound *reason* and *divine* truth, doe thereby verily thinke and beleeve, that the damnable *act* of *self-murder* doth bring the *committers* thereof into the wofull and fearefull estate of eternall *perdition* in the world to come.

Thus farre I have laboured to discover the *motives* abused to *self-murder*, and have shewed the *insufficiency* of them.

Where we may observe, how men encourage themselves, and pretend reason for all their wicked and unreasonable courses, and how weake and unwarrantable their grounds and excuses are for the same; which, like smoke or a shadow, vanishes in the tryall of impartiall truth; and so leaves the *sinner* stript naked from his shifts, and subjected to just judgement of condemnation at the last. *Observe.*

Chap. 16.

The introducement and entrance into self-murderer.

§. 1. *Of the persons subject to self-murder.*

WEE are now to proceed to the *introduction* and beginning of *self-murder*, in the act thereof; about which we are to consider *two things.*

1. Persons subject to self-murder.

First, the persons that are most subject, upon the former grounds, to temptations and acts of *self-murder*, are specially of *foure sorts.*

1. Melancholicke people.

First, *melancholie* people; *because* they are most *cogitabundi & tristes, given to musing and sadnesse*, on whom *Satan* workes most; *and* they are most subject to discontentment, and apt thereupon to entertaine impressions and resolutions of *self-murder*. *So* that *naturall temper* makes much for the *passive* capacity of some vertues and vices, more than others.

2. People under spirituall temptations.

Secondly, the persons most subject to these fits of self-murder, are Christians under great *spirituall temptations*, upon their want of apprehension of the presence of *grace*, and favour of *God*; and upon the sense of the horrour of their owne raging corruptions and lusts, in the seeming prevailing thereof against their opposition, without hope of ability to subdue them, or to have them pardoned. *And* upon conceiving that their crosses, when the same are great, are in wrath from *God*, without any hope of forgivenesse or freedome; which swallowes them up in despaire: temptations incline men contrary to their own tempers.

Thirdly,

Thirdly, the parties most subject to *self-murder*, are *high-minded* and *ambitious persons*, impatient of disgrace and crosses; as was *Abitophel*, and all such as place their chiefe happinesse in earthly things; whereof when they are disappointed, they grow into that degree of discontentment, that they will not out-live their expectation of earthly things, but will rather kill themselves, than endure such a crosse and disappointment in that which they most highly value. 3. Proud ambitious persons.

Fourthly, those that are most subject to fall into this *self-murder*, are people that are most *obnoxious* to a wicked and *flagitious course of life*, imbraced and impenitently lived in; *contrary* both to the *meanes* they have, *and also* to the light and *reluctancy* of their owne *consciences*; with such affection of love to, and zeale for evill, and hatred and opposition of goodnesse and all good people; that they overpitch themselves so farre beyond recovery, that when they are throughly awaked, and doe seriously consider, discerne and feele the wofulnesse of their estates; being under the desperate sense and importable horrour of their sinnes and judgements due for the same; then are they in danger to conclude their wretched dayes by *self-murder*. 4. Wicked persons.

Therefore, people should well *consider* their owne *tempers* and states, with the severall *dangers* that attend upon the same; and are to be *wise* to fortifie themselves, where they are weakest; and so wisely to demeane and behave themselves, that they *neither* entertaine, nor give way to any thing in themselves that may bring them to destruction; but by faith and good workes to walke with *God*, whereby they may be sure to live for ever. *Observ.* To know our tempers, and watch our selves.

§.2. Of

§. 2. *Of the entrance into self-murder.*

2. Entrances into self-murder. *The second* thing considerable in the acting of *self-murder*, is the first entrances, degrees or approaches into it, *which* are specially *foure.*

1. Crying capitall crimes. Parricide proceeds. *First, grievous capitall crying sinnes of blood*; as *murder*, knowne, or secret, *parricide*, which is killing of *parents, children, wives*, or *husbands* : *which* flowes *either* from *exuberancy* of carnall affection to them whom they kill, 1. From love of them that are killed. whereby they take occasion to kill them, by prevention, to free them from miseries; *or* to have them with them out of this world; being by their owne hands about to rid themselves out of this life.

2. From hatred of them. *Or else* it proceeds from *unnaturall*, or *monstrous hatred to them*, for *wrong* sustained by them, for keeping some good from them; *or* for the supposed evill they 3. From love of some other things. may bring upon them : as *whores* that kill their *infants* to avoide *shame* and *punishment* ; *children* that kill their aged *parents* to come to their *estates*; *mothers* in *law* that kill their *children* in *law*, to derive *estates* to their owne; *widdowes* that kill their children to ease themselves of *charge*, and to preferre themselves by *mariage*. *These* persons, as they kill their owne soules by such vile sins; so are they justly given over of *God* in recompense of their owne wayes, to destroy their own bodies by their owne *self-murdering* hands.

2. Desperation. *The second degree* of entrance, or approach into *self-murder*, is *desperation* of pardon of sins, or of freedome from calamities; which rather than some will endure, they will kill themselves; seeing no other way of easing themselves and their minds, whereof some resemblance *Job* 2.9. expounded. may bee seene in *Iobs Wifes* counsell to her *Husband*, advising him in his extremitie to curse *God* and *die*; that is, that he would take a course to be rid out of his miseries; *either* by *blasphemy* provoking *God* to kill him; *or* by

by dispatching himselfe with his owne hands, after that he had blessed *God*, in making peace with him for the safety of his *soule*.

Thirdly, a further degree of *entrance* into *self-murder*, is the advised entertainment of *temptations* and *motions* for a man to kill himselfe, voluntarily suffering the same to seise upon him, with some liking thereof; searching and pleading reasons, and examples to beguile himselfe; whereby he may thinke it lawfull, or lesse evill in that case to kill himselfe : *and* begins to plot the *manner* how he may best accomplish it, with a fluttering wavering resolution to doe it. 3 Entertainment of self-murderous motions.

The fourth degree of entrance into *self-murder*, is the impatient wishing and desiring of *death*, and a lothing and wearisomnesse of life; which so farre prevailes upon some, that their whole study and endeavours are how to get out of their lives, and to dispatch themselves by their owne hands, rather than to live here. 4. Impatient desire of death.

It is here a pertinent *question*, whether it be at all lawfull to *desire* that we were dead? A question concerning desire of death.

For resolution whereof, it is to bee considered that there are *two sorts* of *desires* of *death*; the one is *holy*, the other is *sinfull*. *Answer.*

A holy desire of death is that, which desires not to be *unclothed*, but to be *clothed upon*, 2 *Cor*.5.2,4. the things that make this desire to be holy are *two*. 1 A holy desire of death. How it is holy.

First, when it is *conditionall* and *moderate*, with respect and subordination to the good will of *God*, being content to live if *God* will have it so; *and* while wee are in this life, such holy desires of our dissolution from hence, doe not hinder, but further all such performances as tend to the glorifying of *God*, and to the edification of our selves and others. 1 By subordination to Gods will.

Secondly, the holinesse of the desire of death consists in the *motives* thereof; the which are *two*. 2 In the motives thereof.

The first, is to bee with *Christ*; that we may enjoy 1

God in him, to our full happinesse. *Philip.* 1. 23.

The *second* is, that we may be wholly *freed* from *sinning* against God, and may be *beatifically* perfit; in having the fulnesse of that, whereof we now have the first fruits, as the Apostle professes touching himselfe; that *he did forget those things that are behinde, and did reach forth to those that are before, and did presse toward the marke, for the price of the high calling of God in Christ Iesus* [a]: yet, for to be translated no man is purposely to doe any thing to hasten his death; *nor* to omit any thing due for preservation of his life; *or* to bee more negligent in doing the things which are pertinent for him to doe in this life.

[a] *Phil.* 3. 13, 14.

Vnlawfull desires of death.

A sinfull desire of death consists in *three* things.

First, in absolutely *desiring* it, according to our owne *wills*, how, and when to die; with using meanes as wee list to effect it, neglecting the preservation of life, and well imployment of the same in doing all those duties, for which *God* doth give it to us.

2 *Secondly*, when our desire of dying is from *lothing* of life, and *envying* the benefit of it to ones selfe, for *Gods glory*, and the good of others; which wee postpone and subject to our owne *self-wills*.

3. *Thirdly*, when our eager desire of the same, is more for *freedome* from some temporary evills [b]; than for to enjoy spirituall and eternall good: which ought not to be, *because God* is as much, if not more glorified, and our selves and others truly benefited by our *passive obedience*, as by our *active*: *for*, by the *former God* hath his *will* more than by the *latter*.

[b] 1 *Kings* 19. 4. *Job* 3. 3. *Jer.* 20. 14. *Rev* 6. 16.

Note. *Non pro vitandis naturæ vel fortunæ malis; sed pro vitando malo animi, & assequendo potiore bono.*

Our chiefe care should be for the happy estate of our soules, and of both soule and body for evermore. *And therefore*, as *one* saith, *Wee may not desire death, to shunne and escape the evills of nature or fortune; but to avoide the evill of the soule, and to obtaine a more excellent good.*

An objection out of *Marke* 14. 21.

An objection may here be made from *Mark.* 14. 21. where

where it is said, *That it had been good that Iudas had never been borne*; *therefore* it may seeme to be lawfull for such to wish and hasten death; that what was good it had not beene, may (as soone as may be) be brought to *not being*.

Hereunto I answer, for a man to *bee*, (although miserable) absolutely considered, is better than not to *bee* at all; *because* God doth nothing in vaine, and but what is good that it should *bee*: *also being* is better than *not being*, in regard of the neerer *proximity* thereof to God. Nor to *bee* is *negative* of all goodnesse, *Non-entis nulla sunt affectiones*: *A non-ens hath no positive properties*: whereas, *being* is good, and capable of good; *ens* and *bonum, metaphysically* considered, are reciprocall. *Answ.* The goodnesse of being.

It is not *good*, with the goodnesse of profit for some men in particular that they are, or *bee*; in regard of their owne private wretched estate, and of the evills that their beeing subjects them unto, and makes them capable of.

Yet it is *good*, in respect of the *Vniverse*, consisting of contraries, and benefited by the same; and for the farther manifestation of the glory of *God*; and *because* it is his will that such men should *bee*.

The publike and more eminent *good preponderates* to give denomination, against the more private and lesser evill.

It is by mans owne fault, abusing his *esse* and *being*, that he is miserable; *both* by *deprivation* of *good*, *and* also by *subjection* to wretchednesse: *esse* or *being* is good to those that use it well, and is evill onely *accidentally* to those that abuse it. *Note.*

§. 3. *Of the signes of self-murder.*

The signes of *self-murder*, are specially *foure*. Signes of self-murder.

First, the unwoonted affectation of *solitarinesse* by persons disposed and fit for *self-murder*, upon some of the 1. Solitarinesse.

 prece-

precedent *motives*, whereby they eſtrange themſelves from all company and meanes, whereby they might bee comforted and upheld; and doe give the greater advantages and entertainment to *ſelf-murderous motions* and temptations, raiſed or injected by the *devill*; or elaborated and wrought out by a diſcontented ſelf-muſing minde.

2. Signe of ſelf-murder. Neglect of duties and regardleſneſſe.

The ſecond forerunning *note* of *ſelf-murder* is a ſtrange and ſudden *neglect* of neceſſary duties of a mans calling, *civill* and *divine*, and a *regardleſſeneſſe* of thoſe perſons, and things in the world that he moſt affected; *having* his thoughts and mentall diſcourſes and determinations imployed about *murdering* of himſelfe; *ſo as neither* his diſcourſes about *religion*, or his *civill* affaires, nor his performances in, or about either of them, is ſo diſcreet, as it was wont to be; *but* as of things that he doth not minde; or whereabouts he is with ſome other thoughts and reſolutions diſturbed.

3. Signe of ſelf-murder. Strange behaviour.

The third ſigne foregoing *ſelf-murder*, is a ſtrange change in outward *behaviour*, with gaſtly lookes, wilde frights and flaights, neſtling and reſtleſſe behaviour, a mindleſſeneſſe and cloſe dumpiſhneſſe, both in company and in good imployments; a diſtracted countenance and cariage; ſpeaking and talking to, and with themſelves, in their ſolitary places and dumps; reaſoning and reſolving with themſelves about that fact, and their motives to it, in a perplexed diſturbed manner, with the like.

4. Signe of ſelf-murder. Speeches and actions.

The fourth precedent note of *ſelf-murder*, is the *ſpeeches* and *actions* of ſuch perſons immediately before the fact: which are ſome words of *threatning* or *fore-telling* ſomething that may import ſo much; as that his friends ſhall not have him long to trouble them; or he will very ſhortly be rid out of all theſe troubles; *or* he deſires the abſence, or ſends away thoſe that he thinkes may hinder him; or he moves queſtions of that nature; he provides himselfe of meanes to doe it; *seekes* opportunities, hee pretends many excuses to be here, or there, to do this, or that, whereby he thinks he may be able to do that vile fact upon himselfe: and sometime he is taken attempting to do it; which is a sufficient warning what he will do, if it be not seasonably prevented.

It is to be *observed*, that *self-murder* comes *ague-like*, by *fits*; and that none, or very few doe fall into that horrible sinne to accomplish it upon themselves, but by *degrees*. *For*, no man at an instant falls into the fowlest crimes in the highest degree; *but* by *meanes*, from step to step, as he is able to overcome the opposition of *reason* and *grace*, that stands in his way. *So then*, suddenly trust not him, that once advisedly attempts to kill himselfe, although he seeme to repent, and promise faire never to do it, when either he himselfe gave over the attempt for the present, or was prevented by others. *Note.* Practises of self-murder comes by fits.

For, except the *cause* thereof bee soundly cured; and he confirmed, in length of time, against the temptation, it will more furiously recoyle upon him; and he, when hee thinks hee is secure of others from interrupting of him, will doe that indeed, which before hee did but attempt for a triall and an essay: so subtill and indivertible is man to destroy himselfe, with whom the devill hath prevailed so far, fully to resolve upon the fact. *Note.*

Chap. 17.

Arguments against self-murder, proving the same to be utterly unlawfull.

§.1. *Self-murder is contrary to Religion.*

First it is against religion, and how.

THat no Men or Women should murder themselves, but that they should abhorre the same, is many waies apparent; *because*, it is unlawfull by *religion*, most harmefull in *effect*, and contrary to *reason*.

1. Against Gods Law.

Non occides: nullus nec ipse utique cui præcipitur, intelligitur exceptus, Tho.

First, that by *religion*, it is unlawfull for people to kill themselves, is manifest by *five particulars*.

First, it is *forbidden* by the *Law* of *God*, in the sixt *Commandement*, *Thou shalt not kill*; *which* prohibits *murder* of man in generall; and that we should kill none, except it be in our owne necessary defence; *or*, by publike *authority*, of *Lawes* and *Magistrates*, to take away a malefactor, in punishment of his sin past, and to prevent mischiefe by him to others, for time to come. For, as *Augustine* saith, *Every one that, without authority of lawfull power, kills a man, is a murderer* [a]; *and* if otherwise we may not by the *Law* of *God* kill any man, then we may not kill our selves: *because*, as the same *Father* saies, *He that kills himselfe, kills no other thing*, in so doing, *but a man* [b]. *For*, we are men, and all the *individuals* are comprehended in, and under their generall.

*Againe, Gen.*9.5. God saies, *That at the hand of man he will require mans blood, even at a mans owne hand*; that is, a *mans* owne blood at his owne hand, if he kill himselfe, as *Peter Martyr* interprets it.

And if, by the Word of *God*, it had beene lawfull for

[a] *Omnis qui sine ulla legitimæ potestatis authoritate hominē occidit homicida est.* Aug. Epist. 61.

[b] *Neque qui se occidit aliud occidit quā hominē.* *Idem* de Civ. D. l. 1. c. 20.

for a man to kill himselfe, then would not the *Apostle Paul* have cryed out to the *Jaylor*, that was about to kill himselfe, *That he should doe himselfe no harme* [a]: *for*, why should he have letted him from doing a lawfull thing, or have called it a doing of himselfe harme, in any *morall* consideration?

[a] *Act* 16.28.

Self-murder is against love the summe of the Law.

Farthermore, *self-murder* is an odious fact, contrary to the generall *summe* of the *Law*; which is *love*, and *justice*: it is against that *love*, that we owe to *God*, in respect whereof wee are to keep his Law, and to affect to enjoy him: *and* it is against that *love*, wherewith wee ought to *love* our *selves*; and whereby we should endeavour our owne wel-fare and happinesse; and according to which we should *love* our *neighbours*. *Who* can expect better measure at a mans hand, than he performes to himselfe? if the *rule* be not straight, all that is measured by it must be crooked: the *Apostle* delivers it as an *axiome*, *no man yet ever hated his owne flesh*, *Ephes.* 5.29. *and againe*, he condemnes those that, under pretence of wil-worship, *did not spare their owne bodies* [b], *Col.* 2.23. *Self-murder* is also contrary to the *love* that we owe to our *neighbours*, by depriving them thereby both of our selves, and of all the good and comfort that they might have by our lives.

[b] ἀφειδίᾳ.

Self-murder is against the generall justice of the Law.

It is likewise against the generall *justice* of the *Law*, which requires that wee should give to every man his *due*. *For*, *self-murder* deprives *God*, our *neighbours* and our *selves* of their *rights*: *God* of obedience and glory, by our lives: and our *neighbours*, and our *selves* of that benefit that both should have by our living.

[c] *Rom.* 13.7.

Question. About Superiours.

Here a *question* may be moved; whether a *Magistrate*, that hath no *superiour* over him on earth, and is guilty of a capitall crime, or crimes, may justly in punishment of himselfe therefore, put himselfe to death, or cause others to do it: *and* whether a *capitall malefactor*, whose hainous offence falls not under mans cognizance; *or* being

ing knowne, is neglected to be punished, as *privy murder*, or *blasphemy* in the highest degree against *God*; may not, in this case, or where he is a subject to none other man, kill himselfe, or cause another to do it, in execution of justice?

Answer.

I *answer*, to the *first branch* of the *question*, with *Thomas Aquinas*, *negatively*; *because*, he cannot be his owne *capitall Judge*, in his owne cause [a]; *and* so, *Magistrates*, that have no earthly *superiour* over them, are lyable to be punished onely by *God*; either immediatly, as was *Herod* [b], or mediatly, by extraordinary meanes of Gods raysing up; *as* was *Belthazzar* by *Darius* [c]. *Magistrates* are under the same *morall Lawes*, in equall strictnesse and extent, as any other men; *for*, before *God* there is no respect of persons; and *therefore*, a *Magistrate*, can no more lawfully kill himselfe, than a private man can kill himselfe: as wee see in King *David*, who neither did put himselfe, nor was put to death by others for his *adultery* and *murder*.

a *Secūda secūdæ*. q. 64. Art 5. *Nullus est Judex sui ipsius*.
b *Act*.12.23.
c *Dan*.5.30,31.

A Magistrate may not kill himselfe, nor may be slaine by his people. 2 *Sam*. 11. & 12.

Reasons.

1. *Finally*, for no crime can a *Magistrate*, in any case, kill himselfe; *because*, he is not his owne, but the *Common-wealths*; and *therefore*, cannot dispose of himselfe in that respect, as he list:
2. *neither* hath the body punitive power of *jurisdiction* over its *head*:
3. *neither* is hee to bee valued and esteemed simply as an *individuall* man; who, as *David* was, may be worth *thousands*; and *therefore*, for crimes punishable in *their* particular subjects by death, is not to be put to death by his *people*, nor yet to kill *himselfe*; whose losse that way may bring farre more damage, than such an execution of *Justice* upon him can do good, in such a *temerarious* manner. *For answer* to the *second branch*, I referre the reader to that which is said before, touching insufficiency of the *third* generall *motive* to *self-murder*; *And* further adde, that things secret belong to *God*; and the *Magistrates omissions*, and *aberrations* belong to *God*, and not to private men, from private

Magistrates neglect, and secret capitall crimes belong not to any to redresse by death upon themselves.

private motion, in authoritative manner to amend. *Such* a man, if to punish himselfe he kill himselfe, cannot do it, but either as a *Magistrate*; *or* as a private man: then in neither respects can he do it, as we have heard: and therefore, he cannot lawfully do it at all.

A Case. About persons condemned to death: what they may do to prevent or hasten it.

I would here further *determine* a *case*, which is this: *Suppose* a man be condemned, ignominiously to die; may he *poyson*, or *famish*, or *bleed* himselfe to death; may hee *stab* himselfe, *hang* himselfe, *cut* his owne *throat*, break his neck, or *cast himselfe* off the *ladder*, *leap into* the *water*, or *fire*, *either* to hasten his death, that he is adjudged to, or to prevent it, specially when it is undeserved?

Answer. They may not kill themselves although commanded to do it.

I answer, that, although the *Judge* should command him to do the same, hee ought not to doe it, much lesse may he doe it of his owne accord: *because*, it is against the *Law* of *God*, and of *nature*, for one to kill himselfe; *and* is an *act* of *self-condemnation*, as if, in his owne opinion he were neither worthy, nor fit to live, nor yet to
Reasons. 1.
die, in a warrantable manner, by the hand of *justice*: the 2.
lengthning of *life* is a blessing to be imbraced, for the 3.
good that thereby we may do, or get: *to* prevent *justice*, 4.
in the execution thereof, doth wrong it, by invading and usurping the right thereof, with injury to the *Commonwealth*, by a self-willed cutting off the *members* therof, in such a disorderly course, as opens a way to overthrow the same: death is an act of suffering, and not of *agency*, of him that is to die; *self-murder* is a more shamefull and
uncomfortable death, than any other that a man can 5.
suffer: *and* it is not the death inflicted by others; *but*, the
cause thereof in our selves, that makes it honourable, or 6.
disgracefull, according to the deserts of our lives. *If* a man be undeservedly condemned to die, it is the more honourable and comfortable for him to suffer [a]; and he needs be the more carefull that hee may not hurt or blemish himselfe, by his manner of dying, otherwise than

[a] 1 *Pet.*3.14,17. & c.4.v.15,16.

becomes a good Christian: *although* hee bee innocent in that speciall thing, for which he is adjudged to die; *yet* he is to consider that hee may bee guilty of some other particulars justly deserving death; and in that respect is patiently to acknowledge and submit to the stroke of *divine Iustice*, finding out, and punishing his sins: *or else*, that *God* wisely so orders things that hee shall so die, only for triall of his *passive* obedience; and for the *glorifying* of *God*, both in the cause, and manner of his death, which he is to suffer well, and for well doing.

What men are to consider in suffering innocently.

How a condemned person is to submit to die.

Yet notwithstanding, a *person* condemned to die, and in the hands of the *executioners*, is not to strive, oppose, or withstand them in doing execution upon him: but he may, and ought, upon their command, so to dispose and order himselfe, as he may be fit, and way by him may be made, for them to doe their office in executing of him: *as*, for him quietly to *submit* to be *led* to the place of *execution*, and there to be ordered by them, as they please; for him patiently to receive his death by their hands: *to open* his *mouth* to receive *poyson* of their giving to him; as our *Saviour* did the *vinegar* that was given him upon the *Crosse*, *Iohn* 19.29,30. to *lay bare* his *neck* to the blow; *submit* his neck to the *haltar*, to *embrace* the fire, *entertaine* applied combustible matter, for dispatch of himselfe: *provided* alwaies, that the same be not first kindled, or applied mortally by his own meanes: *the* truth thereof is apparent, by that which our blessed *Saviour* fortold *Peter*, that hee should *stretch forth his hands, and another should gird him: signifying by what death he should glorifie God* [a].

[a] *Ioh.*21.18,19.

Reasons.

1. *The reason* hereof is evident; *because*, a *person* condemned to death is no more his owne, but the *sonne* of *death*, in the hand of *authority*, to be disposed of, as the same pleases; with safety of divine right:

2. *and* the minister of Iustice, that gives the last and *fatall* blow, is he that properly kills the man, and not the man himselfe,

by his *active* and *passive submission* to receive the same; that he may obediently in *charity* and *peace*, leave this world; and patiently resigne his *soule* to *God*, in hope of entring upon a more happy life, in exchange for this. 3.

§. 2. *How self-murder is against God himselfe.*

The second particular, whereby it is apparent that by *religion* a man may not kill himselfe, is *because*, it is a most hainous crime against *God himselfe* immediatly, in *foure* severall *respects*.

2. Self-murder it is against God himselfe. In what respects.

First, *self-murder* destroyes and defaces the *Image* of *God* [a]; in the most expresse forme thereof that is in any humane creature, and in the neerest *proximity* and possession thereof in him, that kills himselfe.

1. It defaces Gods Image. [a] *Gen* 9.6.

It is *treason*, *indignly* to abuse, or demolish the *Kings Image*; much more is it *treason* against the *King* of heaven and earth, to deface, or unworthily to intreat his sacred *Image*; *specially* for them to do it, to whom the entertainment, preservation, and honourable usage of the same is committed.

Secondly, *self-murder* is *peccant* and injurious against *Gods* soveraigne *authority*, who is absolute *Lord* of our *persons*, and of our *lives*, and *therefore*, wee have no power, but from him, and according to his *Word*, to dispose of our selves; *seeing* that wee are not our owne *Superiours*, supreme, nor *subordinate*, which is impossible: *for*, then *one* must be *two*; *or* else, one must bee both *superiour* and *inferiour* to it selfe, at the same instant, and in the same case, and respect; than which, what is more *absurd* to think, and impossible to be?

2. It wrongs Gods soveraigne authority.

If a *private* man should violently take a *malefactor*, that is worthy of death, from the *Kings barre* of Judgment, and upon his owne will and authority put him to death, it would justly be deemed an audacious unlawfull

Comparison.

act, and worthy of exemplary punishment; *both* for usurping the authority that belongs not to him, by thrusting of the *King* out of his place and jurisdiction: *and also*, for depriving of the *King* of opportunity of shewing *mercy*, or executing *justice*, according to his *regall* power. *So* likewise may wee judge of a *self-murderer*, that takes himselfe from the *barre* of *God*, to dispose of himselfe as he list, to the wrong of *Gods* soveraigne authority.

3. Self-murder wrongs Gods goodnesse.

Thirdly, *self-murder*, or wilfull self-killing, which are both one, is against *Gods goodnesse*, whereby he gives us our lives, with meanes of their preservation; which is a most excellent blessing in it selfe; *and* for the good that thereby we may doe: and *therefore*, one sayes well, that *Life is a certaine gift, given to man from above, and is subject to his power, who kills and makes alive*; who is only *God*, as the Scripture tells us[a]; *and therefore*, for a man prodigally to waste, or destroy this life of his, he not only doth an *unlawfull act*, *but* also slights and contemnes *Gods* speciall *goodnesse* to him: which is more damnable than to sin against his other *properties*; *because*, in this consists all our happinesse, and thereby God gaines most *glory*; and for despising whereof the *Apostle* gives a most bitter reproofe; *Despisest thou the riches of his goodnesse? &c. Rom* 2.4.

Vita est quoddã donũ divinitus homini attributum, & ejus potestati subjectum, qui occidit, & vivere facit.

[a] *Deut.* 32.39. 1 *Sam.* 2.6.

The most grievous sins are committed against Gods goodnesse.

4. Self-murder wrongs Gods providence.

Fourthly, *self-murder* is a course against the *providence*, and established *government* of *God* in the world, about mankind; which it doth disturbe by determining the *time*, how long; and the *manner*, after what fashion we should die, or live; according to our owne wills, without any dependence upon, or respect to the will of *God*; which necessarily imports, that a *self-murderer* is *either* an *Atheist*, holding that there is no *God* at all; *or* that God takes no care of the world, nor of men, to order them, or dispose of them; but keepes himselfe onely within the circuite of the *Heavens*: than which, what can

A self-murderer is an Atheist.

can be more contrary to the reason of a good man ?

Or else, by his practise, he proclaimes himselfe a *rebell* against *God*, to whom he will not be subject, nor bee disposed according to his *Word*; *but* like a *devill* sets himselfe in opposition against *God*, to his owne everlasting destruction. Or rebell against God.

§. 3. *How self-murder is against nature.*

3. Self-murder is against nature.

The third particular that makes it apparent that *self-murder* is unlawfull, by the rules of *religion*, is *because* it is against *nature* it selfe, and against that *naturall affection* and propensnesse, whereby it endeavours to preserve and cherish it selfe; and to withstand and repell all that is *destructive* of it, and *inimicall to it* : *that religion* requires the observation of the *law* of *nature*, is manifest; *because* religion and natures law are not repugnant, but differ in extent and degrees of perfection; the law of *nature* being more universall, and lesse divinely perfit. The *Scripture* it selfe commends the keeping, and condemnes the transgressing of the law of *nature*. In which respect the *Apostle* blames the *Gentiles*, that *knowing God by nature, they did not glorifie him as God*[a]. *And* againe, he commends them *for doing by nature the things contained in the Law*[b]; and which naturally was written in their hearts. *Hee* blames the *Incestuous Corinthian* for doing a sin so hainous; as *is not so much as named amongst the Gentiles*[c].

Religion requires the observation of the law of nature.

[a] *Rom.* 1.21.

[b] *Rom.* 2.14,15.

[c] 1 *Cor.* 5.1.

And further, he condemnes mens wearing of *long haire* contrary to the *law* of *nature*; when *he* sayes, *Doth not even nature it selfe teach you, that if a man have long haire it is a shame unto him*[d]?

[d] 1 *Cor.* 11.14.

Thomas Aquinas sayes[e], that *for any man to kill himselfe is against naturall inclination and charity*.

[e] *Quod aliquis seipsum occidat, est contra inclinationem naturalem, & contra charitatem.*

The devill knew that man naturally will give all he hath for his *life*, *Iob* 2. 4. the *soule* and *body* of a man doe naturally affect to be united together; *because* of the unity of of the *person* that consists of them both personally joyned together; by whose dissolution it is destroyed.

The soule and body are neither of them perfit without the other, and therefore affect to be united together.

And the soule and *body* are so made one for another, that they are not, nor can be perfit the one without the other, *neither* with *naturall* nor beatificall perfection; *for* beside a *partiall* perfection, there is that full *perfection* that is *of* the *whole*, and *in* the *whole*. *The soule* doth not willingly leave the *body*, but with respect of advancement of the *person*, whereof it is the *soule*, by entring upon possession of that *partiall* perfection whereof it is capable, and the *whole* for measure and degree, is due to the *person* constituted of soule and body: and for which union and *adeption* of perfit glory of the person, there shall be a *resurrection* of the body at the last day: *and therefore* is the body in the meane time called *Nephesh* [a] by the *Hebrewes*. And *God* is said by our *Saviour* himselfe speaking of the dead, to be the *God of the living* [b]; whose *bodies* although they were dead, yet themselves are said to be alive in regard of their living *soules*, who cannot be *personally* considered, but in their union together, that by death cannot be dissolved; in *Gods* consideration of us, and in respect of the naturall *inclination* of each mans proper soule and body, the one to the other for their full perfection: and in regard of the resurrection, when they shall be united everlastingly to live together; *betweene* which time and the day of our death, there is no sensible distance of time to us, nor length of time with *God*.

נפש

[a] *Psal.16.10.*

[b] *Mat.22.32.*

§. 4. *How self-murder is injurious to mankinde.*

4. Self-murder wrongs mankinde.

The fourth particular that makes it evident that *self-murder* is condemned by *religion*; is *because* it is *injurious* to *mankinde*, and to the *common-wealth*, whereof the *self-murderer* is a *member*; who, by that fact of killing himselfe, hurts humane *society* by such hainous disorders, and

and pernicious *examples* for others to follow to their destruction; *and* by the unrecoverable *damage* and losse of its *members*, and of the good that the same might have by their lives. *For* as *Thomas* sayes, *Every man is a part of a Commonalty, and he that kills himselfe doth an injury to that Commonalty* [a].

a *Quilibet homo est pars cōmunitatis, & qui seipsum interficit injuriam facit communitati.*

Examples.

The commendable *examples*, and *practise* of the *godly*, hath ever beene opposite to *self-murder*, as well as their *opinion*, and have had a care to preserve their lives, not only for their own good, but also for the good of others who had an interest in them: *as* is manifest by the *Apostle Paul*, *Phil.* 1.24,25. *and* 2.17. *Who* seeing his life to be needfull for the *Philippians*, was willing to abide and continue with them, *For the furtherance and joy of their faith; and did joy and rejoyce to be offered upon the sacrifice and service of the same.*

It is hurtfull to the common-wealth.

If *self-murder* were not unlawfull, even in respect of the wrong thereby done to the *common-wealth*; why should *David* have commanded to take away the *life* of the yong man the *Amalekite*, that did help *Saul* to kill himselfe; whom *David* asked, *How he was not affraid to stretch forth his hand to destroy the Lords annointed?* and so caused to put him to death; *not* simply for unjustly killing an innocent man; *but* specially in consideration of killing of the *King*, the head of the *land*, which by his death was wronged, and was a dangerous president to passe unpunished.

§.5. *How self-murder wrongs mans selfe doing it.*

5. It wrongs a mans selfe, and how.

The fifth particular demonstrating how unlawfull *self-murder* is by *religion*, is the *sin* and wrong which the *self-murderer* doth thereby to *himselfe*; in *three* speciall *respects*.

1. *First*, in regard of the principall *saving graces* of God in

It overthrowes faith and love in a man.

in *man*, which are *faith* and *love*: *self-murder* is against *faith* and trust in *God*, and overthrowes the same by *desperation*; that *neither* in adversity can a person that is resolved to kill himselfe, have any true *comfort*, *nor* any *hope* of life eternall, by a course that he knowes is the way to *damnation*.

Touching love, we have heard before how it cannot consist with *self-murder*, they being *contrary*. *For*, as *one* sayes, *Every one ought to love himselfe more than his neighbour*: For, the *neerenesse* of our selves to our selves, and for the *perfection* that should be in the *rule* or measure whereby we are to *love* others.

Quisq; debet plus amare seipsum quam proximum. Filliuc.

2 It marres our duty.

Secondly, in regard of our *duty*; which is not to dispose of, or doe that which is not in our power, nor within our *authority*, such as to kill ones selfe is. *For*, when a man kills himselfe, he either kills an *innocent*, and so in that respect grievously sinnes; *or else*, hee kills a *malefactor*, and then he sinnes that doth it without lawfull *authority* to warrant his action; which no man hath to kill himselfe, but expresse command to the contrary.

3. It destroyes our persons.

Thirdly, *self-murder* is much against our selves; *both* by the *destruction* of our *persons* in this world; *and* by running of our selves into everlasting *damnation* in the world to come, by such a damnable and wicked practise; whereby we are sinners against our owne *soules*.

§. 6. *How self-murder is most harmefull.*

Self-murder is most harmfull.

Now it followes to bee shewed how *self-murder* is most *harmefull* and damageable; which may bee seene in *foure* particulars.

1. To Gods glory

First, it is hurtfull to the *glory* and honour of *God*; who is thereby dishonoured, not only by the transgression of his *Law*; but also by the wrong that thereby is done to the Soveraigne *authority*, and to the image of *God*.

2. *Secondly*, it is hurtfull to the *Church* and *Commonwealth*,

wealth, by bereaving the same unjustly of their *members*; and by drawing downe Gods judgements upon them, for such damnable *facts* committed within the same. (To the Church and common-wealth.)

3. To friends and posterity.

Thirdly, it is harmefull to a mans *friends* and *posterity*; *both* in overshadowing their *credit* and honour by the darke and disgracefull cloud of such a fact, and over-lading them with *troubles, griefe* and *shame* for the same: *And also* by depriving them of that earthly *estate* and *meanes*, whereby otherwise they might have been helpfull to them, for their livelihood or advancement.

4. To a mans selfe.

Fourthly, *self murder* is harmefull to a *mans selfe*; *both* by *depriving* him of life; *and* also by *subjecting* him to misery, with losse of happinesse and good name. *Ierome* sayes in the name of *God*, *I receive not such soules as have come out of their bodies against my will*[a]*: and* the *Philosophers* that did kill themselves, he calls them *Martyrs* of *foolish philosophy*[b]. *Virgil* places *self-murderers* in the third *circle* or region of *hell*.

> *—qui sibi lethum*
> *Insontes peperêre manu—*

For a man wittingly and willingly to doe that, which of it selfe is wholly *morally evill*, and whereof nothing but evill and mischiefe redounds to others, and to the doers thereof especially, is extreame *folly* and *madnesse*. And *therefore self murder*, being a thing of that kinde; those that kill themselves doe thereby proclaime themselves to be damnable *fooles*, or *mad men*, or worse; and so in regard of the damage thereof, self-murder is to be abhorred of all. (Self-murderers are fooles and mad men.)

[a] *Non recipio tales animas quae me nolente exierunt è corpore.* Hierom. ad Marcellam de obitu Blesellæ.

[b] *Martyres stultæ philosophiæ.*

§. 7. *How reason condemnes self-murder.*

It remaines, that it be demonstrated by *reason*, that *self-murder* is *wicked* and *unlawfull*; and that no man may (Self-murder is against reason.)

kill himselfe upon any pretence, whereof the *reasons* are many; some whereof I will here subjoyne.

1. It is evill. 1 Cor. 15.26.

First, that which is every way *evil* is not to be done; *but* to kill ones selfe is every way *evill*; *peccantly* and *penally*; *naturally* and *morally*. The *Apostle* calls death an enemy, it is threatned by *God* as a punishment for sin: it is *privative* of life; and *therefore* opposite to *God*, who is life, and a pure *act* of eternall living. *Life* is promised as a blessing, and in that respect to be desired and imbraced; *It* makes us by our vitall *being*, conformable to the first *being*, and capable of happinesse. *And* the higher that any thing is raised upon the foundation of *being*, the liker it is to *God*: as *vegetables* doe more resemble *God* than *inanimates*, that have but simple *being*; and *sensitives* more than *vegetables*; and *rationall* creatures, as men, approach neerer to *God* than *sensitives*; and *intellectuall* creatures, *or spirituall intelligences*, as *Angels*, are neerer to *God*, than rationall creatures on earth; *and* those that are of the longest lives resemble *the ancient of dayes* most: *So* that to live long in an estate of neerest *proximity* to *God* every man should affect, whereunto *self-murder* is contrary.

The degrees of the creatures being.

2. Self-murder is against faith.

Secondly, whatsoever wee doe, *morally* considered, should be an *act* of *faith* and *obedience*: but *self-murder* cannot be an *act* of *faith* and *obedience*; *both because Gods* word is against it; and *also* for that it proceeds from *desperation*, and mans domineering *self will*; which is contrary to *faith* and holy *obedience*.

3. It is not to bee desired to be done by others, nor to others. [a] Mat. 7.12.

Thirdly, what a man may neither *naturally*, nor *morally* desire, nor endeavour that another should doe to him, nor he to another, that may not he doe to *himselfe*; *because* wee ought to doe, as wee would be done to, which is the summe of the *Law* and the *Prophets* [a]: our *judgement* and *practise* should agree.

But no man rightly disposed in his wits, may, nor can advisedly desire, or endeavour that another should kill him; or that he should kill another undeservedly, and upon on private *motion*: the latter is *literally* forbidden by the sixth *Commandement*: *and* against the *former, nature*, and *religion* bids, and armes a man to defend himselfe, for preservation of his life. *Nature* rightly disposed erres not in, and about its proper *object*, seeing it is a proper *judge* of things properly belonging to it, and is from *God*, and not contrary to his *Word*. *And therefore* a man may not kill himselfe contrary to the *dictate* of *nature*.

Fourthly, no man may do that which makes him most unlike to *God*; *for* the *Creator* and *creature* must hold *proportion* together; and our *happinesse* stands in our *likenesse* to him, and *communion with him*, 1 *Iohn* 3. 2. *But* for a man to kill himselfe makes him most *unlike* to *God*, *both* by his *sinne*, and *also* by the *effect* of his fact. *For*, for a man by his own hands to make himselfe not to *be*, is contrary to him, who hath his *being* and living of himselfe, and doth everlastingly live, he being naturally the fountaine of life: and his *living* and *essence* are *reciprocall*, or *convertible*, and is absolutely immortall; *and* so, the more that any preserves their lives, and the longer they live, the liker they are to *God*; and the more that they are impotently *passive*, and the sooner they cease to bee, the unliker they are to *God*. 4. It makes him unlike to God. How self-murder makes a man unlike to God;

The *being* and *living* of creatures, is the ground of all other blessings wherewith they are, or can be indowed; *therefore* no man should kill himselfe, when death deprives him of so much good.

Fifthly, wee should most carefully keepe the greatest *naturall blessing* that God bestowes upon us, which is our life, and be thankfull to God for it; *because* it is the *first blessing*, and the ground of all the rest that God bestowes upon us; and *therefore* we ought most to abhorre *self-murder*, because it is most contrary to life. 5. Life is a blessing.

Sixthly, no man should doe that whereby hee doth himselfe the greatest *harme*: *for*, all things naturally move for, and towards their owne *perfection*; and where 6. Self-murder most harmfull to a mans selfe, should cause us to avoide it.

 hurt

hurt cannot be avoided, we are ever to choose the least of two *evills of punishment*.

But, to kill our selves doth us the greatest *harme*, both *naturally* and *morally*; *because* it makes us guilty of most hainous *sin*; and subjects us to most fearefull *judgements* for the same; *and* thereby a man destroyes his owne *person*, that is better than all the *accidents* about the same, when the *subject* and *adjuncts* are contra-distinguished.

Aristotle sayes, that *death is the last of terrible things, and the greatest evill of the body* [a]; and *therefore* is most to be abhorred, specially from a mans owne hands.

[a] *Ultimum terribilium, & corporis maximum malum.*

7. Death is not subject to mans free-will.

Seventhly, man may not determine and *order* things as he *list*, which are not left and subjected to his *freewill*; *but dying*, or departing out of this life is not left, or subjected to the *freewill* and lawfull power of man himself, to *die* when, and as he list; *no more* than it is subjected to his *freewill* to make himselfe alive againe when hee is dead. *For*, for to kill and make alive, belongs to *Gods royall prerogative* [b]: *but* as man is onely *passive* in the *latter*, for his *animation*; so should he be in the *former*, that he may not wrong his *preservation*.

[b] *Transitus de hac vita ad aliam non subjacet libero hominis arbitrio.* Thom. Aquinas.

1 *Sam.* 2 6.

8. Avoide self-murder as contrary to nature.

Eighthly, no man may doe that which is most *contrary to pure nature*; *for*, as *Aquinas* saith, *Every thing naturally loves and preserves it selfe.*

Naturaliter quelibet res seipsam amat & conservat.

But to kill ones selfe, is most *contrary to pure nature*; *for* as *Aristotle, lib.* 2. *de anima*, sayes, *generation is a work most agreeable to nature*, and *therefore* death is most contrary to *nature*, which it doth destroy; and to inflict it upon a mans selfe by his owne hand, is monstrous cruelty.

Augustine bids us to *consider how great a good thing life is*, for (saith he) *it is better to be, and to be miserable, than not to be at all*; *therefore, both those that are happy, and those that are miserable, doe desire to be* [c].

[c] *Considera quantum bonum est vita; nam melius est esse, & miserum esse, quam non esse; propterea & beati, & miseri appetunt esse.* August. l. de lib. arb.

Ninthly,

Ninthly, no man is to doe that which all *wise* and *good men*, and *humane* and *ecclesiasticall lawes doe condemne* : *but* all these doe condemne *self-murder*, and *self-murderers*. The *Athenians* would not suffer a *self-murderer* to be buried in their *territories*. 9. It is condemned by men and their laws.

Plato in *Phædone* sayes, that *when our soules are given us to keepe, we must not thrust them out of doores*.

It is an ill recompense, when a man hath abused his *soule* all his life time to sin, at last by a self-murdering hand forcibly to expell it, as incestuous *Amon* served his *sister Tamar* in most ignominious manner [a].

[a] 2 *Sam.* 13.17.

Philolaus the *Pythagorean*, speaking against *self-murder*, was wont to say (as he is cited by *Plato* and *Tullie* in his *Tusculan questions*, and others) *Divide not the tree, or ship in the way, or while it is in the voyage*, for so it must of necessity parish; that is, that we should not part *soule* and *body* before their due time, and happy arrivall at their last port appointed of *God*.

Ne dividas in via lignum.

Ierome upon *Ionas* sayes, that *it is not our duty to snatch death to our selves, but patiently to beare it* [b] when it comes: *Which sentence* is so memorable, that it is inserted into the *Canon Law*.

[b] *Non est nostrũ mortẽ arripere, sed oblatã patienter ferre.* Decret. 2. pars causa 23. c. 11.

The Canons that beare the name of the *Apostles*, doe call those that *geld* themselves *homicides*; *self-murderers* are worse; and therefore homicides in the highest degree.

The first *Councell* of *Bracara* in *Spaine*, about the time of the *Pope Honorius* the *first*, did *decree*, that for those *that doe kill themselves*, either *by weapon*, or *by poyson*, or *by casting themselves from high places*, or *by hanging*, or *by any other manner of violence, there should be no commemoration made of them in the oblation*, .i. *of prayer*, *or sacrament*; *neither should their bodies be conveyed to buriall with psalmes and solemnity* [c]: but they are excluded from *Christian buriall*; which also is assumed and established in the *Canon law* [d]; *seeing self-murderers* doe wilfully deprive

[c] *Placuit qui sibi ipsis, aut per ferrũ aut per venenũ, aut per præcipitiũ; aut suspendium; aut quolibet modo violentiæ, inferunt mortẽ: nulla pro illis in oblatione cõmemoratio fiat: neq; cum psalmis ad sepulturam cadavera eorum deducantur.*

[d] *Decret. secunda part. causa* 23. c. 12.

deprive the living of their company, it is just that the *living* should deprive them of all *honour* of solemnity, and place of *buriall*; holding them in detestation, so as not to have *communion* with them after death in any thing, that were not willing to continue their *communion* with the *living* in this world: *and* so by that act, they die cut off from the *Church*, as *excommunicate ipso facto*, never to be absolved.

Reasons of the confiscation of the goods of self-murderers.

The Civill and *Common Law* confiscates the *estates* of *self-murderers*, specially for *three reasons*.

1. For terror.

First, for *terror* to the living, that they may not attempt the like.

2. For punishmét.

Secondly, for *punishment* of them in their *posterity*, who are deprived of their *estates*; and so the *sinnes of the Parents are visited upon their children without injustice*; *because*, the *children* are both of their parents *naturall* substance, and also part of their *civill*; that so affection to their *posterity* may restraine them from killing themselves.

3. For recōpence to the State.

Thirdly, the worldly estate of *self-murderers* is to be seased upon, by the State of the *Kingdome*, for *recompence* to the *Common-wealth*, for depriving the same of a *member*; and is a *deodand* to *God*, being as *Iericho* was, an execrated thing; because it belonged to such a person, and therefore accursed, and not to be enjoyed from him, but from *God* the true originall owner thereof, to whom, by that vile fact, they are forfaite.

10. Self-murder excludes man from amendment.

Tenthly, what a man hath not power to make, or to *amend*, after it is once ill done, and shall be found to be *evill* and inconvenient, that he ought not to do: *because*, by doing thereof, he excludes himselfe from all possibility and meanes of recovering his losse; as, from the *privation* to the *habit* naturally there is no returne [a]: *but* when a man hath killed himselfe, he cannot make himselfe alive againe, that hee may amend the errors of his course; and therefore expedient it is for him to keepe his

[a] *A privatione ad habitum non datur regressus.*

his life as long as hee can, when hee hath it.

Eleventhly, no man is to doe that, which may crosse his last *ayme* and *end*, which is his *salvation*; but, for a man to kill himselfe, *crosses* him in this end, and deprives him of attaining the same: *because*, thereby he *termines* and finishes his life with, and in an *act* of most damnable *sin*; and also deprives himselfe of all meanes of reformation and salvation in time to come. 11. It crosses a mans last aime.

Twelfthly, *self-murder* is condemned by *Macrobius* and *Picolomineus* under *similies*: as, a *servant* may not kill himselfe; *because*, he is not *sui juris*, his owne. *So*, we being *Gods* servants, not only (as they say) by *creation*, and *subordination* in place and duty, *but also*, by *covenant* and *redemption*, we may not kill our selves. 12. Self-murder is condemned by similies. 1.

No man may *dispose* as hee list of other mens *goods*, although he bee *usu fructuarius* of them for a time, having the *propertie* of them for his profitable *use*, with reservation and preservation of the *substance* of them: we are such; and *therefore*, have not such *soveraigne* and absolute *right* and *authority* over our selves, that we may kill our selves; *seeing* we are bound as Gods tenants, to the *upholding* and *reparations* of our selves, as much as we can. 2.

A man committed to *prison*, by lawfull and just *authority*, although unjustly, may not make an *escape*, by breaking of *ward*, to prevent punishment; *because*, thereby he condemnes and makes himselfe a *transgressor*, and worthy of punishment: *neither* are we to rid our selves out of this life of troubles, into which *God* hath put us, untill he shall againe himselfe call us out, and free us; as *Paul* and *Silas* would not come out of *prison*, untill the *Magistrates* brought them out, that had put them in [a]. 3.

[a] *Act.*16.37,39

Plato sayes, that as wee may not kill another mans *servant*, in regard that thereby we wrong his *Master*; and as *Souldiers* may not forsake their *stations* and places, without order from their *Commander* [b]; so may no man 4.

[b] *Injussa imperatoris deserere stationem.*

man kill *himselfe*, seeing thereby he wrongs *God*, that is his *Master*; and forsakes the place and condition that *God* his *Commander* hath set him in, there to serve him, as a *Souldier* in this world, during his good
a 1 *Tim.* 1.18. pleasure a.

*August.de.*C.D. lib.1.c.20. *Augustine* sayes, that as *he is a false witnesse as well, and rather more, that wittingly deposes falsely against himselfe; so he that kills himselfe is a murderer, as much and more,*
5. *than if he killed another man. Parricide,* as to kill *Wife, Husband*, or *children*, is odious; but *self-murder* is worse, because it is neerest a mans selfe, and *most* against the *rule*.

13. It is the grossest murder. *Thirteenthly*, wee are specially bound to shun the most *grosse* and worst *facts* and sinnes; for that, if we do them, wee are most inexcusable, and culpable, and justly damned: *because*, they are most against *conscience*, they being most within the light of mans *understanding*, *whereby* the conscience being convinced, it inexcusably condemnes the doers of them; *which also* are most within the power of man to resist, and against which he hath most *helps*; and therefore the doing of them imports more wilfulnesse, than frailty, or want of power in those that do the same.

But self-murder is a sinne of this kind: *because*, it is the *grossest* and most odious sort of *murder* that can be, and *therefore* most to be shunned.

14. It makes a bad exchange. *Fourteenthly*, we are advisedly to make no *exchange*, that may be for the *worse*; *but*, a man by killing himselfe, makes an *exchange* for the *worse*: *because*, hee gives his life in exchange for death; *or*, at the best, for freedome from worldly troubles & discontentment; *which* is a *price* farre above the worth of the *purchase*; *and God* never allowed of this kinde of *truckage*, nor appointed *self-murder* to be the means of any *good*; *but* thereby men cast themselves into greater misery and destruction, than otherwise they should ever have beene subject to.

Fifteenthly,

Fifteenthly, every man should strive to be in such an *estate* of favour with *God*, and to bee found of him so doing, when he dies, as may be allowable before *God*, and most comfortable to a mans selfe. *Blessed is that servant whom his Lord, when bee commeth, shall finde so doing*[a]. *But* a *self-murderer*, in his act of killing of himself, can *neither* have any comfort that hee is in the estate of *Gods* favour; *nor* that his *act* is allowable before him; whose law thereby hee transgresses with a high hand, concluding his last gaspe with an *act* of horrible *sinne*; having his *soule* in the passing thereof out of his body, filled with disordered *passions* and *perturbations*, of *discontent, griefe, hatred, feare*, diverted upon *unlawfull objects* and *acts*; and filled with *horror*, and *environed* with *devils*: and *so*, by *self-murder* the soule is most diverted from *God*, and infected; when the same should be most neerely converted to *God*, and bee best fitted and perfited for him at death; that, by the hands of the blessed *Angels*, it may be caryed into *heaven* and eternall happinesse. 15. It puts man into a bad estate to die in.

[a] *Math.* 24. 46.

Sixteenthly, a man is to do no more than hee hath lawfull *right* and *power* to do, lest he make himselfe a *transgressor*: *but* mans *power* over himselfe is not *supreame*, *but* as a *usu-fructuarie*, he hath *dominium utile*, *profitable dominion* of himselfe, being bound by *God* his highest *Lord*, not to commit *waste* upon himselfe. *As* mans *dominion* over the *earth* is not supreame, for the *Lord is King, the earth may be glad of it*; *but* onely to take the *profit* of it, and not to destroy it; the *creatures* he may kill for to enjoy a *better use* of them. 16. Man hath not authority to kil himselfe. *Comparison.*

But the best *use* that a man can have of himselfe, is by his *life*, and not by his *death*; and *therefore*, he is to avoid *self-murder*, *because* it deprives a man of that *use* of himselfe, for which *God* hath given a man to himselfe.

As the wife hath not power of her owne body, to *Comparison.*

dispose thereof as she list, in regard of that interest and proprietie that her *husband* hath over her; *so* cannot man do with himselfe what he pleases, in regard that we are the *members* of *Christ* his body and spouse [a], and *therefore* are subject to him.

[a] Ephes. 5. 23, 24

The object of mans will.

Man is *Lord* of his *naturall* and *morall actions*, *because*, they are the *subjects* of his *will*; and *therefore*, he is culpable and punishable, if they be not well ordered: *and* so to the doing only of that, which hee may well do, he is to be willing; and *therefore* to kill himselfe hee should not be willing; *because*, he cannot well do it, which is against the *Law* both of *God*, and of *nature*.

17. The examples of self-murder are wicked.

Seventeenthly, the *quality* and esteeme of the *persons* that kill themselves, may demonstrate the odiousnesse of that *fact* in any: *for*, generally they are *wicked persons*, and their names execrable in the *Church*; such as were *Saul*, *Abitophel*, *Zimri*, *Iudas*, and the like. *And therefore*, as a man would not bee ranked with them, nor be *subject* to their *infamie* in this world, *nor* would partake with them in their *estate* of misery and damnation in the world to come, *so* he should be most carefull that he have no communion with them in their ill courses and wretched practises in this world; specially that he may not shut up his life with them in the same damnable manner of *self-murder*. *For* any *godly persons* that have killed themselves, whose names are under a *charitable censure* of commendation, it was done by them; *either* out of blamelesse *ignorance* of the *morall* forme of the *fact*; *or* else by speciall *motion* of the holy *Spirit* warranting them to do what they did [a]: and are charitably *excused* or *commended*, not for their *fact* of killing themselves, but for their *precedent* good *lives*, and for their *heavenly mindednesse*, and holy *dispositions*, which apparently they had; for which they did, and when they did, out of their weakenesse, that unlawfull *fact*: *extraordinary* and *exempt cases*, which stand upon some speciall and transcendent

b *Ex ignorantia inculpata, vel motu speciali Spiritus sancti.*

transcendent *circumstances*, are not to be made *rules* and *precedents*, nor to bee imitated, for, and in ordinary practise; none can dispense, or make *exceptions*, but he that hath power over the *Law*, which is the *rule* of our lives, who is *God* alone.

Eighteenthly, *self-murder* is abominated and condemned by the generall *verdite* of the *furie* of all the *creatures*, *inanimate* and *irrationall*; whose universall practise, for *self-preservation*, utterly condemnes all *self-murderers*, upon *natures* evidence against them. 18. The verdit of nature in the creatures condemnes self-murder.

We see how the *Hare* flees before the *Hound*, and useth many naturall slights and *stratagems* to escape the danger. *So* doth the *Partridge* to avoyd the talons of the *Falcon*; yea a worme trod upon, turnes againe.

The like is *observable* also in senselesse *creatures*, we see every *element* fleeing from its *contrary*, to the place of the *conservation* of it selfe.

Yea, even also in *man* himselfe, it is apparent how nature abhorres and shuns *self-murder*, where we see how by naturall instinct, in suddaine *perils*, when a man hath leasure to thinke of avoyding of them; *as*, when a *blow* is suddenly and *unexspectedly* reached at a man, the hand, naturally, and of it selfe, will instantly object it self, to save *life*: which demonstrates that for a man to turne his hands against himself to kill himself, is unnaturall and monstrous.

Lastly, those *indowments*, *abilities*, and *meanes*, that man hath naturally to preserve himselfe and his life, utterly condemnes his self-killing, as impious and monstrous. 19. Mans own indowments condemnes self-murder.

For, *first*, he is indowed with *self-love*; *every man naturally is a friend to himselfe*; sayes the *Philosopher*[a]; whereby every man may have a desire to preserve himselfe.

[a] φίλος ἑαυτῷ πᾶς ἄνθρωπος φύσει ἐστί.

Secondly, man is indowed with *feare* of whatsoever may hurt or destroy him. Feare is φυλακτικόν τι a certaine

 preservative,

preservative, whereby men labour to preserve themselves.

Thirdly, man is qualified and furnished with *understanding* and *memory*, which gives knowledge and experience, whence flowes the *morall habit* of *prudence*, by which man is enabled both to foresee, and to prevent dangers, and to be *Iudge* and *Master* of his owne actions, for his owne good and preservation; so that a man cannot kill himselfe without being self-condemned, in the doing of the act, contrary to *naturall instinct*, to reason, and to all the indowments and meanes that he hath to the contrary; and must perish without all *plea* of excuse.

I will conclude the *arguments* against *self-murder*, with the grave and most serious judgement and determination of *Iosephus*, disswading his *Countrey-men* from the same; when they were most desperately and instantly urging the doing thereof; to whom he said as followeth.

De bello Iudaico. lib. 3. cap. 14.

Wherefore, ô my friends, (quoth he) *are wee become murderers of our selves? Wherefore doe we make war betweene things so united, as are the soule and the body? If the Romans (our adversaries) thinke good to spare their enemies, should not we think it good likewise to spare our owne selves? ——— it is meere folly to do that to our owne selves, for which we fight against our enemies. ———*

He is not onely to be judged a coward, who refuseth to die, when need requireth; but also he that will die when no need urgeth. ———

Shall we make that certaine to our selves, that wee feare at our enemies hands?

You will say it is the part of him that is valiant to kill himselfe: nay truly, it is the part of a very coward. For, I thinke him to bee a timorous sea-man, who perceiving a tempest coming, before it fall, sinketh the ship wherein he is.

Moreover, it is against the Law of nature, and the nature of of all creatures to kill themselves; and thereby wee should commit a hainous crime against God: there is no living creature that of his owne seeking would willingly die: for, every one feeleth in himselfe the strong and forcible law of nature, whereby they desire to live: and for this cause wee judge them for our enemies, that seeke to take it from us; and doe punish them that doe take it indeed. And doe you thinke it is not a greater contempt of God for a man to despise his gift? For, we of him received our first beeing, and from him let us expect our ending. The body is mortall, framed of corruptible matter; but our soules are immortall, and there is a little part of God placed in our bodies. If any one abuseth that which another man putteth him in trust with, presently we thinke him a perfidious and wicked man: and shall we thinke, that if we cast away out of our bodies that which God hath put us in trust withall and placed in the same, that he shall not know of it, whom we have so abused? we hold those slaves worthy to be punished, that run away from bad masters: and shall not we then be held for impious, who flee from so good a master as God is? doe you not know that they who according to the Law of nature depart out of this life, and render that to God, which they received of him, when he who gave it requires it, shall leave behind them a perpetuall name to their posterity and family?

And that unto those soules who are obedient to their Creator when he calls them, he gives a holy and sacred mansion in heaven? and that they who wrought their owne death, goe into dark hell? and that God punisheth this their offence upon all their posterity?

Hence it is that God is displeased therewith, and it is forbidden by our most wise Law-giver. For, if any amongst us kill themselves, it is decreed that till the Sunne goe downe they shall be unburyed; yet we hold it lawfull to bury our enemies. Other nations cause their right hands to be cut off, who have killed themselves; Iudging that as the soule thereby was made a stranger to the body, even so by that fact was *the hand made a stranger unto it.* Thus farre *Iosephus.*

§. 8. *Of certaine uses.*

The uses, or *observations* from all these arguments, proving the unlawfulnesse of *self-murder*, are *three.*

First, hereby we may see the *hainousnesse* and damnablenesse of *self-murder*. For, the more *lawes* that any sin *transgresses*, the greater it is; and the *more directly*, and in the *higher degrees* it violates those *lawes*; and the more and eminenter the *persons* bee that it *wronges*, and the more and greater the reasons be, that are against it, the more grievous it is.

Self-murder transgresses the *lawes* of *God*, of *nature* and of *men*: it is against them in their most *prime* and *literall sense*; so smiting justice spightfully on the *face* of it: *it* is against *God*, and against *men*; *it* is against all *publicke bodyes* of *society*, and against every *private person*: *it* is against *heaven*, and against *earth*; it empties these to fill *hell*: in so much that well it may be a question, or rather a certaine conclusion, that not any who hath true *grace*, can in its full *formality*, commit this *sinne*; neither any that doth so perpetrate this sinne can be *saved*.

2. Self-murderers doe sinne most grievously.

Secondly, from the consideration of that which is said against *self-murder*, it is to be *observed*, that they that kill themselves *wittingly* and *willingly*, doe sinne thereby against a great light and strength of *arguments* to the contrary, whereby they are *self-convinced* in their *consciences*, that it is a grievous sinne; and are *self-condemned*, upon their resolution to doe it: and *therefore*, they must have a great and horrible conflict within themselves before they doe it; *that* they may first overcome and remove the many and strong *obstacles*, that stand in their way to hinder them; that they may blind-fold themselves from sight of the *truth*, and may subdue their *wills* and *faculties*, against all *reason*, to bee obedient to doe it.

Whereby,

Whereby, a *self-murderer* is guilty and damnable, not onely for his horrible fact of *self-murder*, simply considered; *but*, also, for his *holding of the truth in unrighteousnesse*;[a] opposing, checking and withstanding the *graces* and *worke of God* in him, and by others, which tend to, and labour for his preservation: *and* for his abusing and perverting of Gods *ordinances*, and *blessings*, to his owne destruction: so that in spight of *heaven* and *earth*, hee will not be saved: *but* in a high and uncontrouleable manner will domineere; to over-rule all things according to his owne peevish *self-will*, to his owne wicked ends and ruine, that safety may not save him: having heaven and earth; God and Angells; men and himselfe against himselfe. Rom.1.18.

3. To take heed of self-murder.

Thirdly, we are here to *observe*, how much it concerns all men to take *heed*; and beware of *self murder*. For, we being *reasonable creatures* and *Christians*, it concernes us that we doe nothing contrary to *reason* and *religion*; *but* that we doe advise with, and frame all our courses according to the same: *that*, being in *qualification*, *men*, and in *profession Christians*; we may not, in degenerate manner, bee in our practice worse than *brute beasts*, or incarnate *devils*; who will not be divided against themselves, or destroy themselves.[a] a Math.12.26

Now, we see that there is no one point that hath more *reason* & *religion* against it, than *self-murder* hath; & *therefore*, one might think that there is no feare that any *Christian creature* should bee in danger of it: but alas, the *devill* labours to make men break their necks over the highest rocks; that so they may be unrecoverable; when they shal have climbed & past over so many obstacles & lets of *arguments*; & over the top of them all have cast themselves headlong into the *gulph* of *self-murder*. *And man*, that is a *rationall* creature, having transgressed and rejected the direction and command of *reason* and *religion*, is subject to breake out into the most damnable *exorbitances*, and unbounded

unbounded excesses; having nothing left to stay him from comming into most horrible *extremities:* and *therefore*, to be preserved from *self-murder*, it is requisite to keep our selves, and our courses within the compasse of sound *reason* and true *religion*. *For*, such sinnes as are done against the greatest *reason* and power of resistance; and upon the least *temptation*, and those that are more from *self-will*, than from *frailtie* and want of power; are neerest to the sinne of the *devill*; and makes men likest to him, in quality, state, and damnation.

Note.

Chap. 18.

Whether all self-murderers bee damned everlastingly, with the Devill in hell.

§. 1. *Of the extent of self-murder to the soules hurt.*

Circumspection in determining.

IN determining of this *question*, about the finall estate of *salvation*, or *damnation* of *self-murderers*, wee must deale warily: that wee may neither dash our selves against the rocke of extreamity, rigorous *uncharitablenesse*, in adjudging all to *damnation*, whereof wee may finde some at the last day to be *inheritours* of *heaven*: and contrariwise, that we may not, by an excesse of charity, extenuate that horrible sinne, or excuse the doers thereof; whereby wee may adjudge those to heaven, which are fire-brands of *hell*; and may encourage others to doe the like *fact*; or at least to make men lesse to regard, or to abhorre and beware of it.

Self-murder doth prejudice the soule most.

I will begin and shew, that the execrable *fact* of detestable *self-murder* concernes not onely the *body*, the life and

and substance whereof it destroyes; but also it specially, in a higher nature, touches the soule; both in polluting of it with a most shamefull and odious sinne: and also, by thrusting of it out off its bodily habitation and condition; wherein it was placed, and injoyed peaceable possession by *God* himselfe; and where it might doe good; and get *grace* and *salvation*; most wretchedly and desperately expelling it to its unavoydable place of the darkest *hell* and everlasting destruction.

It respects not onely this *life* present, whereof, and of all blessings and comforts in this *world* it utterly deprives the man that commits it: *but* also, it farre more neerely concernes a mans future and eternall estate in the *world* to come; wherein a *self-murderer* debarres himselfe from all beatificall happinesse, & subjects himself to everlasting misery, by that woefull exchange.

And therefore, are all men that have any care of the good and comfort of their soules, or of their eternall future happinesse in the *world* to come, to abandon all thoughts of *self-murder*; that consideration of present things may not wholy possesse and take them up from minding and intending the spirituall good of their soules, and the future felicity of a better *life*: *but* that they may order all their wayes and actions so, as the same may not prejudice, but advantage the good of their *soules*; and advance them to, and in the estate of glory. *Observe.* Whereof men should be most carefull.

But, it seemes by the practice of *self-murder*, that *self-murderers* either thinke that they have no *soules*; but are as irrationall *brutes*: of whom death ends all; or else, that they undervalue their *soules*, as things nought worth: *and* are regardlesse of their future *estate* in the world to come; as if neither of them were worth their care and respect; that for the same they should frame their course, and order their practice any otherwise than they list themselves: and in that respect are wilfull *mad Atheists*. Selfe-murderers regard not their soules.

If *self-murderers* doe conceive that they have *soules*, What they should consider

 that

that are *superstites* remaining after their death; and beleeve that there is a life of *happinesse*, or misery to come after this; then should they be mindfull of the same; and consider what shall become of their poore *soules*, and what their *state* shall be, if they doe kill and rid themselves out of this life and world; and whether *salvation*, or *damnation* is the portion of *self-murderers*.

§. 2. *That all that kill themselves are not properly Self-murderers, nor in their estate of damnation.*

All self-killers are not properly self-murderers.

About determining this great *question*, concerning the *finall estate* of *self-murderers*, whether they bee all damned in hell; or any of them saved in heaven; we are *first* to consider that all that fall by their owne hands, or meanes are not *self-murderers*; as hath beene formerly shewed in divers *exempt cases* in the chapter of *direct bodily self-murder*; to which I referre the *reader*. For, although all *self-murderers* are *self-killers*, yet all *self-killers* are not *self-murderers*: they are not termes convertible, or reciprocall; *because*, although they may agree, and be the same in the materiall part, or substance of the *action*; yet they doe differ in their forme and nature of *Anomy*, or sinfulnesse: which doeth varie and alter the *kinde*, that it is not the same properly with the other; and so, it is not simply subject to the same *effects*, and *Consequences* thereof.

Chap. 12. §. 5.

They differ formally.

Whereupon, not only by the *verdict* of *divine* reason; but even also by the *Courts* of humane *Iudicature*, about *feloes de se*, such are acquitted, as are expressed, Chap. 12. §. 5. In the exempt cases.

As if a *Child* kill itselfe, that hath not attained to age of discretion, or to use of reason; *or*, if a man, or woman kill himselfe, that is an *Ideote*, or naturall *foole*; or is *mad*, constantly, or in a fit of *Lunacie*; or of a *Fever*; or *Calenture*;

ture; or in a fit of *Phrensie* (how ever involuntarily contracted;) or by mischance; no *Court* of *equity*, or Iustice, in advised well informed proceeding, will condemne such an one for a *self murderer*; and accordingly so dispose of his body, and goods, as of self-murderers.

For, for them to exempt such from the number and censures of *self-murderers*, their reason is good, because, it is most *inhumane* and unreasonable so ignominiously to condemne and censure persons for self-murderers; whose case deserves pitty and commiseration, for their lamentable suffering; both in their death, and also in that evill of calamity, which is the cause of it; against, or (at least) without the free consent of their *wills*; and therefore, to punish a fact neither of their proper effecting, nor advised approving, by addition of more misery, were most unjust.

Hereupon it necessarily followes, that the persons justly acquitted and exempted from the number and censure of self-murderers, by the *verdict* and Judgement of men; as such to whom usually the *Church* grants communion of *Christian buriall*, with other priviledges of holy *Church*, after their death; cannot in charity be denyed by it, the happinesse of salvation.

§. 3. *That proper and direct self-murderers are all reprobates, and without the state of grace.*

The proper *subject* of this *question* about *salvation*, are not the persons aforesaid, falling by their owne hands, in the foresaid cases; who are not properly *self-murderers*: *But* those only that out of deliberate *Judgement*, doe *advisedly*, *wittingly* and *willingly* kill themselves; contrary to the meanes and power, that they have to the contrary; if they list to use the same, as they might; of these I say and doe peremptorily conclude, *that they all, and every of them that so murder themselves*; *are certainly, and infalli-* All self-murderers are damned.

 bly,

bly damned soule and body for evermore without redemption; which I will pregnantly prove by *five* strong and undenyable *arguments*, and *reasons*.

Reasons.

I.

None in the state of salvation can be properly a self-murderer.

First, because none doe, nor can so murder themselves but *unregenerated* and *reprobate* persons; who dying in that estate cannot possibly be saved.

For, both the *transcendent greatnesse* of that sinne of *self murder*, in it selfe, and perfect forme considered, and in all the circumstances thereof, for manner of doing of it; And also, the full measure of the *wills exorbitancy* in a plenary consent, and the indivertible indeavours of the minde, and all the powers and faculties of these *self murderers* presumptuously to doe this vile execrable act, against all resistance and helps to the contrarie; is such as cannot be incident to any godly body that shall be saved.

Of the regenerated preserved.

Because, in those that are truly adopted of God; *both* the power of sinne, formally considered, in that degree of *Anomie* and excesse of enormity, is, by saving grace, and the *Spirits* working in them, broken, and bridled; that they cannot breake out into the same so extremely, as others doe.

And also, their *wills* are brought under such conformity to the rule and command of *God*, and of his spirit; and all their powers, faculties, and dispositions, are in some measure, so inclined to goodnesse, and divine obedience; that they can never transgresse into any odious grosse sin, without far more reluctancy, opposition, and hinderance in themselves against it; from light of *Judgement*, divine restraint; and from *antipathy* of renewed inclination, than can be in any that is wicked, or unconverted; who running in an unregenerate estate, with such a full *Careere* sometimes upon the rock of *self-murder*; doe therein outstrip others so farre, that they overshoote themselves beyond all bounds of salvation; and are all certainly damned, even in the judgement of men here on earth; who have no better esteeme of them, but as of damned *Reprobates*;

bates, who by their owne meanes and procurement, perish for ever, not onely by and for the odious *act* of murdering themselves; but together with that, for their former wicked impenitent life, and are not saved; principally for their unbeliefe: as our *Saviour Christ* saith, *He that beleeveth not, is condemned already* [a].

[a] *Ioh.* 3.18.

§. 4. *Of the examples of self-murderers in Scripture.*

The second argument, proving that all proper *self-murderers* are damned; is, the *examples* of those recorded in the *Scriptures*, who did murder thẽselves: as, *Saul*, *Abitophel*, *Zimri*, *Iudas*, *&c.* that were all reprobates and damned persons. For, the *Scripture* speakes not onely of their fact of *self-murder*, with condemning and detesting of the same; but also, it so describes the *persons* themselves that do it, that it makes it apparent that they are damned; and gives instance in none other that did it, but reprobately damned wretches.

2. *Reason.* Proving that all self-murderers are damned. *Examples.*

So that, by *induction* of particular *self-murderers* in *Scripture*, who were all reprobates and damned, we may safely conclude, that no *self-murderer* is, or can be saved; seeing there can no *Authentick* instance be given of any such, that ever was saved. And therefore, we should not be *conformable* to those in their damnable practise, with whom wee would not *communicate* in their last and finall *estate* of everlasting *damnation*: but of this see more, *cap.* 15. §. 23. *cap.* 17. §. 7. *argument* 17.

§. 5. *Self-murder is a sin transcendent beyond Law and mercy.*

The third reason and ground, whereupon it is evident, that no *self-murderer* can be saved, but are all damned, is the very *nature* of this horrible sinne of *self-murder* it selfe,

3. *Reason.* Proving that all self-murderers are damned.

selfe, taken in the full *latitude* thereof, in manner and *forme* of the greatest *anomie* and enormity of it, which neither can here consist with true grace, in those that so perpetrate it, nor will permit any that so do it to enter into Heaven, in regard of the *hainousnesse* of it, whereby it is without the pale and *verge* of mercy to be shewed to any that commit it.

The excessive hainousnesse of that sinne.

Reason.

The reason whereof is this; by the *Gospell*, *God* offers *mercy*, upon repentance, to those onely, that transgresse against the *Law* of naturall reason, and of the positive *Commandements* of *God*, in those *kindes* and *degrees* of sinnes, the highest and most grievous whereof exceeds not, nor transcends the utmost limits and bounds of that, which *humane reason* properly, and *Gods Law* expresly forbids and condemnes, and whereof instances may be given, that some in that estate, or in one *parallel* to it, have repented and beene saved.

The Lawes given to man have bounds.

Because, (to restraine mans presumption in evill) *mercy* is intended and offered to penitent men, for sinnes contained within certaine bounds, and limits, and not extended to infinitnesse of excesse, or malignity, with overthrow either of the universall Law of *nature*, or of the Law whereby *God* is, subsists, and acts his works: which would import that there must be neither *God*, nor *Creature*.

These limits of mans pardonable sins, are those lawes of *reason*, or of *Divine imposition*, which are proportionable, and reciprocally proper for men, binding them onely to keepe them; (as every kinde of creatures are bound by their owne proper lawes; and the *universe* by the lawes that binds the whole and all its parts;) beyond or above the height of enormitie forbidden directly by them, for men to transgresse; they wrong and overthrow what they can, the very being and happinesse both of the *Creature* and *Creator*, in which excesse of iniquity, beyond the highest kinds and degrees directly forbidden

den in the Law, there is no salvation to be had: because, in that case, men are without and beyond the highest expresse extent of the lawes proper to men; for breaches whereof, *mercy* may be had by the *Gospell*.

For, the *Gospell* and *Law* have respect thus farre one to another, for their bounds and extent, that the vertue and benefit of the *Gospell* extends onely to save those penitents, that are in danger to perish, by sinnes directly under, and within the compasse of the law proper to man: but, if man do sin transcendently-presumptiously, and properly against more *universall*, or higher Lawes, that concernes the *being* of *God*, or of the whole frame of the *creation*; the violating whereof naturall *instinct*, and divine *horror* may make us abominate; there is no comfort of the *Gospell*, nor salvation to such, as is apparent in the *devils*; into whose qualities, and order such men do degenerate, by their transcendent sinnes, beyond the list of those, for which mercy may be had by the *Gospell*, which respects pardon of sinnes, limited only within compasse of that Law, which is properly given to man; and requires a modified justice, sutable to the power man had at first to performe dutie.

For sinnes beyond the Law, no mercy.

Now, *self-murder* properly so called, is such an *extracategorian* and transcendent sinne, beyond or above the law of reason, or of divine imposition proper to man, that it violates the frame of the *Creation* and the Majesty of God himselfe, (as well as his Law,) in endeavouring the destruction of both; from which horrible fact, both naturall instinct, and divine horror might restraine a man, if he had not put off humanity.

Self-murder, is a transcendent sinne, beyond Law.

The sinne of *self-murder* is forbidden by Gods Law: *Thou shalt do no murder*. Whereunto it belongs only by *reduction* and *Analogie*, or proportion that it hath to *murder*, and not properly, but is a *nameless* sinne, properly belonging to a more universall and higher Law, that concernes God himselfe, and the frame of the *Creation*: the

the transcendency of which sin puts the doers thereof, without the pale of mercy.

§. 6. *Self-murderers want true repentance.*

4. *Reason.* Proving that all proper self-murderers are damned.

The fourth reason and argument, whereupon it is evident, that all *proper self-murderer's,* in that transcendent extent and forme, spoken of before, cannot be saved, but are all damned; *is their want of true repentance for their sinnes:* without which there can be no salvation.

They want true repentance.

That they want true *repentance,* and all other subsequent saving graces, neither in that estate can have the same, is thus apparent; *if* they have *repentance,* it must be either *habituall* and *implicite* in their disposition; or *actuall* and explicite in expressions and deeds; or in *both.*

But, if it be *neither* way in them, then it cannot be in them at all, but it is *neither* way in them, *ergo.*

1. Habituall repentance.

First, habituall repentance they cannot have; because, it is a penitent disposition, that must be either *infused* by the *holy Spirit;* or *acquired* and purchased, by frequent *acts* and practise of repentance: but, neither doth the *holy Ghost* indow such with the *habituall* disposition of true *repentance;* because, it is an *Evangelicall grace* whereof sinners of that transcendencie beyond the Law are not capable; and where it is, it is accompanied with the body of other saving graces, which all such persons do want: nor yet have they got *habituall* repentance, by their long and constant practise thereof; seeing such do alwaies live impenitent wretches in their sins, without godly remorse and new life.

2. Actuall repentance.

Secondly, for such persons *actually* and indeed to repent soundly, and to *life,* at, or in their *act* of this transcendent *self-murder,* they cannot; in regard that either they want time to doe it, if it were possible for them to repent; or, they want rather a heart savingly to repent; which requires both a *divine principle* within them, whereby

whereby they may be able to do it, and also some blessed meanes of Gods ordination, to exuscitate and stirre up that power into act: the former a *self-murderer* hath not; for the latter, *God* never ordained vile *self-murder* to be a meanes of a *self-murderers* repentance; neither attends such mens leisure, to give them repentance, when they list; who would not repent at his call.

By the transcendency of their sin, these *self-murderers* over-set themselves, beyond the pitch of recovery. *And* if any such should happen to have time, betweene his vile act and his expiration, his sorrow for such an extraordinary and odious fact cannot be true saving repentance: because, repentance in such extremities, and also late, where there is no time to trie, and give proofe of the soundnesse of it, is forced, and rarely true, and also repentance for one grosse fact, or for a few, is not sound, nor sufficient for salvation; where a man stands guilty and impenitent for abundance of other sinnes and corruptions, whereof he ought to repent, as well as of the other. And when and where was it ever knowne certainly, that any such transcendent *self-murderer* did savingly repent, although he had time betweene the blow and his departure?

And *therefore*, as no proper and transcendent *self-murderer* doth, or can truly repent, so can he not be saved, but is damned, by and upon accomplishment of that enormious and odious *fact*.

§. 7. *The Churches Iudgement of self-murderers.*

The fifth and last *argument*, that makes it apparent that no proper *self-murderer* is saved, is the ancient and constantly continued *Iudgement* of the *Church* touching the finall estate of such *persons*, which is expressed by her *order* and *practise*, in excluding them from the priviledges

5. Reason. That all self-murderers are damned. By the Iudgment of the Church.

viledges of *Christian* buriall, as hath beene formerly said[a]; that she will neither permit, nor allow that their bodies shall be brought to the grave with Christian solemnity; as, *with ringing of Bells*, or *singing of Psalmes*, or the like: nor that they shall be interred or *buried* in *consecrate* ground or *Christian buriall*, in common with the bodies of those, all whose soules the *Church* hopes, in *charity*, are saved in Heaven: neither at their *buriall*, (where ever it be else) will the *Church* suffer any *prayers*, or reading of *Scriptures* to be used, as may intimate to others any comfort, or hope of their salvation.

[a] Chap. 17. §. 7. Argument 9.

Decreti secunda pars. causa. 23. quaest. 5. c. 12. Placuit.

Qui se laqueo perimunt, aut ense necant, manifestum si scelus horum sit, nobiscum non tumulentur. Raimundus.

Barring them from Christian buriall.

Their *wills* she makes void, as of persons that, having cast away their soules, have nothing left, nor power to dispose of any thing, she deemes it unreasonable for such to have their *wills* stand, who do, in so high a degree, withstand and counterveen the *will* of *God*.

Neither, at any time after their *buriall*, will the *Church* allow, or permit that any *commemoration* shall be made of the names of any such, in the suffrages or solemnities of her *divine service*, (as anciently the manner was to deale with those, of whose salvation shee did not despaire.)

That by this omission it might be manifest, how shee abhorred *self-murderers*, and their vile practise, and that their names might bee extinct, and rot, whose soules shee conceived were damned: she would not have them remembred, or registred by her to their *honor*, that were so dead; or to the comfort of the living, either in regard of the fact, or in respect of the finall estate of the persons, whose names she conceives are razed out of the *booke of life*.

For, if so bee that the *Church* did, in charity, conceive that the soules of any proper *self-murderers* had communion after death, in place, state and blessednesse, with the soules of those that are saved; why then should shee, or could shee justly exclude the bodies of those *self-*

self-murderers from communion, in *Christian buriall*, with the bodies of the godly, and heires of salvation?

And, if the *Church* had any hope of the salvation of *self-murderers*, why should she deny the use of those meanes of solemnities, of reading of *Scripture*, of saying godly *prayers*, and of making honourable *commemorations* of their *names* in publick *divine assemblies* and *service*, whereby the *Church* her self might be comforted, and also the disconsolate friends of such parties might be cheered, touching the goodnesse of the finall estate of such self-murderers?

Why should the *Church* deny any of her common *priviledges* to any that she conceives to inherit the priviledge of enjoying the kingdome of Heaven? it cannot be done, only for *terror* to the living, that they may not dare to do the like; because, the *Church, the pillar and ground of truth* [a], will not do so much wrong and injustice to the dead, to effect any good; for doing whereof she hath other, and those warrantable meanes sufficient; yea, even the *Roman Church* leaves no place of hope for *self-murderers*, so much as in *purgatory*; but abandons them all to *hell* without redemption, by all which the *Church* makes it manifest, that it is her Judgement that none such are saved; *but* are all damned: whose very externall goods are judged, by the *Church* and *Commonwealth*, to be execrable; and, in that respect, are made a *deodand*.

[a] 1 *Tim.* 3.15.

And *therefore*, upon all the foresaid *reasons*, and arguments, I conclude that no proper *self-murderer*, in manner aforesaid, can be saved, but are all damned.

§. 8. *Of certaine uses.*

Observe.

1. From what hath beene said, touching the finall estate of proper *self-murderers*, we may *observe*, for our *use*; *first*, that none but *reprobates* and damned persons do

breake out into this transcendent, direct and proper *self-murder* : so that, it is proper only for *reprobates* and damned persons to do it, in the perfit height, and greatest enormity of it ; and is not incident to any good body that shall be saved, to do it, in that *manner*.

2. *Secondly*, the consideration of the finall damnable estate of those *self-murderers*, in respect of that fact, may make *self-murder* odious and formidable to all people ; lest by their venturing and approaching neere to the brinks of that desperate gulph, they should fall in; to the everlasting destruction both of soule and body : which shewes the desperate madnesse of those, that wilfully ruinate themselves for ever, in this manner, by *self-murder*.

§. 9. *Certaine objections answered ; and first touching the nature of self-murder.*

Objections. There remaines now certaine *objections* to be answered, which may be made in favour of proper *self-murderers*, for their *salvation*, which are especially *three*.

The *first* of them may be pretended to be taken from the *nature* of *self-murder*, alledging that the same is not so hainous a sinne, but that the doers thereof may bee saved.

1. From the nature of self-murder. *First*, because, if we consider sinnes as they are committed against the *Gospell*, onely the sinne against the *holy Ghost* is called a *sinne unto death* [a], which never shall be pardoned [b]. *Self-murder* is not that sinne, and therefore may seeme to bee pardonable, and the doers thereof saved.

[a] 1 *Joh*.5.16.
[b] *Mat*.12.31.

2. *Againe*, if wee do consider the sinnes committed directly agaist the *Law*, there is none of them desperately unpardonable ; because they all, and every of them may, upon repentance, be cured by the *Gospell*, which is of

equall

equall extent to the Law, to be able to repleave and save all that the *Law* condemnes.

And of the *sinnes* committed against the *Law*, some (as spitefull *blasphemy* against the *Majesty* of *God*, and the like;) may in the true nature of them seeme to be more hainous than *self-murder*; both, in regard of their more direct and malignant *opposition* against *God*: and also for their greater *distance* in *nature* from pardon.

Answ. 1. The sin against the holy Ghost.

To this *objection*, that caries with it a countenance of probability: I *answer*, *first*, touching the argument taken from the sin against the *holy Ghost*, it is to be considered that, that sin is *unpardonable*, and they damned that do it, onely in respect of that desperate *opposition*, whereby the committers of it do spitefully oppose and reject *Christ* and his *Gospell*, the very only meanes whereby they can be saved; so that there remaines no further, or other way, or help for salvation; and also because, *that sinne* is ever infallibly accompanied with finall *impenitency*; which alwaies makes a man uncapable of grace and salvation, which none can have but true *penitents*.

How self-murder is equivalet to the sinne against the holy Ghost.

Self-murder hath that in it, which is in the sin against the *holy Ghost*, in respect whereof it damnes, and is unpardonable; which is both *finall impenitency*, in regard that a *self-murderer*, by that sinne in the perfection of the *anomie* of it, doth so *indispose* himselfe, and shuts up and ends his life by, and in such a horrible transgression, that hee cannot possibly repent, nor consequently bee saved. And also, equivalent and answerable to that spitefull rejection of Christ, his grace, and Gospell, in the sin against the *holy Ghost*, by the living; there is in *self-murder* the cutting off of ones selfe (by his owne hands in this death,) from grace and salvation, to be gotten only in, and by life.

So that, in these respects, *self-murder* is as certainly damnable, and the doers thereof reprobated, as is the sin against the *holy Ghost*, and the committers thereof. For, although of the sin against the *holy Ghost* it be precisely said, that it shall *never* be *forgiven*, and that the committers thereof are certainely damned; yet, it is neither said, nor is true that none, but sinners against the holy Ghost, have their sinnes not forgiven to them, and are damned, seeing the contrary is abundantly certaine; and the wicked quality, and impenitent disposition of some persons, so depraved and vitiated by their sins, makes the same to be in them unpardonable; which brings them to the same finall state with sinners against the *holy Ghost*; it matters little for a mans comfort, that is to be put to death, whether he be hanged for *felonie*, or for *burglarie*, seeing for *either* of them his death is the same.

2. Self-murder a transcendent great sin.

Secondly, I answer touching the comparison made betweene *self-murder* and other sinnes, committed against the *Law*, that *self-murder* is a greater sin, than any that can be directly and properly committed against and within any precept of the Law, for which the committers of the same may have grounded hope of forgivenesse; because, *self-murder* is a *transcendent sinne*, as hath beene shewed in the *third reason*; *transcendents* are ever larger and greater than *subordinates*; and it is a sinne condemnable by more, and stronger *reasons* and *arguments*, than any other sinne committed against and within the compasse of the *Law*: as the same is more grievously injurious to more *objects*, and transgresses more Lawes, naturall, divine, and humane; and therefore, it must needs be the greater sinne.

Also the estimate of the greatnesse and unpardonablenesse of sinnes as they are in *offenders*, is not wholly to be made by consideration of their *abstract nature*; but specially the same is to bee made by the *quality* and *disposition* of the *committers* of them, whose *personall* and *actionall* circumstances in doing of thẽ, much *aggravats*, or extenuats the same. For, *pardon*, or not *pardon* of *sins* depends more upon the penitencie, or impenitency of the

the *offenders*, than upon the *nature* of their sins; absolutly and abstractly considered, the *fact* of *self-murder* is such a sinne, as no man penitently disposed can commit, and it cuts him (that doth it) off finally from all repentance, and consequently from salvation.

Of all sinnes against the *Law*, *self-murder* is most dangerous and pernicious for a mans soule, to bring it to damnation: both because, it excludes all care, and meanes of a mans salvation, which if a *self-murderer* did regard, he would not venture in the last period of his life, upon a course so contrary to it; and also, it puts the *self-murderer* into such an estate and disposition of sinfulnesse and aversenesse from God and his will, in pursuing of his owne wicked lust, that he is not, nor can be capable of grace, nor is in the way of salvation, whereunto self-murder is most contrary, by his last act of horrible sin, in the closure of his life. Self-murder most dangerous for a mans soule.

And *therefore*, it is apparent that, for any thing in this *objection* alledged, there is nothing from the nature of the sin of self-murder, properly so called, that can give any comfort of salvation to *self-murderers*, or can warrant us to hold probably, and in the judgement of charity, that they are not all (generally considered) utterly damned.

§. 10. *Touching Examples of self-killers.*

The *second objection*, that may be made, in favour of the *salvation* of *self-murderers*, is taken from *examples* of *Sampson*, *Pelagia*, and many others that in the *Primitive Church* killed themselves, and are acknowledged to be saved. Therefore, it may seeme *probable* that some *self-murderers* may be saved. 2. *Object.* Is from examples.

Answers.

To this *objection* I *answer*, first, touching *Sampson*, that he was no *self-murderer directly*; nor, in that point of so dying, *indirectly*; the reasons whereof are evident. 1. That *Sampson* is no self-murderer.

First,

Reasons.

1\. *First*, because his *intention*, *will* and *endeavours* were not directly, or primarily, but only accidentally to kill himselfe; but, in all the aforesaid respects, he was wholly bent to destroy his enemies the *Philistims*; which he could not doe, but with, and by the death of himselfe: which is apparent by the story, *Iudg*.16.28.

2\. *Secondly*, he was a *Iudge* of the people of *Israel*, to free and avenge them of their enemies the *Philistims*; and *therefore*, by vertue of his *office*, was warranted to destroy them, as he should be able; in which execution, although he perished through his owne voluntary act, according to his owne certaine foreknowledge; he could not be a *self-murderer*; from which sinne his *office* and calling of *God* to that work freed him.

3\. *Thirdly*, for that act, and last worke of *Sampson*, whereby himselfe died; *God* called him to it, that then and there he might so do it, both by his providence, giving him such an opportunitie against his enemies so assembled, as he could never have the like againe; and also, by the extraordinary supernaturall assistance of the *Spirit* of *God* that came upon him, and strengthned him to do the *deed*: which it never doth for any wicked act; which is rather the work of the *devill*. Whereby it is manifest that *Sampsons act* was not self-murder.

Spiritus latenter hoc jusserat. Decreti secunda pars, causa.23. c.9. si non licet.

4\. That *Sampsons* act was warrantable, and no fact of *self-murder*, is evident, by his intending, and going about it in subordination to *God*, and his will, manifested by his Spirits assistance, and obtained by lawfull and pious prayer, which no *self-murderer* doth; who preferre their owne wills above Gods; in satisfying whereof, they cannot comfortably pray for Gods assistance to doe the deed, which in their owne consciences they know is unlawfull and wicked; and *therefore*, were horrible to entreat him to be an *actor* of the same with them.

5\. *Fiftly*, this last *act* of *Sampson* is spoken of in the *history* of it, *Iudg*.16.30. with commendation; when it is is said that the *dead which he slew at his death, were more than they which he slew in his life* : and *Heb.* 11.32. himselfe is honoured among the *faithfull*, as being one of them: whereas the facts of *self-murder*; and the persons of *self-murderers* are never spoken of, but with aspersion of blame and disgrace; and therefore, *Sampson* is no *self-murderer*.

Sixtly, things may be done lawfully in a *type* or figure upon divine instinct, or ordination; which otherwise were unlawfull to be done: as, a *Certaine man of the sonnes of the Prophets, said unto his neighbour, in the word of the Lord, smite me, I pray thee: and the man refused to smite him: then said he unto him, because thou hast not obeyed the voice of the Lord, behold, assoone as thou art departed from me, a Lyon shall slay thee: and assoone as he was departed from him, a Lyon found him, and slew him. Then he found another man, and said, smite me, I pray thee; and the man smote him, so that in smiting he wounded him*, 1 *King*.20.35,36,37. Which act otherwise had beene unlawfull; that here, done upon divine command, and for a *type*, or figure, was good. 6.

Sampsons manner of so dying was a *type* or *figure* of *Christ*; who by his death slew more, than in his life: and therefore, in this respect, it was lawfull, and he no *self-murderer*.

Secondly, I answer, touching *Pelagia*, and others in the *Primitive Church*, who killed themselves to avoid, either doing of sin themselves, or suffering sin to be done upon them, that they were charitably thought of, and favourably censured; because of their precedent pious godly life, and of their good intention, although the act were wicked; and are excused, 1. By allegation of their *ignorance* of the morall nature, and of the danger of the fact to their soules: 2. And by the suddaine invasion and surprisall of them, by violence of their unadvised *passions*: which can be no president for ordinary practise, 2. About *Pelagia* and others, not self-murderers.

 either

either to warrant the fact to be lawfull, or to comfort the *persons* doing it with expectation of the like event, and safety. But of this see more *cap.*12§.5. and *cap.*15. §.23. and *cap.*19.§.7. *argument* 17. & *supra* § 4.

Whereby it appeares evidently that those, and such *persons* were not proper *self-murderers*, and so not of that number, and ranck of *self-killers*, that are, certainely, and finally, excluded from salvation. And so, this *objection* is of no force against the former *conclusion* of the damnation of all *proper* and *transcendent self-murderers*; because, the *instances* given are insufficient, and impertinent to make proofe, or to give any comfort and hope of salvation to any proper *self-murderer*, in regard that the same are of another kinde; for, although, by falling by their owne hands, or meanes, they were *self-killers*; yet they were not *proper* and *direct self-murderers*; seeing these two are not alwaies convertible, and of equall extent, as hath beene shewed.

§. 11. *About antecedent Prayer and repentance for pardon of sinnes to come.*

3. *Object.* From mens preparation to God-ward, before they murder themselves.

The *third objection*, that may be alledged in favour of the *salvation* of *self-murderers*, is that a *self-murderer* purposing, and resolved to murder himselfe; may, before the *fact* make his peace with *God*, by *humiliation* and *repentance* for all his sinnes past, and in particular for his hainous sin of *self murder* to come; praying instantly to *God* to forgive him both the guiltinesse and punishment of that vile fact, that he is bent suddainely to do; and beseeching him, through *Christ* and his merits, to receive him into mercy, and to save his soule; for the same, casting himselfe upon, and beleeving in *Christ*. And so, thereupon dispatches and murders himselfe, by his owne meanes, or hands; hoping and expecting to be saved: whereby, and in which case, such an one seemes to to die in a good minde, in peace with God, and in charity with all the world; and in an estate sure enough of heaven for his *soule*, and of perfection of salvation for both, at the resurrection, and great day of Judgement.

To this *objection*, I *answer*, that no man can make, or be at *peace* with *God*; when and so long as he wilfully intends and persists in such a sinfull course, or practise, as offends, enrages, and makes *God* his implacable enemie, in that case: such is the state of an indivertibly-resolved *self-murderer*; and therefore, it is impossible that, so long as he is in that minde to murder himselfe, he can make, or be at peace with *God*; whom, by his vile sin, he inrages against him, so that he cannot die that way, but in vengeance from *God*; both thereby punishing his former sinnes, and also thus dispatching him away to *hell*.

Answer. A self-murderer cannot make peace with God.

Neither can any man truly *repent* before hand, for that grosse sinne, which he is purposed, and fully bent to do afterward; notwithstanding that he knowes the same to be directly contrary to Gods will, and to his own salvation. *Neither* can any mans precedent *prayer* be effectuall with *God*, for to obtaine pardon of a vile enormious sin, that he desperatly and unresistably intends to perpetrate against the *will* of *God*; which I will manifest by *three* strong *reasons*.

Antecedent prayer and repentance for self-murder is uneffectuall.

First, Repentance, and *Prayer* to *God* for pardon of the vile sin of *self-murder*, that a man purposes to do; doth manifest, it is in him, not a sinne of *infirmity*, but a most *presumptuous* sin, which he doth so advisedly, deliberatly, wittingly, and willingly go about: and therefore, in that case, is farre from true *repentance*, and hath no ground for him to dare to come before *God*, to pray for such a thing, neither can he hope to be heard in such a *prayer*, which helps onely to condemne him, if he do the same: because, thereby he witnesses and testifies against himself, that such an act of *self-murder* is wicked and sinfull, and

Reasons. 1. Such prayer condemnes the self-murderer.

 that

that he doth advisedly and presumptuously intend, and do it; and therefore, for his doing of it, may most justly and certainely looke to be damned.

And againe, by such an *antecedent prayer*, *repentance* and *pretended reconciliation* to *God*, such a *self-murderer* doth but beg of *God* leave, that he may securely sinne, in that horrible manner, and fact, without feare, or check of conscience, or touch of punishment: which is to desire, that *God* would be *unjust*; by shewing *mercy*, contrary to his *nature* and *truth*, to presumptuous sinners, in their act of so sinning: and so by that kinde of *humiliation*, and *prayer* to *God*, for favour in their purpose and act of *self-murder*, they make *God* a partie accessary to their sinne, and to be sinfull, by his assistance of them in their vile practise.

Such persons abhorre not the *sinne*, but the *punishment*; and would have *heaven* by their owne way, contrary to Gods; which cannot be.

2. Such prayer is not of faith.

The *second reason*, proving the unlawfulnesse, and uneffectualnesse of the *antecedent repentance*, and *prayer* of *self-murderers*, for pardon for the sin, that they purpose to commit, is; because, such a *prayer* cannot be of *faith*, whereby they sue to *God* for a pardon *ante factum* before the deed be done; which is nothing else but the grant of a *dispensation* for them to sin, in most vile manner, which is most unlawfull to be desired; for which there is no warrant, and it is most impossible for God to grant; because, thereby hee must not onely dispense with the *punishment* of the fact, contrary to his *justice*: but also he must approve of the *deed* to be done, as lawfull; contrary to his *nature*, and *will*. For, both the *allowance* of the *fact*, and also *exemption* from *punishment* are comprehended in a *dispensation*.

But, *God* can neither lye, by shewing mercy contrary to his truth, nor yet can approve any sin, so as it should be no sin in the *doer*, and *act* of it: which is a *contradiction*.

True

True *repentance* lyes specially in abhorring, forsaking and reforming of sin; both for the *habit*, and for the *act* of it; which, in this case, a *self-murderer* doth not; and therefore, doth not repent, neither of his other former sins, nor of this; for the same reason of repenting for the one, is for the other.

The *third reason* of the vainnesse of such *repentance* and *prayer*, made by *self-murderers*, is; because, the same wants all *warrant* : For, *repentance* can be onely of sins committed and past, or present, and not of sins to come; whereof a man (in that respect) cannot be guilty; because, a thing to come is yet a *non ens*, or nothing; it is not certaine it shall be: and all sins for time to come should be utterly resolved against, and withstood, with prayer to *God* for grace, that wee may never bee able to doe them. 3. It is unwarrantable.

Pardon of sins is craved by *prayer*, and granted by *God*, onely for sinnes commited; and not before they be done: for, *pardon* followes upon *repentance*; which is properly of sins done, and not of sinnes purposed to be done. True *repentance* changes, both a mans ill purposes and practise; contrary to the course and disposition of such a *self-murderer*, whose *repentance* and *prayer* tends to incourage him more boldly to sinne; by a most vile fact of *self-murder*: he cleaves to the *sinne*, and practises it; the *punishment* whereof he would avoid, which are individuall companions.

It is a strange madnesse for a *self-murderer* to conceit, or presume, that *God*, upon his prayer proceeding out of a wicked minde, and from an ill intent, will grant him his request and *will*, for the salvation of his *soule*, when as he will not yeild to the *will* of God, who forbids the horrible sin of *self-murder*.

Touching such *self-murderers* beleeving, hoping, and casting themselves upon *Christ* for salvation; I grant, they may have desires of *salvation*; but it is onely to be had *Note.*

 had

had in *Gods* way, and therefore, they cannot have it in their own. True *faith* and *hope* they cannot have; because, the same cannot consist with such raigning and advised presumptuous sins; neither have they any ground to *beleeve*, or *hope* that any, in that case, can be saved.

To cast themselves upon *Christ* for salvation I deny not; as the foolish *Virgins* that knocked to be let in; but *Christ* will be *Saviour* to none, that will not submit to him for to be their *King*; to be ordered by him, in all things.

Although *multitudes* come and cast themselves upon *Christ* for *salvation* by him, yet hee receives, and saves none but such as come first to him, in all humilitie and obedience, to be *cured* of their *sinnes*, and to be *ruled* by his *Lawes*.

Presumption. The *hope* and *expectation* of the salvation of such self-murdering persons when they die; is but groundlesse *presumption*, in regard that their abuse of religious practises of *prayer* and the like, and wretched dallying with *God*, in so wicked a minde, and to so vile an end, doth aggravate their sin, and makes them much more culpable and subject to eternall damnation, than if they had forborne the same: the expectation and desire of the wicked, and hope of the hypocrites shall perish [a].

[a] *Prov.* 10.28. *Job.* 8.13. *Psal.* 112.10.

They that do to themselves an act of the greatest hatred and hostility in the world, in murdering themselves, cannot properly be in charity with others; God, or men.

And to die in peace, and in a good minde they cannot, whose mindes at their last gaspe, are perturbed, troubled, and set upon a most horrible vile act of *self-murder*; attended upon with all horror from Heaven and hell, to their everlasting confusion.

So then it is apparent, for ought that can be said in favour, or hope of the salvation of any proper *self-murderer*; that there is no probability of the salvation of any of of them, but that they are all damned; according to the former *conclusion*.

And therefore, we are to beware that, upon no pretence, we approach neere to that sin, which brings to so certaine and eternall destruction.

CHAP. 19.

Antidotes for prevention of self-murder.

§. 1. *What we are to do of our selves, to prevent self-murder.*

IT followes now that wee consider the *Antidotes* and *meanes* whereby *self-murder* may be *prevented: which* are of *three* sorts. The kinds of Antidotes. three.

First, that which wee are to use in *private* by our selves.

Secondly, those that we are to use *joyntly* with others.

Thirdly, those that are to be used by *others*, about those that are under the strong *temptations* of *self-murder*.

The meanes that we are to use by our *selves*, whereby we may prevent *self-murder* are specially *eight*. 1. Meanes by our selves to prevēt self-murder.

First, to prevent the prevailing *temptations* of *self-murder*, we should be carefull of our *spirituall* and *morall estates*, that the same be good: *both*, by being in the *state* of grace and favour of *God*, by *faith* in *Christ*, whereby we may have comfort, in the *forgivenesse* of our sins, and in assurance of *Gods promises*, 1 *Cor*.3.22. *Rom*.8.28. and may have supply of all necessary strength against all execrable *temptations*, by our depending upon *God* in *Christ*, who will not suffer us to bee tempted above that which we are able to beare. 1. To be in state of grace. [a] *Psal*.32.1.

And

Holy lives. *And* also, our care for our *morall estate*, that the same may be good, should be, that our *lives* and conversations be *holy*, in compleat *obedience* to *Gods Word*: *and* that, for the sinnes that trouble our *consciences*, we should in true *repentance* labour to get the pardon of them; *resolving* and striving against all sin and iniquity for time to come, whereof *self-murder* is one, and so it will be detestable to us, as we are regenerated.

Repentance.

By this course, we shall not onely cut off the *occasions* of *self-murder*, such as the *horror* of conscience, and matter of sin; *but* shall also be accomplished with all needfull *strength* against that evill; *besides* that, hereby wee shall be in an estate more specially priviledged from *self-murder*; and out of which a man can have no security, no not against himselfe, from this *fact*.

2. Indowment of vertues. 1. Humility. 2. Contentment.

Secondly, to prevent *self-murder*, we should labour for *humility* and *self-deniall*, which our *Saviour* commended to his *Disciples*, *Mark.* 9. 35. and *Mark.* 8. 34. *For, pride*, in over-valuing our selves, and *self-will*, in headstrongnesse in our owne way, do often bring men to *self-murder*.

[a] *Rom.* 5. 3. 1 *Tim.* 6. 6.

We should also endeavour to be *content* and *cheerefull* in our present estates[a], whatsoever the same be, so long as we are in *Christ*: *these* vertues are so contrary to the temptations of *self-murder*, and doe so indispose the *subjects*, wherein they are, to such a fact, that they utterly exclude *self-murder*.

How to get these vertues. 1. Consideration of Gods wisdome and goodnesse. [b] *Rom.* 8. 28.

The way for a man to attaine these *vertues*, is

First, the serious consideration of the infinite *Wisdom* and *Goodnesse* of *God*; *whereby* we may know that his *will* in all things is the best; *both*, for the *rightnesse* and *goodnesse* thereof to us, in all his dealings with, and concerning us; to whom, we know, all things worke together for good while we serve him.

2. Our estates better than our deserts.

Secondly, wee are to consider that our *estates* and troubles, what ever they be, are much better, than wee do do *deserve*, which wee cannot amend, but make much worse by *self-murder*.

Thirdly, wee are to cast our eyes upon many *others*, who are farre better than wee; and doe patiently *suffer* much worse, and heavier things than we doe, at the hands of *God*, in this world. 3. Others better suffer more.

Fourthly, wee are to *observe* in all the matters of our discontentment, that the same is wholy *ordered* by our loving *Father*; without whose *providence a haire cannot fall from our heads*; *who* moderates our *afflictions* and crosses, how great and how long they shall be; gives strength to beare them; grace to profit by them; and directs them all to an happy end. 4. God our Father orders all things.

Fiftly, we are to consider the *end* of all our *crosses* and *troubles*; *both* that which God intends and propounds; and *also* that which we, by patient waiting for, shall at last obtaine: which is (in those that feare God) ever *glory* to *God*, and increase of happinesse to our selves, as the *Apostle Paul* tells us, 2 *Cor*.4. 17. and also *St. James* tells us of *Iob*, *Iam*.5.11. 5. The end of our troubles good.

Therefore, in all troubles, we must be carefull that we fixe not our eyes upon their beginnings and present countenance; lest wee despaire, or faint; but that we looke through them, to the comfortable fruit and end thereof; which will contentedly uphold our hearts in hope; as did our Saviour. *Heb*. 12.2. *Note.*

Thirdly, to prevent *self-murder*, we must be carefull to *live by faith* in all estates; after that we are first thereby spiritually made alive in *Christ*. 3. live by faith. *Habakuk* 2 4.

Fourthly, to prevent *self-murder*, when we are under the *temptations* of it, wee must not yeeld too much to them; *or* be *negligent* and faint-hearted to resist, or shake them off: as those doe, who give too much way to the *feare* of killing themselves; which they manifest divers wayes, *as* 1. *In forbearing lawfull use of weapons, or knives*. 2. *Shunning to goe upon lawfull calling, into solitary retired* 4. Withstand temptations and feare.

 places;

places ; over waters, bridges, upon battlements of houses ; or neere steepe downe places ; when they have motions of self-murder in their minds. 3. *Shunning to be alone, or in darke places.*

Feare entertained is harmfull.

These entertained *feares* of *self-murder* doe much incourage and advantage the *devill* against us, *and* doe hurt our selves ; seeing that what evill men doe strongly conceit, and *feare* they shall doe, they cannot be quiet untill they fall upon attempting the doing of it indeed.

[b] Iam.4.7.

And therefore, wee must remember to resist the *devill that hee may fly from us* [b]: at first, wee should despise and outface the temptations of *self-murder*, that wee may expell the feare of it ; which by resistance and contempt, doth often vanish away.

Note.

But, if so be that the *temptations* of it doe prevaile; to some kind of resolution to kill ones selfe ; then are such to avoide all the meanes and opportunities, whereby they may accomplish that wicked designe ; and to use all the helps they can against it.

5. Good imploiment.

Fiftly, to prevent *self-murder*, we should be constantly and diligently *imployed* in *holy* and *civill* exercises of our *callings*, that wee may ever bee found in Gods way, and well imployed : as *Ierome* adviseth his *Friend*, that *hee should alwayes be doing some good worke,* [c] *that the devill,* when he comes upon us, may alwaies find us well *occupied. And* that we may not be weary with any one exercise; *or* that the *devill* should intermingle his temptations with it ; it is good for those, that are under *temptations* of this kind, to *shift* their exercises often, that *Satan* may never find us within his *verge* of *idlenesse*, or bad imployment ; whereby he may sease upon us, or challenge us, for that he found us within his walke, or precincts.

c *Facito aliquid operis, ut te semper inveniat diabolus occupatum.* Hieron: ad Rusticum.

Note.

Inveni in meo.

Give not way to horrible motions.

If wee be in *prayer, reading, meditation*, or any other lawfull necessary imployment ; we must beware that wee give not way to *horrible motions* of the *devill*, perswading us to kill our selves ; *so* that thereupon we should breake off

off our exercises, or neglect the duties of our callings; to pore and muse upon, or to bee taken up with such motions; which are better defeated by our abhorring and contemning of them, and by our proceeding in the pursuit of the duties of *religion*, and our *callings*, from one thing to another, whereby wee may banish those motions of *self murder*; cast them off, and out of sight, which cannot consist with such good thoughts and imploiments.

6. Fasting and prayer.

Sixtly, that we may prevent *self-murder*, when we are in conflict with the *temptations* thereof, wee are to *fast* and *pray* against it: *for the motions* thereof are like to that kind of unclean *spirits, that are not cast out, but by fasting & prayer* [a]. *The* more unnaturall and horrible that any evill motions are, the more hardly are they ejected, when they have possession of a man: *because* of the greatnesse and violence of their strength; and of the weaknesse and subjection of that which should withstand, or expell them; that now the same must be done by a more powerfull and immediate hand of *God*, when man is insufficient.

a Mark 9 29.

Note.

Application of the word against temptations.

Also, application must bee made of the *Word* of *God* against such *temptations* of *self-murder*, by well considering the *precepts*, *promises*, and *threatnings* of the *Scripture*; whereby the feare of offending *God*, and of the damnation of our *soules* may powerfully restraine us, from any such wicked *act*; when wee consider the extreame and unrecoverable evils of it, farre exceeding any good, or profit that can be had thereby.

7. Right ordering of our thoughts.

Seventhly, for *antidotes* against *self-murder*, we should carefully consider *what we would say, out of advised Iudgement to another, in that case*, labouring under strong temptations to kill himselfe; and desiring our counsell and help what to doe therein. Would any sober, or reasonable man *perswade* such an one to yeeld to the *temptation*, and kill himselfe? *or* would he not rather *disswade* him, by all the *arguments* and *reasons* he could, from doing of it? *for*, if he may perswade one man to kill himselfe, then why may

As we would say to another in that case.

he not likewise perswade all men, in the same case, to do the like?

A man under *temptations* of *self-murder*, should urge upon himselfe the same *conclusion*, not to kill himselfe; forced and backed by the same *reasons* and *arguments*, that he doth upon another in the like case; *by* which *application* to himselfe, he may well resolve, and fortifie himselfe against all such *temptations* and *intentions* of *self-murder*.

Note. *And* againe, wee should consider, what we would, or could reply to another man; if any such should perswade us to kill our selves, upon those *reasons* and *arguments*; whereupon our temptations are grounded, that move us to *self-murder*. And so, we should apply the same to answer our owne self-murdering *motives* and motions: whereby we should smother and destroy the first conceptions of a monstrous brood.

To make self-murder vile in our eyes. *And finally*, we should upon every motion of *self-murder*, think and consider of all the things and reasons, that we can, to make that *fact* vile and odious in our eyes; and to terrifie us from daring to resolve to doe it; *and* withall we should not entertaine, but reject the least thought of any thing, that may arise in our mindes; *or* be otherwise suggested to incline us; *or* be a *pretence*, or starting hole to encourage us to doe such a vile fact, or any other evill, contrary to *Gods* sacred word. By which ordering of our thoughts, the resolutions of *self-murder* would bee utterly excluded and dashed.

8. Confession. *Eighthly*, the last *antidote* that a man alone by himselfe can use, to prevent *self-murder* is, when all his other private endeavours prove uneffectuall, (or rather in the first place, when he feeles his soule troubled) and not able to overcome his *temptations* of *self-murder*; which by secresie and concealment of them, doe still more and more grow upon him, and prevaile; that hee is in great danger to be overcome by them, and to yeeld to kill himselfe: *then*

then is hee to open his estate, and *confesse* the same to others, who can and may help him; according to the *Apostles* commandement, *Iam.* 5.16. *For*, both the worke is easily done, and the burthen lightly borne, that hath the help of many hands: *and* also vent of the minde, by *confession*, doth often give ease to an oppressed heart; and upon discovery, the *devill* many times gets him gone; and his *temptations* vanish; *as thieves*, that dare not harbour where they are revealed; and the Country is up, by a *hubbub* raised in pursuit of them; *and* as the foggie *vapoures*, that are dissolved and scattered by the heat of the Sunne risen, and shining upon them. Comparison.

§. 2. *Caveats and observations about confession.*

Touching this *confession*, in this case *fower* things as *Caveats* are to bee carefully observed; that men under such temptations may have good by this course. Caveats about confession.

1. *Caveat.*

First, they are to bee circumspect and warie whom they choose to open their state, and confesse themselves to.

That they be not people undiscreet; *or* of *weake* Judgments, and little experience in such cases of conscience; *Whereby* such an afflicted person shall have no benefit by them; *but*, both he and they perhaps much hurt, by such *Physitians* of no value; who may be infected themselves with that mans disease which they cannot cure: as were the *Egyptian Magicians.* Not to undiscreet.

Neither must such a man make choice of *blabs* of their tongues; whose knowledge of secrets is but fuell of common *scandall* and *offence*. *But* of all persons that a man in this case should open and confesse his state unto; he should specially make choice of his owne Minister, *because*, hee is nearest in *relation* and duty to him; as a *Father* to his *Child*; he knowes best, for understanding and experience, how to discerne his griefe; and how to speake fitly, and seasonably to his comfort: from whom helpe and conso- Not to blabs. To whom to confesse. 1. To his owne Minister.

 lation

lation may be better expected, and come with more authority and sweetnesse, than from another; *in* regard of his *office*, and *parts*; *being one of a thousand, Iob.* 33. 23. *The words of whose mouth God creates to bee a comfort* [a].

[a] Esay. 57. 19.

The promise for effecting such a worke is specially made to the *Ministers* of *Gods word*; *when* our *Saviour* sayes, *Whose soever sins ye remit, they are remitted unto them* [b], *and whatsoever thou shalt loose on earth, shalbe loosed in heaven* [c]. *Thus God* is pleased specially to grace his owne ordinances and servants, by powerful effecting that by them, which ordinarily he will not doe without them.

b Ioh. 20. 23.

c Mat. 16. 19.

2. To a godly private Christian.

For want of such a *Minister* to confesse to; then a man in this case may lay open his *state* to some other reverend *Divine*, or to some other private, godly, wise, faithfull *Christian, one*, or *more*; according to the direction of the *Apostle Iames*; *for*, although such have lesse learning and authority than *Ministers*; yet they may have more *experience*, in that case; *and* the *Lord* may, for his owne glory, manifest his power by weake meanes; when the same are used without contempt, or neglect of better.

d Iam. 5. 16.

The properties of those to whom we are to confesse.

The qualities of the *parties*, to whom a man under pressure of such temptations is to *confesse*, and open his estate, are diverse.

1. Godly humble minded men.

First, that they be *godly humble minded men*, who have themselves beene exercised under afflictions and temptations; wherein they have well quit themselves, in a victorious manner; whereby wee may the more confidently open our state to them; and comfortably expect to be comforted by them, *with the same comfort*, wherewith themselves were comforted and upheld [e].

e 2 Cor. 1. 4.

2. Assured friends and experimented.

Secondly, those *private* men that, in this case, we are to confesse to, should be both assured *friends* to us; as *Ionathan* was to *David*, if it be possible; and also *tried* men, in like cases and imployment, *approved* by good successe that way with others.

Thirdly,

Thirdly, such as, in this case, wee are to make our *spirituall Physitians*, should bee *advised*, *grave*, *sober-spirited persons*, and *reserved* from needlesly divulging mens *secrets* to others : *whereof* they give assurance, by their *confessing* to the afflicted, like, or worse things of their owne, with discovery of the *meanes*, and manner of their recovery : which gives some comfort to the distressed, that they may belong to *God*, and may recover, as well as such. 3. Wise and reserved.

The *second caveat*, in the case of *confession* under temptations of *self-murder*, is, touching *what* the afflicted is to *confesse* : *which* is 2. *Caveat*. What to confesse.

First, the *fact* that he is tempted to do. 1.

Secondly the *motives* and *arguments* whereupon he is moved to the same. 2.

Thirdly, he is to discover how farre the temptation hath *prevailed* with him, in the entertainment thereof, and in his purposes and attempts to effect *self-murder*. 3.

And withall, he is to make his confession *freely*, whereby he may shew his confidence in the party, to whom he makes it. How to confes for manner. 1. Freely.

And also, he is to do it *plainly*, that he may be throughly understood. 2. Plainly.

And to make it *fully*, that he may reserve nothing undiscovered, that may hinder the perfit cure of his griefe, and may afterwards breake out in more violent manner to effect the deed : *as* some that confesse a little by peece-meales; whereupon finding some ease, they suppressing the worst of their estates, are thereby overthrowne, after that they have thought themselves quite escaped and safe. *So dangerous* are the recoyles and reverses of those aguish fits of *self-murder*, when the dregs of that pestilent disease have not been well purged out. 3. Fully. *Note.*

The third caveat in this *confession* is, the observing of the right *end* and *use* of it; *which* is, that those that are under- 3. *Caveat*. To observe the right end and use of confession.

under *such temptations may bee holpen against the same, and be preserved from that vile fact of self-murder*; *both*, by such *reasons* and *perswasions* as may settle their judgments, and resolve their hearts against the same;*and also*, by the effectuall *prayers* of such godly *friends*, that they may be assisted and freed, by Gods gracious goodnesse and power, against, and from such vile temptations, and horrible conclusions of *self-murder* against themselves.

Note. *The* minding, and intending of the *end* of our course, that we take, will incline us unto, and hasten and facilitate the accomplishment of the same, in the happy atchievement of our desired preservation and cure.

4. *Caveat.* Removeall of impediments. *The fourth caveat* observable about this *confession* is, that those that are under such temptations of *self-murder*, do strive to *remove* the impediments in *themselves*, that may hinder the benefit that may be had by this *confession*, in this *case: which* are *two.*

1. Prejudicate opinions. *First, prejudicate opinions* against the *judgement*, and *reasons* of others disswading the afflicted from the *fact*; and confuting their *motives* and *arguments*. *For*, when the pretensed *reasons* and motives of *self-murder* have, in temptations, made such deepe impressions upon mens mindes; and have got such entertainment and liking in their hearts; that the same is predominant above all other meanes and arguments to the contrary.

Then, by the help of depraved *fancie* and *affection*, all sound *reasons*, that crosse that *humour*, are sleighted; and the contrary are magnified. *And therefore*, in this case, we should labour to see the weight and worth of the *reasons*, and *counsell* of others; and endeavour to entertaine, and be guided by the same.

2. Stiffnesse of resolution to kill ones selfe. *The second let* to be removed is, *stiffnesse of purpose, and resolution of committing self-murder*. Which unnaturall and wicked *conclusion* is many times obstinately held, without respect of, and against all good *premises*, or *arguments*. *For*, commonly the more *unnaturall* and unreasonable

unreasonable that any opinion and resolution is, it is the more backed with *obstinacie*; *and therefore*, men under *temptations* of *self-murder* should, not only *passively* submit to bee wrought upon, and to bee drawne from their wicked *conclusion*, by the help of others; *but* should also endevour to *convert* their *resolutions* in, and by the course this way taken. *For*, there is no *morall conversion*, or change, neither can bee, against a mans *will*; or without his *will* concurring to effect the same; but that a man must be *active* in the same.

The benefits of this *confession* are great; first *mutuall ingagement of Christians one to another* thereby; in their *trust*, *affection*, and *helpe*; which increaseth *comfort* and *love*; *secondly*, thereby the *graces* and *experience* of all the *members* of the *Church*, are communicated and improved to the common use and good one of another: and so the *stronger* helps to beare the burdens of the *weaker*.

Benefits of confession.

1. Mutuall ingagement.

2. Communion of graces. Gal. 6. 2.

The devill labours to keep men in these *temptations* of *self-murder*, from disclosing the same, as hath beene shewed; *that so*, the same by concealement prevailing against them, they may in the end certainly perish. The *motives* he uses to effect it, are *first feare of shame* and *disgrace* with men, if they should know it, which such persons cannot endure; as they suppose: it is certaine that the more vile, and unreasonable that any *opinion* and *practice* is, the more loath and ashamed are men to discover the same, in regard of *shame* and *punishment*. *But*, if it be a *disgrace* and *shame* to be knowne to be tainted with such *temptations*, how much more *shamefull* is it willingly to harbour them, and to bee overcome by them to kill themselves? *When*, upon *confession*, such *afflicted* persons shall understand from others, that such *temptations* are incident to many that are *godly*, the shame of the same will vanish; not only by knowledge of the *commonnesse* of them; but specially because in such *temptations* men are rather *sufferers* than *agents*; which is manifest by our sorrowfull confessing

Satan hinders confession.

His motives.

1. Feare of shame.

Note.

fessing of them, and striving against them.

2. Self-murderers desire to have their will.

The second motive, that *Satan* useth to make men to conceale these *temptations* is, that the *tempted* may have their *will* to accomplish their *designes*, in killing themselves, without interruption, or hinderance: *there is nothing that a man so affects, as not to be crossed in his will*; and by that it is that the *devill* prevailes; our care therefore should be to have our *wils* subordinate to *Gods, and* freed out of the power of the *devill*; and that we be not *selfe-willed*, to prosecute an ill course.

3. Suspicion of all men, that he dares not trust them.

The third motive, whereby *Satan* works upon a man, under these *temptations*, to conceale them; is *misprision* and *suspicion* of all men; *that he knowes none that hee dares trust, or trouble so farre; or that is able to doe him any good: conceiting that they are not so trusty, nor well affected to him; nor so humbly compassionate towards him; nor sufficient to help him*; and *therefore*, hee will not *communicate* his griefe to them.

Observe.

From whence we may *observe*, that as a man growes into inimicall and unnaturall *resolutions* against himselfe; so he growes into *strangenesse*, and *alienation* in heart and conversation, from all *mankinde*. *The* more indisposed that any under self-murdering temptations, is to discover his estate by *confession* to others; *and* the longer that hee deferres it by concealement, the more dangerous is his estate, and the more incurable: *therefore*, men in that case, should shake off that loathnesse; and against all these *obstacles*, use *confession*; the meanes appointed of *God*, in such difficulties and distresse, for certaine help.

Self-murderers grow strange to men.

§. 3. *Of the meanes to be used with others against temptations to self-murder.*

The second kinde of Antidotes are with others.

The second sort of *Antidotes* and *meanes* to be used for *prevention* of *self-murder*, is the course that they, that labour

labour under such *temptations*, are to take jointly with *others*: *which* is *either privatly* with a few, or publickly with the *Church*.

First, with a *few*, (to whom by *confession* such a *partie* so afflicted hath discovered his estate,as hath been said,) he is *both* to *advise* by conference, for setling his judgement, resolving and comforting his conscience; *and* for right ordering of his practise: *and also*, to use *fasting* and *prayer* together with such *friends* in private; *whereby* he may get power from *God* to overcome the temptation, and to be freed from danger of the fact.

1. With a few. To advise, and pray.

For, we have a *promise*, *that where there are two or three assembled together in Christs name, there he will be in the midst of them, and will grant them whatsoever they shall aske in his name* [a].

[a] *Mat.* 18. 19, 20.

The care of private *friends*, so farre interessed by *confession* in this case, should be, not only to *advise*, and *pray* for those that are under these *temptations*, in company with them: *but also* to *pray* for them by themselves: *and* towards such they should shew themselves *pitifull*, and compassionate, about their estate; such persons *distemper* is better allayed *palpando quam pulsando*, by *gentlenesse*, than by *rigour*: *they* should often *deale* with them, and *question* them about their successe against their *temptations*: *for*, what cannot be effected at once, repetition may worke; and the victory be got, and the cure be accomplished; *suddaine cures are commonly unsound*: and to leave them over-soone argues too much neglect of them; and also the disease is not fully discovered, when they suppose the same is healed.

Note. The care of friends to the tempted.

Note.

Self-murder is prevented, not so much by *arguments* against the *fact*; which disswades from the *conclusion*; as by the discovery and removall of the *motives* and *causes*, whereupon they are tempted to do the same: *as* diseases are cured by removing of the *causes*, rather than of their *symptomes*: *and practicall conclusions* are overthrowne by

How self-murder is best prevented by removall of the motives to it. *Comparison.*

solid *confutation* of the *premises* and *arguments*, upon which they do depend; *in logicall discourse, conclusions* are neither properly the matter of denyall, nor of confutation, so long as the *premises*, and *reasons*, whereupon the same stands, are passed by, as allowed, or granted.

2. With the Church.

Secondly, when as the *temptations* of *self-murder* still prevaile against all the former meanes; then it remaines for the *tempted* to flee unto, and to make use of the more publick helps and assistance of the *Church*: which (as a tender *Mother*) both compassionatly pities her distressed Children; and also by her *counsell* and *comfort* to them, and by her *intercession* and prayers to God with, and for them; is ever readie, as well in her publick assemblies, as in private to relieve and succour all those that resort to her for the same: which from, and by her meanes is more certainly and comfortably to bee expected, and to be had, than by any other course; as the publick Church is more prevalent with God, than private Christians; and the promises of God more ample to her for regard and audience, than to her particular members.

§. 4. *Of the course that others without the tempted are to take to save him.*

3. By others powerfull restraint.

The *third* sort of *Antidotes*, or *preservatives* against *self-murder* is, when after the use of all the foresaid meanes, the temptation of *self-murder* still continues and prevailes in a party resolved to kill himselfe; and seeking and attempting all the meanes that he can to do it: *then* all others are to be carefull;

1. Required of God by Prayer.

First, not to cease to *pray* to *God* instantly for him, that he would keepe him and deliver him by his over-ruling providence, hindering the execution, and turning his will.

2. Be observant of the tempted.

Secondly, men should bee *observant* of such persons; *both*

both to *fish* and *spie* out the outmost hidden lurking undiscovered *causes* thereof, that the same may be removed, that hinders the cure; *and also*, to watch him, against all *oppertunities* and meanes, whereby hee may accomplish his act of *self-murder*. — 1. To spie out the causes. 2. To watch him that he do it not.

Thirdly, they are to use outward *forcible restraint* to such an *one*, as to a mad man; *shutting him up, and keeping meanes of self-destruction from him*; as much as may be. *The* putting by of the violent attempts and *passions* of *self-murder*, which comes by *fits*, *ague-like*, not only *restraines* the *act*, for the time beeing, *but* may also counter-check and *abate* the *rage* of it, that by degrees it may be prevailed against, and asswaged; *as agues*, many times, are cured *accidentally*, by very impertinent *medicines*, putting by the *fits*. — 3. Humane forcible restraint. *Comparison.*

From that which hath beene said, touching the *Antidotes* for *self-murder*, we may *observe* that it is a mans owne fault if he perish by *self-murder*, in *neglect* of using the *meanes* against it. *For*, as there are *medicines* for all diseases; *so* are there *meanes* of preservation against all sinnes too, how great soever they be, to prevent them: *and*, these *meanes* are within the reach of a mans power to use. — *Observe.* None are self-murdered but by their owne fault. *Comparison.*

If a man once deeply *plunged* into these *temptations* of *self-murder*, do *christianly* overcome the same, and be soundly recovered; he hath thereby a good pledge never to be so tried againe; *and* hath a *pawne* and evidence of *victory* against other sinnes, if he doe his best against them. — *Note.* The benefits of recovery frō the temptatiōs of self-murder.

And also, for this *deliverance*, such a one is bound to be ever exceeding *thankefull* to *God*. — Vse of it.

Upon *preservation* and *freedome* out of these temptations of *self-murder*, a man is to take heed of *two* great *dangers*. — Vpon the cure, dangers.

First, *security*, *self-confidence* and *presumption*, whereby those corruptions and sinnes may closely grow upon him, — 1. Security, &c.

him, that may bring him into as *dangerous* a condition for his *salvation*; *as* we see how *Hezechia* after his recovery out of his mortall sicknesse, fell into other sins, (as he manifested, by his ostentation to the *messengers* of *Babylon*, in boastingly-shewing them his *treasure* and *strength*) all which cost him deare.[a]

[a] 2 *King*. 20. 13.

2. Vnprofitable life to goodnesse.

The second danger to be avoided, after such a *recovery*, is *unprofitable living*; *when* such a man spends not the *life* that *God* hath given him, in speciall manner, to *Gods glory*, to the *good* of *others*, and to his owne *salvation*; which is the maine *end* why *God* gives us our lives; *and* for the attainement thereof, if we spend them not, it were better for us not to live.

Observe.

The various states, and great *dangers* that *God* carieth *man* through are very remarkable: *and Gods* worke therein is gracious and *wonderfull*; *for* which we should ever praise his glorious and blessed name, with constant dependance upon, and dutifull obsequiousnesse to him, in all our life, and wayes: which God grant we may do. *Amen*.

FINIS.

AN ALPHABETICALL Table of the materiall Contents of this Treatise, directing to the Page where the same is contained, or begun.

Xx Assizes.

How

For

Igno-

K

L

Some

Wagering

The faults of the Presse thus amend.

Pag. 21. *l.* 1. *r.* mans life. *p.* 26. *l.* 31. Citie. The *p.* 39 *l.* 23. *r.* so a man *p.* 40. *margine*, *r.* weakeners of zeale. *p.* 41. *l.* 2. *r.* ill examples. and *l.* 3. *r.* from the prevailing. *ibid.* *l.* 13. Antiperistasis. *p.* 44. *In the margine against* § 2. set, First, of the body. *ibid.* *l.* 19 *r.* the taking away. *p.* 45. *l.* 5. *r.* Courses. *ibid.* *l.* 7. *r.* are guilty *p.* 51. *In the margine against* *l.* 17. *set downe*, Secondly, from the Divell. *p.* 64. *after* *l.* 14. *and before the uses, insert* §. 9. *p.* 65. *l.* 34. *After the word*, things; *adde*, proper to their estates. *p.* 72 *l.* 27. crooked wayes. *p.* 88 *l.* 11. *r.* is directly under a common *Genus* or *generall*, partakes *p.* 94. *l.* 5. omission, *p.* 123 *l.* 32. *r.* and some, *p.* 126. *l.* 33. *r.* cut off; *p.* 130. *l.* 19. *r.* Tollet. *p.* 138. *l. ult.* *r.* overcharged. *p.* 142 *l.* 13. *r.* opportunity, to teach *p.* 147. *l.* 33. the will of superiour *ib.* *l.* 34. *r.* concurre, if it plainly *ibid.* *l.* 35. *dele* to *p.* 152. *l.* 25. *r.* subjecto *p.* 153. *l.* 29. *for* properly, *r.* peremptorily *p.* 162. *l.* 12. *for* conclude *r.* include *p.* 172. *l.* 6. *for* fower *r.* five *p.* 184. *l.* 13. *r.* forwardnesse *p.* 197. *l.* 14. *for* ore *r.* over *p.* 204. *l.* 1. *for* greater *r.* great *p.* 207. *l.* 29. *for* God *r.* Good *p.* 235. *l.* 2. *r.* debilitating *p.* 261. *l.* 23. *for* Essay *r.* Assay. *p.* 272. *l.* 10. For the *p.* 283. *l.* 7. *for* fury *r.* Iury.

PErlegi hoc Opus cui Titulus [Lifes preservative against Self-killing] *in quo non reperio quicquam sanæ doctrinæ aut bonis moribus contrarium, quo minus publicè cum utilitate imprimi queat.*

Octob. 29. 1636.

Gulielm. Haywood
RR. P. Archiepisc.
Cantuar. Cap.
Domest.

For Product Safety Concerns and Information please contact our EU
representative GPSR@taylorandfrancis.com
Taylor & Francis Verlag GmbH, Kaufingerstraße 24, 80331 München, Germany

www.ingramcontent.com/pod-product-compliance
Lightning Source LLC
LaVergne TN
LVHW011105300926
849160LV00008B/287

* 9 7 8 0 4 1 5 7 3 0 8 3 9 *